11/03

More praise for *Teen*

"Year after year the Gallup Polls show how devastating alcohol and other drug addictions are to individuals and our society as a whole. The new big threat is adolescent drug use and addiction, a problem that affects our society at all levels. *Teens Under the Influence* will be welcomed and applauded by parents, educators, judges, probation officers, and adolescents themselves. It will be a wonderful teaching tool, helping us to educate our children and ourselves about the facts, eliminating the many myths that cloud our thinking, and helping to eradicate the stigma of alcohol and other drug addictions."

> —GEORGE GALLUP, Chairman
> The George H. Gallup International Institute
> Princeton, New Jersey

"It is difficult to overestimate the importance and severity of adolescent alcohol and drug addiction, which is growing continually and also contributing to an increased rate of adolescent suicide. Strong parental leadership can make an enormous difference, but many parents do not know how to assert that kind of positive influence. *Teens Under the Influence* will save lives."

> —ROBERT CANCRO, M.D.
> Lucius N. Littauer Professor of Psychiatry
> and Department Chair, NYU School of Medicine

Please turn the page for more acclaim . . .

"What we lack in the addiction field is a comprehensive guidebook written for parents and kids in a language they can understand. This book will fill that need."

> —SCOTT MUNSON, Executive Director
> Sundown M. Ranch Treatment Center
> Past Chairperson, National Association of
> Addiction Treatment Providers

"Underage drinking, which includes most college binge drinking, is one of the greatest problems we are facing in this country. The tragic results—carnage on the highways, college date rapes, deaths, homicides, suicide, teenage pregnancy, and the spread of AIDS— could be prevented with education, and *Teens Under the Influence* is just what the doctor ordered."

> —ADELE C. SMITHERS-FORNACI, President
> The Christopher D. Smithers Foundations, Inc.

"There is a critical need for a book addressing guidelines for parents dealing with drug problems in their adolescents. *Teens Under the Influence* is a current valuable contribution to parents and to the field of addiction and medicine."

> —G. DOUGLAS TALBOTT, M.D.
> Founder and Medical Director
> The Talbott Recovery Campus

Teens Under the Influence

THE TRUTH ABOUT KIDS,
ALCOHOL, AND OTHER DRUGS—
HOW TO RECOGNIZE THE PROBLEM
AND WHAT TO DO ABOUT IT

Katherine Ketcham and
Nicholas A. Pace, M.D.

BALLANTINE BOOKS • NEW YORK

A Ballantine Book
Published by The Random House Publishing Group

Copyright © 2003 by Katherine Ketcham and Nicholas A. Pace, M.D.

Ballantine and colophon are registered trademarks of Random House, Inc.

www.ballantinebooks.com

Library of Congress Control Number: 2003109360

ISBN 0-345-45734-X

Text design by Kris Tobiassen

Manufactured in the United States of America

First Edition: September 2003

10   9   8   7   6   5   4   3   2   1

Acknowledgments

Our debt of gratitude is deep and wide. This book could not have been written without the following people, who told us their stories, offered their wisdom and experience, and inspired us at every loop and twist along the way.

To the kids, especially Aaron, AJ, Allen, Alicia, Amanda, Anastasia, Andrew, Anthony, April, Autumn, Ben G., Ben S., Benny, Bethany, BJ, Blythe, Brad, Brenda, Brittany, Camille, Carl, Carlos, Carol, Caroline, Chad, Chance, Charra, Chelsie, Chris, Christina, Christy, Cody, Colin, Colleen, Curtis, Daniel, Debra, Derek, Derrick, Domingo, Doug, Ed, Elmer, Emily, Evian, Foster, Francisco, Frank, Gary, Geneva, Gilbert, Hannah, James, Jason G., Jason C-II., Javi, JD, Jeffrey, Jenna, Jennifer, Jeremy C., Jeremy M., Jerry, Jessica, Joanna, Joe, John, Johnny, Jolan, Joleen, Jordan, José, Joseph, Josh, Juan, Kate, Katie, Kim, Kirby, Kristina, Kristle, Latasha, Laura, Lisa, Leo, Lori, Lucy, Luis, Luke, Marc B., Marc L., Marcus, Margarita, Mario, Mark, Marquelle, Matt, Melissa, Michael, Michelle, Molly, Monica, Natalie, Nicole, Noshka, Paul, Peter, Robert, Ron, Ross, Sabrina, Samantha, Seth, Sharon, Shawn, Shalynn, Stacy, Stepfanie, Stephanie, Steven, Tania, Thaddeus, Tiffany, Tim, Todd, Tony, Tyler, Vanessa L., Vanessa R., Vincent, Wade, Will, and so many others.

To the parents, especially Lenna Buissink, Kathleen McCaw and Mark Grandstuff, former senator George and his wife Eleanor McGovern, Diana and Randy Pierce, and Sandra Reavis.

To the staff at the Walla Walla Juvenile Justice Center:

Michael Bates, Norris Gregoire, George Wiese; and Avril Atkinson, Brian Bieren, Steve Boese, Bill Boggs, Jon Cassetto, Donna Coffeen, Dondi Cortinas, Julie Elmenhurst, Jamila Gordon, Ralph Harris, Craig Isitt, Joette Jones, Debra Kelley, Gina Laib, Anne Lierley, Kevin Magnaghi, Frank Martinez, Jan McCaw, Cindy Mercado, Tiffany Michaels, Vance Norsworthy, Becky Renwick, Angela Reyna, Judy Roy, Julio Tapia, Kim Throw, and Christy Young.

To the staff and students at Summit High School in Spokane, Washington; and special thanks to Andy Finch, director of the Association of Recovery Schools.

To the physicians and researchers who are changing the world for children and their families: Daniel Amen, M.D.; Henri Begleiter, Ph.D.; Joseph A. Califano, Jr.; Robert Cancro, M.D.; Marc Fishman, M.D.; Stanley Gitlow, M.D.; Fred Goodwin, M.D.; Enoch Gordis, M.D.; Steven Jaffe, M.D.; Ting-Kai Li, M.D.; Herbert D. Kleber, M.D.; Alan I. Leshner, Ph.D.; David Lewis, M.D.; Charles Lieber, M.D.; Howard A. Liddle, Ed.D.; Howard Marquelle, M.D.; Kenneth Minkoff, M.D.; Ernest Noble, M.D., Ph.D.; Bert Pepper, M.D.; Richard Ries, M.D.; Steven Schroeder, M.D.; Marc Schuckit, M.D.; David E. Smith, M.D.; G. Douglas Talbott, M.D.; Nora Volkow, M.D.; James W. West, M.D.; Aaron White, Ph.D.; Ken Winters, Ph.D.

To the treatment specialists who offered their advice and experience: Judy Bixby; Mike Early; Jeannette Friedman; Terence Gorski; Diane Hall; Jeff and Debra Jay; Vernon Johnson; Jerry Moe; Ed Mosshart; Ira Mothner; Scott Munson; Michael Osbourne; Rick Risberg; David Rosenker; Mitchell S. Rosenthal, M.D.; John Schwarzlose; Marvin Seppala, M.D.; Adele C. Smithers-Fornaci; James Steinhagen; Bill Teuteberg; Joseph Ward; Randall Webber; Harvey Weiss; Sis Wenger; and Stephen Wyatt.

To those who led the way: John B. Alfieri; Sidney Cohen; M.D.; Luther Cloud, M.D.; Charles A. Dana; Ruth Fox, M.D.; Louis Fugazy; Senator Harold Hughes; George Meany; Thomas H. Meikle, Jr., M.D.; R. Brinkley Smithers.

To our friends and mentors: William Asbury, Teri Barila, Doug Barram, Dave Beebe, Laurie Becker, Melinda Burgess,

Kathy Covey, Jack Delaney, Marilyn Dickinson, George H. Gallup, Jr., John Glase, Peggy Gutierrez, Jeff and Debra Jay, Elizabeth R. Kabler, Sharon and Timothy Kaufman-Osborn, Jane Kelly, Charles Kester, Ernest Kurtz, Mary Ann LaFazia, Alan Luks, James R. Milam, Richard Morgan, Ann Mueller, Kathy Lowe Petersen, Richard Nagle, Nancy Reagan, Jason and Lois Robards, James Roche, Charles Rosenberry, Neil Scott, Mel Schulstad, Kenneth D. Stark, Susan Stewart-Rickelman, Doug Thorburn, Joseph Ward, Robert Warren, William S. White, Cynthia Witman, Jason Zelus.

To the foundations, institutes, and organizations dedicated to helping troubled teenagers and their families, including the Annie E. Casey Foundation, Bill and Melinda Gates Foundation, Big Brothers Big Sisters of America, Caron Foundation, Charles Stewart Mott Foundation, Christopher D. Smithers Foundation, Edna McConnell Clark Foundation, George H. Gallup International Institute, Hazelden Foundation, Henry J. Kaiser Family Foundation, John D. and Catherine T. MacArthur Foundation, Josiah Macy Foundation, Lowe Family Foundation, Marin Institute, Rush Recovery Institute, Robert Wood Johnson Foundation, Terry McGovern Foundation, and William T. Grant Foundation.

To the wonderfully capable and caring staff at Ballantine Books, especially Elisabeth Dyssegaard, Julia Cheiffetz, Elizabeth Cochrane, Kim Hovey, Laura Jorstad, Gene Mydlowski, and Patricia K. Nicolescu.

To our literary agents, past and present: Carole Abel, Kathleen Anderson, Jane Dystel, and Sarah Jane Freymann.

To our families: Katherine Ketcham's husband Patrick Spencer and her children Robyn, Alison, and Benjamin Spencer; and Nicholas A. Pace's wife Carolyn and his children Victoria, Gregory, and Anthony.

And special thanks to William L. White, who truly does know it all.

Contents

PART THREE: WHAT PARENTS CAN DO

Introduction

*D*iana is sitting in the waiting room of the Juvenile Justice Detention Center. In ten minutes she will be able to visit with her daughter, Samantha, who is locked up for a probation violation.

Samantha, seventeen, has curly blond hair and a beautiful smile. She likes to write in her journal, read, draw, and play with her three-year-old niece, whom she loves more than anything in the world.

Samantha is addicted to methamphetamines. She started using "meth" in ninth grade in an attempt to lose weight. She lost sixty pounds, but then she couldn't stop using the drug. She tried, many times, but the withdrawal symptoms were too painful and the craving too intense.

This is Samantha's third stay in detention. Three weeks earlier, she ran away from home and went on a meth binge. When she finally returned home, late on a Sunday evening, she was physically ill, mentally confused, and deeply, suicidally depressed. She collapsed, sobbing, in her mother's arms.

That night Diana called Samantha's probation officer, who picked up Samantha the next morning and booked her into detention. Diana and her husband were relieved—in detention, at least, they knew Samantha would be safe, because she couldn't use drugs and she couldn't run away.

Three days later, waiting to see her daughter, Diana sits with her hands clasped, her eyes glued to the floor. The other parents in the room are also staring at the floor in silence.

"It was like an unspoken rule—no talking or making eye contact with other parents," Diana remembers. "I felt so alone. I didn't have anyone to *confide in who could really understand how our family was being torn apart. I was embarrassed and ashamed to tell anyone how horrible our lives had become. I secretly wondered if other parents were going through the same emotions, but I was afraid to ask for fear that I would have to reveal the terrible truth about our lives."*

This day, though, Diana decides to break the silence. She turns to the woman next to her, whom she saw in court the day before and whose son was being sentenced to a year in a juvenile institution for drug-related charges.

"I told her how sorry I was about her son," Diana recalls. "She told me he'd been using alcohol and marijuana since he was twelve years old, and he'd recently started using cocaine. As his drug use escalated, his criminal behavior increased. 'At least he'll be safe from drugs while he's in the institution,' she told me."

Another parent shyly joins in the conversation. Her son has just been arrested for breaking into a liquor store. He was drunk at the time.

"My son just got kicked out of school for marijuana possession," says another parent. "This is his fifth time in detention."

Before long, everyone in the waiting room is talking about his or her fears and frustrations. They all admit to feeling embarrassed, humiliated, helpless, ashamed, and, worst of all, alone.

For Diana, those conversations with other parents mark both an end and a beginning—an end to silence, secrecy, and shame, and the beginning of freedom and empowerment.

"I finally opened up about my problems," she says, "and I felt an incredible sense of release—I felt free from guilt, from secrets, from fear. I realized I was not alone. And that changed everything."

I met Diana several months ago, when I was working with her daughter at the Walla Walla, Washington, Juvenile Justice Center. After the publication of my eleventh book, *Beyond the Influence: Understanding and Defeating Alcoholism* I decided to put my pen aside for a while and "walk the walk," volunteering several hours a week in the detention center. A year later I was hired part time to work with kids in trouble with drugs in both detention and on probation.

I knew a lot about alcohol and other drugs when I started working with the kids, but I was not prepared for the magnitude of the drug problem I would encounter. Virtually every adolescent I meet has had some experience with alcohol and/or other drugs. Most of the kids are in trouble with drugs, and an astonishingly high percentage of them are addicted.

Kids are starting to use drugs at ten, eleven, and twelve years old. Some of them start much earlier—smoking weed with older brothers and sisters or huffing glue or nail polish remover while they are still in elementary school. They frequently combine drugs—marijuana and alcohol are "the regulars," but you name a combination and the kids have tried it. Some kids are using four, five, or more drugs at one time.

Their lives are complicated and filled with stress. They talk about bullying at school, gang members who threaten them, family members who are addicted, friends who overdose or die in car crashes. They use drugs, they say, to cope, to get by, to kick back, to forget, to escape the "drama" of ordinary life.

After talking to the kids for a few weeks, I put aside my carefully organized notes and mini lectures and just listened. When there was silence, I would ask questions. I scribbled down their answers, asking first for permission. "You want to write about me?" they would say. "That's cool, go ahead, quote me, write it all down. I give you permission."

They want to tell their stories. They want adults to listen, to understand, to relate. They need us to help them help themselves.

Over the past three years, I have worked with hundreds of adolescent boys and girls ranging in age from ten to eighteen. I've spent many hours with the so-called good kids—the relatively healthy, happy, well-adjusted adolescents who come from high-functioning families and who did something stupid, maybe even life threatening, because they were high on alcohol or other drugs.

I have also spent many hours with the so-called bad kids—the kids with seven, ten, or twenty (I'm not exaggerating) "priors"; the tattooed gang members who tell me about their bulletproof vests and their "homies" whom, they say, they would die for without a second thought; the middle school girls riddled with sexually transmitted diseases who use sex as a substitute for love; and the thirteen-, fourteen-, and fifteen-year-olds hooked on inhalants, cigarettes, marijuana, cocaine, crank (methamphetamines), heroin, prescription drugs, or the granddaddy of all, the drug that is almost always there, alone or in combination with other drugs—alcohol.

Listening to these kids quickly blurs the distinction between good and bad. For when kids start using drugs on a regular basis, they start doing bad things. They start looking and acting like "bad" kids.

The more I listened to the kids, the more I realized how desperate they were for accurate, easy-to-understand information about drugs, addiction, treatment, and recovery. When I offered them the facts, they were fascinated. They asked a lot of questions, and they wondered aloud if their drug use might be causing some of their problems at home, at school, and with the law.

They talked openly about values—honesty, trust, respect, responsibility, forgiveness, tolerance, and compassion. Most of them said they were sick and tired of the fear and loneliness, the sickness and confusion, the depression and anxiety of their lives. They were tired of feeling abnormal, set apart, treated by so many people with disgust or disdain. Even as they expressed the desire to be unique and wholly themselves, they also wanted to be normal—part of the orderly, healthy, sane world.

They talked about God, forgiveness, and freedom. When things seemed most hopeless, they told me, they would get down on their knees and pray, saying the shortest of all prayers: *"Help me."*

Slowly, over a period of several years, this book came into being. One day, in the spring of 2001, I called my friend and colleague Dr. Nicholas A. Pace. Nick is one of the foremost authorities in the world on alcoholism and other drug addictions. He has been working in the addiction field for more than thirty years, and he is personally responsible for helping thousands of people in trouble with drugs, young and old alike, into treatment and recovery programs. Through his writings, his teachings, and his daily work as a physician and expert in the field of chemical dependency, he has served as an invaluable resource and beacon of hope for addicted people and their family members.

I told Nick I wanted to write a book for parents focused specifically on adolescent drug problems, and I asked if he would consider collaborating with me. We talked about how desperate parents are for accurate facts and positive guidance, and we discussed the burgeoning field of adolescent addiction medicine and the wealth of research locked up in scholarly journals.

Nick didn't hesitate for a moment. "There is a great need for a book that will speak directly to parents and teenagers, making the scientific facts about adolescent drug use and addiction clear and understandable," he told me. "By helping parents understand what can and must be done to help their children, this book could prevent much pain and anguish."

And so we have dedicated the last three years to researching and writing this book. Our primary goal is to educate parents and other family members about the realities of adolescent drug use and addiction. With an understanding of the facts, parents will know what must be done to help their children and stop the downward spiral. Empowered by knowledge, possessing the wisdom of their own experience, they will be able to initiate positive changes in their own lives and reach out to others who are confused and despairing.

We have divided our book into three sections. In part 1, "Why Kids Get Hooked," we separate myth from fact, presenting the most up-to-date research on the biological and environmental influences affecting adolescent drug use and addiction.

In part 2, we take a detailed look at the drugs kids are using. We explain who uses these drugs and why, and we explore each drug's short-term effects on the brain and body, the potential long-term damage to vital organs, the danger of combining different drugs, the risk of addiction, and the telltale signs and symptoms associated with regular drug use and addiction.

In part 3, we offer practical advice about what you can do, as parents and concerned citizens, to help children and young adults in trouble with drugs. We include detailed information about diagnosis, intervention, treatment, relapses, and the recovery process, and we give parents step-by-step guidelines to help them understand what they can do to intervene and save their families from further harm. We end the book with "words of wisdom" from kids themselves.

We fervently hope that the information in this book will contribute to a revolution in the way our society approaches adolescent drug use and addiction, and the way the institutions and organizations empowered with helping our nation's children treat adolescents with substance-use disorders and their families.

As parents, you are an integral part of that revolution. This book is your invitation to change the world, not only for your family, but also for the millions of other families who are suffering in ignorance, confusion, fear, and shame.

For, as so many parents are discovering, you are not alone.

—*Katherine Ketcham*

A Note to Kids

This book is written primarily for the people who love and care for you—your parents, grandparents, guardians, and other close relatives.

The book is also directed to your teachers, doctors, counselors, clergy members, lawyers, probation officers, and others who need to understand the unique problems related to adolescent drug use, addiction, treatment, and recovery.

But you are the book's heart and soul. Your voices are heard throughout. Your insights give the book any wisdom it might have.

"I go to school to youth to learn the future," wrote poet Robert Frost.

You are our teachers.

You are our future.

PART ONE

Why Kids Get Hooked

Fighting the stigma of alcohol and drug problems in youth presents us with a real challenge because there are really two pervasive stigmas—abusing alcohol and other drugs and being an adolescent.

Coupled with the stigma is our imperfect understanding of the reasons and mechanisms that lead to these problems. Substance-use disorders are truly complex and involve an interaction of biological and environmental forces. When we add in the influence of the family, peers, boredom, the natural risk-taking of adolescents, serious co-occurring emotional and behavioral disorders, and the sheer availability of alcohol and other drugs, we've clearly got a complicated situation on our hands.

On the other hand, this very complexity gives us more choices for early intervention and treatment tailored specifically to the individual adolescent's needs, and these innovative methods are showing more and more promise.

A seven-year-old friend of mine named Chandler put it best: "Kids need health."

—DAVID LEWIS, M.D.
Professor of Medicine and Community Health, Donald G. Millar
Distinguished Professor of Alcohol and Addiction Studies at
Brown University, and project director of the Physician
Leadership on National Drug Policy

The Road Less Traveled

The only good is knowledge, and
the only evil is ignorance

—SOCRATES

The beginning of knowledge is the
discovery of something we do not
understand.

—FRANK HERBERT

Thomas is a tall, good-looking kid with a winning smile and a cocky attitude. Intelligent and articulate, he seems much older than his sixteen years.

In the last four years, Thomas has been arrested eleven times for assault, malicious mischief, reckless endangerment, minor-in-possession and minor-in-consumption charges, and various probation violations. This time he's locked up in the Juvenile Justice Detention Center for thirty days; it's the fourth time he's been in detention in the last seven months.

Thomas knows he has a problem with alcohol, but he isn't worried. He thinks he can quit whenever he wants.

"I just don't want to," he says with a confident smile. "Alcohol makes me feel good, you know, happy, crazy, full of myself. It gives me liquid courage—I feel like I can be and do anything."

He drinks, he says, for all sorts of reasons—to get high, to get numb, to get crazy with his friends, to forget about his troubles, to feel good, to feel better. "I don't always like myself when I'm sober," he admits, the cocky attitude disappearing for a moment. "But after a few six-packs, I feel much better about myself."

On what Thomas calls a "normal" night, he'll drink three forties (120 ounces of beer). On a party night, he'll drink a case of beer or more.

When he drinks, he does stupid things. He drives drunk, or he gets into cars with other drunk drivers. He has sex with girls he doesn't know and doesn't care about.

He doesn't use condoms when he's drunk because they're "too much trouble." He steals money and possessions from his friends and neighbors or he sells his own CDs, clothes, or PlayStation games to get money to buy more beer.

He gets belligerent when he drinks and often gets into fights with his friends or with strangers. "I get angry and aggressive," he admits. "People tell me I get 'that stupid look.' That's when I start arguing and fighting with everyone, even with my best friends.

"I think I'm so tough, you know," he adds with a sideways grin.

Thomas has blackouts ("lots of them") when he doesn't remember a single detail of the night before. He's frightened by the fact that he feels like he's in control when he's drinking but says and does things that show he's out of control. He's afraid he'll kill himself or someone else in a car wreck, get sent away to an institution, get a girl pregnant, or get AIDS from having unprotected sex.

But worse than the fear is the guilt and the shame.

"I feel ashamed because of the people I've hurt and the stupid things I've done and the way I've let my family down. I'm the outcast of the family. They don't trust me anymore," he admits.

Thomas is quiet for a few moments. "I thought loving someone meant that you forgive them and trust them, but maybe I've broken my parents' trust so often that they just can't believe me anymore. It's hard to live with yourself when you feel like you're letting everyone down, like you're a failure in everything you do. You know what I mean?"

* * *

Thomas is a troubled adolescent who uses drugs to have fun, to loosen his inhibitions, and to ease his emotional pain.

He is also an alcoholic. The signs and symptoms point to an early-stage addiction. First, there's the genetic evidence. Thomas's father is an alcoholic who has been in and out of treatment several times. Both his brother and his sister have a history of alcohol problems.

While Thomas's family history of alcoholism puts him at risk—scientific research conclusively shows that alcoholism is a genetically influenced disease—his drinking patterns also point to an early-stage addiction. He loves to drink ("I feel like I'm on top of the world after a few beers"), and he drinks whenever he has the opportunity. As hard as he tried, he can't stop after four or five beers—he keeps drinking until he gets drunk. He has a high tolerance for alcohol, putting away a case of beer or more in one evening. Always the life of the party, he's the person others turn to when everyone else is too drunk to drive.

Preoccupation with alcohol, continued drinking despite the desire to quit or cut down, and high tolerance are all early-stage symptoms of alcoholism. The symptoms are so subtle and seem so harmless, however, that they escape almost everyone's notice. "What's the big deal?" Thomas asks. "All my friends love to drink, none of them want to quit, and almost all of them have a high tolerance."

His parents admit that Thomas has problems, but they do not believe he is "addicted." His father refuses to acknowledge his own alcoholism, insisting that he isn't anything like "those bums who have no morals and no self-control." Both his mother and father think that Thomas drinks because he's a risk-taking adolescent with numerous behavioral, psychological, and social problems. They don't realize that Thomas's drinking is the primary cause of most of his problems.

After all, they reason, he could quit if he really wanted to, he doesn't drink all the time, he goes to school, and he gets decent grades. He's a good kid, down deep, they say, and he's trying hard to get his act together. He just has to work through his problems, get through the challenges of adolescence, and eventually he'll grow up, learn how to drink responsibly, and turn his life around.

Professionals (mental health counselors, educators, probation officers, doctors, clergy members) also focus exclusively on Thomas's emotional and behavioral problems, insisting that he needs to learn how to control his impulses and take responsibility for his actions. They believe his excessive drinking is merely a response to his multiple life problems, and that once these problems are addressed, he will be able to moderate his alcohol use.

During his freshman year in high school, the principal called Thomas into his office for a conference and warned him about the school's zero-tolerance policy. "If you cause any more problems here," the principal said, literally wagging his finger in Thomas's face, "you will be expelled, and you will not be welcomed back."

A mental health counselor diagnosed Thomas as clinically depressed and asked him if he had ever been suicidal. When Thomas admitted that he had thought about suicide, the counselor recommended antidepressant medication and long-term counseling to get at the root of his mental health problems. The counselor never thought to ask about his drinking.

In a recent juvenile court appearance, the judge said, "Young man, if you don't pull things together, I will have no choice but to institutionalize you." His lawyer agreed that sending Thomas to a juvenile institution might be the best course of action for everyone involved. "At least if he's locked up, he'll be safe from himself, and the community will be safe from him," the lawyer reasoned.

Thomas is angered by outsiders' interference in what he feels are "my personal problems." He insists he can handle his own problems, and he wishes everyone would just leave him alone. He's convinced he's not hooked on drugs—how could he be a drug addict when he's only sixteen years old? How could he be addicted when he doesn't drink in the morning or even every day?

Yet he is also afraid that something terrible is happening to him. He worries that he may have some kind of mental problem. Filled with shame and guilt, he detests himself for his inability to control his drinking. He knows what he should do to stay out of trouble, but he can't seem to do it. He listens to everyone's advice, but none of it makes any sense to him. He feels like a failure and a disgrace to his family.

"I'm not sure there's much hope for me," he admits.

What will happen to Thomas? His future will follow one of two divergent pathways. If he continues to use drugs—alcohol, in his case—he will experience increasingly severe emotional, behavioral, and physical problems. If, on the other hand, he stops using alcohol and other drugs, receives appropriate and effective treatment for his drug problem and any co-occurring emotional or behavioral disorders that might exist, and is offered ongoing support and encouragement in recovery, he can improve his relationships with his parents and friends, rebuild his self-confidence, and gradually work through the problems in his life.

Let's look at the first option, which is, unfortunately and often tragically, the more common pathway. As his parents, physician, mental health counselor, and teachers continue to search for ways to control Thomas's self-destructive behavior, they will unwittingly deflect attention away from his alcohol problem. These diversions from the primary problem—drug (alcohol) dependence—to the symptoms that are caused or exacerbated by his drug use (angry outbursts, violent behaviors, irritability, mood changes, anxiety, paranoia, depression, suicidal thoughts) will serve as a smoke screen, preventing Thomas from receiving appropriate help.

As he continues to drink, his emotional and behavioral problems will increase. He will have trouble at school with his peers, teachers, and administrators. His grades will fall, and he may be kicked out of school or drop out on his own. He will become sullen and withdrawn. He will stop talking to his parents and refuse to follow their advice. Tormented by self-loathing, he will wonder if he is going crazy and fear that there is no way out of the hole he is in.

As time goes by and the disease progresses, he will begin to suffer mild and moderate withdrawal symptoms—shaking, sweating, nausea, insomnia, mood swings, moderate or intense craving for alcohol or other drugs.

He will have accidents—falls, car accidents, burns, broken bones. These mishaps may involve minor scrapes and bruises, or they may require trips to the emergency room. They may be life threatening.

His relationships with family members will slowly but surely deteriorate. His teachers, coaches, friends, and relatives will lose faith in him. He will be called, by people who do not understand the nature and extent of his drug problems, "a bad kid," "a juvenile delinquent," or even "a lost cause."

His self-hatred will deepen, and his sense of hopelessness will increase. As his shame and guilt intensify, he will become increasingly depressed. He may try to take his own life.

For too many young people addicted to alcohol and/or other drugs, this is the common pathway. Everyone is unique, of course, and no adolescent's experience is exactly like another's, but the general descent into more serious problems—and the one-dimensional focus on emotional and behavioral problems that are, in many cases, caused or exacerbated by the primary disease of drug addiction—is typical. Only one in ten adolescents who need treatment for alcohol and/or other drug addictions are getting it.

But there is another way. If Thomas is fortunate enough to be evaluated by someone who understands the unique problems associated with adolescent drug use and addiction, he and his parents will receive help in the form of fact-based education, counseling, treatment, and continuing care. He will be screened for emotional and behavioral disorders and for past and/or current victimization or maltreatment. He will be referred for appropriate treatment—with careful attention paid to both chemical dependency and co-occurring emotional or behavioral problems—and he will take part in a structured, long-term continuing care program.

If Thomas drops out of treatment or suffers a relapse after treatment, it is critically important that his family members and helping professionals do not dismiss him as a treatment "failure." Substance-use disorders are chronic in nature, and treatment specialists advise a "never give up" attitude and a firm commitment to continuing care.

Statistics show that treatment programs based on current scientific evidence work. Treatment may not work miracles right here, right now, but over time it saves lives—and even short episodes of treatment dramatically reduce the damage to individuals, families, and our society as a whole.

Every bit of factual information about the disease and every period of sobriety, no matter how brief, can serve to "inoculate" adolescents against future problems. When kids know the facts about drugs and their effect on the developing brain and body, they also know what they must do to protect themselves. They know that if they use alcohol or other drugs, they put their physical, emotional, and spiritual health at risk. They know how drugs affect behavior, mood, motivation, and personality. They know that help is available, and they know what they can do to help themselves.

Once you know the facts, it ruins the fun of using drugs. After my fifth stay in detention—I kept running away from home and getting MIP [minor-in-possession] and MIC [minor-in-consumption] charges—my probation officer gave me the choice of treatment or spending a year in an institution. At the time, I hated her for forcing me into treatment. I was so angry and felt so powerless. But treatment changed my life. I learned all this stuff about my brain and the power of addiction to take over your mind and spirit, and now I know what I should do—not just for this moment, day, week, or month, but for my entire life.

My life is on the line, it's that simple, and knowing that one fact changes everything. Now I'm thinking about my life and the person I want to become. I'm also thinking about all the people who love me and who suffer when I use drugs. I'm not going to say it will be easy, but I do know this—if I can stay clean, I'll live a lot longer, my life will be a lot happier, and I will be able to wake up in the morning and look in the mirror without wanting to cry.

—MICHELLE, *fourteen*

Knowledge is the master key to helping adolescents in trouble with alcohol and other drugs. Adolescents—and, just as important, the adults who care for them and make decisions about their futures—must know the facts. For without the facts, we are hobbled by myths and misconceptions. We make decisions that will harm others, and ourselves, and we allow drugs to maintain their control over all our lives.

The primary purpose of this book is to present the facts as the scientific research has reported them, undistorted by myth and misconception. Separating myth from fact is not an easy or simple task, for misconceptions about addiction have persisted for hundreds, even thousands, of years. Myths are, in truth, reality for many people, and when we suggest that a different reality exists, we turn their world upside down. Few of us are comfortable when we discover that our beliefs and the decisions we have made based on those beliefs are rooted in error and misconception.

Yet only when we rely on the facts can we release our children, and ourselves, from the shame and disgrace that have surrounded drug use and addiction for thousands of years. Only with the facts can we help kids understand what drugs do to their bodies, minds, and spirits, and offer them the tools they need to protect themselves.

Only with the facts—and the willingness to use them to dismantle the prevailing myths and misconceptions—can we put an end to the death and destruction caused by drugs and the chronic, progressive disease of drug addiction . . . a disease that destroys the lives of tens of thousands of Americans, young and old alike, year after year after year.

"If You Could Only See Inside Me"

We must not be hampered by yesterday's myths in concentrating on today's needs.

—HAROLD GENEEN

Only as you do know yourself can your brain serve you as a sharp and efficient tool. Know your own failings, passions, and prejudices so you can separate them from what you see.

—BERNARD M. BARUCH

Eric, eighteen, wears baggy pants and shuffles when he walks, hands in his pockets. His eyes—narrowed, challenging—are dark brown, almost black. He shaves his head and wears a goatee. His arms, legs, back, and chest are decorated with more than a dozen tattoos.

When Eric was fifteen, he became a member of the Hispanic gang in his small town. Two of his closest friends in the gang died recently. One friend was shot dead at a party, and the other died in a car wreck after a night of heavy drinking and partying.

Eric has been arrested ten times and has six felony charges. Just before his eighteenth birthday, a juvenile court judge told him he had run out of options.

"In the eyes of the law, you're about to become an adult," the judge said. "One more mistake—that's all it will take—and you'll spend time in the county jail or the state penitentiary."

Drugs have been part of Eric's life since he started drinking at age twelve. He smokes weed and has experimented with cocaine and methamphetamine, but his favorite drug—the drug he just can't seem to give up—is alcohol.

"I don't like those other drugs," he explains, "too nasty, too much trouble. But beer—oh, man, what can I say? I just love beer."

Even though his drinking invariably gets him into trouble—fights, drunk driving, "killer" hangovers, and periodic blackouts—he can't stop. At least not for very long. He tried to quit a few months ago and stayed sober for ten days before he started drinking again.

"It's hard to stay away from it," he says. "I try, but I just can't seem to stop. I just like it too much, I guess."

A gang member, a convicted felon, a drug user, and, in the judge's words, "a risk to the community," Eric could be considered the epitome of a "bad kid."

At least on the outside. But what about the inside?

If you take the time to get to know Eric, you learn about his inherent goodness. If he trusts you, Eric will tell you about his life and his struggles to "do good." He has an eighteen-month-old daughter, and he is working hard to hold down a full-time job so that he can help take care of her. He talks often and with deep regret about the pain he has caused his family. He believes that he can prove to them, with luck and over time, that he is not a failure and he can change his ways.

His favorite book is Father Greg and the Homeboys, *about a Jesuit priest's relationships with Los Angeles gang members. Eric's favorite character in the book is Cisco.*

"Listen," he says, reading Cisco's own words:

I started gang banging when I was eleven, that's when I got jumped in to TMC [a Los Angeles gang]. When I got jumped in there was seven people hitting me and I was small. I broke two of my home-boys' noses and a couple of their teeth. But they couldn't take me down. I've been shot six times.

"That's bad, huh?" Eric asks, his brown eyes wide and wondering. It's clear that he's thinking about the relative safety of the small town where he lives and wondering how—and if—he would survive in a big-city gang.

Eric openly admits that he is responsible for the choices he has made in his life, and he talks without shame about his fears. "I don't know what I'm afraid of," he says, "but sooner or later something bad is going to happen."

He gets choked up when he talks about his friends who have been "sent up" to juvenile institutions or when he recalls the events of the night when Stranger, one of his closest friends, died. Eric was standing on the lawn of a friend's house, "just drinking beer and shooting the bull," when a car pulled up. Five strangers got out of the car, and a fight broke out. Then there was a "pop," and Stranger was lying on the ground, shot in the chest. Eric helped carry his friend inside; he was holding Stranger's head in his lap when he died.

In lighter moments Eric likes to talk about his tattoos. He'll even lift up his shirt (laughing, asking you not to make fun of his beer belly) and show you the colorful words and pictures on his back and chest.

He's especially proud of the tattoo on his chest that runs from one shoul-der blade to the other and reads: IF YOU COULD ONLY SEE INSIDE ME.

Why did Eric have those words permanently engraved on his chest?

He raises his eyebrows and smiles, slowly, thoughtfully, and in that moment, he looks about ten years old.

"Because people don't see the real me—they only see the outside," he ex-plains. "You got to know me from the inside, too. You know what I mean?"

The inside versus the outside—how many of us make judg-ments based on what we see from the outside? How many of us bother to look, with patience and compassionate concern, at the inside?

Eric knows that he is judged by the way he looks on the outside—the brown skin and dark eyes, the baggy pants, shaved head, and tattoos. He is also judged for his gang involvement, drug use, and criminal record, which follow him from school to school, from one court appearance to another, and from one job interview to the next. People who look at the black-and-white facts of Eric's life and then match those facts with his appearance almost invariably conclude, "This is a bad kid."

Adolescents who regularly use drugs—and who cannot seem to quit no matter how many problems they experience—are inevitably judged from the outside. Labeled drug abusers, juvenile delinquents, and threats to the community, they are kicked out of schools, bounced around from one helping agency to another, cycled through the juvenile justice system, and, in many cases, incarcerated in juvenile institutions for months, even years.

Because they keep drinking and using, they are considered irresponsible, careless, self-centered, and immature. The labels "drug abusers" and "addicts" isolate them from the rest of normal society and undermine their identity as people of merit and worth. They are branded with the stigma of a disorder that is not recognized as a true medical condition but as a symptom of moral degeneration, a character defect or personality flaw.

This one word—*stigma*—is extremely important in understanding substance-use disorders and the reasons why they have been so difficult to diagnose and treat. The *Oxford English Dictionary* defines *stigma* as "a mark of infamy or subjection, a sign of public abhorrence," and cites the stigma inflicted on African-American slaves as an example. Hundreds of years ago, slave owners branded their slaves with the "stigma" of scars and cuts, making it easier for their owners to catch them if they ran away. Slaves carried these visible signs of shame and debasement for life.

The stigma of drug addiction, like all stigmas, creates a permanent if invisible stain on a person's character and reputation.

Branded by censure and condemnation, the addict's identity is spoiled, scarred, and disgraced, as he or she is "reduced in our minds from a whole and usual person to a tainted, discounted one," as Canadian sociologist Erving Goffman wrote several decades ago.

The stigma associated with drug problems and drug addiction has existed from the beginning of recorded time. The Bible warns that whoever is led astray by strong drink is "not wise." (Proverbs 20:1). Good men and women are advised to "not associate" with drunkards. "With such a man do not even eat" (1 Corinthians 5:11). Heaven's doors are closed to drunkards; for, as the Bible reminds us, those who engage in drunkenness, debauchery, and the like "shall not inherit the Kingdom of God" (Galatians 5;19-21).

Thousands of years later—despite the scientific research demonstrating that drug addiction is a genetically influenced, physiological disease—we continue to view drunkenness and drug disorders as signs of moral weakness, character defects, or personality disorders. In a 1979 survey, 67 percent of 2,187 respondents expressed the belief that alcoholism is a sign of "personal emotional weakness." Only 19 percent of people surveyed believed alcoholism is solely a health problem.

A survey conducted nearly twenty years later reveals that our attitudes toward alcoholics have not changed significantly over the years. Based on telephone and one on-one interviews with more than two thousand people, the survey concludes:

Most people see alcoholism as having elements of both disease and weakness. Fewer than one in four say alcoholism is 100 percent disease. In fact, the majority of every group surveyed, except psychiatrists and counselors, said alcoholism is at least 25 percent due to moral or personal weakness.

Counselors are most likely to accept alcoholism as a physical or mental illness, attributing an average 70 percent to disease and 20 percent to weakness. Doctors see alcoholism as 64 percent disease and 31 percent weakness, and family members view it as 56 percent disease and 39 percent weakness.

Even people who have been clean and sober for years feel the sting of stigma. A 2001 survey reveals that one in four people in recovery have experienced discrimination in the workplace or in seeking health care, and one in five fear being fired if their employer finds out they are recovering alcoholics or addicts.

For family members, it is guilt by association. Helping professionals often focus exclusively on family dynamics, implicitly or explicitly blaming parents for the child's misbehaviors. Parents also blame themselves, fearing that their parenting style contributed to their children's emotional and behavioral problems. Self-blame and feelings of anger, guilt, and fear that the family as a whole will be judged as abnormal isolate parents and other family members and prevent them from seeking help for their children.

In a comprehensive 1999 review of the literature on the stigma of drug use and drug users, researchers describe the painful paradox confronting family members:

> The family member is part of the "normal" social world of the non-stigmatized. Yet, on the other hand, the family member shares the stigma of his/her loved one and also has membership in the social world of the stigmatized . . . families of stigmatized people are seen as "normal" yet "different."

Parents and other family members generally respond to this "normal yet different" label in one of two ways, according to the researchers. They either accept their drug-dependent family member "in the hopes of showing the world how to treat their loved one with compassion," or they distance themselves from the addicted person "in order to shield themselves against stigma."

Family members appear to suffer the most stigma when dealing with professionals, including teachers, school administrators, police officers, lawyers, judges, and employees of the criminal justice system. Researchers report that parents often feel "ignored, blamed and de-valued when dealing with people in these agencies," and frequently experience difficulty getting professionals "to respond appropriately to their child's drug abuse."

Most frustrating of all, many parents feel that bureaucratic agencies and helping professionals blame them for their children's drug problems and hold them responsible for finding solutions. University of Colorado researcher Judith A. Barton discusses the gap between what parents want from helping agencies and what they receive:

> The parents wanted these supposedly impersonal bureaucratic organizations to enforce the rules and laws, to charge the child with wrongdoing so that the child could be socialized about the consequences of drug abuse. Instead, the bureaucrats appeared to be reacting personally against the parents. The message parents received was that it was their responsibility to control the child, with minimal support from community institutions.

When researchers at the Centre for Addiction and Mental Health in Canada asked family members to respond to the question, "What is it that you would really like other people to know or think about someone who has (or has had) a problem with substance use?" they received some fascinating answers.

- "They're not all bad. There is good in them. Look past that part to see what else is there."
- "Look beyond the obvious and view the underlying problem."
- "Families expend a lot of energy to keep the problem quiet."
- "I like the expression: 'It takes a whole village to raise a family.' But that's not the way it is."
- "Behaviors are a symptom of something. Instead of just looking at the person as a user or abuser, wonder why."
- "They probably have a deeper problem than the one you're seeing. They need help and understanding rather than being shunned or having backs turned on them."
- "Blame doesn't help. It doesn't help them to say, 'You should do this.' They're enmeshed and entangled in this whole set of behaviors."

Responding to the same question, people addicted to drugs gave these revealing answers:

- "I am much more than my addiction."
- "Don't push me to the back of the line. I'm just the same person as you are—only I had an addiction problem."
- "I'm a human being. These are just some of my warts—we all have them."
- "The Greek concept of 'agape' means to 'love in spite of.' I want people to care about me and each other in that way. That makes recovering a lot easier."

The blame and shame intensify when adolescents suffer from co-occurring emotional or behavioral disorders—and researchers estimate that between 50 and 90 percent of adolescents in treatment for substance-use disorders have diagnosable mental health disorders. A 2001 report by the Federation of Families for Children's Mental Health explores the problem.

[Y]outh and family members were severely blamed and shamed by providers and systems when what they needed was nonjudgmental recognition of their struggle to find caring help and support. Both youth and their parents pointed out that blaming one another hurts deeply and contributes to the complex array of problems they face (i.e., anger, hurt, frustration, lack of services and support, isolation, disappointment, conflict, etc.). . . .

Many youth want to get better, but react strongly to the inhumane way in which they feel they are treated. They become resistant to participation or, at best, they "fake it" to get through a program. The result is release from treatment (after the standard period of time) without any change—often resulting in a relapse.

The stigma leveled on both drug-using adolescents and their parents is persistent, and it is deeply painful. Most problematic of all, this pervasive stigma breeds numerous myths and misconceptions that prevent young people and their family members from understanding the complexities of their problems and the essential elements required for accurate and effective assessment, diagnosis, intervention, treatment, and recovery. Branded by the stigma of drug abuse and addiction, fearful of censure, filled with shame and self-blame, adolescents and their parents come to believe that they have no place to turn, nowhere to go.

How do we break the cycle? We replace myths with facts. Relying on factual information that is firmly rooted in scientific research, we can educate ourselves and others, dismantle the prevailing myths and misconceptions, and release our children, and ourselves, from hopelessness and despair.

In the remainder of this chapter, we will present the most pervasive myths about adolescent drug use and addiction. A brief factual statement and page references guiding the reader to sections of the book where the facts are elaborated follow each myth. We ask you to read this section on myths and facts with great care and thoughtful reflection. Like all prejudices and biases, these myths directly affect the way we think about ourselves, and the way we treat each other. Only with an open mind and the willingness to accept a different reality can we know the truth and absorb it into our everyday thoughts and behavior. Only then can we make a real and lasting difference in our efforts to help kids in trouble with alcohol and other drugs.

The Myths and Facts
About Adolescent Drug Use and Addiction

MYTH: Alcohol isn't really a drug—at least it's not as bad as LSD, cocaine, marijuana, methamphetamines, or heroin.
FACT: Alcohol is a toxic, potentially addictive drug that causes more damage to the individual and society than all illegal drugs combined—in fact, alcohol kills nearly seven times more young Americans than all illegal drugs combined. *(See pages 69–88.)*

MYTH: Marijuana is not physically addictive.

FACT: Although physical withdrawal symptoms are generally subtle compared to other addictive drugs, recent research clearly shows that marijuana can be physically addicting. Furthermore, studies indicate that regular marijuana use can have profoundly damaging long-term effects on adolescents' physical, mental, and emotional health. (*See pages 115–119.*)

MYTH: Alcoholism and other drug addictions progress in similar ways in adolescents and adults.

FACT: Addiction progresses much faster in adolescents (we call it hyperspeed addiction) for three basic reasons: (1) The adolescent's developing brain and other vital organs are extremely vulnerable to the toxic effects of drugs; (2) adolescents start using drugs at an early age, often beginning in middle school or even in elementary school; and (3) adolescents often combine drugs, taking two, three, four, or more drugs at a time, which dramatically increases the risk of brain damage and drug addiction. (*See pages 38–42.*)

MYTH: Raging hormones trigger the majority of problems associated with adolescent drug use.

FACT: Brain development and reorganization is the major culprit. Around the age of eleven and continuing for the next decade, the brain undergoes major reorganization and maturation. During this stage of brain growth and consolidation, adolescents are extremely vulnerable to drug addiction. (*See pages 42–45.*)

MYTH: Parents' approval or disapproval of their children's drug use has little or no impact on whether or not their kids will use.

FACT: When parents are concerned and actively involved in their children's lives, they can have a powerful influence on adolescent drug use. Recent research confirms that when parents are educated about substance-use disorders and become involved in constructive ways in their children's lives, they can exert a strong and enduring influence on their children's decision to use drugs and their willingness to seek help for drug problems. (*See pages 237–252; 339–363.*)

MYTH: Adolescents and adults require the same kind of treatment for their drug problems.

FACT: Adolescents differ from adults in the drugs they use, patterns of drug use, physical and emotional development, cognitive abilities, values, and belief systems. Co-occurring emotional and behavioral disorders including depression, anxiety disorders, and eating disorders are more common among adolescents. Involvement with peers who use drugs often triggers relapses. Family issues often complicate treatment and recovery. For all these reasons, treatment must be tailored to the adolescent's unique developmental, psychological, social, and environmental needs. *(See pages 270–300.)*

MYTH: Treatment doesn't work because the majority of adolescents relapse.

FACT: Success rates in treatment will vary depending on the type of treatment adolescents receive and the severity of their physical, emotional, and behavioral problems. Adolescents may receive inappropriate or ineffective treatment, and many adolescents who need treatment for co-occurring emotional or behavioral disorders never receive it. Relapses must not be regarded as failures, but as signs that more intensive treatment is needed. Continuing care programs are an essential element of treatment and can dramatically reduce relapses. *(See pages 301–316.)*

MYTH: Treatment doesn't work unless the adolescent is ready for it.

FACT: Adolescents who are coerced or forced into treatment by their parents, school administrators, probation officers, or the legal system are just as successful in treatment and recovery as adolescents who willingly enter treatment. *(See pages 297–300.)*

MYTH: Adolescents who get into trouble with drugs cause most if not all of their problems by their irresponsible behaviors and decisions.

FACT: When adolescents (and adults) use drugs—even if they use them "responsibly"—they are likely to make irresponsible decisions because alcohol and other drugs disrupt the brain's chemical and electrical functions, dramatically altering our thoughts, feelings, and behaviors and undermining our ability to make healthy choices and decisions. *(See pages 23–65.)*

Why Kids Get Hooked

I have a need inside my head.

WILL, *seventeen*

*D*erek, *thirteen, Janelle, fourteen, and Lisa, fourteen, are talking about why kids use drugs. Dressed in orange overalls and blue Velcro slippers, the three teenagers are locked up in the Juvenile Justice Detention Center.*

Janelle is the most experienced drug user. She was six years old when her alcoholic mother gave her a wine cooler, eight years old when she first tried marijuana, and twelve years old when she became addicted to methamphetamines. This is her fifteenth stay in the detention center in three years.

Derek used marijuana for the first time when his father took him on a camping trip and shared a joint with him. He was eight years old at the time.

Lisa began drinking when she was eleven. She is the quietest member of the group and will not talk about her past. "Something very bad happened," she explains.

Derek and Janelle nod their heads respectfully. They, too, have bad things in their past that they don't want to talk about.

But talking about drugs is easy. They know this subject, and they are eager to show off their knowledge and experience.

"Why do kids use drugs?" Derek repeats the question. "That's easy—to feel relaxed, get rid of stress, be happy."

"Some kids use drugs to get rid of pain, you know, to make them forget about their childhood," says Lisa.

Derek nods his head in agreement. "Yeah, to forget our troubles, you know, ease the pain."

Janelle looks impatient. "Look, I can tell you exactly why kids start using drugs; I can give you twenty reasons, are you ready?" She starts ticking off the reasons, and for each one she holds up a finger. "To feel good. To feel less stressed and more relaxed. To feel normal. Because your parents use, or your brothers or sisters use. Because you're curious about how this drug or that drug will make you feel. Because you want to be like older kids you admire who use drugs. Because other kids make fun of you and won't leave you alone if you don't use. Because drugs are everywhere."

She takes a deep breath and then continues adding up the reasons. "To forget about family problems. To be bad, which, you know, means to be good—if you're bad, you're good, right?"

Derek and Lisa nod their heads and smile; they know what she means.

"To have fun, to be cool, to go into a different world, to be a rebel, to get away from adults who keep telling you what you should be doing and who think they can control your life."

Janelle smiles, proud of her ability to come up with so many different reasons why kids use drugs. But then she frowns and adds an interesting observation. "You know, really, it's kind of a stupid question, asking why kids use drugs. We use drugs because they're there and because they make you feel good, or at least different for a while. I don't know anyone who hasn't used drugs."

Why Kids Use Drugs

Janelle is close to the truth. According to the 2002 Monitoring the Future Survey, nearly 25 percent of eighth-graders have used illegal drugs, 47 percent have used alcohol, and more than 31 percent have smoked cigarettes. For twelfth-graders, those alarming statistics become even more frightening—53 percent of high school seniors admit to having used illegal drugs, 78 percent have used alcohol, and 57 percent have smoked cigarettes.

Columbia University researchers recently reported that more than five million high school students (31 percent of all high schoolers) say they binge drink at least once a month. Male and female ninth-graders are just as likely to drink (40 percent versus 41 percent), and one-third of sixth- and ninth-graders say they get their alcohol from home.

These statistics alert us to the epidemic of adolescent drug use and addiction that threatens our children, but they still don't answer the question—"Why are so many kids using alcohol and other drugs?" The answer to this simple query is extraordinarily complex. Many kids use drugs for the same general reasons adults use drugs—to get high, to feel happy, stimulated, relaxed, or intoxicated; to ease stress, frustration, tension, disappointment, fear, or anger; to take their minds off their pain or their troubles.

Kids may start drinking or using other drugs to impress their friends, to rebel against their parents or society, or because they don't want to be seen as preppies or suck-ups.

If their friends have a few beers or smoke a bowl on Friday night, adolescents may join in to keep them company, to fit in, or to avoid drawing attention to themselves. If they belong to a gang, they may use drugs to win respect, to be cool, or just because that's what everyone else is doing.

When adolescents are particularly tense, stressed, or upset—say, after they get a bad grade or following a tearful argument with parents or friends—they may use more drugs than normal in an attempt to ease their distress. Adolescents who are anxious or fearful may use alcohol and/or other drugs to boost their self-confidence. Extroverted, outgoing teenagers may use drugs because they like the company of other fun-loving, risk-taking kids.

Adolescents may change their drug habits—using more, cutting back, or quitting altogether—because of life changes, the death of a family member or friend, parent problems (divorce, illness, drug problems), failing grades, suspension from school, or legal troubles.

Emotional and psychological problems such as loneliness, depression, fears, and insecurities will affect the adolescent's drug use. When everything is going well, many adolescents experience no desire to use, but when problems arise, their drug use may increase.

Adolescents who have diagnosed or undiagnosed behavioral and/or emotional disorders such as conduct disorder, oppositional defiant disorder, chronic depression, chronic anxiety, or attention deficit hyperactivity disorder are even more likely to experiment with drugs and to continue using despite recurrent problems related to their drug use.

Adolescents who have been or continue to be victimized or maltreated are more likely to use drugs at an earlier age and have higher levels of use.

To sum it up, adolescents use drugs for numerous reasons. But at some point, something different happens to the kids who get in trouble with drugs. They may want to cut back or stop using, but they can't, at least not for very long. Their personalities begin to change. The sensitive boy may become insensitive, the extroverted girl turns introverted, the gentle child is suddenly belligerent, the friendly kid becomes hostile, and the compassionate friend suddenly couldn't care less.

When they use drugs often enough and in large-enough amounts, formerly happy, high-functioning, well-adjusted kids become irritable, moody, and depressed. They angrily deny that drinking alcohol or smoking marijuana is affecting their mood or personality, and they blame their rebellious behavior on anyone and everyone else—the too-strict parent, the teachers who don't understand them, the bullies who won't leave them alone, the friends who have deserted them, the coaches who give up on them, the counselors who, they say, don't have a clue what they are thinking or feeling.

When they can no longer deny that their drug use is causing problems, they solemnly vow to quit or cut down. Within days or weeks, their promises are broken. Family relationships begin to slowly, painfully deteriorate, old friendships dissolve, and interest in schoolwork fades away.

What's happening? The answer is extremely complex, for there are multiple pathways—physical, emotional, behavioral, social, developmental, familial—that can lead to drug use and potential drug problems in adolescents. In this chapter, we will focus on the biological and genetic factors that control the adolescent's reaction to drugs and susceptibility to addiction. In the next chapter, we will explore the numerous environmental influences that can affect the onset and progression of adolescent drug problems.

Why Some Kids Get Hooked

Psychological and sociological research indicates that the environment can trigger, worsen, or to some degree alleviate the genetic predisposition [to alcoholism and other drug addictions], but the determining factors are biogenetic and biochemical.

— KENNETH BLUM, Ph.D.

While no one is predestined to become addicted to drugs, we all enter life with varying degrees of vulnerability to drug dependence. Just as some people are more susceptible to diabetes, heart disease, and cancer, so are certain people more physically vulnerable to alcohol and other drug addictions. We inherit this predisposition to certain diseases or disorders from the genes passed down to us by our parents, grandparents, great-grandparents, and on down the line.

Most research studies dealing with the biogenetic aspects of drug addiction focus on the drug alcohol, because beer, wine, and distilled spirits are legal and readily available, and because people (young and old) have been drinking alcohol in one form or another for thousands of years. Almost half of all Americans age twelve or over—109 million people—are current drinkers. More than ten million youths between the ages of twelve and twenty (28.5 percent of that age group) use alcohol, and of this number, 6.8 million (19 percent) are considered binge drinkers, drinking five or more drinks on one occasion.

While alcohol is the drug most often studied by researchers, most experts agree that addiction is addiction is addiction no matter what drug is used. Thus, the basic facts about alcohol dependence also hold true for addiction to nicotine, marijuana, cocaine, heroin, methamphetamines, prescription painkillers, tranquilizers, and sedatives, and all other addictive drugs. Different genes and gene combinations are almost certainly involved, but the basic neurological and biological changes that underlie drug addiction remain the same for all addictive drugs.

You don't need to be a geneticist to understand the basic and most essential point underlying addiction—your likelihood of becoming addicted to drugs is determined, in large part, by the genes you inherit from your parents. In alcoholism, for example, we know that the children of alcoholics have a much greater risk of addiction. If one parent is alcoholic, the risk of addiction for the child is approximately 40 percent, or about four times the risk in the general population. If both parents are alcoholics, the risk increases to about 60 percent.

What, exactly, do the children of alcoholics inherit? Multiple genes are involved—perhaps dozens of genes. Some genes may increase the risk of inheriting a predisposition to drug addiction while others decrease the risk, and all these complicated genetic factors interact with various environmental influences to create each individual's unique response to drugs.

We will attempt to simplify the genetic research by focusing on certain key findings. This brief review of the genetic territory can be compared to a quick tour through a foreign country in which you visit only the big cities and popular tourist attractions. You'll get a general sense of the place, but if you want to travel farther and wider into the outlying countryside, we suggest you look in "Resources" at the back of this book for recommended books and educational Web sites.

Preference for Alcohol

Tampering with the genetic code of rodents, researchers have created strains of rats and mice that love the taste of alcohol and others that can't stand it. The DBA and C3H strains of mice, for example, consistently prefer water over alcohol when given a choice, while the C57 and C58 strains will choose alcohol over water almost every time. The offspring of the alcohol-loving rodents inherit their parents' fondness for booze, while the descendants of the alcohol-hating mice simply don't like the stuff.

The same thing happens in the world of human beings—some people love the effect of alcohol (even if they can't stand the taste), while others might enjoy a glass of wine or a beer every now and then, and still others have no desire to drink, period.

Animal studies and our own very human experience confirm that genes have a profound effect on *preference*—the desire to drink or abstain from drinking alcohol.

Adoption Studies

In the 1970s, scientists began studying the drinking patterns of adopted children of alcoholics to determine if heredity or environment is most influential in the development of alcoholism. Numerous studies by internationally renowned researchers provide strong confirmation of the genetic link. The important findings generated by this line of research are summarized below:

- Adopted children whose biological parents were alcoholics are *four* times more likely than adopted children of nonalcoholics to become addicted to alcohol.
- Personal contact with the alcoholic biological parent does not affect the likelihood of developing a drinking problem.
- When children whose biological parents were *not* alcoholics are adopted into alcoholic households, they do *not* have an increased risk of alcoholism associated with being raised by alcoholics.
- Adopted children whose biological parents were alcoholics were no more likely to have a psychiatric disturbance than the adopted children whose biological parents were not alcoholics.

Three decades of adoption studies provide clear and unequivocal evidence that predisposition to alcoholism can be passed down from parent to child through the genes. Thus, if you inherit the genes that increase susceptibility to alcoholism, you are significantly more likely to become an alcoholic if you drink.

Brain Wave Abnormalities

In the late 1970s, Henri Begleiter and his colleagues at New York State University in Brooklyn began studying certain brain abnormalities in what is called the P3 brain wave. In a series of studies that continue to this day, Dr. Begleiter's research team discovered that certain deficits in the P3 brain wave exist in alcoholics even many years after they stop drinking.

The researchers then compared the sons of alcoholics, ages seven to thirteen, with the sons of nonalcoholics. Though neither group had ever been exposed to alcohol or other drugs, the sons of alcoholics also had abnormalities in their P3 brain wave.

These electrophysiological "brain marker" studies strongly suggest, in Dr. Begleiter's words, "that decrements in P3 activity are not a consequence of years of heavy drinking but are genetic antecedents of alcohol abuse." In other words, certain brain abnormalities that predispose people to alcoholism are passed from the alcoholic parent to the child—they are part of our genetic inheritance.

Acetaldehyde Buildup

When alcohol is metabolized in the liver, it is converted first to acetaldehyde, a highly toxic (poisonous) substance, and then to acetate. Research teams led by Charles S. Lieber, M.D., have discovered that the same amount of alcohol produces very different blood acetaldehyde levels in alcoholics and nonalcoholics— approximately 50 percent higher in alcoholics. Unfortunately, acetaldehyde is a nasty troublemaker, creating havoc in the liver, the brain, the heart, and other vital organs.

Why are the acetaldehyde levels so much higher in alcoholics? A superefficient metabolic system (called the microsomal ethanol oxidizing system or MEOS) appears to be responsible. Adolescents who are genetically predisposed to alcoholism and who drink heavily and/or regularly may unknowingly set this system into motion, causing the toxic acetaldehyde to build up in the liver. A vicious cycle develops—as alcohol consumption increases, metabolic activity revs up and increased amounts of acetaldehyde are produced, causing damage to the cells responsible for breaking down and eliminating acetaldehyde, which results in more acetaldehyde buildup.

In the liver, a buildup of acetaldehyde causes widespread cell destruction and death. But the damage isn't confined solely to the liver, for some acetaldehyde also travels to the heart, the brain, and other vital organs. In the heart, acetaldehyde inhibits the synthesis of proteins in the heart muscle, which can lead to impaired cardiac functioning. And in the brain, acetaldehyde interacts with certain chemical messengers called neurotransmitters, leading some researchers to theorize that acetaldehyde buildup may be at least partly responsible for the development of neurological addiction and the symptoms of increased tolerance, craving, withdrawal, and progressive loss of control.

Dopamine Deficiencies

Dopamine is a natural brain chemical (neurotransmitter) that makes us feel good. Like its close cousins serotonin, norepinephrine, and GABA, dopamine is one of many mood-lifting, pleasure-inducing chemical messengers that regularly course through our brains, regulating our moods, reducing compulsive behavior, and generally increasing feelings of well-being.

Some people are born with naturally higher levels of these neurotransmitters than others; they are blessed with an abundance of feel-good chemicals from birth. Other people inherit deficiencies in dopamine and other neurotransmitters; they have less dopamine surging through their brains, which may contribute to chronic feelings of depression, anxiety, irritability, and moodiness.

Alcoholics appear to inherit several genes that influence their natural dopamine levels. In 1990, a team of researchers led by Kenneth Blum, Ph.D., and Ernest Noble, M.D., discovered one gene mutation (the D2 dopamine receptor gene) associated with alcoholism. They theorized that a genetically transmitted defect in this gene leads to deficiencies in dopamine receptors in the brain, which in turn leads to a reduced supply of the feel-good chemical dopamine.

Alcoholics are much more likely to have this genetic abnormality than nonalcoholics, the researchers discovered. Because alcohol works almost instantaneously to open up the dopamine faucets, flooding the brain with the pleasure-creating brain chemical, children who inherit this gene mutation may use alcohol in an attempt to restore a "normal" dopamine balance.

Thus, when kids say they use alcohol in order to feel normal, they may be expressing a scientific truth. For alcohol works quickly and efficiently to raise dopamine levels, thereby creating immediate and intense sensations of pleasure, euphoria, and general well-being. Unfortunately and often tragically, this "wow" reaction to alcohol may be a sign of an underlying chemical imbalance in the brain—which is, in turn, regulated by genetic variations that predispose certain individuals to alcoholism and/or other drug addictions.

Dopamine also plays an important role when adolescents use other dopamine-boosting drugs such as marijuana, nicotine, cocaine, methamphetamines, and heroin. Kids who have low levels of certain dopamine receptors in the brain respond to these drugs in different ways than kids with high levels, and researchers believe these abnormalities in brain dopamine activity may explain why some kids get hooked on drugs. Research by Nora Volkow, M.D., current director of the National Institute on Drug Abuse and an expert on the brain's dopamine system, strongly supports the theory that impairments in the brain's dopamine system affect whether or not an adolescent is likely to continue to use drugs and eventually become addicted to drugs.

Low-Intensity Reaction

Do you have a high tolerance for alcohol? Can you drink a lot and still function somewhat normally? Are you known as the life of the party?

If you answered yes to these questions, you may be insensitive to the effects of alcohol and thus at greater risk of developing alcoholism. In several long-term studies, researchers discovered that the children of alcoholics are much more likely than children of nonalcoholics to experience this lower-intensity reaction to alcohol's effects. In a ten-year study conducted between 1978 and 1988, psychiatrist-researcher Marc Schuckit evaluated the effects of three to five drinks (the amount depended on the subject's weight) on the behavioral and perceptual reactions of 453 college age men. Half of the men had severely impaired alcoholic fathers, while the other half (the control group) had no known alcoholic biological relatives.

Reactions were measured by subjective feelings of intoxication, measures of brain activity, hormone levels, and motor performance (coordination) tests that calculated body sway when under the influence. Forty percent of the young men with a positive family history of alcoholism demonstrated remarkably low levels of response to alcohol, as compared to 10 percent of the control group. From his research, Schuckit concluded that "reduced sensitivity to lower doses of alcohol makes it more likely that excessive alcohol consumption and subsequent alcohol-related difficulties will occur in about half of the children of alcoholics."

A follow-up study conducted ten years later confirmed Schuckit's preliminary conclusions. Fifty-six percent of the group with a family history of alcoholism and low levels of alcohol response was diagnosed as alcoholics, compared to 14 percent of the men with high levels of sensitivity to alcohol and no family history of alcoholism. From these studies, we can conclude that an adolescent's initial level of response to alcohol appears to be a potent predictor of future alcoholism risk.

Dr. Schuckit has been very careful to point out in his discussions of this research that the future risk of alcoholism for these young men was *not* related to any higher risk for psychiatric disorders such as severe depression or anxiety.

Summary of the Biological and Genetic Evidence

The scientific evidence clearly shows that the interactions among different hereditary and physiological factors underlie an individual's susceptibility to alcoholism and other drug addictions. The interplay among these factors is extremely complex and cannot be reduced to a simple formula, nor can it be explained by singling out a defective gene or abnormal enzyme. Many different neurophysiological and biochemical events are operating simultaneously to influence your or your child's unique reaction to alcohol and other drugs.

While biogenetic factors are fundamental to understanding why adolescents respond in different ways to the physical and mind-altering effects of alcohol and other drugs, numerous environmental factors also play an important role as they influence the onset, progression, and severity of drug-related problems and chemical dependency. This is the story we will tell in the next chapter.

4.

Beyond the Genes

We do not know, in most cases, how
far social failure and success are due
to heredity, and how far to environment. But environment is the easier
of the two to improve.

—J. B. S. HALDANE

B iology is not destiny. Because you have a predisposition to a
certain disorder or disease does not mean that you are doomed
to get it. Your unique and highly individual chemical makeup will
play an important role in your susceptibility to alcohol and other
drug problems, as will your general health, diet, stress level, exercise patterns, exposure to environmental toxins, and so on. As
Ting-Kai Li, M.D., director of the National Institute on Alcohol
Abuse and Alcoholism, explains: "The development of alcoholism
is not a case of genetics versus the environment; it is one of genetics and the environment."

The environment plays a significant role in substance-use disorders because anything that increases an individual's exposure to
alcohol or other drugs will affect his or her risk of using and, therefore, experiencing serious, even life-threatening drug problems.
We begin this chapter by focusing on the three major environmental factors contributing to an increased risk of drug problems and

chemical dependence in adolescents: (1) prenatal exposure to alcohol or other drugs; (2) early age of first drink (AFD); and (3) multidrug use (using more than one drug at a time).

We will then look briefly at other developmental, social, emotional, and familial risk factors for adolescents, including adolescent brain development; sensitivity to alcohol and/or other drugs; parental drug use; victimization and maltreatment; emotional and behavioral disorders; attention deficient hyperactivity disorder; learning disabilities; head injuries; stress and post-traumatic stress disorder; gang involvement; poverty; and gender differences.

Prenatal Exposure

Born three months early to an alcoholic mother, Carrie barely survived serious respiratory problems, jaundice, and spinal meningitis.

From the time she can remember, her mother beat her with a belt; she was always careful, though, to hit Carrie only on her chest, back, and buttocks, so no one could see the bruises and welts.

When she was twelve, Carrie started drinking beer and cheap wine. By age fourteen, she was having regular blackouts and drinking to the point of passing out several times a week. She ran away from home half a dozen times. One day she got drunk, stole a car, and crashed into a telephone pole. Now fifteen, she is serving a one-year sentence in a juvenile institution.

Children who inherit a genetic predisposition to alcoholism must start drinking in order to fire up the addictive process. If they never use alcohol or other drugs, they will never become addicted to them. Yet, tragically for many children, the first exposure to alcohol and/or other drugs occurs before they are even born.

Despite widespread educational efforts to increase public awareness of the risks to the developing fetus, increasing numbers of women are using alcohol and/or other drugs during pregnancy. Researchers estimate that as many as one-tenth of all infants may have been exposed to an illegal drug in utero (before birth).

Many more unborn children are exposed to legal drugs such as alcohol and nicotine. According to a 1998 national survey, 59 percent of women between the ages of fifteen and forty-four drank while pregnant. Sixty-six percent drank alcohol in their first trimester, 57 percent used alcohol in their second trimester, and 54 percent reported using alcohol in their third trimester. In the first research to link prenatal alcohol exposure to later drinking problems, a 2003 University of Washington study shows that 14 percent of twenty-one-year-olds whose mothers drank heavily during pregnancy showed signs of alcohol dependence compared to 4.5 percent of children whose mothers drank less or not at all.

The American Lung Association reports that 12.3 percent of the women who gave birth in 1999 smoked during pregnancy.

Young pregnant women are more likely than older women to use alcohol and other drugs during pregnancy, according to a recent study conducted by researchers at the Centers for Disease Control and Prevention.

Because the mother's blood is shared with the fetus, whenever the mother uses drugs, the unborn child does, too. Regular use of alcohol or other drugs during pregnancy and/or periodic binge drinking damage the developing child's brain. The specific effects and their impact, both short and long term, depend on the type of drugs being used as well as the dosage and frequency of use, but there is no doubt that using alcohol or other drugs in large amounts or over a long period of time can seriously and perhaps permanently damage the developing child's brain and other vital organs and increase his or her risk of developing drug problems and addiction later in life.

Most women who use drugs during pregnancy fail to disclose their drug use during prenatal exams. Whatever their reasons for withholding the truth—shame, guilt, fear of intervention and/or legal consequences—it is critically important that doctors, nurses, chemical dependency counselors, mental health workers, and other health care practitioners provide pregnant women with facts about drug use during pregnancy and offer counseling, treatment, and ongoing support services to women with drug problems.

Age of First Drink (AFD)

Adolescents who start drinking before age fifteen have a greatly increased risk of becoming alcohol-dependent.

In a landmark study published in 1998, researchers discovered that more than 40 percent of people who began drinking before age fifteen were later classified as alcohol-dependent (alcoholics), while only 10 percent of those who started drinking after age twenty-one became alcoholics. This conclusion points a heavy finger of blame at the liquor industry (including the makers of beer and wine), which spends many millions of dollars every year trying to lure young people to drink.

The research on early drinking continues. In a 2001 study, researchers at the University of Minnesota discovered that an early AFD (age of first drink) might be a symptom of an underlying physiological vulnerability to alcoholism. The researchers found that early AFD is associated with certain brain wave abnormalities (see page 30) that are considered "markers" for alcoholism. This means that children or adolescents who have this abnormal brain wave can be considered at high risk for developing alcoholism.

Adolescents with at least one parent with an early AFD are more likely to become early drinkers themselves—and this genetic vulnerability to addiction is associated with characterological disorders such as conduct disorder or oppositional defiant disorder. Boys with an early AFD are more likely to exhibit rebellious behaviors and symptoms of conduct disorder, such as bullying, physical cruelty to people or animals, lying, stealing, and deliberate destruction of property. For adolescent boys whose mothers and fathers both had an early AFD, 60 percent showed symptoms of conduct disorder and an early AFD themselves. Yet if neither parent had an early AFD, just 13 percent of boys had one or both of these conditions.

Traditionally, psychologists and mental health counselors would describe these children and adolescents as having "low behavioral constraint," meaning that they often act impulsively and seem to have little or no regard for social norms—the generally accepted rules for normal behavior. We might conclude, then, that adolescents who start drinking early are rebels and rule breakers. We might be tempted to label them deviant, abnormal, delinquent, or just plain bad kids. We might then leap to the conclusion that because they act impulsively and have such little regard for society's rules, they "abuse" alcohol and other drugs, thus running the risk of getting addicted.

If we look at the research, however, we see how these psychological labels and mental health diagnoses obscure a much more complicated truth. For scientists now believe that certain genetic mutations or variations may lead in early childhood to behavioral problems; then later, in adolescence, these same genetic variations (or closely related gene mutations) may contribute to alcohol and other drug problems.

Multidrug Use

"It's like a science experiment," says Rob, seventeen. "You drink alcohol and then take some Ecstasy, pop some OxyContin, or smoke some marijuana and wait to see what happens. Sometimes it's just a nice mellow buzz—but sometimes it's like an explosion and you're just gone—you feel completely out of it."

Rob sticks his tongue out the side of his mouth and rolls his eyes around to get a laugh. Then, suddenly, he's serious.

"It's weird, because you never know exactly what's going to happen. I've had some great times when I combined drugs, and I've had some really bad times. *Really* bad times," he repeats. "You just never know what's going to happen when you mix drugs."

Combining drugs can be deadly. You may have heard the story of Karen Ann Quinlan. One night in 1975, the twenty-one-year-old collapsed after combining alcohol and tranquilizers at a party. Doctors saved her life, but she suffered brain damage from oxygen deprivation and lapsed into a "persistent vegetative state." Quinlan remained in a coma for almost ten years in a New Jersey nursing home until her parents were successful in their legal battle to have her removed from all life-support equipment. She died in 1985.

Combining drugs killed actor-comedian John Belushi. Belushi, thirty-three, died in 1982 after ingesting a speedball (a potent combination of heroin and cocaine).

In 1997, actor-comedian Chris Farley died from a lethal combination of morphine and cocaine. An autopsy showed that Farley's liver was scarred by heavy drinking. Like his idol John Belushi, Farley was thirty-three years old.

Yet celebrity deaths pale in comparison to the thousands upon thousands of people in small towns and big cities throughout this country who have died from unintentional overdoses caused by combining different drugs. And there are many, many more people who have been rushed to hospital emergency rooms, had their stomachs pumped, and then been sent home (typically with no intervention for their drug problem), perhaps unaware how close they were to death.

Most adolescent drug users combine drugs. Why? Perhaps the most obvious answer is that they are curious about how high they can get and how much they can handle. It's a chemistry experiment, of sorts, with the thrill of risk taking being the main ingredient.

> I stopped getting really high on marijuana after a while. It just didn't do much for me, so I started combining it with alcohol and then I used marijuana with LSD and Ecstasy. I think the most drugs I've ever combined are five—marijuana, Ecstasy, alcohol, Vicodin, and mushrooms. I was flying that night. But that's nothing, really. I have some friends who have used eight drugs at one time. It's just something kids do, and it's both fun and scary because you never know what's going to happen.
>
> —JOHN, *sixteen*

For adolescents, the most common drug combination is marijuana and alcohol. Kids call these drugs "the regulars."

Most of my friends drink and smoke weed at the same time. Not many kids that I hang out with mess around with cocaine or heroin, but weed and beer—those are the regulars, the ones we use all the time.

—ALAINA, *fifteen*

Adolescents—and younger children—need to know about the dangers of combining drugs. When two or more drugs are used together, the individual effects of each drug are "potentiated." This means that one beer plus one bowl of marijuana doesn't equal the effects of two drinks or two bowls—instead the potency of the drugs is multiplied three times, four times, or more. It's like throwing gasoline on a smoldering fire. Maybe you'll get really lit. Maybe you'll black out, vomit, lose bladder control, or pass out.

Or maybe the drugs will interact explosively, and you'll have a seizure or stop breathing. It happens a whole lot more often than parents and kids would like to think. There's no predicting exactly what will happen when you combine drugs, even if you're using drugs that you've used many times before.

The first time I used alcohol, I mixed it with one of my mother's pain pills. She has arthritis bad. I was thirteen and I didn't know what I was doing, so I just drank a bunch of vodka and took the pill and the next thing I knew I was in the hospital with my mother and my uncle sobbing over me. I'd been in a coma for two days. The doctors and nurses told me they didn't think I would make it.

That scared me, but I didn't stop using drugs. They're just out there, and you can say no for a while but then you just sort of give in because everybody else is using them. I know drugs aren't doing me any good, but I can't sit in my room alone all day playing video games. You get lonely. You miss your friends. And when your friends use, believe me, eventually you will, too.

—BRIAN, *fifteen*

Combining drugs is dangerous and unpredictable for another reason. When adolescents regularly use two or more drugs together, they are much more vulnerable to becoming addicted. Multidrug use leads to a speeded-up addiction process, even in adolescents who may not have a genetic predisposition. These days it is not unusual to find children as young as eleven and twelve with full-blown addictions in inpatient and outpatient drug treatment centers. Virtually all these young adolescents combine drugs.

(For more information on multidrug use, see the sections on combining drugs in chapters 5 through 14.)

Adolescent Brain Development

If a teen is doing music or sports or academics, those are the cells and connections that will be hard-wired. If they're lying on the couch or playing video games or MTV, those are the cells and connections that are going [to] survive. . . .

It's a particularly cruel irony of nature that right at this time when the brain is most vulnerable is also the time when teens are most likely to experiment with drugs or alcohol. Sometimes when I'm working with teens, I actually show them these brain development curves, how they peak at puberty and then prune down and try to reason with them that if they're doing drugs or alcohol that evening, it may not just be affecting their brains for that night or even for that weekend, but for the next eighty years of their life.

—JAY GIEDD, M.D.
Neuroscientist with the National
Institute of Mental Health

In our lives we get two opportunities to develop brainpower. In early childhood our brains develop at an astonishing rate, reaching about 95 percent of adult volume by age five. Until relatively recently, researchers believed that this was the end of the growth spurt, but new studies show that we get one additional opportunity to grow more gray matter and, even more important, to organize the electrical and chemical brain circuitry that underlies maturity, self-control, emotional balance, rational decision making, memory formation, social skills, intelligence, and personality. This second round of brain development and reorganization occurs between the ages of ten and twenty-one.

To understand what happens to our brains in adolescence, we need to think in terms of *growth* and, equally as important, *pruning*. During adolescence the brain grows in quantity, packing in some extra gray matter (dense concentrations of brain tissue), adding new nerve fibers, and creating denser connections. At the same time, the brain starts cutting back on "deadweight," snipping off useless or nonessential branches and bundling nerve fibers together so they can function more efficiently. Like pruning a rosebush, these snips and cuts help the brain reorganize itself to function more efficiently, thereby allowing personality, emotional control, and reasoning skills to blossom.

The selective pruning process eventually results in less gray matter—between the ages of thirteen and eighteen, adolescents actually lose about 1 percent of their brain tissue every year—but helps to create a more highly coordinated, extremely efficient brain.

What do these structural brain changes, which take place in our second decade, mean in terms of adolescent drug use?

We know, first of all, that alcohol and other drugs interfere with normal brain function. Because the adolescent brain is still developing and maturing in ways that allow us to function as rational, reasonable, mature adults, drugs threaten our very survival by short-circuiting the normal processes of development and leading to long-term problems with memory, learning, speech, mood, and personality. Depending on the amount and frequency of drug use, these changes may be subtle and barely noticeable, or they may be profound and exert lasting influence on the adolescent's intellectual abilities, social skills, and personality development.

Drugs also interfere with what scientists call "neural plasticity"— the brain's ability to adapt and adjust to life experiences. Every experience we have reorganizes our brain circuitry, and that shuffling and sorting process allows us to form memories and learn from our experience. Alcohol, marijuana, cocaine, heroin, methamphetamines, and other drugs disrupt this neural plasticity. Connections that should bend and flex, yielding and adapting to experience, may become brittle and hard. Other connections may be cut off completely or short-circuited by the toxic effects of drugs. As a result, the communication lines between brain cells may be weak and fuzzy, like a bad phone connection, and memories may be only partially formed or never stored at all.

Because the adolescent's brain is still maturing, alcohol and other drugs affect kids in more profound and potentially damaging ways than they do adults. Throughout adolescence, as we've noted, the brain is adapting and flexing, simultaneously growing and cutting back as it matures in response to life experiences. These adaptive responses eventually become hard-wired, meaning that the electrical and chemical circuitry established in adolescence will be with you for the rest of your life. While you can change the "software" through experience—reading, traveling, meeting new people, and expanding your horizons in any number of ways—you will not be able to replace or recapture the hardware that has been damaged or destroyed by drug use.

Insensitivity and Ultrasensitivity to Alcohol

Adolescents and adults respond in different ways to the same amount of alcohol. Compared to adults, adolescents tend to be less sensitive to alcohol's calming effects, and they are also less sensitive to alcohol's effects on motor coordination. But when it comes to reasoning, logic, and memory—skills controlled by different brain structures—adolescents are much more vulnerable to alcohol-induced impairment. As one adolescent explains, "When I get loaded, I can walk and talk pretty good, but I can't think or remember much of anything."

Because their brains are still growing and maturing, adolescents are more sensitive than adults to the effects of alcohol on learning and memory. Because their bodies tend to mature earlier than their brains and because they are young, flexible, and physically agile, however, adolescents tend to be less sensitive to the effects of alcohol on motor performance and coordination.

This is a dangerous combination, a double whammy of sorts, for while adolescents may be able to stay awake and keep drinking long after adult drinkers stumble into bed, their decision-making skills, judgment, and memory are more profoundly affected by the drug. They will think they can do things that they cannot do safely under the influence of drugs, and they may make decisions that put their lives or the lives of others at risk.

> You should see me skateboard when I'm high. I swear, I can fly. All the fear is gone, but I don't lose any of my skill. That means I do all sorts of crazy things. Fun things. But I have to admit, I've made some really stupid decisions. Like this one time I decided to skate down these stairs, there must have been a hundred of them, and I just flipped out. I broke a couple teeth, knocked myself out, got cuts and scrapes everywhere—but for a while there, I was really flying. It was amazing.
>
> —CHRIS, *sixteen*

Parental Drug Use and Addiction

> The conscience of children is formed by the influences that surround them; their notions of good and evil are the result of the moral atmosphere they breathe.
>
> —RICHTER

Children who grow up with parents who use alcohol and other drugs are at greater risk for drug use and addiction for the following basic reasons:

- **HEREDITY:** Children may inherit their parents' genetic predisposition to alcohol and other drug addictions.
- **EXPOSURE:** Children whose parents use drugs are more likely to be exposed to drugs and drug users than children

whose parents abstain from using drugs. Children also tend to adopt their parents' attitudes toward drugs. If drugs are part of their everyday life, they may begin to view drug use as "normal."

- **STRESS:** When parents regularly use alcohol and/or other drugs, the child's home life is more likely to be stressful and chaotic. If one or both parents are addicted to drugs, stress levels are bound to be high and the risk of physical, sexual, and emotional abuse increases dramatically.

- **LACK OF DISCIPLINE:** Because people who are dependent on drugs spend a relatively large percentage of their time either high or preoccupied with getting high, they will have less time to spend with their children. Drugs profoundly affect the brain, impairing the parent's ability to reason and react in a reasonable way, control impulses, remember important dates and responsibilities, and keep emotions under control.

Adolescents whose parents are addicted to drugs have one additional risk factor—any attempt they make themselves to stop using drugs may be derailed by their parents or other drug-using family members, including brothers, sisters, cousins, aunts, uncles, and grandparents.

I want to quit drinking and smoking weed. I never admitted that to anybody, but I hate my life and I hate the person I'm becoming under the influence of drugs. You know, I steal and I lie and I treat people bad.

My parents are divorced, and I live with my father because my mother thinks I'm a total loser. My dad's an alcoholic. He drinks two six-packs a day, at least. And he thinks marijuana is a great drug. He's an aging hippie, you know. Anyway, he tells me to stay away from booze and smoke marijuana instead. I don't know. I think about getting clean, but then I think about living with my dad while he's drinking and smoking weed, and I just don't know if I can make it.

—DOUGLAS, *sixteen*

Victimization and Maltreatment

Numerous studies link sexual and physical victimization during childhood with drug use in adolescence. The research also suggests that victimization (especially sexual abuse) is linked to earlier onset of alcohol and/or drug use and higher levels of use. And early onset of use is directly related to an increased risk of addiction, legal involvement, behavioral and emotional problems, and poor post-treatment outcomes.

Here are the most recent facts about physical and sexual abuse:

- In 1999, an estimated 826,000 children younger than age eighteen were victims of abuse or neglect in the United States. Because this figure is based solely on reports to state agencies, researchers believe it grossly underestimates the number of children who are being victimized.
- Girls are four times more likely to be sexually victimized, but researchers believe boys underreport the prevalence of sexual trauma.
- Among adolescents treated for alcohol and/or other drug addictions, 39 percent of boys and 59 percent of girls reported current or past sexual and/or physical abuse.
- Adolescent alcohol addiction is strongly associated with conduct disorder, depression, anxiety, and post-traumatic stress disorder, but a history of childhood sexual abuse magnifies the severity of problems and adds to the risk of continued problems and poor treatment outcomes.
- Despite the high rates of maltreatment and victimization among adolescent drug users, questions about victimization experiences are not routinely included in standard assessments.

Emotional and Behavioral Disorders

When an emotionally troubled kid self-medicates with pot and alcohol, the interaction can be explosive and catastrophic. It can start with a depressed, scared, lonely eleven-year-old girl or boy who drinks and smokes pot for temporary relief; who finds that drinking and drugging is the admission fee to get into the crowd; who messes up at school; who gets into trouble with the law; who may end up in a psychiatric hospital, looking more mentally ill than they really are, or in a drug rehab center, or homeless. And by sixteen or seventeen you wouldn't know it's the same nice but unhappy eleven-year-old who needed help, didn't get it, and took slow poison instead.

—BERT PEPPER, M.D.
Clinical Professor of Psychiatry
at NYU Medical School

- One in ten children and adolescents in the United States suffer from serious emotional disorders, yet fewer than one in five receive appropriate treatment.
- Experts estimate that approximately half of all adolescents who are receiving mental health services have a co-occurring drug problem.
- Alcohol is the substance most commonly used by adolescents with serious emotional disturbances.
- Children with serious emotional problems are four times more likely to use and be dependent on illegal drugs than children without serious emotional problems.
- Forty to 60 percent of adolescents in alcohol and other drug treatment programs need attention for psychological or psychiatric problems.
- Frequent use of alcohol, marijuana, and other illegal drugs during adolescence increases the risk of psychological and emotional disorders later in life.

Drugs and serious emotional disturbances go hand in hand. Children and adolescents with undiagnosed mental health problems often turn to alcohol and other drugs as a way of self-medicating their anxiety, depression, insecurity, loneliness, or fear. While alcohol and other drugs may temporarily alleviate certain distressing symptoms, they inevitably and invariably make the mental health problem worse in the long run, intensifying the original symptoms and creating even more serious problems.

The interactions between drug use and specific mental health disorders are discussed below:

- **DEPRESSION:** An estimated 32 percent of adolescents and adults have depressive disorders, which can be primary or secondary to drug use. In adolescents, secondary or substance-induced mood disorders are approximately twice as common as primary depression; and in one study, researchers found that secondary depression in adolescents does not improve with abstinence, a finding that strongly suggests the need for accurate assessment and intensive, ongoing treatment of adolescent depression.

- **ANXIETY DISORDERS, INCLUDING SOCIAL PHOBIA, OBSESSIVE-COMPULSIVE DISORDER, AND PANIC DISORDER:** Adolescents with anxiety and panic disorders often use alcohol and/or other drugs to medicate their anxiety, alleviate their distress, and/or overcome shyness or social phobias. Yet drugs often intensify anxiety, fear, and panic.

- **CHARACTEROLOGICAL (CONDUCT) DISORDERS:** Adolescents with conduct disorders (characterized by deceitfulness, impulsivity, aggressiveness, irresponsibility, cruelty to animals and humans, and a pervasive pattern of disregard and violation of the rights of others) are thirteen times more likely to have a drug problem than kids who do not suffer from these disorders. Using drugs during adolescence also increases the risk of antisocial and disruptive disorders later in adolescence and adulthood.

- **BORDERLINE PERSONALITY DISORDER (BPD):** This disorder is characterized by impulsive and self-destructive behaviors, unstable moods, intense anger, and chronic feelings of emptiness. Adolescents with BPD often use alcohol and other drugs in an attempt to alleviate their fear, anger, and loneliness, but drug use only intensifies their symptoms and contributes to greater impulsivity. Adolescents with BPD and characterological disorders are more likely to drop out of treatment or relapse soon after treatment, and they also experience a greater risk of suicide.
- **BIPOLAR DISORDER (PREVIOUSLY KNOWN AS MANIC-DEPRESSIVE ILLNESS):** An estimated 30 to 60 percent of adolescents with bipolar disorder also have substance-use disorders. Bipolar disorders often begin during late adolescence, and symptoms include unstable moods, inflated self-esteem, racing thoughts, and excessive involvement in pleasurable activities (spending money, sex, using drugs, and so on). In an attempt to control the highs and lows associated with bipolar disease, adolescents may self-medicate with alcohol, stimulants, or depressant drugs. Recent research shows that bipolar disorder patients who are also dependent on alcohol and/or other drugs have a 40 percent lifetime rate of attempted suicide.
- **SCHIZOPHRENIA:** Schizophrenia, which may include symptoms such as auditory hallucinations, illusions, delusions, and disordered thinking, is rare in children under twelve but occurs in about three out of every thousand adolescents. Up to 60 percent of people with schizophrenia use drugs in an attempt to manage or deny their symptoms. While most experts agree that alcohol and other drugs do not cause schizophrenia, certain drugs such as PCP and LSD can create schizophrenia-like symptoms in otherwise healthy adolescents. Alcohol and other drugs can also make schizophrenic symptoms worse or trigger psychotic episodes in adolescents suffering from schizophrenia.

Eating Disorders
(Anorexia Nervosa, Bulimia, and Body Dysmorphic Disorder)

Adolescence is the time when young people, particularly women, are most vulnerable to eating disorders. Adolescence is also the time when girls and boys are at the greatest risk of substance use or are currently experiencing drug problems. Ninety to 95 percent of all eating disorders occur in females.

Bulimia, the most common eating disorder in adolescents, involves binge eating, sometimes accompanied by vomiting and laxative abuse, and a preoccupation with food and weight. Anorexia involves weight restriction, increased activity, distorted body image, and intense fears of losing control and gaining weight. Body dysmorphic disorder involves obsessive worrying about perceived flaws or defects in physical appearance.

Adolescents with eating disorders may use alcohol and/or other drugs as a coping mechanism in an attempt to relieve psychological pain and cope with stress, anxiety, guilt, depression, and shame. Adolescents, and young women in particular, may also use appetite-suppressant drugs such as nicotine, cocaine, diet pills, and methamphetamines in an attempt to lose weight.

Columbia University researchers cite the following facts linking drug use/dependence and eating disorders:

- Between 12 and 18 percent of individuals with anorexia and between 30 and 70 percent of those with bulimia abuse tobacco, alcohol, pills, or over-the-counter substances.
- During treatment for substance-use disorders and in early recovery, it is not unusual for an individual to turn to binge eating.
- A student who has dieted in sixth grade is more than 20 percent likelier to drink alcohol in the ninth grade than one who has never dieted.

- The more often and more severely an incoming college female diets, the more likely she is to use alcohol and other drugs. Seventy-two percent of severe freshmen dieters and bulimics have used alcohol in the past month, compared to less than 44 percent of those who did not diet. Freshmen women with bulimia are more than four times likelier to have smoked in the last month than those who did not diet. The more severe the dieter, the more likely she is to use more than one drug.
- More than twice as many individuals with a history of weight-control issues respond positively to two or more questions on the C.A.G.E. Questionnaire* assessing alcoholism, signaling the likelihood of a serious alcohol problem, than those without such a history.
- A *People* magazine survey revealed that 12 percent of women consider smoking a weight-reduction method.
- Girls who smoke to suppress their appetites are among the largest group of new nicotine addicts. Among white teenagers who smoke, girls are three times likelier than boys to smoke to suppress their appetites.
- Women who smoke are more than twice as likely as men to cite weight concerns as a reason not to quit.

Attention Deficit Hyperactivity Disorder (ADHD/ADD)

Attention deficit hyperactivity disorder (ADHD) is a genetically influenced neurological disorder in the part of the brain called the prefrontal cortex. If one person in a family is diagnosed with

---

*The C.A.G.E. Questionnaire consists of four questions: Have you ever felt you should Cut down on your drinking? Have people Annoyed you by criticizing your drinking? Have you ever felt bad or Guilty about your drinking? Have you ever had a drink first thing in the morning to steady your nerves or to get rid of a hang-over (Eye-opener)?

ADHD, there is a 25 to 35 percent probability that another family member also has ADHD, compared to a 4 to 6 percent probability for someone in the general population. Many experts believe the neurological dysfunctions associated with ADHD are due, at least in part, to abnormalities in brain dopamine activity; dopamine is a pleasure-creating brain chemical that is linked to drug use, addiction, and craving. (See page 31.)

The most common symptoms associated with ADHD are distractibility (short attention span); impulsivity (inability to delay gratification, tendency to interrupt); and hyperactivity (excessive activity and physical restlessness). Other symptoms include disorganization; difficulty learning from past mistakes, lack of forethought; poor judgment; procrastination; conflict seeking; moodiness; irritability; negative thinking; a tendency to worry; anxiety; difficulty expressing emotions; and lack of empathy for others.

Although many people in the general public use the term *ADD*, the official clinical diagnosis for this disorder is attention deficit hyperactivity disorder, or ADHD. Approximately one-third of people with ADHD do not have the hyperactive or overactive behavior component. Experts estimate that ADHD affects 4 to 6 percent of the U.S. population, or approximately seventeen million Americans.

Adolescents with ADHD (which may or may not be diagnosed) do not feel right because their brains do not work right. In an attempt to create at least a temporary state of balance, they may seek out activities and substances that make them feel normal or at least "better than bad," as one adolescent put it. And that's where the trouble comes in, for alcohol, nicotine, caffeine, marijuana, and other drugs relieve many of the distressing physical and psychological symptoms associated with ADHD, at least for short periods of time, and the adolescent appears to have discovered an instant, magical cure for his or her distress.

I was diagnosed with ADHD in the fourth grade and the doctor prescribed Ritalin. But I was still all over the place. I just couldn't stay still. In sixth grade, a friend brought some marijuana into school in his backpack. We got high in the boy's bathroom at school, and that's when I knew, for the first time it seems, that life can be really, really good. I felt calm and happy. My worries just melted away. Just one or two hits, and I felt like everything was just the way it should be.

—RUDY, *sixteen*

But drugs work their magic for only a short time and then the symptoms return, often with a vengeance. This can lead to a vicious cycle of drug use to relieve the distress of the underlying brain disorder, followed by drug-intensified symptoms, which lead to more drug use, leading to more symptoms, and on and on and on. According to Daniel Amen, a child and adolescent psychiatrist who specializes in ADD and ADHD, 50 percent of people with ADHD develop problems with drug use, and a high percentage of them use marijuana.

If your child has been diagnosed with ADD or ADHD (or if you suspect a problem based on the symptoms listed on the previous page), be aware that many adolescents will attempt to medicate their symptoms with legal and illegal drugs. While drugs may help in the short run, they inevitably and invariably make problems worse—much worse—in the long run.

Learning Disabilities

Learning disabilities affect approximately 10.8 million children, or 20 percent of the nearly 54 million children in the United States.

Broadly defined, learning disabilities are disorders of the brain that affect the child's ability to absorb, process, or communicate information. A large number of children who suffer from learning disabilities also suffer from behavioral disorders such as ADHD and conduct disorder. Furthermore, scientists have discovered that children with learning disorders are significantly more likely to use alcohol and other drugs.

The connection between learning disabilities and drug use is complicated and involves both genetic and environmental influences. We know for a fact that prenatal exposure to alcohol or other drugs can damage the child's developing brain, leading to a range of neurological disorders. Learning disabilities may be a relatively minor fetal drug effect, showing up later in childhood and adolescence and causing difficulties in the child's ability to process and communicate information.

We know, too, that exposure to environmental toxins can cause moderate to severe learning disabilities. Because children raised in poverty are more likely to encounter lead and other toxic substances in their environment, poverty itself is often associated with learning disabilities (see pages 61–62).

Finally, and most significantly in terms of this book, we know that when children and adolescents use drugs, the toxic chemicals in these drugs can have both direct and dramatic effects on their ability to learn, store, and retrieve information. These effects may be short-lived and reversible, or long lasting and irreversible, depending on the particular drug used and the amount and duration of use.

Head Injuries

[The] brain is more sophisticated than any computer we can think of designing. You can't drop a computer without the potential of causing serious damage. In the same way, the brain is fragile, and if trauma occurs in sensitive parts of the brain, it has the potential to alter one's ability to function.

—DANIEL AMEN, M.D.

The way we think, act, react, and feel is directly related to the health and functioning of our brains. All behaviors—and that includes actions, thoughts, and emotions—are generated by the brain's electrical and chemical impulses. When the brain functions normally, we are thoughtful and considerate of others. Our moods tend to be stable, our emotions balanced. We are able to set goals, focus on the work at hand, and finish our projects on time. At times we may get angry, fearful, anxious, or depressed, but in most cases we are capable of controlling these emotions and working through them. When our brains are healthy, mature, and drug-free, we tend to make good choices and learn quickly from past mistakes.

When the brain is injured, our ability to maintain balance and control is compromised and our thoughts, moods, and behaviors are affected in both subtle and profound ways. Every year, an estimated 2 million people sustain a head injury, and approximately 500,000 to 750,000 of these traumatic brain injuries are severe enough to require hospitalization. Head injuries are most common among males between the ages of fifteen and twenty-four. Motor vehicle accidents account for 28 percent of traumatic brain injuries, while sports and physical activity are responsible for 20 percent, and assaults are responsible for 9 percent. For brain injuries severe enough to require hospitalization, almost half (49 percent) are caused by motor vehicle accidents.

Even minor head injuries can lead to short- or long-term behavioral problems (hyperactivity, distractibility, lack of impulse control, violent or aggressive tendencies), psychological and emotional problems (fear, anxiety, depression, erratic mood swings), learning problems (short-term and long-term memory problems), and spiritual problems (hopelessness, sense of worthlessness, despair, suicidal tendencies).

Because drugs can ease or mask many of these symptoms, adolescents with head injuries may be using alcohol, marijuana, nicotine, caffeine, and other drugs in an attempt to self-medicate an underlying brain disorder. Once again, while both legal and illegal drugs may offer short-term relief, excessive or prolonged drug use will intensify the original symptoms. Of even greater concern, of course, is the fact that when adolescents use drugs regularly, and especially if they combine different drugs, they are in great danger of becoming physically addicted to the drugs, even if they have no genetic predisposition.

The other side of the coin is that adolescents and young adults who use alcohol and/or other drugs are obviously at much greater risk of sustaining a head injury. According to researchers at Boston University School of Public Health, twelve hundred college students in the United States die each year from car crashes or other alcohol-related incidents. Every year five hundred thousand eighteen- to twenty-four-year-olds suffer drinking-related injuries, and more than six hundred thousand are assaulted by students under the influence.

Stress and Trauma

After the September 11, 2001, terrorist attacks on New York City and Washington, D.C., doctors saw an immediate upswing in drug use in their patients. Stress created fear, anxiety, depression, and hopelessness, which in turn triggered a desire for alcohol or other drugs to ease the physical and emotional distress.

While adults often have well-developed relationships and the experience of knowing how to deal with different levels of stress, adolescents have relatively few outlets for relieving stress. They can exercise and eat well, get lots of sleep, talk out their problems with counselors, and find comfort and consolation in relationships with friends, teachers, parents, and other relatives, but many adolescents do not have the inclination and/or the opportunity to take advantage of these natural routes to stress relief. All too often adolescents attempt to relieve their stress with drugs, which work magic in the short term but end up creating even more problems in the long run.

Experts agree that stress is the number one cause of relapse for chemically dependent people. When experiencing chronic or acute periods of stress, smokers start smoking again, drinkers start drinking again, and cocaine, methamphetamine, and heroin users experience an intense craving to start using again. Stress is not merely (or even mostly) psychological; in fact, recent research emphasizes the physiological events that underlie the stress response.

The research shows that stress increases our vulnerability to drug use and dependence in the following ways:

- The brain circuits that respond to drugs and those that respond to stress overlap, meaning that increased stress may lead to increased drug-seeking behavior.
- Animal studies confirm that stress increases drug-seeking behavior. In animals with no previous drug exposure, physical and emotional stress increase the likelihood that the animal will self-administer drugs. Stress can also induce relapse to drugs after animals have been abstinent for long periods of time.
- People exposed to stress are more likely to use alcohol and other drugs and more likely to relapse.
- Teens who are directly threatened with violence or witness threats or acts of violence between others are more likely to use alcohol, nicotine, marijuana, and/or other drugs.
- Craving for alcohol or other drugs is also affected by stress—in one study of drug-free cocaine users in treatment, exposure to personal stress situations led to consistent and significant increases in cocaine craving.
- People who have developed resources for coping with stress are significantly more likely to stay clean and sober in stressful situations.

Post-Traumatic Stress Disorder (PTSD)

While every human being on this planet is exposed to stress in one form or another, some of us have undergone extraordinarily stressful experiences. Adults and children who experience life-threatening events such as terrorist incidents, military combat, natural disasters (floods, earthquakes, fires), serious accidents, or violent personal assaults (rape, assault, physical or sexual abuse) may develop post-traumatic stress disorder (PTSD).

Symptoms of PTSD include flashbacks; nightmares; night terrors; exaggerated startle response; hypervigilance; anxiety, irritability, mood swings; panic attacks; and avoidance of people, places, and thoughts connected to the traumatic event.

PTSD is remarkably common in adolescents. In one study, lifetime rates of PTSD ranged from more than 6 percent of older adolescents in a community sample to nearly 30 percent in drug-dependent adolescents between the ages of fifteen and nineteen. Among the drug-dependent adolescents, over 19 percent currently suffered from PTSD. And in a study of 1,007 young adults, researchers found that PTSD was associated with more than a fourfold increased risk of drug use and dependence.

> I was scared as a kid. I don't ever remember not being scared. But then I started using weed when I was eight or nine years old, and I felt so powerful, so alive. Weed helped me forget the fact that my mom was doing meth, coke, and heroin. It made me forget about having to take care of my brother, clean up the house, cook the meals. It helped me forget about being molested by my mother's boyfriend. I wasn't scared anymore. Drugs worked.
>
> —MARY, *fourteen*

Why is drug use so common in PTSD patients? Researchers and clinicians generally agree that people suffering from PTSD may use drugs in an attempt to relieve their symptoms. For adolescents with a strong genetic predisposition to addiction, stress may be the initial trigger leading to drug use and, eventually, drug dependence. For adolescents with no genetic predisposition, acute or chronic stress may lead to experimentation with drugs, regular use, and combining drugs to increase the stress-relieving effects.

Gangs

When I was going to school, at first, I was staying away from gangs. But I started needing money. See, my mother stopped having any money, so I used to go out there and make it myself. That's when I started selling dope. I started getting closer to the gangs because they were the, you know, connection. That's when I started getting their ways, being like them.

—GREEN EYES, *quoted in*
Father Greg and the Homeboys

If your child belongs to a gang, there's a good chance that he or she is involved with using and/or selling drugs. Gangs, drugs, and crime are intimately connected. According to the National Youth Gang Survey, more than 40 percent of the youth gangs in the United States are involved in the street sale of drugs. Large cities have the highest percentage of youth gangs involved in drug sales (49 percent), followed by suburban counties (43 percent), rural counties (35 percent), and small cities (31 percent).

Why are gangs and drugs almost synonymous? Marc, a fifteen-year-old gang member, put it this way:

Gangs are like drugs. Drugs are an addiction. Gangs are a part of that. It's a rush—it's all a rush. And that's what we're looking for. Something to take us away, to make us forget, for a little while, what we don't have or what we're running away from.

Adolescents (and younger children) get involved in gangs for many reasons. For some kids, gangs hold the allure of risk, danger, and constant excitement. For others, gangs may seem like the only answer to loneliness and fear. If they don't join, they fear they will get beaten up. If they do join, they know they'll get beaten up, but at least they will have the protection and friendship of their "homies." Only later, after they've been in the gang for a while, do they realize how hard it can be to get away from the gang and start a new life.

The truth is, I'm tired of banging. . . . I'm bored with the homies. I'm bored with dressing like a gangster. I want to dress normal. I just want a normal life. I want to get away from the bad and go toward the good. I don't want to be down here in the projects no more. I want to go to Job Corps because when I come back I'll be different. I registered already but it takes a long time for them to call you. . . . If I can just get away from here—get away from the projects, get away from the homies—I'll be different. I guarantee it. If I can just get away. That's the hard part. How do you find someplace else to go?

—TURTLE, *quoted in*
Father Greg and the Homeboys

Poverty

Poverty does not cause drug use and addiction, but it can contribute to an environment in which drugs are readily available and where drug use and drug addiction affect entire families, even entire communities.

According to the latest census, taken in 2000, more than thirty-one million Americans (approximately 11 percent) live in poverty. (The average poverty threshold for a family of four in 2000 was $17,603 in annual income; for a family of three, it was $14,738.) Minorities are much more likely to grow up in poverty. Over one-quarter of American Indian and Native Alaskans, 22 percent of African Americans, and 21 percent of Hispanics are considered to be poverty-stricken.

But the most astonishing statistic of all involves our country's youth. For children under the age of eighteen, the poverty rate in the U.S. is 16.2 percent. That's twelve million children, or approximately one in six, who currently live in poverty. And things are getting worse, not better—the number of children living in poverty has increased by 1.6 million since 1979.

When we think about poverty, it's important to keep in mind that we're not just talking about a shortage of financial resources. Poverty also involves a lack of emotional, spiritual, mental, and physical resources. As educator Ruby Payne puts it, "A working definition of poverty is the extent to which an individual does without resources."

Children growing up in poverty, Payne and other poverty experts emphasize, frequently lack the education, support systems, relationships, and role models that help to nurture their emotional and spiritual growth. Without these resources and relationships, children are at greater risk for physical and emotional harm, including exposure to environmental toxins; physical, sexual, and/or emotional abuse or trauma; inadequate nutrition; and regular exposure to drugs, drug dealers, and the ravages of drug addiction. Each of these risk factors has the potential to affect a child's neurological development, physical health, emotional resiliency, and susceptibility to drug use and addiction.

Children growing up in poverty are also much more likely to be subjected to the lure of "drug money" or "easy money"—the big bucks that can be made from dealing drugs. In fact, dealing drugs is one way some children and adolescents hope to escape poverty.

Gender

Girls and young women get hooked faster, they get hooked using lesser amounts of alcohol and [other] drugs, and they suffer the consequences faster and more severely.

—JOSEPH A. CALIFANO, JR.
President and Chairman of the National
Center on Addiction and Substance
Abuse at Columbia University

A nationwide survey released in 2003 found that boys typically start experimenting with drugs for thrills or heightened social status. Girls, on the other hand, tend to experiment with drugs if they reach puberty early, have eating disorders, want to reduce stress or alleviate depression, or have been physically or sexually abused.

Research on gender differences in drug use and addiction is still in its infancy, but here's what we know so far:

- Over the years, drug use and drug addiction have increased steadily among adolescent girls. Surveys conducted in 2001 show that female ninth-graders are just as likely to drink alcohol as males (40 percent versus 41 percent), and even more likely to smoke cigarettes. Studies with college-age women show that binge drinking increased by 125 percent from 1993 to 2001, and the number of women who report being drunk on ten or more occasions during those same years increased threefold.
- Even if a boy and a girl weigh the same and drink the same amount, the woman will experience a higher blood alcohol concentration (BAC) for two basic reasons. (1) Females have a deficient or missing alcohol-eliminating enzyme in their stomachs; as a result, more unmetabolized alcohol is released directly into a woman's bloodstream, which leads to higher concentrations of alcohol. (2) Females typically have a higher proportion of body fat and a lower percentage of body water than boys. Alcohol is easily dissolved in water but not in fatty tissue, which means that people with more body fat will experience higher BACs when they drink.
- The hippocampus, the area of the brain that forms and preserves memories, grows faster in girls than in boys, probably in response to the female hormone estrogen. The amygdala, which controls emotions such as fear, anger, and anxiety, responds to the male hormone androgen and grows faster in boys than in girls. These hormonally influenced neurological effects undoubtedly influence behavior (including learning, memory, fear or anxiety responses, aggression, and violent tendencies) in both subtle and profound ways.
- In women, BACs vary according to the phases of the menstrual cycle. The highest BACs occur during the premenstrual phase. Because hormone levels can vary day to day and month to month (and BACs fluctuate with them), women are less able to predict accurately the effect of a given amount of alcohol.

- The female hormone estrogen may increase sensitization to drugs, which in turn increases craving for drugs. Fluctuations in estrogen levels may impact the areas of the brain that control addictive behaviors. Once a woman is sensitized to drugs when her estrogen level is elevated, the increased sensitivity remains even when the estrogen levels are reduced.
- A recent study shows that girls who witness or experience violence (robbery, assault, rape) are two to three times more likely than girls with no exposure to violence to use legal and illegal drugs, and three to four times more likely to engage in risky health behaviors such as having sex at an early age, having multiple sex partners, or having sex with strangers.
- Unplanned sexual activity, date rape, and sexual assault among college-age women who drink has recently increased 150 percent, according to a study published in 2002 in the *Journal of American College Health*.
- Girls under the age of eighteen are the fastest-growing segment of the juvenile justice population: In 2001, 442,255 girls under the age of eighteen were arrested for crimes ranging from curfew violations to burglary, vandalism, and assault.
- Girls are more likely than boys to use and become addicted to prescription painkillers, stimulants, and tranquilizers.
- Suicide attempts are more common among females than males and more common among females who are alcoholics. According to one study, 40 percent of alcoholic women attempt to commit suicide, compared to approximately 9 percent of nonalcoholic women.
- Suicide attempts are even more common among young women alcoholics. Approximately 50 percent of young women alcoholics attempt suicide.
- Girls and young women are more susceptible than boys and young men to experiencing adverse health consequences related to drug use, including greater smoking-related lung

damage, alcohol-induced brain damage, cardiac problems, and liver disease.

The information in this chapter reveals the extraordinary complexity of adolescent drug use and addiction. When you combine biological and genetic factors that we explored in chapter 3 and the developmental, social, emotional, and familial influences discussed in this chapter, you can begin to understand why so many people are confused about the nature and progression of alcoholism and other drug addictions.

Having read this far, you are in a powerful position. Now you know the basic facts about why kids use alcohol and other drugs and why so many teenagers experience serious drug problems. Armed with this knowledge and the wisdom of your own experience, you will be able to act as an effective advocate for your child. In every interaction with others—doctors, mental health professionals, juvenile justice workers, judges, lawyers, clergy members, teachers, school administrators, relatives, neighbors, and friends— you will be able to speak from a position of knowledge rather than ignorance, with facts rather than myths and misconceptions guiding your thinking.

There is still much to learn, however, for you need to know the basic facts about the legal and illegal drugs kids are using today and how these drugs can damage your child's physical, mental, emotional, and spiritual health. This is the story we will tell in part 2.

PART TWO

The Drugs

Cigarettes brought me to weed.
Weed brought me to alcohol.
Alcohol brought me to crank.
Crank brought me to 'shrooms.
'Shrooms brought me to coke.
And coke brought me to this decision to stop it all.

—KATIE, *thirteen*

If we sit down with kids who use drugs and ask them questions—and if they trust us and know that their answers will be safe with us—we learn amazing things about the world they live in.

This world of drugs—surreal, bizarre, horrifying—is so far removed from what we imagine childhood should be. Our own adolescence was filled, at times, with indescribable joys and inexpressible torments, but the highs and the lows that adolescent drug users experience are so far off the charts that most of us just can't relate. We listen with our mouths dropped open, our minds numb, our hearts racing, and the question—*can this really be happening?*—circling round and round our uncomprehending brains.

And when we hear how many kids are using drugs—rich and

poor kids, males and females, athletes and musicians, valedictorians and dropouts, "good" and "bad" kids, loving and hostile kids, kids with bright futures, and kids who have lost hope—we have to confront our own prejudices and stereotypes. We have to realize "we don't know nothing" and start back at square one.

We can't begin to comprehend the enormity of what it is we are facing until we understand the complexity, variety, and sheer abundance of the drugs our kids can choose from.

What, exactly, are these drugs?

What do they do to the adolescent's developing brain and body?

How many kids use them, and when do they start using them?

What is the high like?

What are the bad effects, both short-term and long-term, including the risk of overdose and death?

What happens when kids combine certain drugs?

Are all these drugs physically addicting?

How can you know for sure if your child is using a particular drug? What are the telltale signs and symptoms associated with using these drugs?

These are the questions we will answer in the next ten chapters.

Alcohol

I don't use drugs. I only use alcohol.

—KIDS EVERYWHERE

The media focuses on illegal drugs
[such as] heroin, but that's the tail.
The dog is alcohol and the dog is
really biting our kids.

—JOSEPH A. CALIFANO, JR.

In the adolescent's vocabulary, alcohol is "the regular"—the everyday, always available, ever-present drug, the old standby that fills in when you can't find (or afford) marijuana, meth, or cocaine. When there's nothing else around, there's always alcohol.

Yet most kids are of two minds about alcohol. On the one hand, they insist that it is not a drug because it's legal and because it's everywhere.

- "Everybody uses it—how can it be a drug?"
- "People go to bars, have a few drinks, drive home, and nobody cares—because they're only drinking alcohol."
- "At my house the beer and wine in the refrigerator are right

next to the milk and the orange juice—you don't see cocaine or heroin sitting in people's refrigerators!"

■ "Alcohol is only a drug for people who can't handle it."

Even while they insist that alcohol isn't really a drug, however, kids know that beer, wine, and hard liquor can get you into big trouble. They'll talk openly about the stupid things they do when they get drunk—the fights, the unprotected sex, the close calls driving drunk, and the wicked hangovers. They also see the glaring hypocrisy in the fact that their alcohol-drinking parents lecture, scold, and punish them for using marijuana, tobacco, and even cocaine—drugs that they perceive are much less dangerous than alcohol.

> People don't die from smoking weed. But they do die from drinking alcohol. My uncle drowned. He was drunk and went swimming and that was it for him. My friend's father fell down the stairs when he was drunk and cracked his head; he was in the hospital for weeks and almost died. My parents drink and get drunk and then they get all stupid and yell at each other and at us kids.
>
> And adults think we're bad because we smoke weed or have a cigarette now and then? Give me a break.
>
> —ANTHONY, *fourteen*

Adolescents know that of all the drugs available to them, alcohol is the most devastating and destructive of all. It is legal (for people over age twenty-one), it is everywhere, it is addictive, and drinking it can make you stupid, aggressive, and violent. Statistics confirm the fact that alcohol is a dangerous drug for both the people who are using it and anyone who happens to get in their way.

■ An estimated 3.3 million children between twelve and seventeen years of age will start drinking alcohol each year.
■ Five percent of all deaths of young people between the ages of fifteen and twenty-nine, worldwide, are attributable to alcohol.

- Almost half of all ninth-grade boys and girls (40 and 41 percent, respectively) drink alcohol, and one-fifth are binge drinkers (drinking four, five, or more drinks at a time).
- Two of every five college students (43 percent) are binge drinkers, drinking five or more drinks at a time; 52 percent of college students who drink say a major motivation is "to get drunk."
- Teens who drink are seven times more likely to have sex, and twice as likely to have sex with four or more partners. Teens who use alcohol also tend to become sexually active at a younger age.
- Almost half of all college students who are victims of campus crimes said they were drinking and/or using other drugs when they were victimized.
- The economic cost of alcohol use by youth—traffic accidents, violent crime, burns, drownings, suicide attempts, alcohol poisoning, fetal alcohol syndrome, and alcohol addiction treatment—is $53 billion dollars a year.
- An estimated 6.6 million children under the age of eighteen live in households with at least one alcoholic parent.

The High

I don't drink to feel a little high. I drink to get drunk.

—JOHNNY, *seventeen*

Within minutes of drinking alcohol, you feel the effects—a sense of well-being, relaxation, increased confidence, and reduced anxiety. Yet along with these benefits come serious penalties—recent research confirms that just one or two drinks can slow down brain activity to the point of clouding judgment and affecting self-control.

Few adolescents stop at just one or two drinks, however. More than five million high school kids—or 31 percent—admit to binge drinking at least once a month. Researchers define binge drinking as four or more drinks in a row for females and five or more drinks in a row for males.

Beer, the adolescent's beverage of choice, accounts for more than 80 percent of excessive alcohol consumption in the United States. Sixty-three percent of beer drinkers under age twenty-four report binge drinking.

> If one beer is good, four is better, and ten or fifteen is right where you want to be.
>
> —ROBERT, *seventeen*

Alcohol's dose-related effects on behavior are summarized below. Remember, though, that gender, body size, stress level, fatigue, recent illness, food content in stomach, age, and use of other drugs (including prescription medications) can dramatically affect individual reactions to alcohol.

Blood Alcohol Concentrations (BAC) and Behavior

- **.02–.05:** After one to two drinks* in an hour (depending on your tolerance), most people experience a mild lift in mood and an overall feeling of warmth and relaxation. You may feel happy, talkative, less inhibited, and more open to communicating your thoughts and feelings. Some drinkers get cocky at this level, bragging about past achievements or boasting about sexual conquests. At .04 BAC, alcohol can impair reaction time, decision making, and judgment.
- **.08:** After three to five drinks in one hour, your muscle coordination will be impaired and your reflexes will slow down. You may feel light-headed, giddy, and have less control over your thoughts and feelings. Inhibitions

---

*A *drink* is defined as one ounce of eighty-proof distilled spirits (vodka, rum, gin, whiskey, and so on), five ounces of wine, or one twelve-ounce can or bottle of beer.

continue to disappear along with reason and judgment—you will start to do stupid things and put yourself or others at risk. In most states you are considered legally drunk at .08 BAC.

- **.10:** After about five drinks consumed in an hour, other people will notice that your reactions are slowed and your muscle control is impaired. You may begin to slur your words and appear clumsy or uncoordinated. Yet you may also feel that you are completely in control and that your behavior isn't being affected in the slightest degree.

- **.15:** After five to seven drinks in an hour—the equivalent of about a six-pack of beer or a half-pint of whiskey circulating through the bloodstream—the average drinker is obviously intoxicated. You may find it hard to maintain balance and, when you walk, you may trip over your own feet. Just standing still, you will sway slightly from one side to the other, even though the body sway may not be noticeable to you or others. Your speech may be slurred, your memory may be affected, and you may get that dumb look that tells your friends you're getting wasted.

- **.20–.25:** After seven to ten drinks in an hour, your control over your ability to move, think, and react is seriously compromised. You will lose control over your emotions, and you may start crying or become angry or upset over the slightest provocation. When you walk, you stagger. Just standing still, you feel off balance. At this BAC level, some drinkers will start vomiting, lose bladder control, become extremely tired, or pass out.

- **.30–.40:** After ten to fifteen drinks in an hour, your body temperature drops, your breathing becomes erratic, your blood pressure falls, and your skin feels clammy to the touch. You don't understand what is happening around you, and you may lose consciousness and lapse into a coma.

For approximately 50 percent of people, .40 is a lethal dose. Many early- and middle-stage alcoholics, however, can walk, talk, and react somewhat "normally," even with a BAC that would seriously disable nonalcoholics.

My cousin is an alcoholic. He can drink half a case of beer and a quart of rum and still keep drinking. One night he was driving too fast on a country road, and he flipped his pickup. It rolled over twice. The car was totaled, but he just opened the door and walked away. The cops arrived, and they didn't even know he was drunk. Then they found some beer cans in his truck and gave him a Breathalyzer test. He blew a .38.

—JERRY, *eighteen*

- **.50:** After fourteen to twenty drinks in an hour, even people who drink heavily and chronically and who have a high tolerance for alcohol (that is, alcoholics) may lose consciousness or lapse into a coma. For three out of four people, .50 is a lethal dose.

Who Uses Alcohol?

Who uses alcohol? I think the better question is: Who doesn't? Everyone drinks. I mean it—everyone.

—CARL, *sixteen*

Underage drinking, researchers say, has reached "epidemic proportions." A 2002 report issued by the National Center on Addiction and Substance Abuse (CASA) shows that 81 percent of high school students have consumed alcohol compared to 70 percent who have smoked cigarettes and 47 percent who have used marijuana. The researchers also found that adolescents who experiment with alcohol continue using it—91.3 percent of the students who said they had consumed alcohol still were drinking in twelfth grade. Thirty-one percent of high school students in this study said they engaged in binge drinking at least once a month.

Recent studies also indicate that girls today are drinking almost as much as boys. The 2001 Youth Risk Behavior Survey reports that among ninth-graders, 40 percent of girls are current drinkers compared to 42 percent of boys; in twelfth grade, 53.9 percent of girls are current drinkers compared to 56.6 percent of boys.

The annual Monitoring the Future Survey reports the following alcohol use statistics for eighth-, tenth-, and twelfth-graders.

Alcohol Use by Students, 2002: Monitoring the Future Survey

	8TH-GRADERS	10TH-GRADERS	12TH-GRADERS
Ever Used	47.0%	66.9%	78.4%
Used in Past Year	38.7	60.0	71.5
Used in Past Month	19.6	35.4	48.6

Bad Effects

Alcohol damages the young brain, interferes with mental and social development, and interrupts academic progress. Alcohol is the fatal attraction for many teens, a major factor in the three leading causes of teen death—accidents, homicide, and suicide.

—JOSEPH A. CALIFANO, JR.

Drinking—even in small amounts—is clearly hazardous to the adolescent's health, impairing judgment, distorting vision, hearing, and coordination, and altering perceptions, moods, and emotions.

- "I do crazy things when I'm drinking. One time I jumped off the roof of my friends' house into their swimming pool. Another time I rode my bike off this ten-foot embankment and broke my arm. I'm lucky I haven't killed myself."
- "I don't know why, but I get really depressed when I drink. Even after just a few beers, I get moody, paranoid, and lonely. Even the next day I feel depressed."
- "I like to fight when I'm drunk. Alcohol gives me liquid

nuts—you know, I think I'm so big and strong and tough. I got in one fight and this guy broke my nose. I've been to the emergency room twice because of fighting when I'm drunk."

- "I swore I'd never get in a car with a drunk driver, but this one night I had too much to drink and I thought my friend was relatively sober. He started driving crazy and then hit some gravel on the side of the road, overcorrected, and ran into a tree at eighty miles an hour. We both survived, but we were pretty banged up. I was in the hospital for three weeks."

Short-Term Effects

- **HANGOVER:** Pounding headache, nausea, and other flu-like symptoms, shaky hands, inner trembling, insomnia.
- **MEMORY PROBLEMS:** Bits and pieces of events or big chunks of time that occurred while drinking may be completely erased from your memory. In truth, these events were never recorded. Alcohol and acetaldehyde (the toxic chemical created when alcohol is broken down in the liver) destroy cells in the hippocampus, the long-term memory storage areas of the brain. Cell destruction is usually associated with a rising blood alcohol level and may be related to oxygen deprivation in certain crucial areas of the brain.
- **BLACKOUTS:** Blackouts—total memory loss for minutes, hours, or even days—are a form of drug-induced brain damage. Severe electrical shock, brain concussions, and anesthesia can also cause blackouts.

    When you use drugs in large amounts, the chemical and electrical signals in your brain are disrupted. With a drug-induced electrical storm fouling up the communication lines in the brain, memory storage is interrupted. Short-term memories, which are temporarily stored as electrical signals, can't be converted into permanent or long-term memories. They are lost forever. Says musician Ozzy Osbourne:

The blackout thing scared me to death. At times during binges, I would just disappear. I woke up in a different town. I didn't know where . . . I was. I became a chronic blackout drinker. I woke up one morning in . . . jail in my hometown, charged with attempted murder. Apparently I attacked my wife and tried to strangle her. The police came in and actually charged me with attempted murder, but my wife dropped the charges. I went to court and everything, and I have zero recollection of it. What always frightened me was that some good person would someday say, "That's the man that ran my brother over," or "That's the man that put a . . . axe through my son's head." That's frightening.

A new study on college drinking found that 40 percent of college students had experienced alcohol-related blackouts in the past year. "It is very possible for social drinkers to experience blackouts if they overdo their consumption of alcohol," said Aaron White, Ph.D., lead author of the study. During alcohol-related blackouts, students, especially females, are more at risk for engaging in risky behaviors such as unprotected sexual intercourse, vandalizing property, or driving under the influence.

- **BRAIN DAMAGE:** If you go on a three- or four-day binge, drinking five or more drinks a day (four or more if you're female), you can damage your brain. In a 2002 study, researchers gave rats the equivalent of ten drinks a day for several days in a row. After two days, the area of the brain responsible for smell was damaged, and after four days, other brain areas showed significant damage.

Binge drinking is common, especially among adolescents. According to a May 2002 fact sheet published by the Center for Substance Abuse Treatment, one-third to nearly half of white and Hispanic twelfth-graders and approximately 20 percent of African-American twelfth-graders reported past-thirty-day binge drinking.

Long-Term Effects

Adolescents are generally strong and resilient, bouncing back from physical and emotional blows that would devastate adults. This innate resiliency leads many adolescents to believe they are invulnerable. Unless life has taught them otherwise, they are convinced that bad things happen to other people, not to them. Besides, they can handle the surreal world of drugs—it's the real world they can't control.

"Reality," some people like to say, quoting a popular bumper sticker, "is for people who can't handle drugs." But the reality is that drinking alcohol in large amounts either chronically (frequently) or acutely (once a week or once a month) can damage the adolescent's developing cells, tissues, and organs. Sometimes the internal devastation goes on for years before outsiders begin to realize something is wrong. But all too often with adolescents, the damage tends to progress quickly, within years or even months, leading to serious physical and emotional problems that cannot be denied.

- **BRAIN**: Until recently, the only way we could measure the extent of drug-induced brain damage was to conduct an autopsy after the person died. Today, however, we have sophisticated brain-imaging techniques that can assess brain damage in living subjects. From these images, called SPECT scans, we know that alcohol tends to shrink the brain. In adolescents and adults who regularly use large amounts of alcohol, blood vessels in the brain constrict and brain activity slows down.

  Alcohol-induced brain damage is most extensive in the prefrontal cortex, the area of the brain that helps us stay focused, make plans, control impulses, and make decisions. Decreased activity in this part of the brain leads to problems with attention span, focus, organization, self-discipline, and the ability to follow through and complete tasks.

Alcohol also directly affects the hippocampus, leading to memory and learning impairments. Heavy or chronic use of alcohol during adolescence has been associated with a permanent decrease in the size of the hippocampus.

A recent study suggests that drinking beer can increase the likelihood of dementia (mental confusion) later in life. People who drink beer, either infrequently or regularly, were more than twice as likely as non-beer-drinkers to experience dementia after age sixty-five.

- **LIVER:** Alcohol causes fat to build up in the liver, a condition called fatty infiltration of the liver. If you drink heavily and regularly, the fat accumulates and begins to crowd out and suffocate liver cells. The liver may become inflamed, swollen, and extremely tender, a condition known as alcoholic hepatitis. At this point, liver disease can be reversed through abstinence and good nutrition, but if drinking continues, scar tissue may begin to form in the liver, leading to the irreversible, potentially deadly disease of cirrhosis.

- **HEART:** Alcohol and its metabolite acetaldehyde can directly damage the heart muscle. Symptoms of alcoholic cardiomyopathy (disease of the heart muscle) are heart palpitations and labored or difficult breathing. Cardiac arrhythmia (abnormal variations of the heartbeat) and high blood pressure are common in people who drink heavily; both conditions can lead to heart failure.

- **MUSCLES:** Long-term drinking damages not only the heart muscle but also muscles in the gastrointestinal system and in the legs by slowing muscle-protein formation, disrupting calcium regulation, and producing cell-damaging substances.

- **GASTROINTESTINAL SYSTEM:** Alcohol can weaken the mucous membrane lining the stomach, which acts as a protective barrier to prevent digestive juices from leaking out. Inflammation of the stomach lining is called gastritis, and symptoms include indigestion, bloating, nausea, vomiting, diarrhea, headache, appetite changes, and internal bleeding. Stomach and intestinal ulcers and colitis are also common in early- and middle-stage alcoholics. Alcoholic myopathy (muscle damage) in the gastrointestinal system impairs digestion and the body's ability to absorb nutrients.

- **RESPIRATORY TRACT:** Alcohol can interfere with the lung's normal defense mechanisms, leading to lung infections, chronic bronchitis, emphysema, and pneumonia.
- **PANCREAS:** Heavy and continuous drinking can injure the pancreas and cause pancreatitis, a serious, potentially life-threatening illness characterized by severe pain in the upper abdomen, back, and lower chest, along with nausea, vomiting, and constipation.
- **CANCER:** People who drink regularly and in large amounts have an increased risk of head and neck, esophageal, lung, bladder, colon, and liver cancers.
- **MALNUTRITION:** Large doses of alcohol interfere with digestion and reduce the liver's ability to make nutrients available to the body's cells and vital organs. Experts agree that most alcoholics (young and old alike) are malnourished. Symptoms can range from mental confusion, fatigue, loss of appetite, irritability, emotional instability, and memory loss, to nerve damage, muscular incoordination, hallucinations, blurring or dimness of vision, and brain hemorrhage.
- **PSYCHOLOGICAL PROBLEMS:** Regular and/or heavy alcohol use will cause or contribute to numerous emotional and behavioral problems, including chronic anxiety, panic attacks, depression, irritability, violent outbursts, paranoia, mental confusion, foggy thinking, and suicidal thoughts and/or attempts.

My smart, adorable, gentle son—where did he go? He started drinking at fourteen, and now it's as if some monstrous process has re-created him from the inside out, and it happened so fast. He doesn't care about school, sports, his old friends, the way he looks.

He doesn't seem to care about anything. He's angry all the time and he can be very aggressive. I can't talk to him or reason with him. To be truthful, I'm scared of him.

Can you tell me what happened?

—SUSAN, *thirty-nine*

Combining Drugs

One night I started drinking and mixing drugs. I used crank [methamphetamines], Ecstasy, marijuana, and beer—lots of beer. I felt incredibly, amazingly good, I was really high. But then, oh, man, I can't even explain it, I was just off somewhere, tripping, and I felt sick and my heart was pounding, and I thought for sure I was gonna die.

—KIM, *fifteen*

One of the big problems with alcohol is that it is everywhere—it's the standard, the regular, always available drug.

Alcohol is the drug kids use when they're on probation and can't use marijuana or methamphetamines because those drugs are stored in fat cells and show up days or even weeks later on urine screens. Unlike most drugs, alcohol is water-soluble and is thus rapidly eliminated from the body. Even if you get stinking drunk on Thursday night, a urine test conducted Friday afternoon will be clean—that is, unless you continue to drink well into the morning hours.

Alcohol is also the drug kids combine with other drugs to see how high they can get. What are the combinations? You name them. Alcohol and weed. Alcohol and weed dipped in PCP or fry (embalming fluid) or dusted with heroin, cocaine, or meth. Alcohol and NyQuil, Robitussin, or Coricidin. Alcohol and OxyContin or Vicodin. Alcohol and LSD, Ecstasy, psychedelic mushrooms, GHB, or Rohypnol. Alcohol and meth. Alcohol and Ritalin. Alcohol and cocaine. Alcohol and heroin.

Combining alcohol and other drugs can be dangerous, even deadly. When two drugs are taken together, their effects are potentiated, which means that the effects of each drug are significantly increased. Here are some of the most lethal combinations:

- **ALCOHOL AND SEDATIVES**: Alcohol is a sedative drug at moderate and high doses. If you combine alcohol with other sedative drugs, your heart rate and respiration will slow down, increasing the risk of coma, convulsions, and death.

  Prescription drugs with sedative-hypnotic effects include the barbiturate drugs (phenobarbital, Nembutal, Seconal, Amytal); chloral hydrate (Notec, Somnos); Quaalude, Equanil, Miltown; and the benzodiazepines (Valium, Librium, Xanax, Klonopin, Halcion, Restoril, and so on).

- **ALCOHOL AND GHB OR ROHYPNOL**: GHB (gamma hydroxybutrate) and Rohypnol are powerful sedatives that are commonly called "date rape drugs." When combined with alcohol—both GHB and Rohypnol are odorless and tasteless and can be added to a person's drink without that person's knowledge—they can cause weakness, dizziness, light-headedness, and mental confusion. Higher doses can lead to unconsciousness, coma, and death.

- **ALCOHOL AND OPIATE-BASED DRUGS**: Like sedatives and barbiturates, the opiate-based narcotic drugs (heroin, morphine, codeine, Darvon, Demerol) slow down breathing and heart rate. They also make you sleepy and can cause vomiting. Combining opiates and alcohol can lead to unconsciousness, coma, and death.

- **ALCOHOL AND STIMULANTS**: Adolescents sometimes use alcohol to calm the jitters associated with withdrawal from methamphetamines, cocaine, Ritalin, and other stimulants. Taking a stimulant and sedative at the same time can lead to unexpected reactions, including nausea, vomiting, loss of consciousness, coma, and death.

- **ALCOHOL AND ANTIHISTAMINES (BENADRYL AND OTHERS)**: Over-the-counter drugs used to treat allergic symptoms and insomnia have sedative effects that are often intensified by alcohol.

■ **ALCOHOL AND ANTIDEPRESSANTS:** Alcohol increases the sedative effects of "tricyclic antidepressants" such as Elavil (amitriptyline), Tofranil (imipramine), Pertofrane (desipramine), and the SSRIs (selective serotonin reuptake inhibitors) such as Prozac, Paxil, and Zoloft. These drugs may also cause blood pressure problems and increase the negative effects alcohol alone has on the liver.

I describe a lot of my last years drinking and using like this: being on a speeding train at night—pitch-black night—riding through the country where there's no street lights and there's a storm going on outside, a very violent storm. Every once in a while there's a flash of lightning and it wakes you up. You look out the window and see the world illuminated by this flash of lightning. You see the rain pouring down, and there's a fierce wind. Then you go back to sleep. That's what my life was like for the last two-and-a-half years of drinking and using. I had this flash of images, and everything filtered through some kind of madness—drunken madness or heroin madness or cocaine madness or combinations of all of them.

—DOUG FIEGER, *recovering alcoholic and
drug addict, lead singer of The Knack*

Physical Dependence

Is alcohol an addictive drug? Yes *and* no. Alcohol is a selectively addictive drug, meaning that while many people can drink without becoming addicted, certain people—those who are genetically predisposed to addiction—will become addicted if they continue to drink. (See pages 28–31 for a discussion of the metabolic differences between alcoholics and nonalcoholics.) For approximately 10 to 15 percent of people, alcohol does something different—it makes them feel so good that even if the taste is repulsive and the consequences are unpleasant, they want to repeat the experience.

At least that was the way it worked twenty or thirty years ago. Today we have a different situation. People are becoming addicted to alcohol who have no family history or genetic evidence of alcoholism. Adolescents are at greatest risk because their brains are still developing, they often start using at an early age, and they frequently combine alcohol and other drugs to intensify the high. Kids with emotional and/or behavioral disorders may use alcohol and other drugs to feel normal and, over time, develop drug problems that exacerbate their mental health problems.

We have always known that combining drugs can lead to a hyperspeed addiction; in the past, for most people, the most common drug combination included alcohol and drugs prescribed by doctors for pain, insomnia, depression, and anxiety. But today there are so many drugs available to adolescents that the combinations are endless. Marijuana and alcohol comprise the most common combination, but from there, almost anything goes. Listen to this conversation between Gary and Shawn, both sixteen years old.

> "The most drugs I've ever combined is seven. Let's see—alcohol, marijuana, Coricidin, Dramamine, Ecstacy, OxyContin, and acid." Gary grimaces and rolls his eyes. "That was a night, let me tell you. I've never been that high—or that sick."
>
> "I've only done five drugs at once," Shawn says. "Weed dipped in heroin, cocaine, a prescription painkiller, can't tell you exactly what it was, and alcohol. Lots of alcohol. Was I high? Oh, yeah, I was high."

If an adolescent starts using alcohol or other drugs before age fifteen and frequently uses alcohol and marijuana or some other drug combination, the risk of addiction is very high—even if there is no history of drug addiction in the family. Furthermore, binge drinking—five or more drinks at a time for boys or four or more drinks for girls—can damage the adolescent's developing brain and increase the possibility of addiction.

When I was twelve years old I felt the need for escape. I didn't run but I formed a taste for alcohol. Mainly I drank what was in the house at the time. My parents never caught me. If they only knew they would have killed me on the spot. I drank vodka and Jack Daniel's and rum and wine along with a lot of beer and wine coolers and many other types of alcohol.

I'm now fifteen and my addiction has worsened. I'm trying to cut down, but not much. Alcohol gives me a kind of freedom I've never had before. I enjoy my drunken self.

The only downfall to my drinking is that sometimes I black out and can't remember things. When I was thirteen, I got in trouble with the law and got put in counseling and then inpatient treatment. I was angry because I couldn't drink. I just wanted my booze. The day I got out of treatment, I went home, and drank myself into a stupor. My parents still didn't notice that I was drunk.*

—BETHANY, *fifteen*

The two classic signs of physical addiction are tolerance and withdrawal.

Tolerance

I have an amazing tolerance. I can drink a quart of vodka and still keep drinking!

—JOHNNY, *seventeen*

The ability to drink a lot of alcohol without feeling or showing the effects is a common symptom of early- and middle-stage alcohol addiction. High tolerance for alcohol is a clear sign of the brain's early, adaptive responses to alcohol—the brain, in other words, welcomes alcohol as a regular guest, changing its structure and functioning to accommodate large amounts of the drug.

---

*Bethany, now seventeen, spent a year in a juvenile institution, where she received treatment for her alcoholism; she was sober for twenty months and then relapsed.

Many adolescents have a high tolerance for alcohol and take pride in the fact that they can keep putting it away while some of their friends are passed out cold or hugging the toilet bowl. They don't know that the ability to drink large quantities of alcohol and still function somewhat "normally" may be a classic, early sign of physical addiction.

Withdrawal

In the early and middle stages of addiction, the acute symptoms of alcohol withdrawal include a shaky, agitated feeling, along with nervousness, weakness, nausea, diarrhea, excessive perspiration, loss of appetite, memory impairment, vivid dreams, insomnia, hangovers (headaches, eyeaches, dizziness), gastrointestinal distress, and psychological anguish (guilt, shame, anxiety, self-loathing, sense of hopelessness and despair).

Feelings of anguish and despair are particularly disturbing to adolescents who have no way of knowing that their anxiety, fear, and depression are related to the fact that their brains are in an agitated, abnormal state. During withdrawal, the brain cells are in extreme distress, and the brain hurts in the only way it can register pain—with emotional and behavioral symptoms of distress.

As the disease progresses, the withdrawal syndrome becomes more intense and uncontrollable. Late-stage withdrawal symptoms include elevated pulse, heart rate, respiration, and blood pressure; extreme agitation (mental confusion, paranoia, anxiety, fear); disorientation (confusion about time, place, past events); frequent blackouts (complete memory loss for minutes, hours, or even days); high fever; diarrhea; hallucinations (usually involving the sensations of sight, hearing, and touch); severe tremors; and seizures. Severe withdrawal can cause delirium tremens (DTS), which has a 5 to 15 percent mortality rate even when appropriately treated.

Craving is a clear sign that the body needs drugs to function normally. As drug use continues, craving intensifies, metamorphosing from a strong desire to drink in order to experience pleasure and euphoria to an overpowering need to use to relieve the physical and emotional anguish of withdrawal. As time goes by, the adolescent's every action, mood, and emotion is increasingly governed by the need to use alcohol and/or other drugs to relieve the withdrawal symptoms.

When you're hungry, your brain says, "Give me food." When you're addicted to alcohol or other drugs, your brain says, "Give me drugs!" Hungry cells need food—drug-addicted cells need drugs. It's that simple, and that profound.

Acute withdrawal, experienced when alcohol and/or other drugs are being eliminated from the bloodstream, causes great physical and emotional distress and a craving for drugs to relieve the painful symptoms. But protracted withdrawal symptoms, experienced after weeks, months, or even years of abstinence from drugs, can also lead to fierce cravings for drugs.

A seventeen-year-old boy, abstinent for four months, describes his craving for alcohol:

> It's like you're thirsty, but you're not thirsty for water. It sucks. You want it, you want to get drunk or stoned or fried. Like, right now, I'm really thirsty for beer. Just talking about it makes me want it. But it's more than wanting it—it's needing it.

How Can I Tell if My Child Is Using Alcohol?

Because most adolescents drink to get drunk, it's usually not hard to tell if your child has been drinking. Here are some specific signs and symptoms to look for:

- **SMELL:** Most adolescents drink beer because it is cheap and readily available, and beer has a characteristic yeasty smell. If your child drinks a lot of beer, you may be able to smell beer on his or her breath the next morning. Follow the lead of some savvy doctors, who lean close during physical examinations in order to smell their patients' breath for alcohol. Be sure to be awake when your children return home after a night out with their friends and give them a hug or kiss.

- **NAUSEA AND VOMITING:** If your child spends the night at a friend's house and returns home the next morning feeling sick, nauseous, and exhausted . . . if your child throws up in his or her bed after being out the night before . . . if your child stumbles, sways, or slurs words . . . the red flags should go way up the flagpole.

- **PARAPHERNALIA:** Look for beer cans and empty bottles in the trash can. Most kids are smart enough to clean out their rooms or their cars, but look for pop tops, bottle tops, or corkscrews in wastebaskets, garbage cans, or out by the back fence.

- **VIOLENT BEHAVIOR:** Alcohol is the drug most often linked with violent behavior—in a comprehensive review of the scientific literature on violence and drugs, a quarter of violent assaults took place under the influence of alcohol compared to less than 10 percent involving drugs such as heroin, cocaine, or PCP. If your child is involved in a fight or becomes unusually aggressive, be on the lookout for other signs of alcohol use.

- **CIGARETTE SMOKING:** Adolescents and adults who drink are more likely to smoke cigarettes. If your child smokes, watch carefully for behaviors associated with alcohol and/or other drug use.

Nicotine

I think I could give up every other
drug—but how could I live without
my cigarettes?

—PAUL, *sixteen*

I quit for six months once. I didn't
think I'd ever smoke again but then
one day someone offered me a cigarette, I lit up, and that was it for me.

—JENNA, *seventeen*

A colorless liquid that turns brown when burned, nicotine is one
of more than four thousand chemicals found in such tobacco
products as cigarettes, bidis, cigars, pipe tobacco, chewing tobacco,
and snuff. Some of the other toxic chemicals in cigarette smoke include carbon monoxide, carbon dioxide, benzene, formaldehyde,
acetone, hydrogen cyanide, and ammonia.

The High

Nicotine stimulates the adrenal glands to release epinephrine (adrenaline), causing an almost immediate surge of energy and euphoria. Epinephrine then stimulates the central nervous system to release glucose, causing more stimulation. And researchers recently discovered that cigarette smoking leads to decreased levels of monoamine oxidase (MAO), an enzyme that works to break down the mood-enhancing brain chemical dopamine. As a result, dopamine levels increase in the brain.

The high doesn't last very long, however. Within ten seconds, nicotine levels peak in the brain, and then rapidly dissipate over the next few minutes. As nicotine levels drop, users typically experience fatigue and slight depression, which create a desire for more nicotine and continuous dosing throughout the day to maintain the drug's pleasurable effects and to prevent withdrawal symptoms.

The average smoker takes ten drags in the five minutes that it takes for the cigarette to burn down. Someone who smokes ten cigarettes a day will get about one hundred nicotine "hits," while someone who smokes a pack a day will get about two hundred "hits." This constant nicotine up and down helps to explain why cigarettes and other tobacco products are so fiercely addictive.

Who Uses Tobacco Products?

Eighteen percent of teenagers between the ages of thirteen and fifteen in this country smoke cigarettes compared to the worldwide average of 14 percent. Only 56 percent of adolescent smokers say they want to stop smoking. Reluctance to quit may be due, in part, to the fact that teenagers tend to underestimate the risks associated with adolescent smoking. Even among adolescents who believe the majority of adult smokers will die from smoking-related causes, just one in four consider their own smoking to be "very risky."

Although cigarette use has declined among young people in the past several years, more high school students use nicotine in the form of cigarettes than any other drug. Every day, more than two thousand adolescents under the age of eighteen start smoking.

Increasing numbers of adolescents are using unfiltered Asian cigarettes called "bidis" (pronounced *beadies*) because they are flavored (chocolate, vanilla, strawberry, lime, grape, root beer), easier and cheaper to buy (available at head shops and health food stores for about a dollar a pack), and perceived as less dangerous to health. According to the Centers for Disease Control and Prevention, however, smoking bidis produces higher levels of carbon monoxide, nicotine, and tar than smoking regular cigarettes. Nearly 13 percent of high school students and 4.4 percent of middle school students report smoking bidis.

Adolescents tend to associate cigarette smoking with popularity. According to one recent study, 40 percent of young people between the ages of fourteen and twenty-two said that their "popular" peers were more likely to smoke cigarettes than "unpopular" adolescents.

Many kids smoke cigarettes in an effort to lose weight, and girls are especially vulnerable. A 2002 report released by the Centers for Disease Control and Prevention found that girls who are trying to lose weight are 40 percent more likely to smoke cigarettes than girls who are not concerned with weight loss.

More girls are smoking now than ever. In 1999, 35 percent of high school girls smoked cigarettes, compared to 27 percent in 1991. Currently more than 1.5 million adolescent girls in the United States smoke cigarettes. Smoking among pregnant teenagers has been rising since the mid-1990s.

Tobacco Use by Students, 2002: Monitoring the Future Survey

	8TH-GRADERS	10TH-GRADERS	12TH-GRADERS
Ever Used	31.4%	47.4%	57.2%
Used in Past Month	10.7	17.7	26.7

Bad Effects

Short-Term Effects

The list is extensive and includes bad breath; stained teeth and fingers; appetite suppression (many adolescents consider this a positive effect); reduced function of taste buds in the mouth; mental confusion; dizziness; chronic cough; shortness of breath; pain in the chest and/or throat; and/or suppression of the immune system, which can lead to chronic bronchitis, colds, flus, and sinus infections.

Using tobacco products also reduces fertility in men and increases the risk of premature delivery, lower birth weight, and spontaneous abortions in pregnant women.

Long-Term Effects

Sixty-five million Americans use tobacco products, and every year 440,000 of these people die. Tobacco use is the leading preventable cause of death in the United States.

The major medical consequences and diseases related to tobacco use include:

- **CANCER:** Overall death rates from cancer are twice as high among smokers as nonsmokers and four times as high among heavy smokers compared to nonsmokers. Approximately 90 percent of all lung cancers are linked to cigarette smoking.

    Smoking is also associated with cancers of the mouth and tongue, pharynx, larynx, esophagus, stomach, pancreas, liver, kidneys, urethra, bladder, rectum, and lymph glands. Women who start smoking within five years of puberty have an increased risk of breast cancer.
- **BRAIN:** New research shows that male and female smokers

ages eighteen to forty-nine are three times more likely than nonsmokers to have brain hemorrhages.

- **LUNG DISEASE:** Cigarette smoking causes lung cancer, which in 1986 surpassed breast cancer as the leading type of cancer in women, according to the American Lung Association.

  Smoking also causes chronic bronchitis, causes or increases the severity of asthma, and accounts for 90 percent of all deaths from emphysema, a lung disorder characterized by damage and destruction to the air sacs in the lungs.

- **HEART DISEASE:** Smoking causes an estimated 30 percent of deaths attributed to heart and vascular disease as well as causing cardiac arrhythmias. Several chemicals in cigarette smoke are to blame—carbon monoxide decreases the oxygen-carrying capability of the blood, and nicotine stimulates the release of epinephrine, which increases the heart rate and blood pressure. Because the heart is a muscle that requires a rich supply of oxygen in order to pump blood through the body, the cigarette smoker's heart needs to work harder with less oxygen available to do its work. Cigarette smoke is also directly toxic to the inner lining of the blood vessels.

  Recent research tells us that smokers who have a heart attack are less likely to survive than people who don't smoke, and the risk of a second heart attack increases dramatically if the person continues to smoke.

- **OSTEOPOROSIS:** We've known for years that women who are heavy smokers are more likely to develop osteoporosis (brittle, easily breakable bones). New research shows that men who smoke also have lower bone mineral density—a risk factor for osteoporosis—and experience a high risk of spinal curvature.

- **EYES:** Smoking damages cells in the retina and can lead to irreversible deterioration and blindness. Smoking triples the risk of age-related maculopathy (ARM), also known as senile macular degeneration, which involves damage to the part of the retina used to see fine details. Smokers who drink four alcoholic drinks a day—the equivalent of four twelve-ounce beers or four five-ounce glasses of wine—are six times more likely to develop ARM.

- **SKIN:** Smoking appears to decrease the blood supply to the top layers of the skin, which may explain why smokers tend to have more wrinkles than nonsmokers and look older.

- **SEXUAL PERFORMANCE:** A new study reports that men who smoke more than twenty cigarettes a day are 60 percent more likely to have erectile dysfunction than men who never smoked; men who smoke less than ten cigarettes a day have a 16 percent higher risk.

- **MENTAL HEALTH:** Adolescents and young adults who smoke are more likely to develop agoraphobia (fear of open spaces), generalized anxiety disorder (fear of having panicky feelings and avoidance of situations and events that might induce fear or panic), and panic disorder. Studies also show that adolescent smokers are twice as likely as adolescent nonsmokers to be depressed.

The question is—Does depression lead to smoking or does smoking cause depression? We don't know for sure, but we do know that if you smoke, you are significantly more likely to be depressed.

Secondhand and Sidestream Smoke

If you live with smokers—or if you spend a good amount of your time with people who smoke—your health is at risk from both secondhand smoke (the smoke exhaled by the smoker) and sidestream smoke (the smoke that rises off the lit cigarette or cigar). Both kinds of smoke can cause cancer in nonsmokers, but sidestream smoke is particularly dangerous because it has not been filtered through the cigarette filter or the smoker's lungs.

Recent research shows that even when parents smoke outside the house—in the garage or on the porch or deck, for example—

their children are exposed to the effects of secondhand and side-stream smoke.

Regular exposure to secondhand and sidestream smoke:

- Doubles your risk of heart disease—forty thousand deaths from cardiovascular disease are caused by secondhand smoke.
- Damages your lungs—three thousand deaths from lung cancer are caused by secondhand and sidestream smoke.
- Increases the risk of cancers of the lung, uterus, cervix, liver, and kidneys.
- Increases the risk of sudden infant death.
- Causes asthma in children and/or contributes to the severity of childhood asthma.
- Predisposes children to smoking at an early age.

Here are some additional facts parents and pregnant teenagers who smoke need to consider carefully:

- Female smokers take longer to conceive than nonsmokers.
- Smoking during pregnancy is linked to an increased risk of spontaneous abortion, premature delivery, lower-weight babies, respiratory infections in newborns, and infant mortality.
- Children whose mothers smoke during pregnancy are at much greater risk than other children for a number of physical, psychological, and behavioral disorders, including asthma, respiratory problems, diabetes, obesity, drug addiction, anxiety, depression, antisocial behaviors such as hitting and biting others, and the psychological diagnosis of conduct disorder.
- Children whose parents ask them to empty their ashtrays, light their cigarettes, or go to the store to buy their cigarettes are more likely to start smoking.

Overdose and Death

Nicotine is a dangerous poison, and lethal overdoses are possible, although rare. Symptoms of an overdose might include muscular twitching, tremors (internal and external shaking), difficulty breathing, rapid breathing, abdominal cramps, vomiting, rapid heartbeat, agitation, mental confusion, convulsions, paralysis of the breathing muscles, and possible death.

Drug Combinations

One drug leads to another—at least that is certainly the case with cigarettes. According to a 2002 report released by the National Center for Tobacco-Free Kids:

- Adolescent smokers between the ages of twelve and seventeen are more than eleven times as likely to use illegal drugs and sixteen times as likely to drink heavily.
- Cigarette smoking usually comes first. Sixty-five percent of adolescents who use both cigarettes and marijuana by the twelfth grade started smoking cigarettes before they used marijuana. Among adolescents who use both cigarettes and cocaine, 98 percent smoked cigarettes first.
- Kids who start smoking are three times more likely to use marijuana and four times more likely to use cocaine than those who do not start smoking as children.
- More than half of all adolescents who start smoking before age fifteen will use an illegal drug in their lifetime.
- Kids who start smoking before age fifteen are seven times more likely to use cocaine than those who never smoke cigarettes.
- Kids who smoke more than fifteen cigarettes a day are more than twice as likely to use an illegal drug and sixteen times more likely to use cocaine than those who smoke less

frequently. When compared to kids who don't smoke at all, these same adolescents are ten times more likely to use an illegal drug and more than one hundred times more likely to use cocaine.

- Children who smoke a pack a day are thirteen times more likely to use heroin than kids who smoke less heavily.
- Smokers between the ages of twelve and seventeen are fourteen times more likely to have binged on alcohol than nonsmokers, more than one hundred times more likely to have used marijuana at least ten times, and thirty-two times more likely to have used cocaine more than ten times.
- Adolescent smokers are three times more likely to use alcohol than adolescents who do not smoke.
- Between 80 and 95 percent of all alcoholics also smoke cigarettes; 70 percent of alcoholics smoke more than a pack a day.
- High school kids who use smokeless (spit) tobacco twenty to thirty days a month are nearly four times more likely to currently use marijuana than nonusers, almost three times more likely to have used cocaine, and nearly three times more likely to have used inhalants.
- Heavy users of smokeless or spit tobacco are almost sixteen times more likely than nonusers to consume alcohol.

Some drug combinations can be especially dangerous, even deadly. In a study conducted at UCLA, cocaine addicts had 23 percent less blood flowing through their brains than a drug-free control group—and cocaine addicts who also smoked cigarettes had a 45 percent reduction in brain blood flow.

Nicotine combined with other stimulant drugs affects not only blood flow but also the risk of sudden death. When nicotine—a powerful stimulant that affects the heart and circulatory system—is combined with other stimulant drugs, such as cocaine or methamphetamines, the risk of sudden death from a heart attack increases dramatically.

Physical Dependence

I don't fiend for other drugs. Not like I do for cigarettes. Go
ahead, take away the marijuana, the beer, the cocaine, LSD, Ecstasy, painkillers, all of it, but leave me my cigarettes.

—TIM, *seventeen*

Nicotine is fiercely addictive, especially for adolescents—just a
few drags on a cigarette every other day for a few weeks can lead to
addiction in teens, according to a 2002 study that appeared in the
Archives of Pediatrics & Adolescent Medicine. Once hooked, adolescents have a much harder time quitting—according to the same
study, adolescents are twenty-nine times more likely to fail in efforts to quit compared to adult smokers.

Females are also more susceptible to addiction than males
(31.6 percent, compared to 27.4 percent), and Caucasians have
higher addiction rates (31.3 percent) than African Americans (25
percent) and Hispanics (27.5 percent). Thus, Caucasian adolescent
females appear to be the most vulnerable of all people to nicotine
addiction.

Tolerance

Tolerance may be more obvious with nicotine than with any other
drug. Addicted smokers need to smoke more to experience the
pleasure and stimulation created by the drug and to forestall withdrawal symptoms—that's the standard definition of *tolerance*. But
with nicotine, acute tolerance also increases over the period of a
day as the smoker provides the brain with multiple drug "hits." As
nicotine is metabolized and eliminated from the body overnight,
tolerance levels drop. This overnight drop in tolerance may explain
why so many smokers claim that the first cigarette of the day is the
very best of all.

Withdrawal

Withdrawal symptoms include depression, mood swings, nervousness, restlessness, anxiety, insomnia, irritability, difficulty concentrating, increased appetite, and nicotine cravings.

In heavy smokers, withdrawal symptoms begin within hours of the last cigarette. Cravings for nicotine can persist for months and are often so intense and persistent that the great majority of people who try to quit, fail. Nearly thirty-five million smokers make a serious attempt to quit each year, but most relapse within a few days, and less than 7 percent are able to remain abstinent for a year or more.

Women have a harder time quitting than men. Large-scale smoking-cessation trials show that women are less likely to attempt to quit and more likely to relapse if they do quit. Furthermore, nicotine patches and gum do not seem to reduce craving as effectively for women as for men. Researchers believe the withdrawal syndrome may be more intense for women than it is for men.

How Can I Tell if My Child Is Using Tobacco Products?

It's difficult for adolescents (and adults) to hide the fact that they are smoking or chewing tobacco, because the signs tend to be everywhere. Parents should look for:

- Cigarette odor on the breath, hands, or clothes.
- Nicotine stains on teeth and fingers.
- Frequent use of breath mints or breath sprays to disguise the odor.
- Cigarettes in ashtrays, empty packs, cigarette butts outside (in the driveway or backyard).
- Missing cash or depleted checking or savings accounts. Cigarettes are expensive—a pack-a-day habit costs about $140 a month.

- Chronic respiratory problems, including shortness of breath, nagging or hacking cough, frequent colds, bronchitis, or sinus infections.

If you smoke cigarettes but want to prevent your children from smoking, the best thing you can do is quit yourself. At the very least, protect your children from secondhand and sidestream smoke (reread the section in this chapter).

Here's another tip—cut down on the amount of television your children watch. New research shows that adolescents who watch five hours or more of television a day are six times more likely to start smoking, and kids who watch between two and four hours of television a day are two to three times more at risk.

"You're looking at TV as indirect advertising," says Dr. Pradeep Gidwani, the study's lead author. "Rarely is smoking portrayed [on television] in an unattractive manner or associated with negative consequences."

Marijuana

> I don't care what people say about
> marijuana or how bad they say it
> is for my lungs, my liver, or my
> brain—I'm going to have my bong
> next to my bed the day I die. It will
> be the last thing I look at when I
> leave this earth.
>
> —EMILY, *fifteen*

Marijuana is a green (high-quality) or brown (low-quality) mixture of the dried leaves, stems, seeds, and flowers of the hemp plant (*Cannabis sativa*). While there are more than four hundred chemicals in marijuana, the major mind-altering, pleasure-creating chemical is delta-9-tetrahydrocannabinol, or THC.

The strength or potency of THC in different batches of marijuana varies from 1 to 2 percent in "bammer" or "brown" weed—consisting mostly of leaves and stems—to as high as 11 to 12 percent for sinsemilla or "chronic" weed, made from the buds and flowering tops of female plants.

While today's marijuana is significantly stronger than it was in the 1960s and 1970s, the potency is often wildly exaggerated. You may have heard people say that high-grade weed is ten to twenty times stronger than it was in the 1960s and 1970s. Laboratory tests, however, show that the average THC content in marijuana ranges between 2 and 6 percent, while sinsemilla is approximately twice as strong as it was thirty years ago.

Most kids don't realize that marijuana, which is fat-soluble, has a long half-life, meaning that it stays in the body's fat cells and continues to exert its effects for days, weeks and even months. In kids who use infrequently, several days must pass before the amount of marijuana in the blood or urine is reduced by 50 percent, and several weeks before the body completely eliminates the drug. In heavy users, marijuana accumulates in the body's fat tissues; even with complete abstinence, the drug may be detected in urine tests after thirty or forty days, and may continue to affect mental, physical, and emotional functioning for months.

The High

Weed makes you happy. You know, calm, loose, funny. Before you smoke, you're sitting there with your friends talking about how bored you are, how there's nothing to do. Then you get high and everybody's talking at once, you're all talking about your day and how this thing happened or that thing happened, and it's all so funny. Ten people are talking at the same time, and everything seems so hilarious.

—JOLEEN, *sixteen*

The effects of marijuana can vary dramatically from one person to another, depending on a number of factors:

- **THE STRENGTH OF THE DRUG:** Sinsemilla ("chronic"), hashish, and hash oil are much stronger than low-grade brown or bammer weed.
- **THE WAY THE DRUG IS TAKEN:** When you smoke marijuana, you feel the high within minutes; when hash or marijuana is eaten, an hour or two may pass before you feel high.

- **THE EXPERIENCE AND EXPECTATIONS OF THE USER:** Experienced users generally know what to expect when they get high, while new users may feel out of control and get anxious or panicky.
- **THE SETTING WHERE THE DRUG IS USED:** If you are smoking weed with close friends, the high tends to be more enjoyable and relaxing than when you smoke around strangers. Some people experience anxiety, panic attacks, paranoia, or depression when smoking in an uncomfortable setting.
- **USING OTHER DRUGS:** When marijuana is mixed with alcohol, cocaine, methamphetamines, or other drugs, the high is more intense and the user's reactions may be unpredictable.

In most cases, the high occurs within a few minutes of smoking and lasts for one to three hours. Users feel happier and calmer, relaxed and at peace. Ordinary sights, sounds, tastes, smells, and sensations of touch are experienced as extraordinary, and time often seems to pass very slowly.

For many adolescents, the high is hilarious, full of laughter and giggling over silly jokes, strange scenarios, or nothing at all. Hysterical laughter may be accompanied by long moments of silence when adolescents become engrossed in watching television, playing video games, or just walking down the street, thinking about life.

This one time I got stoned watching the movie *Half Baked* with some friends. We kept rewinding this one part because we thought it was so hilarious. I think we watched that part maybe twenty times. I laughed so hard I could hardly breathe. It was like I was laughing myself clean.

—BEN, *fifteen*

The other side of getting the giggles is getting paranoid. Some adolescents routinely feel paranoid when they smoke, while others get "freaked out" only when they smoke excessive amounts or combine other drugs with weed. Feeling out of control and disoriented, the novice user might panic or experience a severe anxiety attack.

Along with the marijuana high comes a powerful sense of hunger called "the munchies," caused by the drug's stimulation of hunger-activating cannabinoid receptors in the brain. Food tastes delicious when you're high on weed, and adolescents tend to pig out on potato chips, crackers, popcorn, cookies, brownies, sweet cereals, or just about anything in the refrigerator.

As the high gradually fades away, many users begin to feel sleepy or drained of energy.

Who Uses Marijuana?

Pretty much anybody who uses drugs uses marijuana. Kids, adults, old people. You might think somebody doesn't use it, but they do. Businesspeople might smoke bud, you know, people walking around in suits. It's sneaky. You never know. How would you know?

—BRAD, *fifteen*

Marijuana is the most frequently used illegal drug in the United States—more than eighty-three million Americans over the age of twelve (37 percent of our population) have tried marijuana at least once. Among teens between the ages of twelve and seventeen, the average age of first use is between thirteen and fourteen.

Marijuana/Hashish Use by Students, 2002: Monitoring the Future Survey

	8TH-GRADERS	10TH-GRADERS	12TH-GRADERS
Ever Used	19.2%	38.7%	47.8%
Used in Past Year	14.6	30.3	36.2
Used in Past Month	8.3	17.8	21.5
Daily	1.2	3.9	6.0

The good news is that marijuana use declined among eighth- and tenth-graders in 2002. The bad news is that the number of adolescents who view the drug as harmful has decreased. In the latest Monitoring the Future Survey, 71.7 percent of eighth-graders believe regular marijuana use is harmful, compared to 74.8 percent in 2000. Among tenth-graders, 60.8 percent perceive regular marijuana smoking to be harmful, compared to 64.7 percent in 2000.

In general, the less harmful a drug is perceived to be, the more willing adolescents are to try it.

Bad Effects

Remember, it's not "How high are you?" It's "Hi, how are you?"

—SIGN SEEN AT A REST STOP
Route 81 in Virginia

Long-term research with adolescents shows that marijuana users are less motivated to achieve, more accepting of and likely to engage in deviant behavior, more aggressive, and more rebellious. They also experience more relationship problems with their parents, and associate more with drug-using friends.

Compared to nonusers, adolescents who use marijuana weekly are six times more likely to run away from home, five times more likely to steal from places other than home, six times more likely to cut classes or skip school, and four times more likely to physically attack others.

Ask the kids, though, and they'll tell you the worst effect associated with smoking weed is laziness.

If you're smoking every day, you don't even try to remember things. You're lazy. Like I'm too lazy to get my driver's permit. I want to drive, but I'm too lazy. I'm too lazy to get up and go to the store with my mom. Too lazy to get up and get a glass of water. Too lazy to ask my mom to buy me a two-liter bottle of soda because I'm too lazy to pour the stuff into the glass.

It sucks. I just drink milk out of the carton, I don't put it in a glass. I try not to use a plate because then you have to clean it and deal with all this stuff, and it's annoying.

I don't want to go to school. 'Cause if you get, like, stoned at lunch or something, you don't want to have to think because thinking is, like, so annoying. It just doesn't work, thinking just doesn't work when you're stoned. You can't retrieve memories; it's all warp style, like an equation in math, you think you've got it the right way and then it's all wrong.

I wish all that laziness made me want to stop. But that's the reason why you do it, so you just don't have to think about things, you don't have to think about the bad things, you don't have to think about things that bother you, you just sit back and do your thing. That's why it's fun to walk when you're stoned, you just walk and you're not even aware of what's going on outside you, you're all in your head. If you try to write and read, it doesn't work because your mind just wanders.

—ROSS, *seventeen*

Short-Term Effects

The short-term effects associated with regularly smoking marijuana can have devastating consequences. Anxiety and panic attacks, depression, and suicidal thoughts can disturb social relationships and personal growth. School performance and grades often drop due to the effects of marijuana on memory, concentration, and the ability to solve problems. Several studies link marijuana smoking with job problems, including increased absences, tardiness, on-the-job accidents, and lower productivity.

Memory problems are common. In addition to exerting its pleasurable effects in the brain, THC also attaches itself to different groups of cannabinoid receptors in the brain, located in the hippocampus (situated within the temporal lobe), the cerebellum, and the basal ganglia. When THC binds with receptors in the hippocampus, which controls short-term memory, it interferes with memory for recent events.

The cerebellum controls coordination, and the basal ganglia controls unconscious muscle movements, and when THC latches onto receptors in these brain structures, motor coordination is affected.

Slower reaction time and reduced concentration can lead to serious, even fatal accidents. Australian researchers who studied thirty-four hundred drivers who died in auto crashes between 1990 and 1999 found that drivers with THC in their bloodstreams were 6.6 times more likely to die in a crash.

When users combine marijuana with alcohol and/or other drugs, as they often do, the risks increase exponentially. In one study of people involved in traffic accidents, 15 percent had been smoking marijuana prior to the accident, while another 17 percent had both THC and alcohol in their blood. In another study of 150 reckless drivers who were tested for drugs at the arrest scene, 33 percent tested positive for marijuana, and 12 percent tested positive for both marijuana and cocaine.

Other short-term effects include dry mouth, increased heart rate, chronic fatigue, social withdrawal, apathy (not caring about anything, including relationships, appearance, or achievement), hallucinations, delusions, depression, and suicidal thoughts.

Long-Term Effects

A number of recent scientific studies raise serious concerns about the long-term health effects of regular marijuana use and the drug's harmful impact on the body's vital organs.

- **BRAIN:** From brain-imaging studies, we know that long-term changes occur in the brains of people who are regular marijuana users. In his book *Change Your Brain, Change Your Life*, psychiatrist and researcher Dr. Daniel Amen describes the damage:

  . . . frequent, long-term marijuana use has the potential to change the perfusion [blood flow] pattern of the brain. While prior studies showed global decreased brain activity, I found focal decreased activity in the temporal lobes . . . [which has] been associated with problems in memory, learning, and motivation—common complaints of teenagers (or at least their parents) and adults who chronically abuse marijuana. Amotivational syndrome, marked by apathy, poor attention span, lethargy, social withdrawal, and loss of interest in achievement, [has] been attributed to marijuana abuse for many years.

In the brains of regular marijuana users, SPECT scans show numerous holes indicating multiple areas of decreased metabolic activity and blood flow. In other words, not much is happening. As Dr. Amen notes in the quotation above, the SPECT scans show that chronic marijuana use leads to decreased activity in the temporal lobes, which are involved with memory, understanding language, facial recognition, and temper control. Problems in this area can lead to temper tantrums, rapid mood shifts, memory and learning problems, and a sense of being out of balance, out of control, and generally confused.

THC also interferes with the normal functioning of the cerebellum, which is responsible for balance, posture, and coordination of body movements.

In the cerebral cortex, marijuana interferes with the reception of sensory messages—touch, sight, hearing, taste, and smell.

Cellular damage and destruction throughout the brain may also lead to problems with memory, learning, and motivation.

- **CANCER:** Marijuana smoke contains many of the same cancer-causing compounds found in tobacco, and sometimes in higher concentrations. A marijuana joint, for example, contains about three times the tar found in a cigarette, as well as other known cancer-causing chemicals such as carbon dioxide, ammonia, vinyl chloride, dimethylnitrosamine, methylethylnitrosamine, benz(a)anthracene, and benzo(a)pyrene.

Several studies show that people who smoke five joints per week may be taking in as many cancer-causing chemicals as someone who smokes a full pack of cigarettes every day. Because marijuana smoke contains 57 percent more carcinogenic hydrocarbons than tobacco smoke, researchers believe smoking marijuana may increase the risk of cancer more than smoking tobacco does. Marijuana smoking also has been linked to early development of head and neck cancers, doubling or tripling the risk of developing these cancers. Because many people who smoke marijuana also smoke cigarettes, however, it is difficult to determine whether marijuana alone causes cancer or whether the increased risk of cancer is due to the combined effect of marijuana and tobacco smoke. Researchers do know that the combination of tobacco and marijuana smoke can work together synergistically to alter the tissues lining the respiratory tract.

- **IMMUNE SYSTEM:** The immune system protects our bodies from many disease-causing agents. While we don't know yet if marijuana causes permanent damage to the immune system, we do know from both animal and human studies that marijuana impairs the ability of T cells in the lungs' immune system to fight off some infections, making it a particularly dangerous drug for anyone whose immune system is impaired.

- **LUNGS:** Regular marijuana smokers often develop the same kinds of breathing problems that cigarette smokers have, including daily cough and phlegm (chronic bronchitis) and frequent chest colds. Chronic, heavy marijuana use can injure or destroy lung tissue, and regular users are also at greater risk of getting lung infections such as pneumonia. A recent study by the British Lung Foundation found that the tar in marijuana contains 50 percent more carcinogens than tobacco, leading researchers to conclude that smoking marijuana may be more harmful to the lungs than smoking cigarettes.

- **SINUSES:** Chronic sinus problems (sinusitis) are common in regular marijuana users.
- **HEART:** Marijuana dramatically increases the heart rate. Recent research shows that the risk of a heart attack for middle-age users is 4.8 times higher in the first hour after smoking marijuana.
- **REPRODUCTIVE ORGANS:** Regular marijuana use in males may result in decreased testosterone levels; decreased sperm count and motility; abnormalities in sperm; and breast enlargement (gynecomastia). Females who are chronic marijuana users may experience abnormal periods, reduced ovulation, and decreased prolactin levels. Prolactin is a hormone that stimulates milk production in nursing females, and researchers believe that it is also involved in fertility and normal immune responses.

  Adolescents who regularly use drugs, including marijuana, may become involved in risky sexual behavior. Numerous research studies have confirmed the strong link between drug use, unsafe sex, and the spread of HIV, the virus that causes AIDS, and other sexually transmitted diseases.
- **EMOTIONAL HEALTH:** Long-term marijuana users show signs of amotivational syndrome and are more likely to be depressed, anxious, irritable, and suicidal than nonusers.

But What About Medical Marijuana Use?

Throughout the years, marijuana has been proposed as a painkiller, antidepressant, anticonvulsant, tranquilizer, and muscle relaxant as well as an appetite stimulant for AIDS patients, a glaucoma aid, and an antinausea drug for patients undergoing cancer chemotherapy. Citing all these potential medical uses, adolescents often argue that marijuana is a harmless drug.

> It's organic! It's a weed! Why would God have put marijuana on this earth if He didn't want us to use it?
>
> —TYLER, *seventeen*

Scientists have been disappointed, however, in their efforts to prove marijuana's therapeutic usefulness. The biggest problem is the harmful side effects stemming from the many toxic compounds (carbon monoxide, acetaldehyde, naphthalene) and carcinogenic (cancer-causing) substances in marijuana smoke, which can have damaging effects on the lungs, heart, brain, reproductive organs, and immune system. Memory impairment, physical dependence, and withdrawal symptoms including irritability, anger, depression, headaches, restlessness, lack of appetite, and craving compound the harmful effects.

And then there's the fact that marijuana simply isn't very effective as a medicine. For glaucoma patients, marijuana can reduce pressure in the eye, but there is also evidence that chronic marijuana use increases pressure in the eye and decreases vision. Studies with AIDS patients show that marijuana does not correlate statistically with any weight gain. And the American Cancer Society has concluded that marijuana has only limited usefulness in the treatment of vomiting caused by cancer chemotherapy, and that modern drugs such as metoclopramide and ondansetron have much greater effectiveness and fewer side effects than THC.

To sum it up, researchers have discovered that the risks of using marijuana as medicine far outweigh any potential benefits.

Overdose and Death

It's almost impossible to overdose on marijuana. In rare cases, small children have gone into comas after unknowingly ingesting large amounts of marijuana in cookies or brownies, but overdosing on marijuana is virtually impossible for adolescents and adults.

Extremely large doses of marijuana can cause a racing heart, anxiety, paranoia, panic attacks, and psychotic symptoms requiring emergency medical treatment. But unlike alcohol, heroin, cocaine, and many other drugs, marijuana won't kill you even if you take it in extraordinarily large amounts.

Drug Combinations

You wanna know what other drugs we use when we're smoking weed? Oh, man, are you ready? Here goes: alcohol, cocaine, cigarettes, opium, codeine, Coricidin, Robitussin, prescription painkillers, PCP, LSD, mushrooms, Ecstasy . . . what's left?

You mix the drugs because you get really, really high. Sometimes you have no idea where you're gonna go when you mix all those drugs, but that's half the fun.

The most drugs I've used at one time is five—weed, alcohol, cigarettes, cocaine, and prescription painkillers. I was so out of it, I fell asleep in my cereal bowl. Froot Loops. My sister had to pull my head out of the bowl.

—MARCUS, *fourteen*

Marijuana has long been called a gateway drug, and few adolescents will dispute the fact that when they started using marijuana, they had more opportunities to use harder drugs such as cocaine, methamphetamines, hallucinogens, and heroin.

Here's what adolescents have to say about marijuana use leading to experimentation with other drugs:

- "Is marijuana a gateway drug? Definitely. It makes you want to have a cooler time, which means taking more drugs."
- "Everyone says marijuana is bad, and it will do this and do that, but then it doesn't do all those bad things. So then you want to try other drugs that are also supposed to be bad,

because you figure since marijuana wasn't so bad, these other drugs probably aren't any worse."

- "Once you start using weed, it feels cool to use drugs. You figure nothing is really bad with marijuana, so why not try other drugs?"
- "You get a certain high from marijuana, and then after you've been smoking it for a while, you don't get as high, so you try acid or some other drug to get a better high."
- "First I started drinking, then I smoked marijuana, and then I was hanging out with a bunch of people who introduced me to cocaine, methamphetamines, LSD, and Ecstasy."
- "Marijuana just stopped doing it for me—I wasn't getting high as much, or enjoying it as much, so I decided to try new drugs so I could get as high as I used to get on marijuana."

Research appears to confirm what adolescents know to be true. National surveys consistently show that most adolescents think marijuana is less dangerous than other illegal drugs—and kids who do not believe there is great risk in smoking marijuana are significantly more likely to use both marijuana and other illegal drugs. Researchers theorize that using marijuana puts kids in contact with others who use and sell illegal drugs, increases peer pressure to use other drugs, and makes it easier for kids to become involved in a "drug culture."

A December 2002 report by the RAND Corporation challenges the gateway theory, however, and cites other reasons why marijuana users become involved with harder drugs.

The people who are predisposed to use drugs and have the opportunity to use drugs are more likely than others to use both marijuana and harder drugs. Marijuana typically comes first because it is more available.

—ANDREW MORRAL, Ph.D.
Senior Behavioral Scientist, RAND

But right after the publication of the RAND Corporation study, a 2003 study published in the *New England Journal of Medi-*

cine bolstered the gateway theory. Australian researchers studied 311 sets of same-sex twins, in which just one twin smoked marijuana before age seventeen. The early marijuana smokers were twice as likely to use opiates like heroin and five times as likely to use hallucinogens such as LSD. Even twins, however, do not share the same environment, and other factors might be at work, including greater access to drugs and willingness to engage in risk-taking behaviors and to break the law.

Whether marijuana changes your brain and makes you crave other drugs or merely increases the opportunity to use other drugs and interact with other drug users, there appears to be little doubt that using one illegal drug makes it easier to use other illegal drugs. That's how Tom Farley, comedian Chris Farley's brother, explains Chris's rapid descent into drug addiction and his eventual death from an overdose.

> [Chris's habit] started with beer, but then he went on to pot.... And yeah, it didn't necessarily mean that he was going to go right from there to cocaine and heroin, but you have to understand that once you start there, once you make the choice to do something illegal or take something somebody else offers you . . . it's very easy to have some guy say, "Why don't you try this now?"
>
> That's what happened to Chris. Literally, he went to New York and found some guy who would sell him pot, and sure enough this guy said, "Here, try this now." There was a very clear progression from one [drug] to the next.

Researchers are currently examining the possibility that long-term marijuana use may change the brain in ways that puts users at greater risk of becoming addicted to other drugs, such as alcohol and cocaine. While not all young people who use marijuana go on to use other illegal drugs, many do—and many adolescents end up experiencing serious physical, emotional, and behavioral problems because they regularly combine marijuana and other drugs.

Physical Dependence

"You'll get used to it in time," said the Caterpillar; and it put the hookah into its mouth and began smoking again.

—LEWIS CARROLL, *Alice in Wonderland*

Almost everyone agrees that marijuana is psychologically addicting, meaning that regular users look forward to getting high even if they don't physically need the drug. But is marijuana physically addicting? Do kids who use marijuana frequently crave the drug to the point that it controls their behavior? Do they have difficulty controlling their marijuana use, even though the drug is causing physical, mental, and/or emotional problems? Do they sacrifice bits and pieces of their lives in order to keep using?

Researchers and addiction medicine specialists answer yes to those questions. The Office of National Drug Control Policy, citing various research reports, publishes the following statistics on marijuana use and dependence in teens:

- Each year, more kids enter treatment with a primary diagnosis of marijuana dependence than for all other illicit drugs combined.
- Sixty percent of teens currently in drug treatment have a primary marijuana diagnosis.
- Research also shows that marijuana use is three times more likely to lead to dependence among adolescents than among adults.
- Among those who have used the drug at least five times, the rates of marijuana dependence are estimated at 20 to 30 percent.
- Among the 220,000 treatment admissions for marijuana in 1999, more than half (57 percent) had first used marijuana by the age of fourteen, and 92 percent by the age of eighteen.

Kids who use marijuana regularly tend to agree with the experts.

- "I fiend for that drug. I fiend for it to the point that I can't think about anything else."
- " I was smoking in the morning, at lunch, and every night. I was just roasted all day. And if I tried to stop for a day, I was a mess—headaches, hands shaking, cravings—I just couldn't take it, so I kept using until I got caught by the cops and thrown in detention."
- "I was flunking out of school and I just didn't care. I used to be a good student. But once marijuana came into my life, that's all I cared about—how to score some weed and kick back with my friends."
- "I developed this tolerance, and suddenly I had to smoke a whole bunch of the stuff to get high. Then, after a while, it was just no fun anymore. I had to go to inpatient treatment to quit. I tried outpatient treatment, but I just couldn't do it on my own."
- "I wanted to quit so bad. I spent twenty-eight days in treatment, and when I got out, I felt so good, I was 100 percent committed to staying clean. But just two weeks after I got out of treatment, a friend offered me a joint, and I swear—I didn't even think twice. I feel incredibly guilty, but I'm still smoking the stuff."

Physical addiction to a drug, as we've noted, is determined by the presence of two basic conditions—tolerance and withdrawal symptoms.

Tolerance

Although tolerance is sometimes difficult to measure, given the wide variation in THC content in marijuana, the research shows that tolerance does increase with continued use, and regular users will tell you that they definitely develop tolerance to the drug.

When I use chronic [high-quality weed], I still get really high but I definitely have to use more than I used to use. It's getting expensive—I spend about four hundred dollars a month on weed. I get my paycheck, and it's gone in one day. I spend it all on weed.

—TYLER, *seventeen*

You start out with just a little bit of bud and get high. Then, as time goes by, you have to smoke more and more to get the same high. With me, it means that I come down really fast; I don't stay high as long. For other people it's different, they have to smoke a lot more bud just to get high. It depends, too, on the quality of the weed. If you've got chronic, you can always get high. Still, even with chronic, I come down much faster now than I used to. It just happens slowly, over time.

—ROSS, *sixteen*

Withdrawal

Recent studies confirm that marijuana smokers experience withdrawal symptoms. In a 1999 study conducted at McLean Hospital in Belmont, Massachusetts, Harvard University researchers identified significant symptoms of withdrawal in 60 percent of regular marijuana users. Withdrawal symptoms include increased irritability, anxiety and physical tension, decreased appetite, and mood swings.

Researchers at Columbia University recently confirmed the existence of withdrawal symptoms in regular users. When daily marijuana smokers stop using the drug, they experience aggression, anxiety, stomach pain, and increased irritability. And a 2001 study appearing in *Archives of General Psychiatry* shows that marijuana smokers suffer withdrawal symptoms (craving, sleep difficulty, decreased appetite, and increases in aggression, anger, irritability, and restlessness) as severe as those experienced by tobacco smokers. According to lead researcher Alan Budney, M.D.:

We found consistent emotional and behavioral symptoms that increased during abstinence and dramatically decreased when marijuana smoking resumed . . . withdrawal from marijuana produces identifiable behavioral and emotional distress that may be as important as, if not more important than, physical symptoms in the development of dependence and undermining attempts to quit using the drug.

Adolescents who frequently use marijuana, and especially those who use daily, may suffer from mild to moderate, and sometimes severe, withdrawal symptoms. Withdrawal can develop within a few hours of use. The user gets jittery, anxious, irritable, and starts "fiending" or "feening" (craving) for the drug. Because these symptoms are relatively mild compared to the withdrawal symptoms associated with alcohol, methamphetamine, cocaine, or heroin, kids often ignore them or blame them on lack of sleep, the flu, depression, family problems, or life in general.

Hey, the only problem I have is that I want more weed. I don't need it— I can get by without it, I do it all the time. But when I want it and can't find it, I get a little jumpy, sure, yeah, and restless and my hands even shake a little. [He laughs.] But that's just the way I always feel when I'm not using.

See, weed makes me feel normal. When I'm not using—well, that's when I feel bad. It has nothing to do with being addicted or anything.

—PAUL, *seventeen*

How long do the withdrawal symptoms last? Because marijuana is stored in the body's fat cells and metabolized slowly, generally over a period of twenty to thirty days, withdrawal symptoms may last for a month, and protracted (long-term) withdrawal symptoms may continue for as long as six months.

Another way to measure physical dependence is to assess the difficulty people experience when they try to stop using a drug. In 1999, more than 220,000 people entering publicly funded drug treatment programs reported marijuana as their primary drug of choice, indicating that they needed help in their efforts to quit. Marijuana admissions represented 14 percent of the 1.6 million people admitted to these treatment programs, up from 7 percent in 1993. Two-thirds of the marijuana admissions were under the age of twenty-five.

> The use of marijuana can produce adverse physical, mental, emotional, and behavioral changes, and—contrary to popular belief—it can be addictive.
>
> —GLEN R. HANSON, Ph.D.
> *Acting Director of the National Institute on Drug Abuse*

How Can I Tell if My Child Is Using Marijuana?

A kid comes home from a party and says, "Hey, I'm really tired," and his eyes are all red, and he has this humungous grin on his face. So the parent says, "Okay, honey, go get some sleep."

Well, that's just plain stupid. That kid is stoned out of his gourd. Parents need to wake up.

—ANDREW, *seventeen*

Here's my advice—put all the signs together. Check out your kids' eyes to see if they're red or squinty. I get all pig-faced when I smoke, you know, my eyes get squinty and my cheeks puff up. If they're totally grubbing food, you know, cleaning out the refrigerator, that's always a good sign. Sometimes kids are just hungry but if they're grubbing out all the time, watch out. See if they laugh over stupid things.

But don't ask your kids if they're using, because they'll just lie to you.

—ROSS, *sixteen*

When kids are regularly using marijuana, parents may notice the following signs and symptoms:

Problems at Home
- Withdrawal from family activities.
- Arguing with siblings and parents.
- Acting sullen or uncommunicative.
- Refusing to do chores, homework.
- Routinely breaking house rules such as meeting curfews, using appropriate language, being respectful of others.

Physical Signs
- Unusual or chronic fatigue.
- Clacking sound when talking.
- Lips stick to teeth.
- Dry mouth.
- Chapped lips.
- Never-ending smile.
- Red, bloodshot eyes.
- Squinty eyes.
- Dilated pupils.

Emotional/Mental Problems
- Anxiety.
- Depression, mild or severe.
- Mood swings.
- Hostility.
- Sudden anger.
- Memory lapses.

Problems at School
- Teachers complain about your child's attitude or behavior in class.
- Low motivation.
- Apathy about school performance.

- Grades begin to drop.
- Absenteeism.
- Truancy.
- Loss of interest in sports or other extracurricular activities.

Behavior Changes
- Carelessness with clothing, hairstyle, or makeup.
- Desire to be with new friends.
- Frequent overnights at other people's houses.
- Excessive laughter or giggling over silly or trivial events.
- Signs of drugs and drug paraphernalia, including pipes and rolling papers.
- Odor on clothes and in the bedroom.
- Use of incense and other deodorizers.
- Use of eyedrops, breath mints, chewing gum, mouthwash.
- Music, clothing, posters, or jewelry promoting drug use.
- Excessive hunger, overeating, or feasting on high-sugar and high-fat foods.

Inhalants

Inhalants are very volatile. You can
die the first time or the fifth time
from abusing inhalants. It's like
playing Russian roulette. . . . I speak
to 100 to 125 parents a year whose
children have died from inhalants.

—HARVEY WEISS, *Founder and*
Executive Director of the National
Inhalant Prevention Coalition (NIPC)

Inhalants are right under our noses. We buy them at hardware,
auto supply, and grocery stores. We keep them in our ga-
rages, under our sinks, and in our medicine cabinets. We think
about them as practical, even indispensable, tools in our daily
lives. And millions of kids in elementary school, middle school, and
high school are "huffing" these toxic chemicals to get a quick,
cheap high.

Adolescents—and kids who are still, literally, children—usually
have no idea that inhaling these products can cause severe headaches, vomiting, accelerated heartbeat, and serious, potentially permanent damage to the brain, lungs, liver, kidneys, and bone
marrow. They don't know that huffing common household chemicals like hair spray, model airplane glue, and spot remover can lead

to permanent brain damage, suffocation, strokes, and sudden death. They think they're in for just a quick, cheap high.

More than a thousand household products can be inhaled for short-lived pleasure—and the ever-present possibility of long-term pain. The most popular inhalants among adolescents between the ages of twelve and seventeen are model airplane glue, rubber cement, shoe polish, paint thinner, gasoline, and lighter fluid. Other commonly used and easily obtained inhalants include nail polish remover, correction fluid, spray paint, the propellant in aerosol whipped cream, and cooking spray.

> When I was eleven, I used to pour nail polish remover on my pillow and then sleep on it.
>
> —VANESSA, *seventeen*

Inhalants are easy to find and easy to use. Young children and adolescents generally use one or all of the following three methods for inhaling toxic chemicals:

- **SNIFFING:** Kids sniff directly from the container of rubber cement, correction fluid, or nail polish remover, or they hold their mouths over the aerosol can as the gas is discharged.
- **HUFFING:** Soaking a rag with hair spray, gasoline, or paint thinner, holding it up to your nose and mouth, and deeply inhaling the vapors.
- **BAGGING:** Spraying or pouring the chemical into a plastic or paper bag or balloon, holding the bag over your nose and mouth, and huffing the fumes. Bagging puts users at risk of suffocation.

Older adolescents and young adults sometimes try torching, which involves inhaling the fumes from a cigarette lighter and then igniting the exhaled air.

That's all it takes—no complex paraphernalia, no dealers or dark-alley transactions, and no difficulty whatsoever obtaining the inexpensive products. All you have to do is open the refrigerator, walk into the garage, or look under the kitchen sink.

The High

Inhalant users sometimes describe the high as a "head rush" of mild euphoria, relaxation and/or stimulation, and perceptual distortions. In general, inhalants produce their effects by temporarily starving the body of oxygen. The heart responds to oxygen deprivation by beating faster in an attempt to get blood flowing back into the brain. Inhalant users often feel tired and weak just moments after using because the body expends a great deal of energy trying to restore blood flow to the brain.

Because the high lasts such a short time, many adolescents continue to use inhalants several times over the period of an hour or two in an attempt to sustain the good feelings. Trying to capture and keep the high, however, is a little bit like a dog chasing its tail in the middle of a busy street. Pain—often severe and all too frequently a sign of serious internal damage—is inevitable.

Who Uses Inhalants?

I was in seventh grade when I started using inhalants. My favorites were nail polish remover, rubber cement, hair spray, and permanent markers. I'd soak a sock with hair spray, put it over my face, and breathe deep. I'd be depressed and then I'd use and I'd feel happy and relieved. I figured it wasn't as bad as coke or crank, because I was using stuff I could buy myself at the grocery store or drugstore.

—KIM, *sixteen*

It's a tragic irony that the substances used most often by young children to get high are among the most lethal substances of all.

Inhalant use is most common among young children and tends to decline as kids get older. Why? Because inhalants are inexpensive, easy to buy or find in the house or garage, and legal. Elementary school children may use inhalants because they do not think they are harmful, and no one has informed them otherwise. Most school systems wait until children reach fourth or fifth grade before they start educating students about the dangers of drugs. Most parents have no idea that their children might be using common household products to get high.

While younger children tend to avoid drugs that they perceive as harmful such as cocaine, methamphetamines, and heroin, they may be tempted to use inhalants because they are, literally, right under their noses. Older adolescents tend to view inhalants as "little-kid drugs" and are much more likely to use nicotine, alcohol, and marijuana. If older teens have difficulty obtaining alcohol, marijuana, cocaine, or methamphetamines, however, they may use inhalants as a cheap, readily available alternative drug.

National surveys indicate that inhalant use is higher for boys than girls in grades four through six. In grades seven through nine—when overall use of inhalants is highest—girls and boys use inhalants at equal rates. In grades ten through twelve, more boys use inhalants than girls, and among young men between the ages of eighteen and twenty-five, the use of inhalants is twice that of females in the same age group.

The statistics on inhalant use are truly horrifying:

- Six percent of fourth-graders have tried inhalants.
- One in five (20 percent) of eighth-graders have used inhalants.
- The average age of first use is twelve.
- Approximately two million adolescents between the ages of twelve and seventeen say they have used inhalants at least once in their lives. That figure represents about 9 percent,

or nearly one in ten, of the twenty-three million adolescents in that age group.

- Between 1994 and 2000, the number of new users increased more than 50 percent—from 618,000 new users in 1994 to 979,000 in 2000.
- From 1999 to 2001, the number of fourteen- and fifteen-year-olds reporting use in the past month increased from 1 percent to 1.3 percent. (Past-month use dropped in that time period for twelve- and thirteen-year-olds and sixteen- and seventeen-year-olds.)
- Since 1996, more than eight hundred people—most of them children and adolescents—have died from using inhalants.

Inhalant Use by Students, 2002: Monitoring the Future Survey

	8TH-GRADERS	10TH-GRADERS	12TH-GRADERS
Ever Used	15.2%	13.5%	11.7%
Used in Past Year	7.7	5.8	4.0
Used in Past Month	3.8	2.4	1.5

Bad Effects

I was trying to stay clean from methamphetamines, but I was having a really hard time. So I used air freshener. I'd get high for fifteen seconds or so, just this rush in my head, and then I would use again. I don't know how many times I used, but I was drawing in my room and then suddenly I was on the floor. I don't remember falling off my chair or anything. I tried to get up but I could hardly walk. I had to put my hand against the wall to walk even a few steps.

—SAM, *seventeen*

Short-Term Effects

After a brief rush of euphoria, users may feel nauseous, start vomiting, feel disoriented and mentally confused, and experience difficulty walking, standing up, and talking intelligently. Wheezing and difficulty breathing are common aftereffects of inhalant use as the body struggles to get oxygen flowing back into the cells, tissues, and vital organs.

- **PHYSICAL SYMPTOMS** include exhaustion, lethargy, insomnia, slurred speech, double vision, rapid and/or jerky eye movements, lurching or staggering when walking, inability to sit or stand, ringing in the ears, abdominal pain, double vision, flushing of the skin, tremors (hands shaking, general feeling of shakiness), rash around the nose and mouth (called "glue sniffer's rash"), and grand mal seizures.
- **EMOTIONAL SYMPTOMS** include mood swings, anxiety, panic attacks, agitation, irritability, and depression.
- **MENTAL SYMPTOMS** include confusion, disorientation, short-term memory loss, and inability to concentrate.

Long-Term Effects

Inhalant users also tend to be disruptive, deviant, or delinquent as a result of the early onset of use, the user's lack of physical and emotional maturation, and the physical consequences that occur from extended use.

—OFFICE OF NATIONAL DRUG CONTROL
POLICY (*June 2001 Fact Sheet*)

In a recent study of twenty-five inhalant users referred for medical treatment, thirteen (52 percent) were diagnosed with central nervous system damage. In another recent study, 55 percent of inhalant users experienced physical damage due to the toxic effects of the drugs.

- **BRAIN**: Inhalants travel directly to the brain, and researchers believe that regular use causes extensive brain damage by dissolving the protective myelin sheath that surrounds the brain cells. Says Carol Falkowski, director of research communications at the Hazelden Foundation:

Inhalant and solvent abuse results in profound, permanent, irreversible brain and nervous system damage. . . . Critical parts of the brain are literally dissolved, and functioning can never be restored.

Frequent use leads to serious decreases in cerebral blood flow. In brain-image scans, the brains of chronic inhalant users look eaten up, with large holes appearing across the entire surface. The holes are actually areas where little or no brain activity is taking place, and the blood flowing through the brain is sharply reduced. In addition to the reduced blood flow and slowed activity, the actual structure of inhalant users' brains is changed, and the cerebral cortex, the cerebellum, and the brain stem are reduced in size.

Chronic use of inhalants can lead to permanent neurological problems, including difficulty thinking and reasoning, learning disabilities, memory impairment, personality changes, hallucinations, motor problems (tremors, uncontrollable shaking, loss of coordination, difficulty walking or running), slurred speech, visual and hearing impairments, and nerve damage with symptoms such as numbness, tingling sensations, and paralysis.

Inhalants alter both the normal structure and functioning of the brain, dramatically affecting the user's behavior, mood, and personality. Behavior problems are common in children and adolescents who use inhalants and include problems in school (failing grades, memory loss, learning problems, chronic absences), and a general sense of apathy or not caring about what happens in life.

Inhalants also disrupt the functioning of the nervous system and can lead to permanent neurological problems, including cognitive and motor difficulties and polyneuropathy (damage to the nerves in the back and legs).

- **LUNGS:** High concentrations of inhalants can cause lung damage and death from suffocation by displacing oxygen in both the lungs and the central nervous system so that breathing slows down and eventually stops.

- **HEART:** Onetime or regular use of inhalants can result in sudden, unexpected disturbances of the heart's rhythm and lead in turn to sudden sniffing death syndrome (SSD). Sniffing, huffing, or bagging highly concentrated amounts of the chemicals in solvents (nail polish remover, paint thinner, felt-tipped markers), aerosol sprays (spray paint, hair spray, air freshener, deodorant, fabric protector), or butane-type gases can directly induce heart failure and death.

- **LIVER:** All inhalants—like all drugs—are broken down in the liver. Regular, long-term use can permanently damage this vital organ.

- **KIDNEYS:** Inhalants containing the chemical toluene (correction fluid, glues, paints and paint thinners, dewaxers) interfere with the kidneys' ability to control the amount of acid in the blood. Kidney damage is reversible when toluene is eliminated from the body, but long-term use can lead to the development of kidney stones.

- **MUSCLES:** Chronic use of inhalants can lead to reduced muscle tone, muscle strength, and loss of muscle tissue.

- **BONE MARROW:** Gasoline contains benzene, a toxic chemical that can cause leukemia, a malignant disease of bone marrow tissues.

- **HEARING LOSS:** The toxic chemicals found in spray paints, glues, dewaxers, cleaning fluid, and correction fluids can lead to hearing loss.

- **IMMUNE SYSTEM:** Research shows that inhaling nitrites (both amyl and butyl) damages the immune system's ability to fight infectious diseases. In research with animals, inhaling nitrites dramatically increases both the incidence and the growth rate of tumors. Thus, adolescents and adults who use nitrites—inhalants typically used to enhance sexual function and pleasure—may be more susceptible to infectious diseases and cancerous tumors. Regular use of nitrites is associated with unsafe sexual practice and a greatly increased risk of HIV/AIDS and hepatitis.

Overdose and Death

When Dr. Richard Heiss, a family practitioner from Bakersfield, California, learned that his twelve-year-old son Wade was using inhalants, he warned him about possible damage to the liver, kidneys, and bone marrow.

Dr. Heiss knew more than most people about the toxic effects of sniffing glue or huffing fumes from a rag soaked in paint thinner. But he didn't know that inhalants can be physically addictive.

He didn't know that sniffing felt-tipped markers or inhaling the gas from a butane lighter can permanently damage the brain.

And he didn't know about sudden sniffing death until December 23, 1995, six days before his son's thirteenth birthday.

That was the day Wade went into cardiac arrest after huffing from a can of air freshener. That was the day Wade died.

"I heard about this huffing," says Dr. Heiss. "But even I didn't know the effects of it, and I'm a medical doctor. Nobody's telling parents about it. Why isn't someone screaming and yelling about this?"

■ **SUDDEN SNIFFING DEATH (SSD)** can occur with first use or after prolonged use of inhalants. The toxic chemicals in inhalants displace oxygen in the lungs, brain, and other vital organs. When the heart is starved of oxygen, it beats faster in an attempt to increase blood flow to the brain, which can cause cardiac arrest and death. The risk of SSD increases if the user is physically active, startled, or anxious—the body responds to these stressors by increasing the flow of adrenaline from the brain to the heart, which can cause heart failure.

First-time users are at great risk of SSD. A British study of one thousand deaths from inhalant use found that two hundred users—one in five—were first-time users.

- **SUFFOCATION**: High concentrations of inhaled fumes, caused by repeated huffing or sniffing, replace oxygen in the lungs and central nervous system and can lead to death by suffocation. Suffocation deaths are most common among adolescents who huff from a paper or plastic bag in an unventilated room.

- **CHOKING**: Inhalant users often become nauseous and start vomiting. If they pass out or lose consciousness, they can choke on their own vomit.

- **SUICIDE**: In the British study mentioned above, 28 percent of inhalant deaths were suicides. Inhalant users frequently become severely depressed and suicidal when coming down from a high. Many experts believe that inhalant deaths are vastly underreported because inhalant use is not linked to death from suicide or accidents.

- **ACCIDENTS**: In one study, 26 percent of inhalant deaths occurred as the result of accidents, including automobile crashes, pedestrian accidents, drowning, and falls.

Not so very long ago, on a half-mile stretch of road called "Dead Man's Curve" near Philadelphia, five teenage girls died when their car hit a utility pole.

The car was traveling at speeds estimated between sixty-six and eighty-eight miles per hour.

There were no beer cans or vodka bottles in the car. Nor was there any evidence of marijuana, cocaine, or methamphetamines. But investigators searching through the twisted wreckage found a can of Duster II, a spray used to clean computer keyboards.

When traces of the toxic chemical difluoroethane were found in the bloodstream of four of the dead girls, including the driver, the medical examiner listed the official cause of death as "intoxication due to inhalant abuse."

Dangerous Combinations

Long-term inhalant users almost always use other drugs, so it is difficult to sort out which toxic effect belongs to which drug or which combination of drugs.

—*BUZZED*, *by Cynthia Kuhn,*
Scott Swartzwelder, and Wilkie Wilson

Because the high from inhalants is so short-lived—and because the headache, depression, and anxiety that follow can be so severe—inhalant users frequently use other drugs.

Combining inhalants with drugs that make you sleepy and slow down breathing—alcohol, opiates, barbiturates, benzodiazepines (Valium, Xanax, Klonopin, Librium), and over-the-counter cold medicines, including sleep-inducing antihistamines—is particularly dangerous.

Physical Dependence

I still get headaches, two months after I quit using inhalants. It's really bad. When I'm at the gas station, I feel really nauseous. I used to love those syrups you put in coffee, but now just smelling them makes me want to throw up.

—JOANNA, *seventeen*

Inhalants can be physically addicting, causing both tolerance and withdrawal symptoms.

Tolerance

Regular users experience increased tolerance, having to use more of the drug to get the same effects they used to get from smaller amounts.

Withdrawal

Regular users may experience some or all of the following withdrawal symptoms: sweating; rapid pulse; hand tremors; insomnia; nausea; vomiting; headaches, often severe; physical agitation; anxiety; hallucinations; and grand mal seizures.

How Can I Tell if My Child Is Using Inhalants?

Be vigilant in looking for signs and symptoms of inhalant use. Start educating your children about the dangers of these common household products when they are in first and second grades. And do not assume that your child, your relatives' children, or your neighbors' children are somehow protected from using these drugs. *Remember—one in five children in the United States has used an inhalant by the time he or she reaches eighth grade.*

The following signs and symptoms are specific to inhalant use:

- **PHYSICAL:** Runny nose; red, watery eyes; rash or sores around the nose and mouth (glue sniffer's rash); poor muscle control; lack of coordination; slurred speech; blurred vision; drunk or dazed appearance; nausea, vomiting, loss of appetite; memory loss; severe headaches.
- **EMOTIONAL:** Manic activity, irritability, excitability, depression, anxiety, violent or unpredictable mood swings, suicidal thoughts or attempts.
- **BEHAVIORAL:** Inappropriate or unexplained laughter; suicidal thoughts or attempts.

- **PROBLEMS AT SCHOOL:** Inhalants cause attention problems, memory loss, and learning disabilities, which may lead, in turn, to low grades, high rates of absenteeism, and school dropout. According to the National Household Survey on Drug Abuse, adolescents whose average grade is D or below are three times more likely than A students to have used inhalants during the past year.
- **OTHER:** Odor of paint or solvents on clothes, skin, or breath; paint or other stains on face, hands, or clothes; bags or rags containing dry plastic cement or other solvents at home, in school locker, at work; discarded whipped cream canisters, cans of spray paint, hair spray, nail polish remover, or air freshener.

Methamphetamines

Go ahead. Use meth. In two months,
maybe it won't take that long, you'll
lose everything. You'll lose twenty
pounds. All your friends will be gone.
Nobody will like you. Nobody will
respect you. You'll be a total jerk. You
won't be able to pay your bills or
keep your appointments.

You wanna love everything you
hate and hate everything you love?
Go ahead, then—use meth.

—HEIDI, *sixteen*

A powerfully addictive stimulant with dramatic effects on the
brain and central nervous system, "meth" is a witch's brew of
toxic chemicals with a high potential for misuse and addiction.

Chemically related to amphetamines ("speed"), methamphetamine delivers an even more powerful jolt to the central nervous
system. The drug releases high levels of the neurotransmitter
dopamine, which stimulates brain cells, enhancing mood and
body movement. Even small amounts of methamphetamine stimulate the central nervous system to create intense euphoria, increased physical activity, and decreased appetite. Other CNS

effects include irritability, insomnia, mental confusion, tremors, hyperthermia (high body temperature), convulsions, anxiety, paranoia, and aggressiveness. Hyperthermia and convulsions can result in death.

Meth has been around for a while. It was first synthesized in Japan in 1919; World War II fighter pilots used methamphetamines to help them stay awake during long missions. So did Adolf Hitler, who allegedly injected himself with meth several times a day. Winston Churchill used speed to give him energy and endurance during World World II, and John F. Kennedy allegedly used it to get through the Cuban Missile Crisis in 1962. And in the recent war against terrorism in Afghanistan, doctors gave U.S. Air Force pilots dextroamphetamine ("go pills") to help them fight battle fatigue; when the pilots returned from battle, doctors gave them sedatives ("no-go pills") to help them sleep.

Most meth available to kids these days is illegally manufactured in makeshift laboratories in the homes and basements of dealers or "cookers." Some of the ingredients in meth include ephedrine or pseudoephedrine (found in over-the-counter cold medications such as Sudafed and Dimetapp), red phosophorus, iodine, acetone, muriatic acid, sulfuric acid, lithium metal from batteries, and anhydrous ammonia (a fertilizer and refrigerant). Cookers who manufacture meth in their homes or backyards commonly use hydrochloric acid, drain cleaner, battery acid, lye, lantern fuel, and antifreeze to make the drug.

> "You can cook it in your bathtub or kitchen sink, man," says Frank, sixteen.
> "What are you talking about, fool? You don't need a tub or a sink—you can cook up a bunch of meth in your car or your closet!" says Ed, fifteen.

In the 1980s, a new form of meth (methamphetamine hydrochloride) called "ice" or "crystal meth" became popular. The crystallized chunks—"they look like snowflakes," the kids say—are heated in a pipe or "boat" (a piece of aluminum foil folded in half), from which the user inhales the fumes. Because "ice" is nearly 100 percent pure methamphetamine, many people believe it is much more potent and addictive than other forms of meth. Yet even inexperienced cooks who brew meth in their backyards and bathtubs can easily create batches of the drug that range between 97 and 98 percent purity.

New users usually start out snorting meth or taking it in pill form (capsules or tablets). Regular users prefer to smoke the pure crystal form or inject a dissolved solution of the drug, because these methods allow the drug to enter the bloodstream quickly, leading to a fast, intense high. Adolescents who use meth tend to prefer smoking because they fear needles and the possibility of HIV/AIDS infection. But as the addiction progresses, injecting the drug becomes more likely. Robert, a former meth addict, explains why:

> As we travel along in our meth addiction, smoking gets old and at times the taste can be horrible. When your level of addiction gets so high, people who say they would never shoot up begin trying injection drug use.
>
> Injecting meth is a different high than smoking. It's not so quick of a rush but it lasts longer and doesn't come with some of the nasty side effects that you get when you smoke or snort the drug—it's a little cleaner rush. The longevity of the meth high is called "having legs," and you can go longer between uses if you're shooting up.
>
> There's nothing good about any method of using, though. One isn't better or worse than another. Snorting, smoking, injecting—some people put meth in their coffee in the morning. Getting the drug into the bloodstream—that's the point.

Both amphetamines and methamphetamines have some medical uses. The prescription drugs Ritalin and Adderall, both forms of methamphetamine, are used in the treatment of attention deficit hyperactivity disorder (ADHD). (See chapter 14 for a discussion of Ritalin.) Amphetamines have also been used in the treatment of obesity, but in most cases the benefits are far outweighed by the penalties associated with using, particularly the high potential for misuse and addiction.

The High

The high—it's unexplainable. After you take a hit or two, you are just ready to go. It makes you talk, feel energetic, opens you up, makes you happy. I love the drug because it makes me feel good. I don't think about my flaws, and I don't feel like a loser when I'm high. I have no fear.

But I hate it, too. I hate it because it screws up your brain and body and tricks you into doing it because you feel so good when you're high. It screws you over fifty times harder than it helps you. The person you become is way not worth it. And you're not right ever after that. Even if you were only high for a day or two, you're twitching and paranoid two months later. You're never the same. You're altered somehow, emotionally, mentally, spiritually.

I have a friend who lost everything because of meth. He got fired from his job. He sold everything he owned for tweak [meth]. He's nineteen years old and he weighs 110 pounds. He was a good kid but his life is dominated by foil [aluminum foil is used to heat up meth in order to snort it]. He bows down to foil. If there was a man made out of foil, that man would be his God.

—CODY, *eighteen*

Whether snorted, smoked, or injected, methamphetamine enters the bloodstream quickly, leading to a fast, intense high. The drug stimulates the release of epinephrine (adrenaline) and norepinephrine, which cause the blood pressure and heart rate to rise, blood vessels to constrict or narrow, breathing tubes in the lungs to expand, and glucose (blood sugar) to be released into the bloodstream. As these physical changes take place, users experience increased energy and alertness.

Methamphetamine also releases dopamine, a feel-good neurotransmitter in the brain that creates powerful sensations of pleasure and euphoria, and serotonin, which increases body temperature, reduces appetite, and stimulates the release of various hormones.

The high varies dramatically depending on how the drug is used. If you swallow meth in pill form, it takes about twenty minutes for the drug to kick in. When meth is snorted, smoked, or injected, the drug surges through the brain and, within minutes, users feel a rush of pleasure. This euphoric rush, which lasts from five to thirty minutes, is related to the release of two chemicals in the brain—the hormone epinephrine and the feel-good brain chemical dopamine, which stimulates the pleasure center in the brain. One user compared the rush to experiencing "ten orgasms."

> What can you say? It's just the best feeling in the whole world.
>
> —TANIA, *sixteen*

After the initial rush comes the longer-lasting high, which includes euphoria, alertness, excitation, the ability to keep going and going ("like the Energizer Bunny," says one fifteen-year-old), and the ability to focus on a particular task for hours.

> You want to get your house cleaned? Hire someone high on meth. Give her ten bucks and then watch her go. When you're high on meth, you can't sleep, you can't stop moving, you love to clean, and you have lots of fun doing it.
>
> —FAITH, *sixteen*

When the drug effects begin to wear off, usually after four to eight hours, pleasure gradually metamorphoses into pain. As meth is metabolized and eliminated from the body, users begin to feel anxious, irritable, depressed, nauseous, shaky, paranoid, and out of control.

Regular users know how to ease the pain—use more meth. Because the rush is so intense and euphoric and because coming down from the peak can be so painful, "chasing the high" is common in regular users. But with each successive use, the rush is weaker because the body's supplies of the feel-good chemicals dopamine and epinephrine have been depleted from the previous rush.

Meth binges last anywhere from a few days to a few weeks, but the crash of coming down is inevitable. Girls tend to crash much sooner than boys, almost certainly for hormonal reasons. For both girls and boys, however, it is not uncommon to hear about meth binges that last for weeks.

> I was high on meth for twenty-seven days straight. I can't remember sleeping at all. I was holed up in a small apartment with other meth addicts, and there were blinds on all the windows. Toward the end of the binge, somebody opened up the blinds. I was blinded. I couldn't see for what seemed like hours.
>
> —JOSH, *sixteen*

By the end of the binge, the brain's stores of dopamine and norepinephrine are exhausted, so there is little if any pleasure from using the drug. But there is a great deal of physical and emotional pain. In the educational film *Life or Meth: What's It Cost?*, a teenage boy talks about the misery he experienced after a binge.

> I couldn't blow my nose without blowing out blood. A lot of times it [meth] would clog up your sweat glands, give you big bumps on your face, your neck, your back. . . . Sometimes I felt like my heart was going to collapse. A lot of times I'd hit the ground and start flopping. I thought I was going to die. My body would shut down, I'd go to sleep and not wake up for a day or so. I'd sleep for twenty-four hours or so. When I'd wake up, I'd feel really sick to my stomach. My bones when I'd get up out of bed from sleeping so long, my bones would pop. I'd feel real bad. I chewed on the whole inside of my mouth.

At the end of the meth binge, when even the drug cannot cure the pain, users enter what is called the "tweaking" stage. Tweakers have often not slept for days, even weeks, and they are extremely anxious, irritable, depressed, paranoid, and aggressive.

"You don't want to make tweakers mad," says one adolescent. "Tweakers are insane." Caroline, a former teenage meth user, explains how dangerous this stage can be.

> When you start tweaking, you get real paranoid. You see shadows and stuff that aren't really there. I've been in places where there's like a gun in this corner and a gun in this corner and a gun sitting under the couch cushion where you're sitting . . . those guns are there for a purpose, they're not there for show, they're there because the people are paranoid about who is there and if they happen to think you're the one who's getting them in trouble, you know, meth makes you delusional, say they thought you're a narc, they're going to hold that gun to your head until you tell them what's going on, and if you can't talk them out of it, then that's it.
>
> If you have to go to the bottom to get [meth], then that's where you're going to go. Your morals and your principles and what's important to you are not anymore important to you. Meth will take you to places where you've never been and it will totally change who you are.

Who Uses Methamphetamines?

Almost five million people have tried methamphetamine at some point in their lives, according to a survey by the National Institute on Drug Abuse. And lots of these meth users are adolescents.

Kids who say they love meth also claim to hate it. They know it's a nasty, repulsive drug with horrific side effects, but they continue to use it. Why? Perhaps the number one reason adolescents use meth is the powerful euphoric high that lasts for many hours.

When I'm high on meth, I find myself thinking about my brain dissolving. And you know what? I don't care, because it feels so good.

—STEVEN, *eighteen*

Kids also use meth because it is easy to find. More than 57 percent of twelfth-graders say amphetamines are "fairly easy" or "very easy" to get, and 28.3 percent say crystal meth (ice) is fairly easy or very easy to get.

Adolescents and college students sometimes start using meth because they believe the drug improves their physical and mental functioning. Cramming for a test by taking meth or speed became popular in the 1960s then fell out of favor for a while, but it is increasingly popular today.

Athletes may experiment with meth, believing it will help them run faster, jump higher, and play with greater concentration.

Some adolescents, girls in particular, may start using meth because it suppresses the appetite and helps them lose weight—fast.

My father was always telling me how fat I was. And I was a big girl, almost two hundred pounds. I started buying Black Beauties and Yellow Jackets—you can get them at 7–Eleven, they're right up front by the cash register—and lost some weight. I liked the buzz, so when someone told me about meth I thought, "Why not try something a little stronger?" I lost about fifty pounds on meth. I'm trying to stay away from it now, but it's so hard. I keep relapsing.

—SAMANTHA, *sixteen*

Other kids start using meth because they have heard that it will heighten sexual experiences and make them sexual superstars by increasing their stamina. Sex and meth can turn into a lethal combination, however, particularly if the meth user becomes involved with multiple sex partners and frequently engages in unprotected sex. Unwanted pregnancies and sexually transmitted diseases including HIV infection are not uncommon among meth addicts.

Methamphetamine Use by Students, 2002: Monitoring the Future Survey

	8TH-GRADERS	10TH-GRADERS	12TH-GRADERS
Ever Used	3.5%	6.1%	6.7%
Used in Past Year	2.8	4.8	4.0
Used in Past Month	1.1	1.8	1.7

Bad Effects

The only good thing about meth is that you get everything done that you need to get done. The bad thing is watching your family and life deteriorate. When I was an addict, I weighed eighty-seven pounds. My face was all sweaty, I had pimples all over my back, neck, and face, scabs on the back of my head and in my mouth. Crank sores, we call them. My face was all sunken in and there were big black circles under my eyes. It was really gross. I've been clean now for fifteen months and nothing—nothing—could make me touch that stuff again.

—COLLEEN, *sixteen*

Short-Term Effects

Physical effects include decreased appetite, shakiness, muscle tightness and cramping, stomach cramps, constipation, insomnia, convulsions, and frightening visual or auditory hallucinations. Other short-term physical effects include:

- **CRANK SORES:** Meth addicts often feel as if there are bugs crawling underneath the skin. They scratch or pick at the imaginary bugs ("It's just that nasty drug trapped inside you trying to get out," explained one user), creating "crank sores," or skin wounds that can be open and bleeding, covered by scabs, or infected.

- **WEIGHT LOSS:** Because meth, like other stimulant drugs, suppresses the appetite for food, users typically don't eat. When you stop eating, your body responds by breaking down fat to mobilize energy, which leads to rapid weight loss.
- **FIGHT-OR-FLIGHT SYNDROME** is caused by meth's effect on the sympathetic nervous system, which leads to increased blood pressure and heart rate, constriction of blood vessels, elevated blood sugar levels, and dilation of breathing tubes in the lungs.
- **INCREASED BODY TEMPERATURE:** Methamphetamines increase body temperature. When meth is combined with extreme physical exertion, which also increases body temperature, the body temperature can rise to dangerous, even fatal levels.

Emotional effects include mood swings, delusions, aggressiveness, violent behavior, depression, anxiety, panic attacks, paranoia, and mental confusion.

Long-Term Effects

Loss of equilibrium, loss of memory, loss of teeth, loss of friends, loss of life—you name it, if you're using meth, you'll lose it.

—ROBERT, *thirty-five,*
former meth addict

- **HEART:** Methamphetamines can directly damage the heart by reducing the oxygen available to the cells and tissues and by increasing the heart rate and raising blood pressure. Effects can range from a disordered heartbeat to failure of the cardiovascular system and death.
- **RESPIRATORY SYSTEM:** Meth addicts often suffer from respiratory problems due to lack of oxygen. Small blood vessels may burst in the nose, throat, and/or lungs, leading to internal bleeding. Ulcers may develop in the lining of the nose.

- **GASTROINTESTINAL SYSTEM:** Meth can directly damage the stomach and intestines, causing stomach ulcers and numerous gastrointestinal disorders.
- **LIVER:** Meth users can contract hepatitis B and C, which attack the liver, through sexual activity and the sharing of drug paraphernalia. The disease can then be transmitted to family members and others who come in contact with the diseased person. Symptoms include nausea, abdominal pain, and jaundice (yellowing of the skin).
- **BRAIN:** Meth has what researchers call a "neurotoxic effect," meaning that the drug directly damages brain cells—particularly those cells that store the feel-good neurotransmitters dopamine and serotonin. Over time, meth appears to reduce dopamine levels in the brain, which can have a disastrous effect on mood and movement and may result in symptoms like those of Parkinson's disease, a severe movement disorder involving uncontrollable shaking (tremors), loss of balance, and difficulty walking.

  Brain-imaging techniques show that methamphetamines have similar effects to cocaine, causing multiple areas of decreased brain activity and reduced blood flow.

  Because meth increases the heart rate and blood pressure, long-term use can permanently damage blood vessels in the brain and lead to strokes. Sometimes called "brain attacks," strokes occur when a blood vessel breaks, interrupting blood flow to part of the brain and killing brain cells in surrounding areas.

  While researchers are careful to emphasize that more studies need to be done to assess the long-term damage caused by methamphetamines, they leave no doubt that the drug causes extensive brain damage.

We can say unequivocally that methamphetamine abusers need to be watched by their physicians as they age to determine whether they begin seeing any effects of neurodegenerative diseases like Parkinson's. The reduction in brain dopamine that occurs as these subjects age, in addition to the loss they experience from use of methamphetamine, may result in symptoms similar to those seen in Parkinson's disease, a severe movement disorder that results from a loss of dopamine in the brain. But our three primary findings—dopamine transporter loss, whole brain inflammation, and loss of motor and cognitive abilities—document the adverse effects of methamphetamine to the human brain.

—NORA VOLKOW, M.D.
Director of the National Institute on Drug Abuse

■ **PSYCHOLOGICAL EFFECTS:** Adolescents who use meth regularly may experience long-term emotional and behavioral symptoms, including anxiety, paranoia, severe depression, suicidal tendencies, aggressiveness, and violent outbursts. Adolescents who are normally gentle and sweet-tempered may suddenly become angry, paranoid, and violent, seemingly overnight.

Chronic methamphetamine use can also cause a prolonged psychosis called "amphetamine delusion disorder" or "amphetamine psychosis." Symptoms include extreme paranoia, severe anxiety, panic attacks, visual and auditory hallucinations, and violent outbursts.

I was coming down off meth and about to jump out of my skin. My foster mother kept asking me what was wrong and staring at me. Just staring at me. I said, "Stop staring at me," and she kept on staring. I kept moving away from her and she kept following me. I was shaking and sweating and felt so sick and I swear I wanted to kill her. She followed me into the kitchen and I picked up a knife and said, "If you don't stop staring at me, I'll kill you." If she hadn't left the room, I would have stabbed her. I was out of my mind.

—SHARON, *sixteen*

Overdose and Death

A single dose will rarely cause an overdose unless the user has an underlying health problem such as coronary artery disease. Meth users, however, often use the drug repeatedly and at fairly close intervals, which can lead to a buildup of toxic levels of the drug in the bloodstream. Combining methamphetamines with other drugs dramatically increases the risk of overdose and death.

Symptoms of toxicity include extreme agitation, internal and external trembling, constant talking, repetitive actions or behaviors, palpitations or chest pains (disturbed heart rhythm), flushing of the skin, headaches, nausea, vomiting, hostility, paranoia, and violent outbursts. If the body temperature or heart rate rises too high, death can come suddenly and without warning. The user collapses, having suffered a fatal heart attack or stroke.

Although methamphetamine overdoses can be medically treated if diagnosed in time, meth addicts typically have a short life span, and a high percentage of addicts will die within ten years of first using the drug. In addition to overdoses, the most common causes of death among meth addicts are malnutrition, motor vehicle accidents, suicide, and murder.

Dangerous Combinations

Combining drugs is a common practice among meth addicts. Because the withdrawal and tweaking phases are so physically and emotionally distressing, meth addicts often use other drugs in an attempt to reduce the painful symptoms.

Meth by itself is a dangerous drug with unpredictable effects on the body and mind, and combining meth with any other drug can be dangerous, even life threatening. The drugs most often used in combination with meth include:

- **MARIJUANA:** Marijuana use is relatively common, especially when users need to calm down the overstimulation and jitteriness.

- **COCAINE:** Both powder and crack cocaine may be used to intensify the high. Because cocaine and meth are both stimulants, combining the two drugs can be extremely dangerous, leading to high blood pressure, disturbances in heart rhythms, seizures, convulsions, and death.
- **DEPRESSANT DRUGS:** The tweaking phase causes both physical pain and emotional instability, and users often take a depressant—alcohol, prescription sedatives or tranquilizers, or heroin—to ease the paranoia, fear, and anxiety.
- **VIAGRA:** Meth users and addicts, especially gay men and teenage ravers, sometimes use Viagra in combination with methamphetamine. Meth stimulates sexual desire but can cause blood vessels in the penis to narrow (vasoconstriction), thus preventing erections. The greatest risk associated with combining these drugs is high-risk sexual behavior and the spread of HIV/AIDS and other sexually transmitted diseases.

Physical Dependence

When it comes down to it, nothing else matters but the drug. I would have killed for meth. I would have died for meth.

—JOSH, *seventeen*

Tolerance

Tolerance can develop rapidly, especially if meth is used regularly or continuously for several days. The brain cells adapt to the presence of the drug and require increasingly large doses in order to feel the euphoric high or rush. Some adolescents will tell you they became addicted the first time they used meth, while others say they used several times before getting hooked.

The first time I tried crank [meth], I didn't like it at all. The second time, I didn't like it but I thought, "Oh well, I'll try this again." But the third time—Wow. I loved it. And I was hooked, just like that.

—ALICIA, *sixteen*

Withdrawal

Withdrawal from methamphetamines is not life threatening, but that's the only positive thing that can be said about it. Withdrawal symptoms include severe depression, anxiety, craving for the drug, irritability, paranoia, violent outbursts, and, eventually, exhaustion and excessive sleep. Intense cravings for the drug can last for weeks, months, or even years.

Perhaps the worst part of withdrawal is the inability to feel pleasure, a state that can last for weeks, months, or even years. Experts call this state anhedonia. A former meth addict describes the hopelessness and despair:

> Withdrawal is the worst feeling I've ever felt. You feel like nothing. The total opposite of the high. No control. You cannot move without aching everywhere, and this is after one full week of sleep. When you do wake up, it's never a fully awake feeling. You actually have no emotion. There's no serotonin being produced in your brain, no endorphins. The depression is so intense. This is when you can make some really rash decision, like hurting yourself or others, because there is this sense of overwhelming doom. I cannot describe it—it's just doom. Life is passing you by with no hope in sight.

How Can I Tell if My Child Is Using Methamphetamines?

Carefully read through this chapter's description of methamphetamine's short-term and long-term effects to understand how the drug affects mood and behavior. And be on the lookout for any of the following changes in your child's appearance, mood, or behavior:

- Excessive talking.
- Constant "hyperactive" movements—fidgeting, jittery movements, repetitive actions, tapping feet, tapping fingers on knees.
- Chronic anxiety and/or acute anxiety attacks.
- Panic attacks.
- Paranoia.
- Aggressive, angry, or violent outbursts.
- Sores, pimples, or scabs on the face, neck, arms, or legs.
- Teeth problems—enamel wearing away, gum problems, loose teeth, decay, bad breath.
- Disrupted sleep patterns—staying up all night, sleeping for days at a time.
- Dark circles under the eyes from lack of sleep, malnutrition.
- Sudden, excessive weight loss.

LSD and Other Hallucinogens

There's high, and there's high, and
to get really high—I mean so high
that you can walk on the water, that
high—that's where I'm goin'.

—GEORGE HARRISON

I hope the fans will take up meditation instead of drugs.

—RINGO STARR

LSD (lysergic acid diethylamide) and other hallucinogens change the way users think, feel, and perceive the world. Of all the hallucinogens, LSD is the most commonly used and by far the most potent—one hundred times more potent that psilocybin mushrooms and four thousand times more potent than mescaline. This doesn't mean the LSD high is hundreds or thousands of times more powerful than that of other hallucinogenic drugs—only that an infinitesimal amount of LSD (which is measured in micrograms, or millionths of a gram) is needed to create powerful, mind-altering effects.

151

Acid absorbs forty-seven times its weight in excess Reality.

Pure, high-potency LSD is a colorless, odorless crystalline substance that is diluted with binding agents or dissolved and diluted in liquids for retail sale in the form of tablets or "microdots," thin gelatin squares called "window panes," or "blotter paper" or "blotter acid," sheets of paper that contain LSD. The drug is occasionally found in capsules, powders, and sugar cubes laced with LSD. The average strength of LSD ranges from twenty to eighty micrograms per dose, considerably less than the one-hundred- to two-hundred-microgram doses commonly used in the 1960s and early 1970s. A twenty-five-microgram dose will produce hallucinogenic effects in most people.

The High

I sat for hours examining the exoticness and magnificence of my right hand. I could see the muscles and the cells and the pores. Each blood vessel was a fascination unto itself, and my mind still flutters with the wonder of it.

—GO ASK ALICE: A REAL DIARY

LSD affects serotonin levels in the brain by blocking some serotonin receptors and stimulating others. Serotonin is one of several feel-good brain chemicals associated with mood, emotional balance, and sleeping behavior.

The drug has a powerful impact on two particular brain structures:

- **THE CEREBRAL CORTEX**, which regulates mood, logical thinking, reasoning, and perception.
- **THE LOCUS CERULEUS**, which receives and integrates sensory signals from all areas of the body.

Between thirty and ninety minutes after taking LSD, users begin to feel the effects. Because the liver metabolizes LSD slowly, the effects can last up to twelve hours.

The nature of the trip varies dramatically from one person to the next and from one trip to the next, depending on the dosage (which can range from twenty to one hundred micrograms); the user's personality, mood, expectations, and experience with the drug; and the environment where the drug is used. In low doses, somewhere between twenty-five and fifty micrograms, LSD creates mild perceptual disturbances. Higher doses (sixty to two-hundred-plus micrograms) can mimic mental illness, making you see and hear things that may not exist in reality. The effects are not entirely dose-dependent, however, for as one research team put it: "Everyone reacts differently to [hallucinogens], and one person's enlightenment can be another person's hell."

- **PHYSICAL REACTIONS** include dilated pupils, nausea, sweating, loss of appetite, sleeplessness, dry mouth, and tremors. Body temperature, heart rate, blood pressure, and blood sugar levels rise.
- **HALLUCINOGENIC EFFECTS** include visual changes, dramatic mood swings, impaired depth and time perception, and distorted perception of the size and shape of objects, movements, color, sound, and touch.
- **EMOTIONAL REACTIONS** to the drug range from euphoria to anxiety to severe paranoia and can shift dramatically from one state to the next. Sensual feelings can cross over or switch places so that the LSD user feels as if he or she can see sounds and hear colors—a condition called synesthesia. While many adolescents enjoy these mind-altering effects, others find the perceptual changes frightening and may become anxious, even panic-stricken. Fear of losing control, intense sensations of despair, and thoughts of insanity or death may occur at the "peak" of the trip—or the user might experience a euphoric sense of

enlightenment and connection with others and with the world itself.

Who Uses LSD?

Adolescents who use LSD say it is an attractive drug because it is inexpensive, with prices per hit around five dollars; it is relatively ease to find—in 2001, almost 45 percent of high school seniors said it would be "fairly easy" or "very easy" for them to get LSD if they wanted it; and it offers a mind-expanding experience without the danger of physical addiction.

Most adolescents, however, agree that regular LSD use is dangerous. In 2002, nearly 40 percent of high school seniors perceived great risk in using LSD once or twice, and 73.9 percent said they saw great risk in using LSD regularly. Nearly 85 percent of twelfth-graders disapproved of experimenting with LSD just once or twice, and 94 percent expressed disapproval of people taking LSD regularly.

LSD Use by Students, 2002: Monitoring the Future Survey

	8TH-GRADERS	10TH-GRADERS	12TH-GRADERS
Ever Used	2.5%	5.0 %	8.4%
Used in Past Year	1.5	2.6	3.5
Used in Past Month	0.7	0.7	0.7

Bad Effects

I am profoundly distrustful of the "pure gifts of the gods." You pay dearly for them.

—CARL JUNG

Short-Term Effects

- **PHYSICAL:** Increased heart rate, elevated blood pressure, body tremors, visual distortions, chills, sweating, dizziness, trembling hands, numbness, nausea, extreme fatigue the day after the trip.
- **PSYCHOLOGICAL:** Intense anxiety, feelings of dread and foreboding, acute panic reactions.
- **INJURIES AND ACCIDENTS:** LSD and other hallucinogenic drugs affect cognitive abilities—thinking and reasoning skills—and may impair the adolescent's ability to understand when a situation is potentially dangerous. Attempting to drive a car, ride a bicycle, play a sport, or even walk down the road while under the influence may lead to accidents or injuries to self or others.
- **BAD TRIP:** Whether you're a first-time or a regular user of LSD, you can have a bad trip, which might include intense feelings of despair, anxiety, panic, paranoia, and fears of losing control, insanity, or death. Bad trips are more likely when taking high doses or multiple doses of LSD. Because the dosage often varies dramatically from one hit to another, however, users cannot always predict how they will react.

Adolescents with underlying mental health problems, including severe anxiety or depression, are more likely to have a bad trip if they take LSD or other hallucinogens, and they are also more likely to suffer long-term consequences from their drug use.

Long-Term Effects

Researchers have identified two long-term effects associated with LSD, both of which can have profoundly disturbing effects on the remainder of the adolescent's life. Both conditions can occur after regular use or after a single drug experience.

- **FLASHBACKS (HALLUCINOGEN PERSISTING PERCEPTUAL DISORDER, OR HPPD):** Days, weeks, months, or years after taking LSD, users may suddenly and without warning experience a flashback or visual disturbance. Flashbacks can be extremely disturbing, both physically and emotionally. Some people fear they may be suffering from brain damage or a severe psychological disorder, while others may have difficulty functioning normally. Why flashbacks occur is not completely understood, although researchers believe the brain stores the hallucinogenic experience as a visual memory, which can suddenly, and without warning, be triggered into consciousness at a later point in time.
- **PERSISTENT PSYCHOSIS:** LSD distorts reality and creates a temporary state of psychosis for some users. In some cases—and it can happen in both regular and onetime users—the effects continue long after the drug wears off, distorting the ability to separate reality from unreality and impairing the ability to think rationally and communicate effectively with others. Long-lasting psychotic disturbances may include fear, paranoia, extreme emotional distress, dramatic mood swings, manic behavior, profound depression, and vivid, visually disturbing hallucinogenic states.

The fear, paranoia, and emotional distress experienced during a bad trip can be profound, and memories of these experiences can persist for life.

If an adolescent has a serious underlying psychological problem or mental illness, taking LSD can intensify and prolong the symptoms.

Overdose and Death

The lethal dose of LSD is so high that it is almost impossible to overdose on the drug. Scientists estimate that a lethal dose for humans would be somewhere between sixteen and eighty milligrams—in street terms, that would mean you'd have to take 50 to 250 hits.

Although extremely rare, LSD overdoses can lead to rapid heartbeat, rise in body temperature to about 106 degrees, low blood pressure, respiratory depression, and respiratory arrest requiring emergency medical care.

Users also don't have to worry about contaminants or adulterants. The typical dose of LSD is usually less than one hundred micrograms, an infinitesimal amount. It's virtually impossible to add a lethal amount of contaminants or adulterants—such as strychnine, PCP, or methamphetamines—to a single LSD dose. Dealers also have little or no incentive to add other chemicals or drugs to LSD because LSD is so inexpensive and easy to market due to the tiny amount needed to get high.

While overdoses and dangerous reactions from contaminants are rare, LSD users are vulnerable to accidents and injuries related to poor judgment, visual disturbances or illusions, hallucinations, paranoia, panic attacks, or psychotic reactions. The October 2002 Drug Abuse Warning Network (DAWN) report lists 2,821 emergency department visits related to LSD. (This figure was 4,016 in 2000 and 5,126 in 1999.) Adolescents between the ages of twelve and seventeen accounted for 34 percent of these emergency room visits.

Dangerous Combinations

It's fun to combine LSD with other drugs. It magnifies the trip, you know, makes everything even more intense.

—JEFFREY, *sixteen*

Adolescents frequently combine LSD with other drugs, a practice that can lead to unexpected reactions and, in rare cases, overdose and death. The most common drugs combined with LSD include other hallucinogens (psychedelic mushrooms, Ecstasy, PCP), marijuana, cocaine, and heroin.

Physical Dependence

LSD is not considered an addictive drug because it does not produce permanent central nervous system adaptation (tolerance), and it does not cause withdrawal symptoms leading to craving and compulsive drug seeking. Tolerance and withdrawal symptoms are considered the classic signs of physical dependence.

LSD does produce "acute" or short-term tolerance, however, meaning that regular users have to take more of the drug to achieve the same effects previously achieved with smaller doses. This tolerance is short-lived and disappears when the user stops taking the drug for several days. If the drug is taken again after several days or weeks, the user will experience a normal sensitivity to its effects. Thus, LSD appears to have a built-in deterrent to physical dependence, and even heavy users generally do not take the drug on a daily or even weekly basis.

How Can I Tell if My Child Is Using LSD?

Adolescents who regularly use LSD and/or other hallucinogens will probably use the drug away from home in order to avoid detection. This is true, of course, for virtually every drug kids use. Adolescents are smart and will do anything they can to avoid getting caught, so they use at other kids' houses when their parents are away from home or asleep, at concerts and all-night dance parties, or on daylong ski trips, fishing trips, or camping trips.

LSD is a long-acting drug, however, with both short-term and long-term aftereffects. Be on the lookout for the following signs and symptoms specifically associated with LSD use:

- Chills or unusual sweating.
- Trembling hands, nausea, and extreme fatigue (usually experienced the day after the trip).
- Intense anxiety and/or panic attacks.
- Fear of insanity or death.
- Visual disturbances that affect the ability to function normally. Flashes of color, halos or mists around objects, and seeing images within images, for example, can affect the ability to read, focus, and concentrate.
- Letters or packages from strangers. LSD is often sold in squares of blotter paper and can be sent through the mail. According to the U.S. Drug Enforcement Administration of the Department of Justice: "A proliferation of mail order sales has created a marketplace where the sellers are virtually unknown to the buyers, giving the highest level traffickers considerable insulation from drug law enforcement operations."

Other Hallucinogens

DMT (Dimethyltryptamine)

DMT is a powerful hallucinogen found in several tropical plants. Most DMT on the streets today is synthetic and made in illegal laboratories. Hallucinogenic effects appear within ten minutes, peak at around thirty minutes, and disappear within an hour, earning the drug the nickname "businessman's special." The high includes euphoria, laughter, and visual hallucinations. Bad effects include anxiety, paranoia, panic, rapid heartbeat, dilated pupils, increased blood pressure, and frightening visual hallucinations.

DMT, like its chemical cousins AMT and DPT, is not considered physically addicting. Acute tolerance often develops immediately after use, so that using DMT again within a few hours will lead to significantly diminished drug effects.

DXM (Dextromethorphan)

Once you've been fried on Coricidin, you don't ever see things the same.

—JOSÉ, *sixteen*

It's cheap, it's legal, it's easy to get, and more and more kids are using DXM to experience an LSD-type high.

The active ingredient in many over-the-counter cough remedies, including Robitussin, Coricidin, and NyQuil, DXM is found in more than 140 nonprescription over-the-counter products, most of which contain between ten and fifteen milligrams per dose. Certain Coricidin products, however, contain up to thirty milligrams per tablet—the largest amount of DXM per dosage unit on the market. As one teenager put it, "Coricidin is like Robitussin on crack."

When taken in high doses (anywhere from eight to fifty or more tablets), DXM acts as a "dissociative anesthetic" similar to ketamine or PCP. The high includes feelings of intoxication, light-headedness, a sense of numbness from the inside out, mild to intense hallucinations involving flashing effects from sights and sounds, and sensations of unreality or disconnection from the real world.

Physical effects include dilated pupils, accelerated heartbeat, increased blood pressure, slurred speech, flushing, loss of motor control (wobbly legs, robotic movements, feelings of being frozen or paralyzed), nausea, itchy skin, and sedation. Adolescents high on DXM tend to have a flat expression and glassy stare.

It's a mind swirl. You feel completely insane. That's why I like it. I think I have supersonic hearing. I swear I can hear stuff blocks away. I sit in the dark, just total darkness, and see all kinds of colors, fireworks. I just sit there and don't move at all, there's just so much stuff going on. You're still in touch with reality but it seems like you have all these powers. Your face gets weird, you have this weird smile, and your movements are all robotic. You forget what happens from one minute to the next. And you stay high for a long time—I was high once for three days.

—MARIO, *sixteen*

Bad effects, which can come right on the heels of the "good" effects, include accelerated heartbeat, high blood pressure, tremors, seizures, and temporary blindness. In extremely high doses—and kids often take this drug in extremely high doses—DXM can cause tremors, loss of consciousness, brain damage, coma, seizures, cerebral hemorrhages, strokes, and death.

Some Coricidin products for colds and flu do not contain DXM but instead contain acetaminophen, the active ingredient in Tylenol. Kids who take these products in high doses, believing they are taking DXM, can damage their livers permanently and even experience liver failure.

Combining DXM with other drugs can be extremely dangerous, even deadly. Because DXM is cheap and easy to obtain, it is sometimes passed off as Ecstasy, or Ecstasy tablets may be adulterated with DXM. If DXM is combined with Ecstasy, the risk of heatstroke increases dramatically, because the same liver enzyme breaks down both drugs and both drugs impair the body's ability to regulate its internal temperature.

To add to the danger, approximately 10 percent of the Caucasian population and between 1 and 10 percent of other ethnic groups are slow metabolizers of DXM, meaning that DXM can build up in the bloodstream of these individuals and cause severe drug reactions.

Ketamine (Ketamine Hydrochloride)

Ketamine was developed in the early 1960s as a tranquilizer and was used during the Vietnam War as an anesthetic. Human use was discontinued because of the drug's powerful hallucinatory effects and the risk of respiratory problems and high blood pressure; veterinarians, however, continue to use ketamine as an animal tranquilizer.

Ketamine, like GHB and Rohypnol, is considered a "date rape drug" because it is colorless, odorless, and tasteless and can be added to someone's drink without his or her knowledge. The high lasts from thirty minutes to two hours and involves powerful visual hallucinations and a distorted sense of time and identity. Although the hallucinogenic effects wear off within an hour or less, the powerful sedative-hypnotic effects of the drug can affect the senses, judgment, and motor coordination for up to twenty-four hours.

Bad effects include agitation, mental confusion, delirium, amnesia, impaired motor function, and potentially fatal respiratory problems. In high doses or when combined with alcohol, marijuana, Ecstasy, or other drugs, ketamine can cause respiratory problems, high blood pressure, brain damage, coma, and death.

Mescaline (Peyote Cactus)

Mescaline's chemical structure is more like amphetamine than LSD, but its effects are similar to those of both drugs. These include increased heart rate and blood pressure, nausea and vomiting, distortions of time and space, flashes of color, and a sense of being separate or distanced from the surrounding environment (sometimes described as "standing outside myself" or "watching myself from a distance"). The high usually lasts from four to six hours, although it can last for as long as twelve hours.

Bad effects are generally psychological and, in most cases, subtler than the bad trips associated with LSD. Anxiety, panic attacks, fear and foreboding, difficulty distinguishing between fantasy and reality, and depression are not uncommon.

Phencyclidine (PCP)

In the 1950s, PCP was used briefly as an anesthetic in humans, but nasty side effects, including extreme mental confusion, paranoia, hallucinations, and delusions, led doctors to discontinue medical use. PCP is sometimes, although rarely, used as a veterinary anesthetic.

The drug produces a state that has been compared to getting drunk, taking hallucinogens, and ingesting amphetamines all at the same time. The high, which lasts for four to six hours, includes amphetamine-like euphoria and stimulation along with a sense of disorientation, altered body perceptions, auditory hallucinations, and reduced sensitivity to pain. Other common effects include coordination problems, slurred speech, blurred vision, drowsiness, and increased body temperature and blood pressure. Users often feel detached from their surroundings and may experience an exaggerated sense of strength and invulnerability. Severe mood disorders, auditory hallucinations, and amnesia are not uncommon.

PCP users often can be recognized by the typical blank stare (sometimes called a mask-like appearance), rapid and involuntary eye movements, clumsy movements, rigid muscles, agitation and/or violence if exposed to sensory stimulation, and reduced sensitivity to pain.

High doses of PCP can cause feelings of being detached and disconnected from your environment; at the other extreme, users may become agitated, belligerent, aggressive, and violent. Aftereffects can last for days or weeks and may include memory loss, anxiety, panic attacks, paranoia, and depression. Long-term use can lead to permanent mental or emotional problems. Extremely high doses can lead to dangerously high blood pressure and body temperature, coma, seizures, and respiratory depression. Just two to five times the normal single dose of PCP can cause serious, even fatal, physical reactions, including strokes, seizures, respiratory depression, and death.

When combined with alcohol or other sedatives, PCP is especially lethal due to the danger of the combined drug effects on heart rate and breathing. Coma and accidental overdose may occur. When combined with stimulants or other drugs that raise body temperature (Ecstasy, amphetamines, mescaline, methamphetamines), PCP can cause dangerous and potentially fatal disruptions of heart rhythms and dangerous spikes in body temperature.

Psilocybin Mushrooms

Psilocybin mushrooms provide a two- to four-hour LSD-type high with feelings of relaxation, visual distortions, light-headedness, sensations of heaviness or lightness, nausea, shivering, sweating, and numbness of the tongue, lips, and mouth. Bad effects are primarily psychological and include anxiety, panic attacks, paranoia, mood changes, disorientation, the inability to distinguish between reality and fantasy, and depression. Accidents and injuries sometimes occur due to loss of coordination and muscle weakness under the influence of the drug.

Psilocybin is not the only mushroom to have hallucinogenic properties, but several other varieties of hallucinogen-producing mushrooms can be extremely dangerous, even lethal. The *Amanita mascara* mushroom, for example, can slow the heart rate and blood pressure to the point of shock and death. Mushrooms containing deadly toxins are also sometimes mistaken for psilocybin mushrooms in the wild.

Ecstasy and Other Club Drugs

I love Ecstasy. I love, love, love it. I know it's bad for my brain, I've seen those brain pictures, but I don't care—give me some and I'll take it, without even thinking about it. Hey, give me two or three, and I'll take them all at once.

—JOE, *fifteen*

Ecstasy or MDMA (short for 3,4–methylene-dioxy-methamphetamine) has been around for almost a century. Created by a German company in 1912 as an experimental amphetamine—its chemical structure is similar to both methamphetamine and mescaline—MDMA was patented in the 1930s as an appetite suppressant but never used clinically.

Ecstasy was rediscovered in the 1970s and was used, for a time, by a small number of psychotherapists who gave it to their clients to produce a temporary state of openness, honesty, and empathy. In the mid-1980s, newspapers and magazines published hundreds of articles on Ecstasy's euphoric and therapeutic qualities, stimulating widespread recreational use and an inevitable crackdown by the

Drug Enforcement Association. In 1985, the federal government classified Ecstasy as a Schedule I narcotic (in the same category as heroin and cocaine) with no acceptable medical use. The drug then went underground, where it quickly spread to college campuses, gay populations, and nightclubs, surfacing several years later at all-night dance parties called "raves."

The High

> I've only used Ecstasy a few times, but I loved it. It was amazing— I could bawl my eyes out, and be happy at the same time.
>
> —LORI, *fourteen*

At normal doses (about a hundred milligrams), Ecstasy's high is experienced as sensations of warmth, peace, love, and connection to others. Like its chemical cousins the amphetamines, Ecstasy produces a sense of euphoria, energy, alertness, and decreased appetite. But Ecstasy is also related to the hallucinogens, and the mind-expanding effects include an enhancement of sensual pleasures connected with sight, sound, taste, smell, and, especially, touch.

That combination of amphetamine-created energy and euphoria and the hallucinogenic experience of enhanced senses gives Ecstasy its reputation as "the love drug" or the "hug drug." Yet the ecstasy high is more sensual than sexual, as a female therapist explains:

> MDMA and sex do not go very well together. For most people, MDMA turns off the ability to function as a lover, to put it indelicately. It's called the love drug because it opens up the capacity to feel loving and affectionate and trusting.

Under the influence of Ecstasy, fear seems to dissolve as self-confidence and self-acceptance increase. A sense of empathy for other people's feelings and experiences and a desire to connect with friends and strangers may be the most unique aspect of the Ecstasy high.

> I felt completely at peace. I sat by a river with my boyfriend, and we just sort of folded into each other. There was no separation between me and him or between me and the river—or even, it seemed, between me and God. I had no sense of time passing. All that mattered was being there, at that moment, at one with myself, my boyfriend, and the whole wide world.
>
> —HANNAH, *nineteen*

Higher-than-normal doses—two hundred milligrams or more—create a different sort of high. The typical amphetamine-like effects kick in hard, causing jaw tension, nausea, vomiting, flushing and sweating, and anxiety or panic attacks. Hallucinogenic symptoms also intensify, creating a sense of unreality and perceptual distortion.

Who Uses Ecstasy?

> It's one thing to talk about an adult, but imagine teenagers. They're full of self-doubt and they take this drug and they're at peace with themselves—maybe for the first time.
>
> —MARSHA ROSENBAUM, *coauthor*
> *of* In Pursuit of Ecstasy

Twelve percent of adolescents between the ages of twelve and eighteen—nearly three million teenagers—have experimented with Ecstasy at least once in their lives, according to a 2002 national survey. Older teens—sixteen- and seventeen-year-olds—are more likely to use Ecstasy than younger teens. Young adults between eighteen and twenty-five years old are the most likely of all to use.

The annual Monitoring the Future Survey reports the following Ecstasy-use statistics for eighth-, tenth-, and twelfth-graders.

Ecstasy Use by Students, 2002:
Monitoring the Future Survey

	8TH-GRADERS	10TH-GRADERS	12TH-GRADERS
Ever Used	4.3%	6.6%	10.5%
Used in Past Year	2.9	4.9	7.4
Used in Past Month	1.4	1.8	2.4

Bad Effects

I used to use Ecstasy a lot. I didn't think there was anything bad about the drug. Then I saw these pictures of the brain, showing big holes in Ecstasy users. That was it for me. Now I won't touch the stuff.

—LEO, *seventeen*

Short-Term Effects

- **PHYSICAL EFFECTS** include muscle tension, involuntary teeth clenching, jaw pain, nausea, blurred vision, rapid eye movements, dizziness, faintness, chills, and sweating.

    Ecstasy increases heart rate and blood pressure and should be considered a special risk for anyone with circulatory or heart disease.

    Some users develop a rash resembling acne. Experts caution that users who develop a rash may be risking serious side effects, including liver damage.

    Although Ecstasy is sometimes called a sex drug, the opposite is true—a common side effect for both men and women is difficulty achieving orgasm.

- **PSYCHOLOGICAL EFFECTS** include sleep problems, mental confusion, depression, severe anxiety, panic attacks, paranoia, psychotic episodes, and drug craving. These symptoms can occur when under the influence of the drug or for weeks or months after taking it.

Long-Term Effects

- **BRAIN:** Brain images show that Ecstasy injures the brain by damaging the neurons that use serotonin to communicate with other brain cells. Because serotonin plays an important role in regulating mood, aggression, sexual activity, sensitivity to pain, sleep, memory, and other high-level cognitive (thinking) processes, regular users may experience mild to severe problems in these areas.

  Dopamine levels may also be affected. Ecstasy is chemically similar to methamphetamine, which directly damages nerve cells containing dopamine. Researchers fear that long-term use may lead to degeneration of the neurons containing dopamine and cause possible Parkinson-like symptoms, including lack of coordination, tremors, and other motor disturbances. Some scientists are concerned that the Ecstasy-induced central nervous system degeneration seen in research animals may also occur in humans. According to Dr. George Ricaurte:

  People should be aware that the use of Ecstasy in doses similar to those used in recreational settings can damage brain cells, and this damage can have serious effects.

- **OTHER VITAL ORGANS:** In high doses, Ecstasy can cause a sharp increase in body temperature, heart rate, and blood pressure, which can, in turn, lead to muscle breakdown, heart problems, kidney failure, and failure of the cardiovascular system.

Overdose and Death

It makes you feel really good, and so I thought if I took another one I'd feel even better. That was a really dumb move. I was like in a trance. It scared the hell out of me.

—MICHAEL, *sixteen*

Overdoses can occur for several different reasons. Because Ecstasy is illegally manufactured and synthesized by underground laboratories, the actual dosage of the drug contained in one tablet can range from fifty to three hundred milligrams.

Ecstasy tablets are also frequently cut with other mind-altering substances such as caffeine, amphetamine, and ephedrine (see the discussion under "Dangerous Combinations" on page 171).

Even if it is relatively pure and uncut, Ecstasy is considered extremely dangerous in high doses—two to three times greater than the normal one-hundred-milligram dose. Adolescents, who are often willing to try anything at least once, may take two or three tablets to intensify the amphetamine-hallucinogenic effects of the drug.

The effects of an Ecstasy overdose are similar to those of an overdose on amphetamines, with such symptoms as jitteriness, loss of appetite, dry mouth, muscle cramping, and nausea. In chronic, high-dose users, Ecstasy can cause panic attacks and paranoid psychotic symptoms, including severe anxiety, paranoia, and mental confusion.

Ecstasy can be extremely dangerous, even deadly for adolescents who attend raves, or all-night dance parties. Rising blood pressure, heart rate, and body temperature along with dehydration from sweating and intense physical activity can have lethal effects on the heart, particularly in people with underlying (and possibly undiagnosed) heart disease. Seizures, heart attacks, and strokes can and do occur.

Statistics highlight the danger. Emergency room visits involving Ecstasy grew ninefold from 319 in 1996 to 2,850 in 1999, and then, in the next two years, nearly doubled to 5,542 in 2001.

Dangerous Combinations

I've tried a candy flip, which is acid and Ecstasy, and a hippie flip, which is mushrooms and Ecstasy. It's fun to combine Ecstasy and other drugs, especially hallucinogenic drugs. You just trip out.

—CODY, *eighteen*

Ecstasy is often cut with other mind-altering chemicals, including amphetamine, ephedrine, caffeine, ketamine, and dextromethorphan (found in over-the-counter cough syrups and pills such as Coricidin, NyQuil, and Robitussin). So even if you think you're using only Ecstasy, you may be swallowing other drugs as well. The interactions between these drugs and your unique body chemistry are often unpredictable.

Compounding the dangers inherent in using a drug that is manufactured illegally, many adolescents combine Ecstasy with other drugs to intensify the high. Drugs that are commonly combined with Ecstasy include:

- **ALCOHOL:** While regular Ecstasy users rarely mix alcohol and Ecstasy, knowing that alcohol's sedative effects diminish Ecstasy's euphoric high, novice users often combine the two drugs. Adolescents and college students frequently "tank up" on alcohol before going to clubs or all-night dance parties, where alcohol is usually banned. And adolescents who are drinking at a party may suddenly decide to use Ecstasy if it is offered to them. Taking a stimulant and sedative drug at the same time can lead to unexpected, potentially deadly consequences, including nausea, vomiting, coma, and death.
- **HALLUCINOGENS:** Because Ecstasy is chemically similar to mescaline, it has mild hallucinogenic effects. Combining Ecstasy with LSD, mescaline, psychedelic mushrooms, and other hallucinogenic drugs intensifies the mind-altering effects of the individual drugs.
- **MARIJUANA:** Marijuana is often used in combination with Ecstasy. Emergency room reports indicate that Ecstasy/marijuana combinations increased from eight cases in 1990 to nearly eight hundred cases in 1999.
- **ANTIDEPRESSANTS:** Millions of adolescents are taking prescription drugs such as Prozac, Paxil, and Zoloft for anxiety disorders, obsessive-compulsive disorders, and depression. Because both Ecstasy and these drugs increase

serotonin, combining the two may intensify the effects of both drugs and lead to serious, potentially harmful side effects.

- **RITALIN:** Millions of adolescents take Ritalin or Adderall for attention deficit hyperactivity disorder. Combining these amphetamine-based drugs with Ecstasy, which is also an amphetamine, intensifies the stimulant effects of both drugs and increases the risk of dangerous side effects.
- **MAO INHIBITORS:** When combined with Ecstasy, antidepressants classified as monoamine oxidase (MAO) inhibitors such as Atapryl, Nardil, and Selpak can have a dangerous, even lethal, effect on heart rate and blood pressure.
- **VIAGRA:** Known as "sextasy," the combination of Ecstasy and Viagra is used to fuel all-night dancing and sexual marathons. Initially used in the U.S. gay club scene, sextasy is gaining popularity with straight clubgoers. Combining the two drugs can cause erections that last for several hours, potentially causing anatomical damage, and can lead to serious, even fatal, heart problems.

Physical Dependence

Chances are good that if your child is a casual Ecstasy user, he or she will not become physically addicted to the drug. The drug seems to have a built-in safeguard against addiction: If you use it too often or in high-enough doses, it simply stops working. As the good effects fade away, the bad effects come sharply into focus. These facts may explain why relatively few adolescents and adults who use Ecstasy could be considered chronic heavy users. The vast majority of people, young and old alike, use Ecstasy infrequently, rarely more than two or three times a month.

Ecstasy is psychologically addicting, however. Many teenagers admit that they crave or "fiend" for the euphoria, serenity, and sense of connection experienced when under the influence of the drug. And we know from the research that even casual use of Ecstasy can change brain structure and functioning. We also know that when Ecstasy is combined with other drugs, as it often is by adolescents, the damage to physical and psychological health can be profound and long lasting.

How Can I Tell if My Child Is Using Ecstasy?

If your kid is out all night, spending mass amounts of money, wears bright-colored clothing, sucks on pacifiers and acts all geeky—you know, that "Wow man, cool, groovy" hippie language, while just sort of floating around on this cloud—well then, you should know that something weird is up.

—AARON, *eighteen*

A 2002 survey conducted by the Partnership for a Drug Free America (PDFA) shows that while 12 percent of teenagers in the United States say they have tried Ecstasy at least once, only 1 percent of parents believe their children have tried the drug. Parents are more likely to discuss alcohol, marijuana, cocaine, and inhalants with their children; in fact, only 29 percent of parents surveyed said they had talked to their children about Ecstasy. Eight percent of parents had never heard of the drug, 49 percent were unclear about Ecstasy's effects on users, and 60 percent didn't know what's in the drug.

Parents should be on the lookout for the following signs and symptoms specifically associated with Ecstasy use:

- Muscle tension (jaw tension, clenched hands, muscle cramps).
- Sore or painful jaw (involuntary jaw clenching).
- Teeth grinding.
- Mouth and tongue sores from grinding teeth or chewing on the inside of the mouth.

- Chills, sweating.
- Dehydration.
- Faintness.
- Acne-like rash.
- Hangover that involves headaches, dizziness, vomiting, nausea.
- Excessive water consumption. Because Ecstasy is dehydrating, bottled water is often sold at raves, and Ecstasy users are counseled to drink lots of water. Look for large numbers of empty water bottles in bedroom or car.
- Unusual or excessive displays of physical affection.
- Sudden and/or unusual exhaustion or depression.
- Memory loss.
- Frequent attendance at all-night "alcohol-free" dance parties.
- Possession of Ecstasy paraphernalia: pacifiers, lollipops, candy necklaces, mentholated rubs, teddy bears, angel wings, glowsticks, glowing jewelry, and children's toys.

Other Club Drugs

Ecstasy is not the only drug being used at clubs, bars, and all-night dance parties or raves. The following "club drugs" are gaining in popularity among adolescents in the United States and overseas. Some of these drugs create an Ecstasy-like high and may be passed off as Ecstasy, with potentially dangerous, even deadly, consequences.

4–MTA (r-Methylthioamphetamine)

An amphetamine that is increasingly popular in the European club scene, 4–MTA produces euphoria and enhances the senses of sight, hearing, smell, and touch. Higher doses can induce LSD-like hallucinations and perceptual disorders, which can be extremely frightening. The drug has been implicated in numerous overdoses and several deaths in Europe.

While 4-MTA is not yet available in the United States, experts fear that it may be the next club drug.

GHB (Gamma Hydroxybutyrate)

GHB is a potent central nervous system depressant that produces relaxation, headache, nausea, and drowsiness. When used in large doses or combined with other drugs, GHB can lead to breathing difficulties, loss of consciousness, seizures, coma, and death.

Frequently called a "date rape drug," GHB is odorless, colorless, and tasteless and can be stirred into a person's drink without his or her knowledge. Adolescents who are unaware that the drug is only mildly euphoric or who are misinformed about its powerful sedative effects may take it to get high and end up in a dangerous, even life-threatening, situation.

> I just wanted to get good and high. I was drinking and decided to take some GHB. I woke up at the hospital two days later. I almost died, and it wasn't like they say it's supposed to be—there were no lights or tunnels or flashing stars. I was just gone.
>
> —JESSICA, *sixteen*

GHB can create physical dependence. Withdrawal symptoms include insomnia, anxiety, tremors, and sweating.

Overdoses can occur easily and without warning, especially if GHB is combined with alcohol or other sedatives. In fact, overdoses are more common on GHB than on Ecstasy. In 2000, 2,482 GHB users visited emergency rooms for an overdose, compared with 1,742 Ecstasy users. Signs of overdose include nausea, vomiting, headache, drowsiness, impaired breathing, loss of consciousness, and death. Since 1995, according to the Drug Enforcement Agency, seventy-three people have died from taking GHB.

According to the 2002 Monitoring the Future Survey, 0.8 percent of eighth-graders, 1.4 percent of tenth-graders, and 1.5 percent of twelfth-graders have experimented with GHB at some time in their lives.

Ketamine (Ketamine HCL)

See chapter 10, LSD and Other Hallucinogens, pages 161–162.

Nexus or 2CB (4–bromo-2, 5–dimethoxyphenethylamine)

Nexus or 2CB is considered a cross between Ecstasy, LSD, and speed. Available in pill, capsule, or powder form, 2CB is ten times more powerful than Ecstasy, with the average dose ranging between five and twenty milligrams.

Doses as low as four milligrams create relaxation and passivity, with effects similar to those created by Ecstasy—euphoria; enhanced visual and auditory perceptions; and increased body awareness including skin sensitivity and heightened responsiveness to smells, tastes, and sexual stimulation.

In higher doses ranging from eight to ten milligrams, 2CB has obvious stimulating and intoxicating effects and may cause mild hallucinations. Doses of twenty to thirty milligrams typically cause intense hallucinations, and higher doses can produce extremely frightening, LSD-type hallucinations, delusional states, extreme anxiety, panic attacks, and mental confusion.

In addition to the risk of a bad trip with frightening hallucinations and delusions, 2CB can cause dehydration and cardiovascular disturbances in high doses or in sensitive individuals.

Paramethoxyamphetamine (PMA)

Often sold as Ecstasy and causing similar hallucinogenic and stimulant effects, PMA is usually swallowed in tablet form, although the powder can also be snorted or dissolved in water and injected.

PMA is often passed off as Ecstasy—the tablets are the same size and color and often share the same trendy designs and logos—or it may be used as an adulterant in some Ecstasy tablets. Because PMA does not create the same euphoric high or empathic sensations, however, unsuspecting users may think they've taken a dose of Ecstasy and pop another pill or two.

But PMA is a much more dangerous drug than Ecstasy. The average dose of PMA is fifty milligrams. In low doses (fifty milligrams or less), PMA increases the pulse rate and blood pressure and causes labored breathing, increased body temperature, nausea, and muscle spasms. At slightly higher doses, between sixty and eighty milligrams, PMA can cause a dangerous rise in body temperature and blood pressure, difficulty breathing, vomiting, convulsions, cardiac arrhythmia, cardiac arrest, kidney failure, coma, and death.

PMA is especially dangerous in combination with other amphetamine-related drugs or with alcohol, cocaine, and prescription medications, including Prozac.

Rohypnol (Flunitrazepam)

Rohypnol is a central nervous system depressant similar to the benzodiazepines Valium and Xanax, but approximately seven to ten times more potent in its sedative effects. Like other benzodiazepines, Rohypnol is physically addicting, and the withdrawal syndrome can be life threatening.

Rohypnol is not available for medical use in the United States but is prescribed in Europe and Latin America for the short-term treatment of severe sleep disorders or as a presurgery anesthetic.

Adolescents use Rohypnol for its intoxicating, relaxing effects and because it is inexpensive—about five dollars per tablet. Rohypnol is also sometimes used by heroin and cocaine addicts to relieve the pain of withdrawal. According to the 2002 Monitoring the Future Survey, 0.3 percent of eighth-graders, 0.7 percent of tenth-graders, and 1.6 percent of twelfth-graders have experimented with Rohypnol at some time in their lives.

The effects—muscle relaxation, decreased blood pressure, extreme sleepiness, and amnesia—occur within thirty minutes of taking the drug, peak within two hours, and can persist for up to eight hours depending on the amount ingested. Other side effects include headaches, dizziness, nightmares, tremors, decreased blood pressure, visual disturbances, mental confusion, and gastrointestinal disturbances. High doses can lead to respiratory depression, coma, and death.

Like GHB, Rohypnol is considered a "date rape drug" because of its sedative and amnesiac qualities. The drug manufacturer has recently added green dye to Rohypnol tablets so that the drug is visible if it is slipped into a drink.

Drug combinations are common with Rohypnol. Adolescents attending all-night dance parties sometimes combine Rohypnol with methamphetamines or mix the drug with alcohol in an attempt to get drunk fast. When combined with alcohol or any other sedative drug, Rohypnol's depressant effects on the central nervous system are multiplied.

Cocaine

> Cocaine is my drug. I love it. I'm
> not hooked or anything I use three
> or four times a week, that's all. I
> don't have to use. I just choose to
> use it. There's a difference, you
> know.
>
> —JENNIFER, *sixteen*

Cocaine is a powerfully addictive stimulant. Extracted from the leaves of several South American plants, the drug has been used for hundreds, perhaps thousands, of years for its stimulant and euphoric effects.

The authors of *Buzzed* offer interesting historical background:

> The natives of South America used cocaine as an important part of their daily life. Cocaine leaves were chewed for their alerting effects and their ability to increase endurance, particularly at the high altitudes in which many of these peoples lived. This practice continues to the present day. When the Spaniards conquered the Incas in the sixteenth century, they attempted to ban the use until they realized that the Indians working in the silver mines would work harder if given their daily allotment of cocaine.

Today, cocaine is purified into a white powder, which is then "cut" with inexpensive, look-alike substances such as sugar, cornstarch, baking soda, or talcum powder. Oral anesthetics such as lidocaine are sometimes used to create the numbing sensation, and studies show that even experienced cocaine users cannot tell the difference between cocaine and lidocaine. Cocaine is also frequently cut or diluted with inexpensive stimulants such as caffeine or amphetamine, which mimic the energizing effects of cocaine. The purity of powder cocaine ranges from 20 to 90 percent

Most adolescents snort or smoke cocaine rather than injecting it. Kids tend to be smart about needles—they've heard plenty of stories about HIV/AIDS, hepatitis, and other blood-borne diseases, and most associate shooting up with hard-core junkies. Many adolescents reason that if they don't shoot up, they can't become addicted.

But shooting up is not necessarily the most destructive way to use cocaine. In the mid-1980s, a new variation on cocaine became popular—crack cocaine, crack, or freebase. Crack is processed by boiling cocaine powder with baking soda (sodium bicarbonate) to create chunks of nearly pure cocaine. When smoked—the term *crack* refers to the crackling noise caused by heating up the baking soda—the drug is rapidly absorbed into the lungs and arrives in the brain within seconds, creating an extraordinarily powerful, and powerfully addictive, high.

Crack is nearly pure cocaine, with purity levels ranging from 85 to 100 percent. Because the euphoric rush is so powerful with crack, the dosage needed to get high is smaller, making the drug cheaper to buy. The cheaper price makes crack attractive to a broader market. And smaller dosages means greater profit for dealers—and thus a major incentive to push the drug.

The crack epidemic hit its peak in the United States in the late 1980s, but cocaine and crack use and addiction remain a major problem. The annual number of new cocaine users has increased over time. In 1975, there were thirty thousand new users. The number increased from 300,000 in 1986 to 361,000 in 2000.

The High

Cocaine increases brain levels of the feel-good chemical dopamine by interfering with the brain cells' ability to reabsorb the neurotransmitter. Cocaine attaches itself to the proteins that are normally used for transporting and eliminating dopamine, causing dopamine levels to increase along with intense sensations of pleasure and excitement.

Cocaine's stimulating and energizing effects are caused by the drug's ability to stimulate the production of stress hormones such as cortisol and norepinephrine (formerly called adrenaline). The high associated with cocaine and other stimulants can be summed up by the acronym *S.T.O.R.M.*.

- **STIMULATION:** All the senses (sight, hearing, smell, taste, and touch) are stimulated and aroused.
- **TALKATIVENESS:** Cocaine users tend to talk nonstop.
- **OBSESSIVENESS:** Users tend to focus on small details, often becoming obsessively involved or concerned with meaningless or trivial events.
- **RUSH:** The high or rush ranges from mild to moderate pleasure when snorting the drug to extreme euphoria when smoking or injecting it. Most regular users reserve the term *rush* for the sudden flash of intense euphoria that occurs when the drug is smoked or injected, methods that deliver the drug immediately to the brain. "It's like the top of your head is coming off," said one crack cocaine user.
- **MANIA:** The hyperactivity, impulsivity, distractability, and mental confusion can range from mild agitation to extreme frenzy and psychotic episodes.

The hyperstimulation, increased energy and alertness, and euphoria last from fifteen to thirty minutes when snorting cocaine. The extreme rush that occurs when smoking or injecting cocaine lasts just five to ten minutes. Then comes the crash—the jittery, anxious, depressed sensations that lead to a craving for more co-caine in order to reexperience the initial high.

Rush-and-crash—that's a quick summary of the cocaine experi-ence. You go up and then you come down, and the down is so un-pleasant that you experience an intense, even overwhelming desire to go back up again. Many people who use cocaine—even people who use infrequently—find themselves chasing the high, trying to achieve the same intense pleasure they experienced the first time they used. The problem is that the brain has only a limited supply of feel-good chemicals that can be released when cocaine or any other pleasure-enhancing drug is taken. With each use, the supply dwindles, leading to a less intense high and a more painful crash.

In the end, cocaine can come to dominate behavior, becoming more important to the adolescent than food, sleep, sex, or love.

> I never wanted to go to sleep. I just kept going. When I was off the drug for a while, I'd feel bad about myself and get depressed. I would promise all the people who were worried about me that I'd stop using. But then I'd use again, and when I was using, I could care less about anybody else. It was all about me, nothing else mat-tered.
>
> —CAROLYN, *eighteen*

Who Uses Cocaine?

> I hated to use cocaine alone, so I was always trying to talk people into using with me. I didn't care how old they were, if they were my good friends, or if I hardly knew them—I just needed some-body with me, to share the experience.
>
> —STEVEN, *seventeen*

Adolescents are using cocaine in record numbers according to a 2002 survey from the Centers for Disease Control and Prevention, which found that the number of teens who have tried cocaine in their lifetime has increased to 9.4 percent, up from 1.7 percent in 1991.

In the 2002 Monitoring the Future Survey, the only significant increases in drug use were past-year sedative use by twelfth-graders and past-year crack use by tenth-graders—crack use increased from 1.8 percent in 2001 to 2.3 percent in 2002. Nearly 24 percent of eighth-graders, 31.3 percent of tenth-graders, and 38.5 percent of high school seniors surveyed in 2002 reported that crack was "fairly easy" or "very easy" to obtain.

According to this survey, the perceived risk and disapproval of using both powder cocaine and crack decreased during the 1990s at all three grade levels surveyed—a factor that researchers believe contributes to the increased use among high school students.

Cocaine Use by Students, 2002: Monitoring the Future Survey

	8TH-GRADERS	10TH-GRADERS	12TH-GRADERS
Ever Used	3.6%	6.1%	7.8%
Used in Past Year	2.3	4.0	5.0
Used in Past Month	1.1	1.6	2.3

Crack Cocaine Use by Students, 2002: Monitoring the Future Survey

	8TH-GRADERS	10TH-GRADERS	12TH-GRADERS
Ever Used	2.5%	3.6%	3.8%
Used in Past Year	1.6	2.3	2.3
Used in Past Month	0.8	1.0	1.2

Important note: Most adolescents start using cocaine only after they have experimented with other drugs, particularly alcohol and marijuana. In most cases, they will try alcohol and/or marijuana first and then move on to cocaine, methamphetamine, hallucinogens, or

Ecstasy. One drug leads to another, which leads to another, and so it goes.

Bad Effects

Using cocaine once is like playing Russian Roulette, but continued use compounds the risk, so it is like adding a second bullet to the chamber of the gun.

—ARTHUR SIEGEL, M.D.
*Director of Internal Medicine
at McLean Hospital, Belmont, MA*

The penalties associated with using cocaine once or twice in your lifetime are all too often the same as the penalties associated with daily or weekly use. Even onetime use can have a devastating effect on the heart and the brain, causing heart arrhythmias, cardiovascular collapse, convulsions, brain hemorrhage, coma, and death.

Keep in mind, then, that while chronic cocaine users are more likely to experience both the short- and long-term effects discussed below, even onetime use can turn out to be a deadly experiment.

Short-Term Effects

Physical effects include the following:

- **GENERAL:** Headaches; increased body temperature due to constriction of small arteries and cocaine's direct effect on the brain's temperature-regulating system; fatigue, insomnia, excessive sleeping.
- **EYES:** Dilated pupils.
- **MUSCLES:** Muscle jerks or spasms.
- **NOSE AND THROAT:** Inflammation, ulceration, sinusitis, sore throat.

- **GASTROINTESTINAL:** Nausea, vomiting.
- **HEART:** Increased heart rate, irregularities of heart rhythm, chest pain.
- **BRAIN:** Convulsions, cerebral hemorrhage.
- **NUTRITIONAL:** Loss of appetite, weight loss.
- **SEXUAL PROBLEMS:** Hypersexuality followed by impotence.

Mental and emotional effects include delusional thinking, paranoia, hallucinations, confusion, difficulty concentrating, impaired memory, depression, anxiety, panic, and suicidal thoughts.

Users may also experience the fight-or-flight response. Like amphetamines and other synthetic stimulants, cocaine mimics the body's natural adrenaline response by increasing blood pressure and heart rate, narrowing blood vessels, and dilating the breathing tubes in the lungs. This natural response to fear or danger prepares the body for emergency situations, but the effects on the body and especially the heart can be profound and result in serious, even fatal, reactions.

Long-Term Effects

- **BRAIN:** When scientists take pictures or scans of cocaine users' brains, they find multiple small holes across the entire surface. The holes are signs of reduced brain activity and decreased blood flow. In one study, researchers noted a 23 percent decrease in cerebral blood flow in crack cocaine users compared to a control group. Crack users who were also cigarette smokers showed a 42 percent decrease in blood flow compared to the control group.

    Interrupting or slowing down the flow of blood through the brain leads to "persistent intellectual compromise," in the words of neuropsychiatrist Daniel Amen. In other words, cocaine users don't think or behave in normal ways because the drug has profoundly disturbed their brains.

Cocaine-induced brain damage is centered in the frontal and temporal-parietal areas of the brain, leading to problems with attention span, ability to concentrate and acquire new learning, visual and verbal memory, word production, and visual-motor integration.

Cocaine also damages the amygdala, an almond-shaped brain structure that regulates our responses to anger, fear, and other negative emotions. Researchers believe that the amygdala's involvement with emotional aspects of memory may help to explain why people addicted to cocaine experience intense and persistent cravings for the drug.

Recent research highlights the long-term dangers, showing that regular cocaine use damages—and may permanently destroy—the brain cells that allow us to feel pleasure. Researchers at the University of Michigan studied brain autopsy specimens from thirty-five cocaine users and thirty-five nonusers of similar age and sex. The cocaine users had significantly less dopamine in their brains; they also had dramatically reduced levels of a transporter protein (VMAT2) used to return dopamine to storage in the neuron.

The conclusion? Chronic cocaine use appears to injure or destroy brain cells, leading to a reduced (and possibly irreversible) ability to experience pleasure—not just the high from cocaine and other drugs, but the normal, everyday happiness and joy associated with eating, love-making, listening to music, watching sunsets, and so on. The researchers believe these findings may help to explain why so many cocaine addicts, even after years of abstinence, suffer from depression, decreased motivation, stunted emotions, and intense craving for cocaine.

■ **HEART:** Recent research shows that using cocaine just twelve times before the age of forty-five increases your risk of having a heart attack by 25 percent.

Cocaine damages the heart muscle by narrowing blood vessels and reducing blood flow. Frequent cocaine use can cause inflammation in the blood vessels, which can lead, in turn, to blood clotting and fatal heart attacks or strokes.

Using cocaine can also cause aortic dissection—a tear in the lining of the heart—and possible rupture of the aorta, the main vessel supplying the body with blood and oxygen. In one review of hospital records, researchers discovered that 37 percent of cases of aortic dissection were related to cocaine use, and that the cocaine users were twice as likely to die from the condition than nonusers.

- **LUNGS:** Cocaine users, particularly crack users, frequently suffer from acute respiratory problems, including coughing, shortness of breath, and severe chest pains. Regular use can lead to internal bleeding, fluid accumulation in the lungs, and respiratory failure.

- **NOSE:** Snorting cocaine can cause ulceration and deterioration of the mucous membrane of the nose, leading to holes in the septum (the main cartilage in the nose) or collapse of this structure. Snorting cocaine on a regular basis can also destroy the sense of smell.

- **PARANOIA, AGGRESSION, AND VIOLENCE:** High doses of cocaine and/or prolonged use can trigger paranoid thoughts and behaviors. Users who smoke crack cocaine are especially likely to experience aggressive paranoid behavior and violent outbursts.

  In a study conducted at the University of Maryland Medical Center over a period of sixteen years with victims of violent injuries from accidents, motor vehicle crashes, and physical attacks, approximately one-third of male victims of violent injuries tested positive for both alcohol and cocaine, and 31 percent of female victims tested positive for cocaine.

- **DEPRESSION:** When addicted individuals stop using cocaine, they often become severely depressed, which leads to an intense craving for the drug to alleviate the depression, and possible relapse. Profound feelings of guilt and shame combined with intense depression and/or anxiety can lead to suicidal thoughts or attempts.

Overdose and Death

That's the thing about cocaine the first time that you come on to it, it's wonderful and it's the last time that it's ever going to be that wonderful. But the interaction with your brain has happened and you're now going to chase it. Monkeys, given a choice between food and cocaine, will do the cocaine until they die of starvation. What does that tell you? . . . I was willing to kill myself for that drug and it was like that from the very first time.

—GREGORY HARRISON, *actor*
and recovering cocaine addict

The warning signs of a potentially lethal overdose include paranoia, hostility, violent behavior, chest pains, severe headaches due to blood vessel constriction, nausea, vomiting, and seizures. Seizures are so common with cocaine overdoses that when adolescents or young adults are admitted to the emergency room with seizures but have no prior history of them, emergency room personnel routinely recommend a drug screening.

Of all the stimulants, cocaine is the most likely to result in sudden death after a single dose. In the 1985 booklet "Cocaine: The Bottom Line," Sidney Cohen, M.D., lists "A Dozen Ways to Die with Cocaine." We have adapted and updated Dr. Cohen's original list.

1. **OVERDOSE**. During cocaine binges, large amounts of cocaine are delivered to the brain and other vital organs. Users may die from respiratory or cardiac arrest.
2. **HYPERSENSITIVITY TO COCAINE**. Cocaine is rapidly broken down in the body by liver and blood esterases (enzymes). Four to 5 percent of people are born with a

congenital absence of these enzymes, which means that they cannot metabolize cocaine efficiently, the drug builds up in the bloodstream, and even small amounts can cause sudden death. A small number of such cases have been reported in the surgical literature when cocaine was used as a local anesthetic.

3. **HYPERTENSION AND CEREBRAL HEMORRHAGE.** The sudden rise in blood pressure that can accompany cocaine use may blow out a weakened blood vessel in the brain, causing paralysis or death.

4. **HYPERPYREXIA.** Some cocaine users, especially those who combine it with physical exertion on hot days or in excessively warm environments, can experience extremely high body temperature and die. Athletes, including bicyclists, runners, and others involved in strenuous sports activities, are particularly susceptible.

5. **MAJOR CONVULSIONS.** Cocaine use can cause epileptic seizures, which can become repetitive and terminate in death.

6. **CORONARY ARTERY DISEASE.** Cocaine decreases coronary blood flow and, in people with preexisting heart disease, can lead to fatal heart attacks.

7. **HOMICIDE.** Paranoid thinking is symptomatic of cocaine addictions and can lead to violent attacks and murder.

8. **SUICIDE.** Postcocaine depression can be profound and can induce suicidal behavior. Regular users, who often feel guilty and become profoundly depressed when they become aware of the harm they have caused to their families, may consider or attempt suicide.

9. **ACCIDENTAL DEATH.** Accidental death in connection with cocaine use is well known. Impaired judgment, irritability, and hyperactivity combine to cause reckless behaviors and serious or fatal accidents.

10. **IMMUNE DEFICIENCY STATES.** The malnutrition and emaciation of some people made anorectic by protracted cocaine use can lead to a variety of infections such as

tuberculosis and fungal diseases because of reduced immune defenses.

11. **BLOOD STREAM INFECTIONS.** Viruses, including hepatitis B and C, AIDS, and bacterial infections of various organs are sometimes found in intravenous users of cocaine.

12. **COCAINE INTERACTIONS WITH OTHER DRUGS.** Using cocaine in combination with drugs that depress breathing—heroin, alcohol, sleeping pills, tranquilizers, sedatives—can paralyze the breathing center, leading to respiratory failure and death.

Dangerous Combinations

I first started using cocaine when I smoked a marijuana joint laced with cocaine. I loved that high—so fast, so intense! I thought, "This is what life is all about!" So I started buying a gram here and another gram there and before I knew it, I was using the stuff all the time. I've probably spent ten thousand dollars on cocaine.

—JAMES, *seventeen*

As with all drug combinations, remember the rule: 1 + 1 = 3 or 4 or 5. The effects of one addictive drug plus the effects of other addictive drugs have an explosive impact, like throwing gasoline on a fire.

Because the up is so euphoric and the crash is so painful—and because the pain follows so closely on the heels of the pleasure—users (including casual or "recreational" users) frequently take other drugs in an attempt to soften or mellow the withdrawal symptoms.

- **ALCOHOL AND COCAINE:** Using alcohol to control cocaine's upper-downer syndrome can lead to toxic interactions between the two drugs and a double drug dependency. In addition, when adolescents and adults use cocaine and alcohol at the same time, they unknowingly create a third chemical in their body. Researchers have discovered that alcohol and cocaine are combined in the liver into cocaethylene—a chemical substance that intensifies cocaine's euphoric effects but also increases the risk of sudden death.

- **OPIATES AND COCAINE**: Searching for the ultimate high, some users combine cocaine with heroin in a "speedball." Cocaine creates tension and heroin induces relaxation and drowsiness, so the idea is that the combination of drugs would increase the euphoria while reducing the unpleasant side effects associated with the individual drugs.

    But heroin slows the brain's breathing center, and in large doses, cocaine also depresses breathing. Combining cocaine with any depressant drug (alcohol, heroin, sleeping pills, tranquilizers, pain medications, sedatives) can paralyze respiration and lead to coma and death.
- **MARIJUANA AND COCAINE**: Research shows that *adolescents who smoke marijuana are eighty-five times more likely to use cocaine.* Unfortunately, this combination is popular with adolescents because marijuana mellows out the cocaine jitters and makes the inevitable cocaine crash less painful.

Physical Dependence

A hundred percent of monkeys no matter what their character structure can be made into insatiable users, and the same can be said of people given plentiful supplies and the willingness to use the drug.

—SIDNEY COHEN, M.D.

Tolerance

When cocaine users say, "I used to get high on a lot less" or "I have to use a lot more cocaine to get high these days," they are describing the effects of tolerance, or central nervous system adaptation to cocaine.

Many cocaine users report that as hard as they try, they cannot ever again get as much pleasure from cocaine as they did the first time they used the drug. Actor Gregory Harrison's experience is not uncommon:

> It hooked me the first time I did it. I remember the very moment that I came onto this first tiny snort of cocaine at a party in the Hollywood Hills in 1978. Within five minutes of snorting that one little spoonful of somebody else's stash—you know, *You gotta try it, it's really fun, it's great, it's harmless*—five minutes later I felt, for the first time in my life . . . perfect.
>
> I had never felt perfect. I had always felt inadequate and like a failure. I thought I should be perfect . . . for all the rest of my addiction, I hunted for that perfection. Occasionally I found it to some degree when I used that drug, but for the most part I was a dog chasing its tail from that point on, always searching for that feeling I once had but would never have again.

Cocaine has a powerful neuropsychological effect, meaning that the drug has a profound effect on the brain, both physically and psychologically. Users keep using despite harmful physical, emotional, and social consequences—as good a definition of addiction as any.

Addiction seems to develop more rapidly when the substance is smoked or injected because these methods deliver high concentrations of the drug to the brain within seconds.

Withdrawal

Withdrawal from cocaine is similar to amphetamine withdrawal. The inevitable crash brings with it aches and pains, irritability, tremors, nausea, weakness, extreme fatigue, and profound depression.

Craving can be fierce and long lasting.

"Man, I'm fiending for some coke." Vincent's legs are jumping up and down and his fingers are playing a wild piano tune on his thighs. He manages a weak smile. "It's better than yesterday, but I don't think I'm going to make it another day. I *need* the drug, man. Do you understand what I'm saying? I need it *now*."

How Can I Tell if My Child Is Using Cocaine?

Parents should look for these signs and symptoms, which are specific to cocaine use:

Physical Symptoms
- **CHANGES IN SLEEP PATTERNS:** Staying up much later than usual, having trouble sleeping, using over-the-counter sleep aids such as Benadryl, melatonin, Excedrin PM, Nytol, Sominex, or Tylenol Extra Strength PM.
- **DRY MOUTH, LIPS, AND NOSE:** Use of moisturizers, lipsticks or lip balms, nasal decongestants.
- **RUNNY NOSE, SINUS AND/OR NASAL PROBLEMS, NOSEBLEEDS.**
- **BAD BREATH:** Use of mints, mouthwash.

Emotional Problems
- **MOOD SWINGS:** Irritability, nervousness, argumentativeness, anxiety, paranoia, hostility, violent behaviors.

Behavioral Changes
- **STUDY HABITS:** Putting off schoolwork and then pulling all-nighters, working nonstop for several hours on a school project.

- **MONEY PROBLEMS:** Savings account disappears, regular ATM withdrawals from checking accounts.
- **NEW POSSESSIONS:** To support their addiction, many adolescents become dealers. They may deal only to their friends and other people they trust, but look for signs of extra money flowing in from unknown sources and expensive new possessions.
- **PARAPHERNALIA:** Razor blades, mirrors, small spoons, little bottles of white powder, and plastic, glass, or metal straws.
- **UNEXPLAINED PHONE CALLS** from strangers or new friends (check your caller ID regularly).
- **REGULAR USE OF OVER-THE-COUNTER PREPARATIONS** for eye or nasal inflammation (Visine or other eyedrops); for dry, chapped lips; or for bad breath.
- **FREQUENT LIP LICKING.**
- **EXCESSIVE ACTIVITY:** Difficulty sitting still, lack of interest in food or sleep.
- **EXCESSIVE TALKING:** Conversations jump from one subject to the next.

Heroin

Choose life. Choose a job. Choose a
career. Choose a family. Choose your
future . . . choose life.

But why would I want to do a
thing like that?

I chose not to choose life. I
chose something else. And the reasons? There are no reasons. Who
needs reasons when you've got
heroin?

—VOICE-OVER
*in the opening scene
of the movie* Trainspotting

Heroin, like all addictive drugs, takes reason away.
Considered a "semi-synthetic opiate," heroin is actually
morphine (a naturally occurring substance in the opium poppy)
that has been chemically altered to enter the brain quickly. Once
heroin enters the brain, it is converted back into morphine. First
marketed commercially by the Bayer Corporation in 1898 as a
cough suppressant and treatment for morphine addiction, the cure
proved worse than the original problem: Heroin turned out to be

even more addictive than morphine. The United States banned heroin manufacturing and importation in 1924.

Typically sold today in clear plastic bags containing about one hundred milligrams of loose powder, heroin's color varies from white (purer) to brown (less pure). The drug is often "cut" with talc, quinine, or baking powder to increase profits for dealers, but today's heroin is incredibly pure—approximately five to ten times purer than it was just a few years ago. The average purity of heroin sold on the street today averages 35 percent and can get as high as 70 to 95 percent. Purer heroin can be snorted or smoked, which means that injection is no longer the only route to the intense heroin high.

> People who may have been deterred are now trying it because it can be put up your nose. It's become mainstream. That line in the sand that used to be drawn between heroin as a hard drug and all other drugs is gone.
>
> —CAROL FALKOWSKI, *Director of Research Communications at Hazelden Foundation*

Most people, adolescents included, believe heroin has to be injected with needles. It's true that ten or twenty years ago, when heroin averaged between 5 and 7 percent purity, injecting the drug was the only way to deliver the full power of the heroin high. But today's heroin is so much purer—and, at this point in time, so much cheaper—that users can smoke or snort the drug and still absorb a sufficient amount to feel the full effect of the heroin high.

According to the 2002 National Drug Assessment Threat published by the National Drug Intelligence Center (NIDC), the recent purity level of heroin available at the retail level nationwide averaged 51.2 percent for South American heroin, 27.3 percent for Mexican, 41.9 percent for Southeast Asian, and 44.0 percent for Southwest Asian heroin. Purity levels today range from 7 to 95 percent.

With the purity levels so high—and the cost remaining relatively low—many users are snorting the drug. And scientific research tells us that adolescents are much more likely to use a drug that can be snorted or smoked. Adolescents link intravenous drug use and needles with hard-core addicts, and most kids know enough about AIDS, hepatitis, and other blood-borne diseases to be extremely wary of injecting drugs. At the same time, many adolescents believe they are protected from addiction and overdose if they snort the drug and don't inject it.

In a recent survey, almost half of high school seniors said they did not believe there was a great risk in trying heroin.

The High

Her eyes closed in spite of herself, and she forgot where she was and fell among the poppies, fast asleep.

"What shall we do?" asked the Tin Woodman.

"If we leave her here she will die," said the Lion. "The smell of the flowers is killing us all. I myself can scarcely keep my eyes open, and the dog is asleep already."

—L. FRANK BAUM
The Wonderful Wizard of Oz

As Dorothy and her companions walk through the poppy fields on their way to Oz, they become sleepy, happy, and dopey (sounds more like the story of the Seven Dwarfs), eventually lying down for a long nap. Only the Scarecrow, who lacks a brain—or at least believes he is brainless—is able to resist the opium poppies' effects.

Heroin and other opiate drugs activate receptors in certain brain structures called the ventral tegmental, nucleus accumbens, and cerebral cortex—the areas that comprise "the reward center" or "pleasure circuit" of the brain. All addictive drugs activate these brain structures, but heroin and other opiates light up the entire switchboard.

The heroin high occurs in several stages. When heroin is injected or smoked, users feel an almost immediate rush of euphoric pleasure.

This rush, which lasts only a minute or two, is intensely pleasurable—users often compare it to a sexual orgasm involving instant relief of tension and sensations of warmth spreading throughout the abdominal region. Snorting heroin takes longer to create a high (with little or no rush), because the drug has to travel through mucous membranes in the nose to the blood vessels beneath before finding its way to the brain.

After the rush and the euphoric high come "the nods," a dreamy state of tranquility, lethargy, and self-absorption that lasts four or five hours. During this stage, users typically feel completely satisfied, with all their needs fulfilled. They also experience a sense of distance from their immediate surroundings and a general lack of concern for whatever is happening around them. Hunger, pain, tension, fear, and sexual desire fade away. Breathing becomes shallow and infrequent.

Heroin is highly addictive: Withdrawal symptoms appear within twenty-four to thirty-six hours of using, and can last between three and five days. As addiction progresses, the euphoria experienced after using the drug is reduced as the pain is increased until eventually the addicted person uses heroin less for pleasure than to relieve the pain and misery of withdrawal.

All opiates cause severe pain in addicted individuals during withdrawal.

Who Uses Heroin?

From 1998, we started seeing heroin spread beyond the cities into the surrounding area with some dealers setting up shop in apartments in the suburbs and smaller towns.

—ERIN ARTIGIANA, *coordinator of the Drug Early Warning System (DAWN)*

In the past, the great majority of adolescents have avoided using heroin because they perceive it to be one of the most dangerous drugs available. In 2002, however, 44 percent of twelfth-graders said they did not believe there is "great risk" involved in using heroin once or twice, and 23.4 percent did not believe there is "great risk" involved in using heroin occasionally.

Teens in 2002 were significantly less likely than in 2001 to "agree strongly" that "heroin can wreck your life," according to the 2002 Partnership Attitude Tracking Study.

Approximately 4 percent of teens have tried heroin, and about 15 percent of teens report having close friends who have tried heroin at least once in their lives.

Heroin Use by Students, 2002: Monitoring the Future Survey

	8TH-GRADERS	10TH-GRADERS	12TH-GRADERS
Ever Used			
with a needle	1.0%	1.0%	0.8%
without a needle	1.0	1.3	1.6
Used in Past Year			
with a needle	0.6	0.6	0.4
without a needle	0.6	0.8	0.8
Used in Past Month			
with a needle	0.3	0.3	0.3
without a needle	0.3	0.4	0.5

Bad Effects

Without you realizing what's happening, heroin sucks the love out of you. The love of life, the love of people, the love of music, the love of whatever it is that you have a love for. It's very deceiving because it'll numb a pain, but it'll numb your love as well. It'll numb your joy and your fervor to discover what it is in life that you were meant to explore.

It kills you, too. Eventually you either die or you end up in a puddle of trouble in the street. You end up in prison or you end up in a loony bin.

—ANTHONY KIEDIS, *recovering drug addict and lead singer of the Red Hot Chili Peppers*

Short-Term Effects

In the gastrointestinal tract, we have opiate receptors that help regulate our ability to digest and eliminate food. When heroin and other opiates occupy these natural receptor sites, drug users experience multiple digestive problems, including abdominal cramping, nausea, vomiting, constipation, and diarrhea.

Other physical effects include constricted pupils, numbness to pain, dizziness, difficulty urinating, skin flushing, itching of the skin, and slow, shallow breathing.

Psychological and emotional effects include irritability, severe anxiety, panic attacks, depression, and suicidal thoughts.

Long-Term Effects

- **BRAIN:** "Brain melt." That's how neurophysiologist Daniel Amen, author of *Change Your Brain, Change Your Life*, describes what happens to the brains of people who regularly use heroin and other opiate drugs. These painkilling drugs "melt the brain" by slowing down blood flow and brain cell activity.

  Opiate drugs also act directly on the respiratory center in the brain stem to slow down breathing. Heroin overdoses are often related to the drug's effect on these respiratory centers, causing the person to stop breathing and die.

  Using heroin regularly or over a long period of time rewires the brain in fundamental and long-lasting ways, leading to a physical craving for the drug that can override all other needs, including the need to eat, have sex, sleep, love, and be loved. Heroin becomes the first, and eventually the only, need.

- **HEART:** Dangers to the heart and cardiovascular system include collapsed blood vessels and infection of the heart lining and valves.
- **LIVER:** The liver detoxifies and breaks down heroin and other drugs so they can be eliminated from the body. Regular use can damage cells and tissues in this vital organ.
- **LUNGS:** Heroin slows down breathing. Regular use, especially when combined with malnutrition and poor health, can lead to pulmonary complications, including various kinds of pneumonia. Also, when heroin addicts inject heroin, they use cotton plugs; the cotton fibers can travel through the bloodstream to the lungs, where they can cause a life-threatening embolism.
- **SEXUAL/REPRODUCTIVE SYSTEMS:** Heroin wreaks havoc with the reproductive system and sexuality, causing impotence, loss of sexual desire, loss of menstrual cycles and spontaneous abortion in women, and lower sperm production in men. If needles are used, the risk of sexually transmitted diseases including hepatitis and HIV/AIDS increases dramatically.
- **INFECTIONS:** Heroin users who share needles are at great risk for bacterial and viral infections, including endocarditis, hepatitis, and HIV/AIDS. Additives and impurities in heroin can also cause serious, even life-threatening, infections.

Overdose and Death

Heroin collapses your lungs if you take too much of it, for whatever reason I'm not sure. Your lungs collapse and they freeze together like sucking the air out of a bag. You're so incredibly unaware under the influence of heroin that you just kind of fall asleep. It's a combination of falling asleep and not breathing. You pass out, your lungs pass out, your brain and lungs pass out together.

—ANTHONY KIEDIS

Death by overdose on heroin is an ever-present possibility for both onetime users and heroin addicts. Heroin and other opiate drugs suppress breathing; within minutes of using, users may become so sedated that they simply stop breathing and slip into a coma.

Symptoms of a heroin overdose include shallow breathing, pinpoint pupils, clammy skin, convulsions, and coma. The latest data on drug-related hospital emergency department visits indicate that heroin/morphine visits increased 15 percent from 1999 to 2000.

The ever-present danger of overdose is compounded by the increasing purity of the drug in recent years. Casual users and addicts can accidentally overdose because they have taken a higher dose of the drug than expected. And since heroin purity varies so dramatically—ranging from 7 to 95 percent—users never know exactly how much heroin they are actually ingesting.

Users and addicts can also die from complications caused by the adulterants (lactose, powdered milk, baking soda, coffee creamer, quinine, sugar, cocaine, rat poison) used to dilute heroin. Additives may not dissolve in the bloodstream and can clog the blood vessels leading to the brain, lungs, liver, kidneys, or heart, and/or lead to life-threatening infections.

Dangerous Combinations

Heroin alone can be deadly—heroin combined with other drugs is even more lethal. A few famous cases make the point:

- In 1970, rock star Janis Joplin died of an accidental overdose of heroin and alcohol. Joplin's death certificate lists "acute heroin-morphine injection" and "injection of overdose" as the cause of death.

- In 1982, actor John Belushi, thirty-three, died after shooting up a "speedball"—a potent combination of heroin and cocaine that slowed down Belushi's breathing and eventually stopped it altogether.
- On October 30, 1993, twenty-three-year-old actor River Phoenix injected himself with a speedball at Johnny Depp's Viper Club on LA's Sunset Strip. After collapsing in convulsions, he was carried outside and allegedly told the doorman, "I'm gonna die, dude." He was pronounced dead later that night at an LA hospital.
- In December 1997, thirty-three-year-old comedian Chris Farley died in his Chicago apartment. Autopsy tests revealed that high levels of morphine and cocaine in Farley's bloodstream triggered a fatal heart attack. Farley's liver was scarred by heavy drinking, although the autopsy showed that he had not been drinking alcohol that night.

Heroin addicts, like other chemically dependent people, often combine drugs because their tolerance levels increase to the point that they experience a less intense, euphoric high when using heroin alone. Seeking the ecstatic rapture that they experienced when they first used heroin, they experiment by combining heroin with other drugs.

But here's the danger: Heroin and other opiates suppress breathing, causing users to breathe shallowly and infrequently, which results in less oxygen available to the brain. Combining heroin with another drug that suppresses breathing—such as alcohol, sedatives, tranquilizers, sleeping pills, prescription painkillers, GHB, PCP, or inhalants—can compound the effects of both drugs, slowing down breathing to the point that it stops and causing respiratory failure, heart failure, coma, brain damage, and death.

Combining heroin with cocaine is common, as the sedating effects of heroin cut the jittery stimulant effects of cocaine. This lethal combination increases the risk of overdose, coma, brain damage, and death.

Physical Dependence

I remember someone saying if you try heroin once you'll become hooked. Of course I laughed and scoffed at the idea but I now believe this to be very true. Not literally, I mean if you do dope once you don't instantly become addicted. . . . But after the first time your mind says ahh that was very pleasant, as long as I don't do it every day I won't have a problem. The problem is it happens over time.

—KURT COBAIN,
who committed suicide in 1994,
from his posthumously published Journals

Addiction to heroin develops rapidly. Daily use for several weeks leads to dramatic increases in tolerance, painful withdrawal symptoms, and powerful drug cravings. Users may be addicted even if they do not experience a noticeable increase in tolerance or obvious withdrawal symptoms. The signs and symptoms of early stage addiction may be mild and easily dismissed with such statements as "I think I have the flu" or "I'm just not feeling well today."

Tolerance

Tolerance develops quickly as the brain adapts to heroin and the brain cells are able to function normally even when large doses of the drug are coursing through the bloodstream.

Withdrawal

Heroin withdrawal can be summed up in this way—it is miserable and miserably long, but it won't kill you.

In the semi-autobiographical book *Junky*, heroin addict William Burroughs describes why so many people addicted to heroin or other opiate drugs can't kick the habit. "The reason it is practically impossible to stop using and cure yourself," he writes, "is that the sickness lasts five to eight days. Twelve hours of it would be easy, 24 possible, but five to eight days is too long."

Burroughs vividly describes the agony of opiate withdrawal in this passage from *Junky*:

> My nose and eyes began to run, sweat soaked through my clothes. Hot and cold flashes hit me as though a furnace door was swinging open and shut. I lay down on the bunk, too weak to move. My legs ached and twitched, so that any position was intolerable, and I moved from one side to the other, sloshing about in my sweaty clothes. . . . Almost worse than the sickness is the depression that goes with it. One afternoon I closed my eyes and saw New York in ruins. Huge centipedes and scorpions crawled in and out of empty bars and cafeterias and drugstores on Forty-second Street. Weeds were growing up though cracks and holes in the pavement. There was no one in sight. After five days I began to feel a little better.

The first signs of withdrawal are sweating, watery eyes, runny nose, and yawning. As withdrawal continues, the physical signs and symptoms intensify. The physical, mental, and emotional agony can last for several days before the withdrawal symptoms begin to wane and decrease in severity.

Symptoms of acute heroin withdrawal include restlessness, irritability, loss of appetite, diarrhea, vomiting, shivering (chills, goose bumps), sweating, flu-like feelings or symptoms, abdominal cramps, muscle and bone pain, increased sensitivity to pain, and difficulty sleeping.

Long-term withdrawal can continue for weeks or even months. The recovering addict may feel physically ill and emotionally unbalanced, with flu-like symptoms, restlessness, irritability, anger, anxiety, and severe depression. The risk of relapse during both acute and protracted withdrawal is high, because the heroin addict knows how to instantly, magically relieve this ongoing pain—use heroin.

Craving for heroin can last many months, long after the acute withdrawal symptoms have disappeared.

How Can I Tell if My Child Is Using Heroin?

If your child uses heroin just once or twice, you may never find out. However, because regular use leads to addiction in such a short time—within weeks or months of first using—it is not difficult to tell if your child is hooked on heroin.

Look for the following signs and symptoms specific to heroin use:

- Gastrointestinal problems—abdominal cramping, constipation, diarrhea.
- Skin flushing or itching.
- Slow, shallow breathing.
- Extreme drowsiness (nodding off) during the day.
- Reduced sensitivity to pain.
- Withdrawal from family and friends.
- Use of other opiate drugs such as codeine, morphine, or prescription drugs such as OxyContin, Vicodin, Percodan, or Percocet to relieve withdrawal symptoms.

OxyContin, Ritalin, and Other Prescription Drugs

> She figures I've slipped back into a
> bad depression. She asks a lot of
> questions about my medication. Does
> it need to be adjusted? Do I need
> some new pill?
> Yeah, sure, I need a new pill. I
> need a lot of them. Oh, Mommy, if
> you only knew.
>
> —ELIZABETH WURTZEL
> *More, Now, Again*

Prescription or psychotherapeutic drugs come in three basic categories: pain relievers, stimulants, and central nervous system depressants.

- **PAINKILLERS** bind to opioid receptors in the brain, spinal cord, and gastrointestinal tract, blocking the transmission of pain and creating euphoria, relaxation, drowsiness, and constipation. Commonly used painkillers include Percocet, Lortab, Vicodin, Darvon, Demerol, Dilaudid, and the superstrength time-release painkiller OxyContin.

- **STIMULANTS** work by enhancing brain activity and increasing heart rate and respiration. Prescription stimulants used to delay the onset of physical or mental fatigue or to increase concentration and focus include the amphetamines Ritalin, Adderall, Dexedrine, and Preludin.
- **CENTRAL NERVOUS SYSTEM DEPRESSANTS (SEDATIVE-HYPNOTIC DRUGS)** act on the neurotransmitter GABA (g-aminobutyrate) to slow down brain activity and are used for their relaxing, anxiety-reducing, hypnotic, and/or sedative effects. The effects of central nervous system depressants or sedatives range on a continuum from relaxation to extreme sedation. In high doses, some depressant drugs can act as general anesthetics.

  These drugs include barbiturates such as Amytal, Luminal, Nembutal, Seconal, and Tuinal; and the benzodiazepines (also called minor tranquilizers), which include Valium, Librium, Xanax, Klonopin, and Ativan. Benzodiazepines with sedating effects are used as sleeping pills and include Restoril, Halcion, Dalmane, Serax, and others. Major tranquilizers or antipsychotics are used to treat symptoms of paranoia, psychosis, hallucinations, or delusions and include Haldol, Navane, Thorazine, and Mellaril.

Many researchers are concerned about the ever-increasing numbers of children being treated with prescription psychiatric drugs. A 2003 study found that from 1987 to 1996, the number of American children being treated with psychiatric drugs such as Prozac, Ritalin, and Risperdal *tripled*. In 1996 more than 6 percent of children were taking these drugs, and the numbers continue to rise.

Other than zonking you, we don't know that behavioral management by drug control is the way to learn to behave properly. If we are using drugs to control behavior, that doesn't change the underlying problem if someone doesn't know how to get along with their peers.

—JULIE ZITO, Ph.D.

The High

The high that adolescents seek on prescription drugs varies from one drug group to another.

- **PAINKILLERS**, particularly narcotic (opiate)–based painkillers, tend to create rapid and intense euphoria, relaxation, and drowsiness.

    OxyContin delivers the most powerful euphoric rush—the drug contains between 10 and 160 milligrams of oxycodone (compared to other painkillers such as Tylox, which contains 5 milligrams) in a time-release tablet that provides up to twelve hours of pain relief. When kids crush the tablet and snort it or dilute it in water and inject it, they bypass the time-release action and experience a powerful euphoric rush. A twenty-one-year-old OxyContin addict quoted in *Newsweek* described the high this way:

    I don't know how to explain the buzz. It's just this utopic feeling. You feel like you can conquer the world. . . . It's a better high than anything else.

- **STIMULANTS** create sensations of energy, excitement, warmth, and stimulation, increased focus, and concentration. When Ritalin is snorted or injected, for example, it delivers a euphoric jolt that users compare to cocaine.

    The following story is told by a sixteen-year-old boy who estimates that he took thirty Adderall pills over a period of ten days while his family was away on vacation. Adderall, like Ritalin, is an amphetamine prescribed for people with attention deficit hyperactivity disorder.

    I stayed up for ten days and ate Popsicles. That's all I ate was Popsicles. I took the Popsicle sticks and a steak knife and spent all day carving the Popsicle sticks. Sitting in the car, I did a drawing of some guy who looked like Jesus. It was so intricate. Crazy.

In the car I would hear the wind, and it sounded like a radio transmission, like a baseball game. I saw things that weren't there, like birds out of the corner of my eyes and people in shadows, and I kept checking.

It was so great not to have to sleep, you don't have to sleep, your life can continue. I didn't sleep for ten days. I pretended like I went to bed and then just dinked around in my room. I smoked cigarettes like a bandit, just chain smoking. I was so high. My body was just pumping.

■ **DEPRESSANTS** ("downers") slow down brain activity to create feelings of relaxation, sedation, numbness, and drowsiness. Adolescents often use depressant drugs to relieve anxiety, decrease inhibitions, and induce euphoria and relaxation.

I took a bunch of Xanax, maybe six or seven pills. I felt like rubber, like I was made out of Jell-O and could just melt into the floor.

—JOANNA, *seventeen*

Who Uses Prescription Drugs?

You want some pills? Just go into your friends' houses and look in the bathrooms. You find all sorts of stuff—pain pills, muscle relaxants, sleeping pills, it's all right there. Nobody catches you 'cause you just take three or four pills out of each bottle.

But it's probably easier just to walk down the street and ask the first kid you run into if he has any pills. You know what he'll say? "What kind do you want? How many?"

—AMANDA, *seventeen*

More than 131 million people—66 percent of all adults in the United States—use prescription drugs. And millions of young people between the ages of twelve and twenty-five are using these drugs for nonmedical purposes.

In January 2003, the U.S. government released statistics showing that in 2001 almost three million adolescents between the ages of twelve and seventeen have used prescription medications nonmedically in their lifetimes.

The 2002 Partnership Attitude Tracking Study reports that one in five, or 20 percent, of teens in grades seven through twelve have used prescription painkillers without a doctor's prescription, and 9 percent say they have used Ritalin or Adderall without a doctor's prescription.

Overall, women and men have about the same rate of nonmedical use of prescription drugs—except in the twelve- to seventeen-year-old category. In this age group, girls are more likely than boys to use illegally obtained prescription drugs—3.8 percent of girls versus 2.7 percent of boys. Researchers also report that women are almost twice as likely to get addicted to central nervous system depressants than men.

- **PAINKILLERS** are statistically the most likely medications to be used illegally. Emergency room visits involving the painkiller hydrocodone (Vicodin, Lortab) increased 131 percent in the last decade, while visits involving oxycodone (Percodan, Tylox, OxyContin) increased 352 percent.
- **OXYCONTIN** misuse is rampant because the drug delivers a powerfully euphoric high, often compared to the rush of heroin. OxyContin, in fact, is often called "poor man's heroin" or "pharmaceutical heroin." On the street, OxyContin tablets sell for about a dollar per milligram; the cost of one pill can range from twenty to eighty dollars. Adolescents who get their hands on a stash of OxyContin pills can make a huge profit.

I have a friend who works at a pharmacy. He's eighteen, and he gets to drive the prescriptions around to all the sick people who can't drive to the pharmacy. So he gets in the drugstore truck, drives a little while, and then finds a safe place to park. He takes one or two pills from every OxyContin bottle and then goes on with his delivery. Then he sells the pills for twenty or forty bucks on the street. He gets paid minimum wage, but he's netting about four hundred dollars a day from selling the pills. Of course, he uses, too, so that cuts down on his profits.

—CARL, *eighteen*

In 1999, approximately 221,000 people age twelve or over had used OxyContin without a prescription. In 2000, that figure jumped to 399,000, and in 2001 it more than doubled again to 957,000 people. In 2002, researchers reported that more than four hundred deaths have been linked to OxyContin.

■ **RITALIN:** On the street, Ritalin tablets are sold for anywhere between two and fifteen dollars. The tablets are crushed and then snorted, or the powder from the crushed tablet is mixed with water and then injected.

When I went to inpatient treatment, I took some Ritalin with me, figuring I could make some fast money. I put the pills between my fingers, so I was able to sneak in eight pills. I sold them for five bucks each. Everything was going great until somebody snitched on me and I got thrown out of treatment.

—MATT, *eighteen*

The Substance Abuse and Mental Health Services Administration (SAMHSA) offers the following data on nonmedical use of prescription drugs.

Prescription Drug Past-Month Nonmedical Use, 1999–2001:
2002 National Household Survey

AGE	1999	2000	2001
12–13	1.8%	1.6%	1.8%
14–15	3.4	3.0	3.5
16–17	3.4	4.3	4.4
18–25	3.7	3.6	4.8

The annual Monitoring the Future Survey reports the following prescription-drug-use statistics for eighth-, tenth-, and twelfth-graders. Long-term declines in nonmedical prescription drug use among adolescents in the 1980s began to level off in the early 1990s and then steadily increased over the next ten years.

Tranquilizer Use by Students, 2002:
Monitoring the Future Survey

	8TH-GRADERS	10TH-GRADERS	12TH-GRADERS
Ever Used	4.3%	8.8%	11.4%
Used in Past Year	2.6	6.3	7.7
Used in Past Month	1.2	2.9	3.3

Barbiturate Use by Students, 2002:
Monitoring the Future Survey

	12TH-GRADERS ONLY
Ever Used	9.5%
Used in Past Year	6.7
Used in Past Month	3.2

OxyContin Use by Students, 2002: Monitoring the Future Survey

	8TH-GRADERS	10TH-GRADERS	12TH-GRADERS
Used in Past Year	1.3%	3.0%	4.0%

Vicodin Use by Students, 2002: Monitoring the Future Survey

	8TH-GRADERS	10TH-GRADERS	12TH-GRADERS
Used in Past Year	1.3%	3.0%	4.0%

Bad Effects

I started using when I was eleven, but now that I'm thirteen it's just not as much fun anymore. Bad things are happening to me. A month ago, I drank a bunch of vodka and took some prescription pain pills. I passed out and some stupid guys took advantage of me. I thought they were my friends.

Lately, my mother and I are fighting all the time. I'm really depressed. I don't know why. Life sucks. I don't know what is happening to me.

—DIANNA, *thirteen*

Short-Term Effects

- **OXYCONTIN AND OTHER NARCOTIC PAINKILLERS:** Constipation, nausea, sedation, dizziness, vomiting, headache, dry mouth, sweating, and weakness.
- **STIMULANTS:** Nervousness, insomnia, loss of appetite, nausea, vomiting, dizziness, headache, changes in heart rate and blood pressure, skin rashes and itching, abdominal pain, weight loss, severe depression, tremors and muscle

twitching, fever, convulsions, anxiety, restlessness, paranoia, hallucinations and delusions, excessive repetition of movements and meaningless tasks, sensation of bugs or worms crawling under the skin (called formication).

- **SEDATIVES:** Memory impairment, drowsiness, mental confusion, personality changes, sleep disturbances, skin rashes, nausea, dizziness.

Long-Term Effects

- **OXYCONTIN:** OxyContin has been on the market only since 1996, so we don't know a great deal about its long-term health effects. Liver damage is a potential risk for regular users.

  Long-term risks for people who inject OxyContin include cardiovascular damage, including endocarditis (life-threatening heart infection), scarred and/or collapsed veins, infections, viruses including HIV/AIDS and hepatitis B and C, and arthritis.

  The most obvious long-term effects are addiction and the extremely painful withdrawal syndrome.

- **RITALIN:** Ritalin tablets are specifically manufactured to be swallowed in pill form. The tablets include "inert" ingredients such as lactose, starch, polyethylene glycol, magnesium stearate, sucrose, talc, cellulose, mineral oil, and various dyes and conditioning agents.

  When the drug is snorted or injected, these ingredients can cause serious, potentially lethal problems. Snorting Ritalin can damage the tissues lining the nasal cavities and air passages and cause open sores, nosebleeds, and deterioration of the nasal cartilage. Injecting Ritalin directly into the veins or body tissues can cause blood clots, pulmonary problems, and skin and circulatory problems. Medical journals contain numerous reports detailing permanent and irreversible lung tissue damage related to injecting Ritalin.

■ **SEDATIVES:** Long-term effects include lethargy, decreased motivation, irritability, vivid or disturbing dreams, nausea, headache, skin rash, impaired sexual functioning, tremors, appetite changes, and menstrual irregularities.

Overdose and Death

■ **PAINKILLERS:** If you take painkillers, stimulants, and/or sedatives in large-enough amounts, you can overdose and die on the drugs. Overdose and death are more likely with narcotic painkillers and sedative drugs, because they slow down brain functions and central nervous system activity and depress breathing.

Because it is such a powerful, "superstrength" narcotic, OxyContin is particularly dangerous. This is especially true when the drug is crushed and snorted, because this method of ingestion stops the time-release action and delivers every milligram of the narcotic to the brain at once. In large-enough doses, or in sensitive individuals, OxyContin can suppress the respiratory system and slow down breathing to the point of coma and death.

Symptoms of an OxyContin overdose include slow breathing, small (pinpoint) pupils, mental confusion, dizziness, weakness, seizures, cold or clammy skin, loss of consciousness, coma, and death.

In April 2002, the U.S. Drug Enforcement Agency reported that more than four hundred deaths had been linked to OxyContin.

■ **RITALIN:** Experts agree that it is difficult to take Ritalin in doses large enough to kill you. It is possible to overdose on the drug, however, and symptoms of an overdose include agitation, confusion, convulsions, elevated blood pressure and body temperature, flushing, hallucinations, headache, muscle twitching, tremors, and vomiting.

- **SEDATIVES:** Overdoses on sedative drugs are not uncommon among adolescents.

January 2002: According to the Philadelphia Police Department, twenty-eight middle school students in Philadelphia, Pennsylvania, were treated at local hospitals after ingesting the benzodiazepine Xanax. A thirteen-year-old stole a bottle of one hundred Xanax tablets from a relative and distributed the tablets during school hours.

Dangerous Combinations

Combining prescription drugs with any other drug—including other prescription drugs, over-the-counter drugs, alcohol, marijuana, cocaine, heroin, hallucinogens, and/or Ecstasy—can be extremely dangerous. Most adolescents who intentionally combine drugs are looking to get blasted, and they want to get there fast—so they often take several drugs at once and then wait to see what happens.

Because there are so many possible combinations, we'll confine our discussion to the drugs adolescents use most often.

- **OXYCONTIN:** When combined with alcohol or other depressant drugs (including over-the-counter drugs such as Coricidin, Robitussin, and NyQuil), the risk of overdose, comas, convulsions, and death increases dramatically.
- **STIMULANTS:** Coming down from stimulant drugs can be extremely painful, especially if you've been taking lots of pills. To ease the pain, many stimulant users take depressant drugs such as alcohol, opiates (prescription painkillers, heroin), marijuana, tranquilizers, or sleeping pills. All these drugs can mellow out the jitters and soften the inevitable crash, but combining stimulants with depressant drugs can slow down breathing to the point of coma and death.

- **SEDATIVES:** Combining sedative drugs with alcohol or other depressant drugs is extremely dangerous and can lead to overdose, coma, convulsions, and death.

Physical Dependence

I like my pills more than I like me, more than I like anybody else. That's the only thing I know that matters.

—ELIZABETH WURTZEL
More, Now, Again

Tolerance

Tolerance can occur with all prescription drugs if the adolescent regularly uses high doses. Tolerance means that the brain and body adapt to the presence of the drug and then need higher and higher doses to achieve the original effects. Once tolerance is established, withdrawal will occur if the adolescent stops taking the drug.

Withdrawal

- **OXYCONTIN:** Withdrawal symptoms are similar to those of heroin, although OxyContin withdrawal is said to be more severe and long lasting than heroin. "It's a living hell, and it goes on for weeks," says one former addict. Withdrawal symptoms include hot and cold sweats, clammy skin, weakness, shaking, buzzing in the head, muscle pain, bone pain, restlessness, involuntary leg movements, severe muscle cramps, diarrhea, fever, vomiting, runny nose and eyes, anxiety, insomnia, and a crushing depression. The physical symptoms often subside within five to ten days—although they can last for thirty days or more—but the depression can linger for weeks, even months. If you are going through withdrawal and do not feel any better after two or three weeks, don't give up—after thirty days, you should be through the worst of it.

Do not attempt to go through OxyContin withdrawal alone. Check yourself into a hospital or a heroin detox center. Withdrawal is simply too painful, and it goes on for too long, to endure it on your own.

- **STIMULANTS:** Stimulant withdrawal can be severe and painful. Withdrawal symptoms, which can last for up to two weeks, include aches and pains, shaking, painful muscle cramps and/or spasms, chills, goose bumps, tremors, nausea, abdominal cramps, diarrhea, weakness, extreme fatigue, insomnia, sweating, runny nose and eyes, extreme sensitivity to noise, profound depression, and suicidal thoughts or attempts.
- **RITALIN:** The manufacturer of Ritalin advises physicians to watch for nervousness and insomnia, loss of appetite, nausea and vomiting, dizziness, palpitations, headaches, changes in heart rate and blood pressure (usually elevation of both), skin rashes and itching, abdominal pain, weight loss and digestive problems, psychotic episodes, drug dependence, and severe depression.
- **SEDATIVES:** Withdrawal symptoms include irritability, headaches, sleep disturbances (nightmares, vivid dreams, insomnia), hallucinations, sweating, nausea, stomach cramps, agitation, anxiety, tremors, delirium, intense cravings, elevated heart and respiration rate, and seizures.

How Can I Tell if My Child Is Misusing Prescription Drugs?

Because the signs and symptoms associated with prescription drug use vary so dramatically from one drug group to another, our basic advice here is to become familiar with the lists of short-term and long-term effects of the drugs in this chapter, as well as the withdrawal syndrome associated with these drugs.

Be sure to carefully monitor all prescription medications; if your child has experienced problems with alcohol, marijuana, cocaine, or any other drug (legal or illegal), keep your medications locked up and be on the lookout for missing pills or bottles of pills.

If your child takes Ritalin or Adderall for ADHD, carefully monitor the pills. Some parents put the prescriptions in a locked safe.

If you suspect your child is crushing up and snorting Ritalin, look for paraphernalia, including small spoons, razor blades, mirrors, and glass or metal straws.

PART THREE

What Parents Can Do

I felt helpless. I didn't know where to turn.

Friends said, "Well, if he were my son . . ." or "Yeah, we had that trouble with our oldest boy."

Family said, "Why doesn't he go live with Uncle Joe in Kentucky?"

Neighbors said, "You've got to get a handle on that kid."

The judge said, "Maybe if we lock him up, he'll learn his lesson."

But nothing helped me see the light at the end of the tunnel. I was searching for a handle to hold on to, a lifesaver for a drowning victim, help instead of pity or, worse, shame and blame. Everyone had an answer, but nothing worked.

—LENNA, *forty-five*

Because alcohol and other drugs affect the brain and body in such profound ways, adolescents and their parents need help, and they need it before serious, life-threatening problems emerge. The widely accepted myth that adolescents in trouble with drugs need to hit bottom before they can successfully turn their lives around is a misguided and potential deadly strategy. If help is delayed until kids are kicked out or flunk out of school, relationships with family members are strained to the breaking point, criminal behaviors (stealing, truancy, possession of drugs, drug dealing) have earned them a reputation as "bad kids" and "lost causes," or drugs have damaged their brains and/or livers, then it has been delayed too long. According to the authors of *Changing for Good*:

> By the time they hit bottom they may be so demoralized and physically debilitated that they do not care about changing. They don't know where, much less have the ability, to begin. . . . Research shows that problems are almost always treated more effectively when they are less rather than more severe, and when they are of shorter rather than longer duration. The longer people wait to change, the more difficult change becomes.

Adolescents who are still in school, who can think clearly enough to slide by with C's and D's in their schoolwork, who pass their physicals, and who have not gotten into any serious problems at school, home, or work may insist that they do not have a problem and stubbornly refuse to get help. They may lie, steal, and cheat to protect their right to continue to use drugs, and they may seem not to care when family members and friends retreat in frustration, anger, or even disgust.

But their deceptions, thoughtlessness, and irresponsibility are no indication that intervention and treatment* will fail. No matter how fiercely adolescents fight those who are trying to help them,

---

*By *treatment*, we mean any number of diagnostic, intervention, and clinical services ranging from once-a-week individualized counseling sessions with an appropriate, credentialed professional to daily or weekly group therapy, family therapy, outpatient treatment, and/or residential (inpatient) treatment lasting from one to six months or more.

they can be helped. In fact, research shows that forcing adolescents to get help for their drug problems is at least as effective as voluntary treatment. Decades of research and clinical experience confirm that adolescents who are coerced into treatment are just as likely to stay sober as adolescents who decide on their own to seek help.

For many adolescents, this coercive force is supplied by the juvenile justice system. In the last ten years, more adolescents have been referred to treatment by the juvenile justice system than by any other source. As the research linking drug use and criminal behavior accumulates, juvenile courts are responding to the scientific facts with enlightened attitudes and policies. Probation officers are recognizing that alcohol and other drugs are often a central factor in juvenile offenses and that many, if not most, of the kids on their caseload are using. Requesting a professional drug assessment for youths convicted of crimes ranging from shoplifting to violent assault is becoming the rule rather than the exception.

The juvenile justice system is now on the front line, advocating for intervention, treatment, and continuing care services for adolescents in trouble with drugs. Enlightened attitudes are also changing policies and programs in our nation's school systems, which are doing away with punitive zero-tolerance policies and focusing on helping kids and families with drug problems through innovative programs and school-based support groups.

Mental health professionals are working hand in hand with chemical dependency experts to address adolescents' physical, mental, emotional, and spiritual needs. Clergy members are reaching out to drug-involved youths, offering support services, counseling, and referrals. And physicians, encouraged by addiction medicine specialists, are recognizing the critical importance of routinely screening children and teenagers for alcohol, tobacco, and other drug use.

Discussion of alcohol, tobacco, and other drug use should be part of the routine health care of all infants, children, and adolescents. Physicians must have a high index of suspicion, as signs and symptoms may be subtle, with numerous manifestations expressed through the pediatric age range.

—MICHELLE PICKETT, M.D.

Parental involvement in this multilevel process of education, assessment, intervention, treatment, and continuing care is essential. Our children desperately need us—more than they need their friends and peers, more than they need their most prized material possessions, more than they need drugs, our children need our compassion, love, support, and firm guidance.

In the next seven chapters, we offer parents, relatives, and other concerned individuals the information they will need to collaborate with teachers, school administrators, physicians, mental health counselors, probation officers, lawyers, clergy members, treatment specialists, and the community as a whole to create appropriate, effective, lifesaving programs to help kids in trouble with drugs.

Sometimes we take a wrong turn. We make mistakes. Sometimes we keep making mistakes. But we're good, in our hearts. We want to do good.

Don't give up on us. If you give up on us, where will we be?

—EVIAN, *sixteen*

Seeing the Problem

Many adults trivialize how bad these drugs really are. They say it's just pot or booze, what's the big deal? But it is a big deal when it involves children.

—MARC FISHMAN, M.D.

It isn't that they can't see the solution. It is that they can't see the problem.

—G. K. CHESTERTON

Your child uses drugs—you know that much.
    Your child is in trouble with drugs—you are also fairly certain about that fact.

But is the problem serious enough to require intervention and treatment? Does your child need professional help? How can you know for sure?

In this chapter, we will help you see the problem by looking at the widespread effects drugs have on emotions, thoughts, personality, physical appearance, and general behavior. When kids use drugs regularly and/or in large amounts, their behavior is affected in certain characteristic ways. And when the brain and body become dependent on drugs—literally, physically needing the drug to function normally—certain telltale symptoms emerge.

Because many of the signs and symptoms listed below can be attributed to adolescence itself, you will need to consider both the quantity of symptoms and progressive deterioration over time. Most healthy, high-functioning teenagers will not experience a large number of these symptoms—even if they are having a tough time negotiating adolescence—and if they do, their problems will tend to improve as they mature and become increasingly capable of making reasonable, sound decisions. Drug-using kids, on the other hand, will spiral downward over a period of weeks, months, or years as drugs gradually eat away at their personalities, judgment, reason, motivation, sense of self, compassion for others, and love of life.

> For me it was just a gradual erosion of my love, my love for everything from human beings to the planet to the animals on the planet. All of my love was slowly eroded because everything was replaced over a ten-year period with only one thing: using.
>
> —ANTHONY KIEDIS

The A to Z of Adolescent Drug Use and Addiction

- **ANXIETY:** Anxiety is universal in adolescents who use drugs regularly. Many drugs cause physical changes (increased pulse rate, sweating, rapid heartbeat) that contribute to anxiety, and all addictive drugs can cause feelings of apprehension, dread, fear, and paranoia, especially during withdrawal. Other symptoms of anxiety include irritability, emotional instability, mood swings, mental confusion, and panic attacks.

Nutritional deficiencies may be contributing to the adolescent's anxiety. Alcohol is notorious for causing blood-sugar ups and downs that contribute to symptoms such as irritability, mood swings, nervousness, and constant worrying. Adolescents who use stimulant drugs such as amphetamines, methamphetamines, or cocaine tend to eat poorly due to these drugs' ability to suppress appetite; when they do eat, they often feast on fat-laden and sugar-rich foods.

- **BLOODSHOT EYES:** Alcohol, marijuana, and inhalants cause tiny blood vessels in the eyes to swell and burst, leading to red, bloodshot eyes. Stimulant drugs interrupt normal sleep patterns, another cause of bloodshot eyes. Regular drug users often attempt to disguise their red eyes by wearing sunglasses, or they use eyedrops to "get the red out."

- **CRAVING:** Kids call it "feening" or "fiending," and like all the symptoms in this A-to-Z list, craving gets worse as drug use intensifies. In the beginning, craving is related to the benefits associated with using—the adolescent desires the pleasure, euphoria, relaxation, and/or stimulation associated with using drugs as well as the good times associated with drinking and partying with friends.

  If the adolescent is addicted to drugs, craving becomes a true physiological need or imperative—the adolescent literally physically needs the drug because his or her brain cells have adapted to its presence and cannot function normally without it.

I can't even talk about drugs without wanting them. Man, my hands are sweating. I'm dying here. I mean it. I need my drugs. It's not even so much that I want them, because I want to quit using, I really do. It's just that I need them.

—KIRBY, *sixteen*

- **DENIAL:** Adolescents deny that they have a drug problem for several reasons. First, "the problem" seems so minor, so easy to control, and so universal. "Sure, yeah, I drink a lot, but everybody drinks—what else is there to do in this town?"

Many adolescents deny they have a problem in order to protect their right to keep using.

You don't want to be addicted, so you don't think about it. You don't listen to people. You don't want to admit it might be true.

—MARK, *fifteen*

Denial may also be a natural, even logical reaction to labels such as "druggie," "drug addict," and "chemically dependent." Most people think of drug addicts as homeless, helpless drunks clutching their brown paper bags or heroin addicts nodding off in the corner of a seedy hotel room. Adolescents match the face staring back at them in the mirror with the stereotypical image of the drug addict and conclude, "Not me."

Look at me—do I look like a druggie? I don't drink in the morning. I don't shoot up on heroin. I don't need drugs—I just love them.

—FRANK, *seventeen*

- **EMOTIONAL HIGHS AND LOWS:** Emotions change rapidly and often take uncharacteristic forms. Adolescents who are normally shy and sensitive may become loudmouthed and belligerent. Friendly, outgoing kids become hostile and paranoid. Intense emotional ups and downs involving depression, anxiety, fear, paranoia, and agitation are often associated with the withdrawal syndrome. Feelings of inferiority and incompetence ("I'm a failure"; "I'm not normal") are also common. When the adolescent is forced to stop using for days or weeks at a time due to illness, family vacations, treatment, or incarceration, emotional highs and lows may increase and cravings for drugs may intensify.

- **FEAR:** As drug use continues, feelings of anxiety and fear gradually metamorphose to suspiciousness, dread, panic, and an overall sense of despair. Paranoia and hostility are particularly acute in adolescents addicted to methamphetamines or cocaine.
- **GASTROINTESTINAL (GI) COMPLAINTS:** The gastrointestinal system—basically all the organs involved in processing food and eliminating wastes—is hit hard by drug use. Symptoms of GI distress may include indigestion, constipation, diarrhea, abdominal cramping, nausea, vomiting, and loss of appetite.
- **HARDHEADEDNESS:** Adolescents who regularly use drugs are notoriously hardheaded—stubborn, willful, headstrong, and obstinate. Every conversation, it seems, ends in a fight. This is fairly typical adolescent behavior but with a twist, for even the simplest questions—"Are you ready for school?"; "Did you do your homework?"; "Have you returned your grandfather's phone call?"—can lead to full-scale battles.

  While we're talking about hard heads, we need to mention the risk of head injuries. A high percentage of adolescents who use drugs regularly will experience a head injury—from motor vehicle accidents to skateboarding while high on acid or " 'shrooms," falling down the stairs when drunk, and violent fights fueled by drug-induced paranoia. (See chapter 4, pages 55–57 for a discussion of head injuries.)

  Headaches, often fierce and long lasting, are also common in kids who use drugs frequently or in large amounts.
- **INSOMNIA:** Drugs interfere with normal sleeping patterns and can cause insomnia, restlessness, interrupted sleep, and vivid nightmares. In an attempt to fix the problem and catch up on sleep, adolescents may use calming or sedating drugs. Those addicted to alcohol, inhalants, marijuana, or prescription painkillers or sedatives often use before

bedtime, believing that the drugs help them sleep. They are much more likely, however, to experience a restless night due to withdrawal symptoms that occur as the drug is metabolized and eliminated from the bloodstream.

- **JOYLESSNESS:** As drug use continues and escalates, feelings of gloom and doom begin to cloud every aspect of life. Relationships with family members, friends, teachers, and coaches are strained or broken, contributing to feelings of despair. Formerly cheerful and energetic behavior gives way to episodes of weeping, guilt, shame, grief, and depression, which become more frequent and more severe as drug use escalates.

- **KEEPING TO ONESELF:** Adolescent drug users begin to spend a great deal of time alone, locked in their rooms, engrossed in their computers or e-mail accounts, or listening to music (often with headphones, to ensure complete isolation). As drug use escalates, the adolescent may become increasingly tight-lipped and secretive. Phone calls and e-mails are jealously guarded. Doors are locked, even bolted. Attempts by parents to find out where the adolescent is going or whom he or she is hanging out with are met with outright lies and deception or angry commands to "mind your own business." (For an accurate, harrowing portrayal of this aspect of adolescent drug-using behavior, watch the movie *Life As a House*.)

- **LEGAL PROBLEMS:** Kids in trouble with drugs are much more likely to be suspended or kicked out of school, run away from home, lie, steal, assault others, take a car without parental permission, and/or drive without a license. Because adolescent drug users typically hang out with other adolescent drug users, they are much more likely to get caught drinking at parties, stashing drugs and/or drug-related paraphernalia in their pockets or backpacks, driving under the influence, getting a "dirty UA" (a urine test that indicates recent drug use), or smoking weed in their cars or backyard alleys—or, as some adolescents claim, in the school parking lot or baseball dugouts. The list of possible offenses goes on and on.

- **MONEY PROBLEMS:** Both legal drugs (alcohol and tobacco products) and illegal drugs are expensive. Take the drug nicotine, for example. Cigarettes cost about five dollars per pack. An adolescent who smokes ten cigarettes a day will spend about seventeen dollars a week, seventy-five dollars a month, or nine hundred dollars a year on cigarettes.

Alcohol isn't cheap, either, and most adolescents who drink, drink a lot. Not many adolescents—addicted or not—limit their partying to one or two bottles of beer.

Marijuana is expensive. A daily marijuana user may spend ten, twenty, fifty, or several hundred dollars a week on high-quality (chronic) weed.

Methamphetamines are relatively cheap, but they are also highly addictive, and many meth addicts use other drugs to alleviate the nasty side effects. If you're on a meth binge, you won't be able to hold down a job, which is one more way to put a hole in your pocket.

Cocaine and heroin are relatively expensive, although the cost has been going down in recent years.

Prescription painkillers such as OxyContin and Vicodin can range between five and one hundred dollars on the street. Ritalin tablets cost between two and twenty dollars when sold illegally.

Adolescents who regularly use drugs go through cash fast. If they become addicted, they may have to use more of the drug to feel the same effects and/or to delay the pain and misery of withdrawal.

Where do kids get money for drugs? They sell their possessions (CDs, DVDs, laptops, video games, jewelry, clothes); they steal money from parents, friends, or relatives; or they start dealing.

- **NERVOUSNESS:** When adolescents use regularly, they are often apprehensive, tense, restless, and jittery. Stimulant drugs such as cocaine, amphetamines, and methamphetamines are most likely to cause physical agitation when the user is high, and all addictive drugs can create jittery nerves during the withdrawal period. Even nonaddicted users will experience shaky hands, tense muscles, and feelings of anxiety and mental confusion after a heavy night of partying.

- **OBLIVION**: Adolescents in trouble with drugs are typically preoccupied, forgetful, and absorbed in their own thoughts. They are literally in their own little world. Careless with their own safety, thoughtless and inconsiderate of others, they seem not to care at all about what others do or think.

  "The only thing that really matters is drugs—getting them, using them, getting more of them," one former user explains. "Everything else fades into oblivion."

- **PROMISES BROKEN**: "I promise I'll cut back." "I promise I'll stay out of trouble." "I promise I'll study harder." Adolescents may sincerely make promises that they are then unable to keep because the addiction subverts their best intentions. That clash between wanting to do the right thing and being unable to follow through on a heartfelt promise often fills the adolescent with shame, guilt, and despair.

- **QUIRKY BEHAVIORS**: While adolescents have always been well known for their bizarre behaviors, hairstyles, and clothing styles—remember the headbands, face paints, and wild outfits of the 1960s?—adolescent drug users tend to go to extremes. Strange or bizarre body movements or gestures including jittery hands and feet, constant lip licking, and scratching or picking at the skin are common. Sudden and dramatic changes in clothing or hairstyles also may be a sign of trouble.

- **RESENTMENTS**: Drug use seems to breed resentment. Old friendships are abandoned in fury or exasperation. The slightest criticism is met with defensiveness and hostility. Grudges are held for weeks or months. Feelings of annoyance, antagonism, and bitterness seem ever-present.

And blame is big—if it's not the teacher, coach, parents, cops, or probation officers who are causing the problem, it's "the system," the community, or the world itself. Blaming others takes the spotlight off the adolescent's drug use, and kids can convince themselves that the real problem exists outside them. "I hate the world," says an eighteen-year-old who regularly uses marijuana, Ecstasy, and hallucinogens. "And I hate all the hypocritical, dishonest, miserable people in it, which is just about everyone."

- **SHAME:** As relationships with family members and friends are strained or ruptured, adolescents' resentments are compounded by intense guilt and shame. While they may try to hide their inner feelings, kids in trouble with drugs often feel inadequate, abnormal, worthless, powerless, and out of control. They may believe they are no good and conclude that they are truly bad kids or lost causes, as they have so often been called. When they get high, they can mask these feelings for a short time, but inevitably shame returns, along with feelings of self-contempt and self-hatred. Mired in self-loathing, many adolescent drug users consider or attempt suicide.

Yet experiences of shame can be positive, even redemptive, forcing adolescents to face the conflict between the person they are and the person they want to become.

Shame interrupts any unquestioning, unaware sense of oneself. But it is possible that experiences of shame if confronted full in the face may throw an unexpected light on who one is and point the way toward who one may become. Fully faced, shame may become not primarily something to be covered, but a positive experience of revelation.

—HELEN MERRELL LYND
On Shame and the Search for Identity

Not every adolescent addicted to drugs will admit to feeling shame, and some never feel remorse or regret about their behavior and its effect on people they love. This lack of conscience may be a sign of deeper emotional problems.

- **TEMPER TANTRUMS:** Temper tantrums are not uncommon among adolescents, but when drugs are involved, sudden violent outbursts are often unprovoked and may occur on a regular basis. The adolescent seems to be angry and annoyed all the time and is often difficult to reason with, restrain, or pacify.

- **UNDERACHIEVEMENT:** This is one of the classic symptoms of drug addiction—kids who once had great energy and potential suddenly couldn't care less about school, grades, old friends, family relationships, or the future.

  Adolescent drug users often stop studying, and their grades drop precipitously. They seem to be unconcerned with the future and are quick to renounce longtime goals such as going to college or finding a steady summer job. They sit passively and watch TV, listen to music, or play video games, and they refuse to become involved in hobbies, sports, or outside activities. All these behaviors may be symptomatic of drug use and addiction.

- **VIOLENT EPISODES:** Certain drugs—alcohol, cocaine, methamphetamines, and PCP, for example—are more likely to make users aggressive and potentially violent. Research shows that alcohol is the drug most likely to cause violent behavior in users. Combining drugs can also lead to paranoid, hostile, aggressive, and violent behaviors.

  Physical and emotional instability increase during the withdrawal period, often leading to violence against others or self-abuse.

- **WEIGHT CHANGES:** Rapid weight loss or sudden weight gain may be a sign of regular drug use. Adolescents who regularly use stimulant drugs such as cocaine and methamphetamines tend to lose weight fast. Kids who regularly use marijuana tend to gain weight, for marijuana is relaxing and kids like to kick back even as they beat a path to the refrigerator to satisfy the munchies. Lack of interest in food, obsession with high-sugar or high-fat foods, and rapid weight loss or weight gain may be warning signs of drug use and possible addiction.

- **XENOPHOBIA:** Xenophobia is a fear or hatred of anything foreign or strange. Many adolescents tend to be distrustful of adults in general, but regular drug use often exacerbates suspicion and paranoia, pulling the adolescent inward, away from others, and creating a sense of alienation and animosity toward strangers or anything out of the ordinary.
- **YEARNING:** A craving for peace and serenity and a longing to be normal are common in adolescents who use drugs.

I never felt "normal" before I started drinking and smoking weed. I didn't realize that until I started using and suddenly felt so much better. It was like a cloud lifted, like I was floating. I thought, "This is the way life should be!" So all you people who are trying to tell me that I have a problem with drugs—you're all wrong. It's only when I'm sober that I feel bad. When I use—that's when I feel on top of the world.

—CHRISTINA, *sixteen*

This yearning can be filled in the short term by drugs and/or material possessions, but inevitably feelings of emptiness—a void at the very center of their being—returns. "At the innermost core of all loneliness is a deep and powerful yearning for union with one's lost self," writes Irish author Brendan Francis. No substance on this earth works as quickly and efficiently as drugs do to separate the body from the soul and the individual from the rest of society.

- **ZONED:** All addictive drugs alter brain chemistry to one extent or another, pulling users into a different reality.

Adolescents high on drugs or in withdrawal from drugs may appear zoned out, spacy, distracted, and off in some other world.

Now that you have read through the A-to-Z list, go back and underline or highlight those descriptions that apply to your child. Looking at those highlighted sections, ask yourself: "Is this normal adolescence, or is something else going on?"

C. S. Lewis once wrote, "It is not until we know our own face that we can turn it towards the light." Understanding the ways in which alcohol and other drugs can create a one-size-fits-all mask that covers the adolescent's body, mind, heart, and soul marks an important first step in the journey to find appropriate, effective help for your child.

Getting Help:
Follow the L.E.A.D.
Guidelines

> There can be no acting or doing of
> any kind, till it be recognized that
> there is a thing to be done; the thing
> once recognized, doing in a thou-
> sand shapes becomes possible.
>
> —THOMAS CARLYLE

A dolescents in trouble with alcohol and/or other drugs want help. They may deny it to your face and tell you that you are the problem. Furious with your "stupid rules," they may pull away in frustration and disgust. Angry that you presume to know what is happening inside them, they will tell you to go away and leave them alone.

> You think you know me. You go around saying you know how I
> feel and you know what I think. But I'm not like everyone else.
> You don't know the first thing about me.
>
> —CARLOS, *seventeen*

They may swear at you and scream at you, and they may even physically attack you. They will almost certainly blame their growing list of problems on you, their teachers, friends, probation officers, lawyers, judges, or the world itself.

> Everybody is driving me up the wall—my grandmother, my drug counselor, my probation officer, even my so-called friends. It's just a screwed-up world. Adults have no idea what it's like for kids these days. Drugs help us cope. I can quit anytime I want, I just don't want to quit. I wish everybody would just leave me alone.
>
> —STACY, *sixteen*

Yet most adolescents in trouble with drugs know, with a deep kind of knowing, that they are lying to you and to themselves. Filled with anxiety, afraid they are not normal, knowing they are in terrible trouble, sick and tired of the lying and covering up, they hang on, helplessly, to the illusion of control.

> I smoke marijuana every day but weed doesn't do much for me anymore. I get high for a little while but then I wonder if getting high is worth all the stuff that's happening in my life. At home, I just walk past my parents—we don't talk to each other, we don't even look at each other.
>
> I love my parents, and they love me. I know they're scared about what's happening to me, and I'm scared, too. But I'm not ready to quit. Someday, maybe. Maybe when I'm eighteen. But not yet.
>
> —ALLEN, *sixteen*

Printed words cannot convey the pain in Allen's voice or the lost, haunted look in his eyes. He knows that marijuana use is destroying his relationships with his parents, teachers, former coaches, and childhood friends. A smart kid, he's failing most of his courses and is in danger of being expelled from school. A former soccer player, he doesn't have the lung power to run fifty yards without wheezing and feeling sick to his stomach. Remembering his past, when he was happy and energetic and loved spending time with his family, he promises himself that he will stop using. He even quit several times, once for two months, but he always starts using again.

Like most adolescents who have experienced serious problems related to their drug use, Allen wants to stop using because drugs are slowly but surely taking his life away from him. But he can't stop, at least not for very long, because the only time he feels really good—normal, relaxed, at home in his own skin—is when he's high. "How can I give up getting high, hanging with my friends, kicking back for a few hours?" he wonders. "Why should I give up drugs when I'm only sixteen years old? What kind of life would I have if I didn't drink or smoke weed?"

Allen's story is typical of many adolescents. He knows drugs are causing problems in his life, and he wants to quit or at least cut back. He wants to be in control, but he seems to be losing control. And he keeps using despite the fact that his life is falling apart.

As parents, our job is to recognize that a problem exists and then use all our skills and compassion to help motivate our child to change. Change progresses through stages, and the adolescent's readiness to change is influenced by both internal and external factors.

> Readiness to change generally is viewed as involving a balance of internal experiential contingency motivations (such as social frustration; symptoms of intoxication or withdrawal; loss of achievements, interests and enjoyment; unpleasant or frightening experiences, including violence, victimization, high-risk motor vehicle use, or unwelcome sexual experiences) and external contingency motivations (such as parental mandates, legal threats, drug testing, peer group affiliations and influences, and loss of status).
>
> —MARC FISHMAN, M.D.
> *Addiction Medicine Specialist*

Motivating adolescents to change usually begins when they are actively resistant to change—this is the stage known as precontemplation, as detailed in the book *Changing for Good*. In the "stages of change model," change then evolves through the stages of contemplation (struggling to understand the problem), preparation (planning to take action), action (modifying behavior and surroundings), maintenance (commitment to a new life or behavior), and recycling (learning from relapse). At each stage, there are unique challenges and opportunities.

No one is in a more powerful position to motivate your child to change his or her life than you are. In the past, you may have been blinded by love, fear, anger, or ignorance. You may have said and done things that you deeply regret. You have almost certainly made mistakes.

But every day offers new hope for change for both you and your child. To help you focus your energies as you prepare to seek help for your family, we have created the L.E.A.D. Guidelines:

L: Listen
E: Educate
A: Avoid moral judgment
D: Develop emotional detachment

Listen

An old saying reminds us that we are given two ears and one mouth so that we will talk only half as much as we listen.

Of all the gifts that parents can offer their children, there is no greater gift than the ability to listen. Why is listening so important? Adolescents understand the most important reasons:

> When someone listens to me—really listens—I feel like I can stop fighting. I just sort of melt inside and all my anger goes away. It's weird, but I suddenly feel at peace.
>
> —RON, *seventeen*

My mother is a good listener, but then she always ends up giving me advice. Sometimes I just want her to listen and not say anything. Just listen. Can parents do that?

—BEN, *fifteen*

My parents never listen to me. Sure, they let me talk sometimes, but then they just go right on with their agenda. It's as if I'm not even there. Sometimes I feel like I'm a stick person to them.

—NATALIE, *fourteen*

To become a better listener, try these simple strategies:

- **CONVEY YOUR SINCERE DESIRE TO UNDERSTAND WHAT YOUR CHILDREN ARE THINKING AND FEELING.** Invite your child into a discussion—not a lecture—and be sure to give him or her time and space to talk.
- **ASK QUESTIONS THAT MOTIVATE YOUR CHILDREN TO EXPLORE THEIR THOUGHTS AND FEELINGS:** For example, you might ask, "What would you have done in that situation?" or "What qualities within you allowed you to see the problem and deal with it so effectively?"
- **LET YOUR CHILDREN TALK WITHOUT INTERRUPTION:** No "ifs, ands, or buts" to this rule. No matter how outrageous the statement, keep your mouth shut and let your children say what they need to say, all the way to the end.
- **WHEN THEY ARE FINISHED TALKING, ASK THEM IF THEY ARE FINISHED TALKING:** This sentence might sound like nonsense, but if you are sure your child has said everything he or she wanted to say, then you are free to respond.
- **REPEAT BACK TO THEM WHAT YOU THINK THEY SAID:** In this way, you will make sure your child agrees you have heard and understood his or her concerns. For

example, you might say: "Do you get the sense that I'm listening to you and that I hear what you are trying to say?" Or you might preface your statements with words such as, "Correct me if I'm wrong, but I think you might be saying . . ." or "Help me fill in the blanks—so far it seems to me that you are concerned about . . ."

These simple strategies invite your child to a discussion rather than a lecture, communicating that you are willing to learn, to be taught, to change your mind, and even, perhaps, to admit that you might be wrong. Listening well builds trust, for your child learns that you honor his or her thoughts and feelings as valid.

In his classic book *On Becoming a Person*, psychologist Carl Rogers suggests a relatively simple strategy to help people strengthen their listening skills:

> The next time you get in an argument . . . just stop the discussion for a moment and for an experiment, institute this rule: "Each person can speak up for himself only after he has first restated the idea and feeling of the previous speaker accurately, and to that speaker's satisfaction." You see what this would mean. It would simply mean that before presenting your own point of view, it would be necessary for you to really achieve the other speaker's frame of reference—to understand his thoughts and feelings so well that you could summarize them for him. Sounds simple, doesn't it? But if you try it you will discover it is one of the most difficult things you have ever tried to do. However, once you have been able to see the other's point of view, your own comments will have to be drastically revised. You will also find the emotion going out of the discussion, the differences being reduced, and those differences which remain being of a rational and understandable sort.

Remember—by your good listening, you build a relationship based on honesty and trust. And you teach your children how to be good listeners, a skill that is essential to developing honest, empathic relationships with everyone in their lives.

Educate

Ignorance and misconception about drugs and addiction are rampant in our society. Even people who are in a position to know a great deal about drugs and their widespread effects on behavior, mood, and personality are often misinformed about the facts.

We live in a society that continues to view drug users and addicts as irresponsible, immature, self-centered, and manipulative human beings. Most people believe alcoholism and other drug addictions are a symptom of a moral failing, character flaw, or serious personality problem.

Your efforts to find appropriate help for your child may be thwarted at various twists and turns by people who believe that your child's drug problems are merely symptoms of some deeper emotional or behavioral disorder. Many adolescents in trouble with drugs do suffer from co-occurring emotional and behavioral disorders, but that does not mean their drug problems are not serious and even, perhaps, primary. As your child's most passionate advocate, you have a great responsibility to educate yourself and communicate the facts to others.

Research scientists at Chestnut Health Systems Lighthouse Institute have identified twelve lessons for parents and others who work with drug-involved adolescents. With their permission, we present their findings below:

1. **MANY ADOLESCENTS MATURE out of substance-related problems in the transition into adult role responsibilities.** This fact, however, does not offset the risks of drug-related developmental delays, disability, and/or death. As a parent, you would be ill advised to assume that using drugs is simply a passing phase that will dissipate over time without enduring harm. The line between experimentation and a serious drug problem is poorly understood.
2. **FOR OTHER ADOLESCENTS, regular drug use already constitutes a chronic, debilitating disorder.** In the recently

completed Cannabis Youth Treatment (CYT) study, 41 percent of adolescents diagnosed with marijuana abuse or dependence reported having failed prior attempts to stop using; 25 percent had prior episodes of formal treatment; and 33 percent were readmitted to treatment during the year following their treatment in the CYT study.

3. **MANY FACTORS INCREASE THE RISK of drug-related problems and inhibit the process of maturing out.** The most significant of these factors include a family history of alcohol and other drug problems, early age of initiation of regular use, co-occurring emotional or behavioral problems, and a low level of positive family and peer support. In the presence of these factors, drug-involved adolescents may need significant and ongoing support to initiate and sustain recovery.

4. **THE EARLIER THE INTERVENTION (in terms of both age and months or years of use) with a substance-use disorder, the better the clinical outcomes and the shorter the addiction career.** These research findings point to the potential usefulness of standardized screening and assessment instruments for early identification of drug problems, and the need for strong connections between schools and addiction treatment and recovery resources.

5. **THERE ARE EVIDENCE-BASED BRIEF THERAPIES that are effective for many drug-involved adolescents.** In a twelve-month follow-up of six hundred adolescents who completed between five and thirteen sessions of outpatient treatments, 24 percent achieved a sustained recovery or achieved recovery after one or more brief post-treatment relapses.

6. **RELAPSE IS OFTEN A PART OF THE PROCESS of long-term recovery and, as with other chronic diseases, multiple interventions may be required to resolve severe and persistent substance-use disorders.** Treatment results in significant enhancements in emotional health and improved functioning in the family, school, and community, and reduced use of alcohol and other drugs.

7. **NOT ALL TREATMENT PROGRAMS** are the same. Programs with the best clinical outcomes:

- Treat a larger number of adolescents.
- Have a larger budget.
- Use evidence-based therapies—those therapies that have been proven effective by scientific research.
- Offer specialized educational, vocational, and psychiatric services.
- Employ counselors with two or more years of experience working with adolescents.
- Offer a larger menu of youth-specific services (such as art therapy or recreational services).
- Are perceived by clients as empathic allies in the recovery process.

8. **MOST ADOLESCENTS ARE PRECARIOUSLY BALANCED between recovery and relapse in the months following treatment.** The period of greatest vulnerability for relapse is in the first thirty days following treatment; adolescents' status at ninety days following treatment is highly predictive of their status at one year following treatment.

   The fragility of early recovery is underscored by the fact that few treated adolescents participate at any significant level in professionally directed continuing care groups or mutual aid groups such as Alcoholics Anonymous or Narcotics Anonymous.

9. **THE STABILITY OF RECOVERY is enhanced by post-treatment monitoring and periodic recovery checkups.** Assertive continuing care is characterized by sustained continuity of contact and support, and assumption of responsibility for such contact by the service professional rather than the adolescent. Placing recovery support services within the adolescent's natural environment (recovery homerooms, in-school recovery meetings,

recovery schools) also enhances the adolescent's chances of long-term recovery.

10. **THE ADOLESCENT'S POST-TREATMENT peer adjustment is a major determinant of treatment outcome.** Adolescents who experience major relapses have the highest density of drug users in their post-treatment social environment.

   Adolescents entering recovery often find themselves in a social limbo. They may have been rejected by their nonusing peers, may be trying to disengage from their drug-using peers, and often have yet to establish a peer-oriented recovery network. Finding ways to renegotiate contact with the existing peer network and getting linked to other recovering adolescents may be crucial for adolescents caught between these social worlds. Parents can help manage the risks of this limbo period by supporting involvement in relationships and activities that do not involve alcohol or other drug use. While a change in friends is a common recommendation for adolescents entering recovery, the truth is that few adolescents are able to completely change their social networks. Parents and others need to find ways to work with adolescents' social networks to enlist their support and neutralize their ability to sabotage recovery efforts.

11. **THE POST-TREATMENT HOME ENVIRONMENT plays a significant role in recovery/relapse outcomes.** Parents can do everything right and still have an adolescent relapse following treatment, but there are things you can do to help tip the scales toward post-treatment recovery. We know, for example, that relapse among adolescents is more common in homes with less family cohesion and more family conflict, and where parents are consuming alcohol or other drugs in the home. The best advice we can give parents wishing to support their child's recovery is to:

- Refrain from using alcohol or other drugs in the home.
- Become involved in your child's recovery activities.
- Actively monitor your child's recovery progress.
- Recognize and praise positives in your child's post-treatment adjustment.
- Participate in your own family recovery meetings.
- Help your child develop pro-recovery supports outside the family.

12. **RECOVERY MUTUAL AID NETWORKS (AA, NA, and so on) can offer considerable support for long-term recovery, but they suffer from low teen participation rates and their effect is dependent upon intensity and duration of participation.** Recovery outcomes improve with increased meeting attendance and participation, increased knowledge of a particular recovery program (say, by reading AA literature, or via AA sponsorship), and involvement in pro-recovery social activities.

Because even these basic facts can be extremely complicated, it helps to have written materials that you can share with people who may be misinformed or uneducated about addiction. Use this book as your ally and read through "Resources" at the back, which lists recommended Web sites, books and other publications, and information sources. You may also want to visit our Web site, www.teensundertheinfluence.com, for additional information and links to treatment centers, community resources, and physician referrals.

One final word of advice regarding education: Human beings are often extremely resistant to change, especially when new facts challenge dearly held belief systems. While you can help educate others about adolescent drug use and addiction, your primary responsibility is to make sure your child gets the most effective, appropriate help available, as soon as possible. If you encounter resistance, be willing to look for help elsewhere. If you believe your health care practitioner, counselor, minister, or lawyer is misinformed and un-willing to change his or her mind, do not continue to wage a hope-less battle.

Seek out professionals who understand and accept the scientific facts about adolescent drug use and addiction and who will serve as advocates for you and your family. Your child's physical, emotional, and spiritual health is on the line, and you cannot afford to settle for anything less than the best-educated and best-qualified profes-sionals to guide you in the right direction and keep you company along the way.

Avoid Moral Judgment

Society stigmatizes people with mental health problems. It sepa-rately and differently stigmatizes people with alcohol abuse prob-lems. And society's stigmatization of people with problems with cocaine and marijuana are yet again different. When the person with co-occurring problems gets pushed into the criminal justice system because of ineffective treatment in the community, an addi-tional stigma is tacked on. The person who has been marked as a criminal has a greater burden to bear, as s/he struggles to find an honorable place in society.

—BERT PEPPER, M.D.
Clinical Professor of Psychiatry at NYU Medical School

The adolescent in trouble with drugs is a sick person, not a bad person. Anytime you hear the words *bad kid*, stand ready to defend not only your adolescent but also all adolescents. Turn the blame game on its head and ask, "Where have we failed these kids?" rather than "Where have our kids failed us?"

All chemically dependent people—adolescents and adults alike—need our compassion and understanding. Let them know you care, *really*, *deeply* care about them. Be honest and straightfor-ward, but always try to avoid harsh words, stern looks, and body movements that convey frustration or anger.

Praise kids when they deserve it. Ask for their thoughts and opinions, and make sure you pay attention when these are offered to you. When you make a mistake and say or do something you regret—and you most certainly will—apologize to your child. The words *I'm sorry*, said with genuine sincerity, can do as much to build and strengthen a relationship as the words *I love you*.

Whenever possible, wherever possible, avoid moralizing. Moral judgments, condescending attitudes, and finger wagging only make adolescents more defensive and hostile, pushing them even further away from treatment and recovery. Adolescents in trouble with drugs don't need preachers and lecturers looking down on them and telling them to clean up their act—they need people who understand what is happening to them to offer a helping hand and walk with them out of the darkness into the light.

A true story may help to illustrate the futility of moralizing.

Chad had been incarcerated in the detention center for four weeks when the pastor of his church paid him a Sunday-afternoon visit. After some small talk, the clergyman got straight to his point.

"Chad," he said, staring into the sixteen-year-old's eyes, "your faith must not be very strong."

"Oh, yeah?" Chad asked, immediately on the defensive. "Why do you say that?"

"Because if your faith in God was strong enough, God would cure you of this addiction."

Retelling the story, Chad looked both amused and perplexed. "I can't figure out why he would say that to me. What if I had scoliosis? Would he tell me that my faith was weak and that's why I had a crooked back?"

Chad managed a weak smile. "I don't think so," he said.

Develop an Emotional Detachment

As parents, our primary duties are to love and care for our children. Sometimes those two responsibilities get mixed up and end up canceling each other out. For when we love our kids with such blind passion that we have trouble seeing their problems and innermost struggles, we may find it difficult to care for them in ways that allow them to grow and change.

If you want to help your child, you will need to develop an emotional detachment. If you become embroiled in your child's denials and excuses, the real problem will get sidetracked. If you convince yourself (or allow someone else to persuade you) that you are primarily responsible for causing your child's unhappiness, then you deflect attention from the immediate problem at hand. If your child uses drugs, but you focus exclusively on the emotional or behavioral symptoms as the source of all the trouble, you unknowingly and unwittingly allow the drug problem to continue and escalate.

If your adolescent is addicted to drugs, it may help to personify the disease so that you can see what you are fighting. Treatment professionals sometimes use the following letter, written by an anonymous person, to help alcoholics and other drug addicts understand what they are up against. The words are equally meaningful and powerful for parents, for they help you to see and understand that your child is in enemy hands.

A Letter from Your Disease

Hello My Friend,

I've come to visit once again. I love to see you suffer mentally, physically, spiritually, and socially. I want to make you restless so you can never relax. I want you jumpy, nervous, and anxious. I want to make you agitated and irritable so everything and everybody makes you uncomfortable. I want you to be confused and depressed so that you can't think clearly or positively.

I want to make you hate everything and everybody—especially yourself. I want you to feel guilty and remorseful for the things you have done in the past that you'll never be able to let go. I want to make you angry and hateful toward the world for the way it is and for the way you are. I want you to feel sorry for yourself and blame everything but *me* for the way things are. I want you to be deceitful and untrustworthy. I want you to manipulate and con as many people as you can. I want to make you fearful and paranoid for no reason at all. I want you to wake up during all hours of the night screaming for *me*. You know you can't sleep without *me* . . . I'm even in your dreams!

I want to be the first thing you wake up to every morning and the last thing you touch before you black out. I would rather kill you than help you, and I'll be happy just putting you back in the hospital, another institution, or jail. I'll be waiting for you when you get out. I love to watch you slowly go insane. I love to see all the physical damage that I'm causing you. I can't help but sneer and chuckle when you shiver and shake, when you freeze and sweat at the same time, and when you wake up with the sheets and blankets soaking wet.

It's amusing to watch you make love to the toilet bowl, heaving and retching and not ever able to hold me down. It is amazing how much destruction I can do to your internal organs while at the same time working on your brain, destroying it bit by bit. I deeply appreciate how much you have sacrificed for *me*. The countless good jobs, all the fine friends you deeply cared for—you gave up for *me*. Especially for the ones you turned against yourself because of your inexcusable actions, I am even more grateful.

Your loved ones—your family, the most important people in the world to you—you threw away for *me*. I cannot express in words the gratitude I have for the loyalty you have for *me*. You sacrificed all these beautiful things in life just to devote yourself completely to *me*. But do not despair, my friend, for on *me* you can always depend. And after all you have lost, you can still depend on *me* to take even more.

You can depend on *me* to keep you in a living hell, to keep you mind, body, and soul—for I will not be satisfied until you are dead, my friend.

Sincerely,
Your Disease

Drugs take a tenacious hold on the adolescent's body, mind, and spirit. You will need to be equally tenacious and determined in your efforts to free your child from the addiction's deadly grip. Look for the small miracles—the light of understanding in a child's eyes, the admission of helplessness, the outstretched hand, the unrequested hug, the whispered "thank you," the moments of peace amid the chaos. Lead by example, creating a home where your child will feel accepted as the flawed, imperfect person he or she is.

For we are all struggling, at one level or another, with our imperfections. In a sense, we are all searching for "home," that place where we are accepted with all our warts, blemishes, defects, and flaws . . . where we fit in and belong . . . where *feeling bad* can be turned into *being good*. As noted in *The Spirituality of Imperfection*:

> Home is the place where we can be ourselves and accept ourselves as both good and bad . . . where we can laugh *and* cry, where we can find some peace within all the chaos and confusion, where we are accepted and, indeed, cherished by others precisely because of our very mixed-up-edness. Home is that place where we *belong*, where we *fit* precisely because of our very unfittingness.

Intervention

A mighty flame followeth a tiny spark.

—DANTE

*C*aroline, *seventeen, is an athlete and a gifted student with an IQ in the genius range. She grew up, wealthy and privileged, in a six-thousand-square-foot house in the suburbs of Boston. Her father is a lawyer, and her mother is a preschool teacher.*

Caroline began to use drugs in seventh grade, when she started drinking with other girls at her private school.

Her parents had no idea she was drinking until one December night during her Christmas vacation, when she came home at three in the morning, threw up on the Oriental rug, and then passed out cold, face-down in her own vomit.

The next day the family had a long talk, and Caroline agreed to see a psychotherapist for weekly sessions.

In ninth grade, Caroline started smoking marijuana. She continued drinking and often combined the two drugs.

In tenth grade, Caroline started acting out at school and getting in trouble at home. Her grades began to fall. Her mother scheduled a physical exam with the family doctor, and Caroline convinced him that she had attention deficit hyperactivity disorder (ADHD). He prescribed Ritalin, which she took by the handful or sold to her friends so she could buy more weed.

After a while, she started snorting Ritalin. When she ran out of pills, she started using cocaine.

Cocaine was a great party drug but coming down was no fun, so she drank or smoked weed or took some painkillers to get through the withdrawal anguish. Whenever she was at someone's house for a party, she'd go through the medicine cabinets and take three or four pills out of each prescription bottle. It didn't matter what kind of pills—tranquilizers, sedatives, sleeping pills, painkillers, she liked them all. And she especially liked them in combination with alcohol and weed. Some days she combined three, four, or five drugs at a time.

In eleventh grade, Caroline became obsessed with her weight. She started bingeing and purging. That was also the year she became deeply depressed and started having panic attacks. Her grades continued to fall.

Her parents knew something was terribly wrong, and they also knew that Caroline was experimenting with drugs, but they had no idea how many drugs she was using and how often she was using them. Then, one night, Caroline's best friend called, in tears, and told them how bad it really was.

That phone call pushed Caroline's parents into high gear. They contacted a treatment facility and arranged for a bed date. Three days later, they presented Caroline with her options.

"We love you," her father said, "but we cannot stand by and watch as alcohol and other drugs destroy your life. You can go into treatment right now, today—or you are on your own. We will not pay for any more of your schooling or your expenses unless you agree to get help for your drug problem."

Caroline protested loudly. She swore at her parents, called them names, and accused them of spying on her. She screamed, slammed doors, stomped her feet, and broke down in tears. But in the end, she knew she had no choice. She couldn't make it on her own out there. Without her parents' financial support, she knew she'd be completely lost.

Caroline started outpatient treatment at a highly respected facility. For eight days she stayed clean and sober, but then she started using again. This time her parents told her she would have to go to inpatient treatment. There were fights, arguments, tears, angry accusations, but once again, Caroline knew she had no choice.

She spent three months in treatment. Within a week of her release, she started drinking and popping pills again.

But now her parents had allies. They called Caroline's counselor in the treatment program, who introduced them to the intervention specialist on staff. Together, they planned a formal intervention.

Early on a Sunday afternoon, Caroline came downstairs to find her parents, grandmother, counselor, and the intervention specialist sitting in a semicircle in the living room. The intervention took all of five minutes. Each person said basically the same thing.

"We are here because we care about you. We can't sit back and watch you destroy yourself. You need to get help."

Caroline stood up, walked out of the room, and slammed the door behind her.

Two hours later she called home and said, simply, "I'll go." Later, she told her counselor that it was her grandmother's presence at the intervention that broke her down. "I felt so ashamed. I just couldn't stand the thought that she looked at me and saw a drug addict," Caroline said.

Because Caroline was almost eighteen, she was admitted into the adult treatment program, which included an intensive relapse program. She finished the three-week program and then willingly entered the extended care program for an additional three weeks.

During her stay at extended care, Caroline began to look at the other problems in her life that were standing in the way of her recovery. With her counselor's help, she accepted the fact that her eating disorder was a serious problem and agreed to get help. The day she left extended care, she entered an eating disorder treatment program, where she stayed for an additional forty-five days.

Today, two years later, Caroline is clean and sober. She attends AA and NA meetings several times a week and shares an apartment with a friend who has been sober for five years. Now in her sophomore year in college, she is planning a career in veterinary medicine.

Caroline's story illustrates both the complexity of adolescent drug addiction and the layers upon layers of interventions that often occur before adolescents are able to see their problem and willingly, wholeheartedly, commit themselves to a new way of life. Intervention in Caroline's case—and, in fact, in most cases—involves a series of events and encounters that take place over a period of several months or years. These interventions may be brief and unorganized or they may be carefully planned and rehearsed. Over time, as the family members become educated about addiction and as they realize the dangers involved in ignoring the symptoms or pretending a problem doesn't exist, there is progress. Ups may be followed by downs, good times by bad times, moments of understanding and intimacy by days of anger and resentment, but in the long run the movement is forward.

There is progress because there is honesty. Stripped down to its basics, intervention is nothing less than an ongoing commitment to live with honesty and integrity. As family members become educated about drug use and addiction, they begin to communicate more openly and honestly with each other. Together—or, in some cases, on their own—they agree to stop hiding, lying, deceiving, and denying. And as they face the truth about the adolescent's drug use, they begin to see how the disease has wrapped them up in its lies and deceptions.

As parents begin to understand how the addiction has taken over the adolescent's body, mind, and spirit and threatens to destroy the family as a whole, they resolve to do whatever is necessary to fight back. They see that by protecting their child from the harmful consequences of drug use, they have allowed the addiction to get stronger. And so they resolve to stop shielding the adolescent from the harmful consequences of addiction through their enabling behaviors such as paying all the bills, lending the adolescent money (and not checking up to see how it is spent), cleaning up after messes, lying to cover up problems, denying the addiction to others, rationalizing and minimizing, arguing, pleading, begging, threatening, and bargaining with the adolescent.

Here's how one mother describes her enabling behaviors.

> I protected my son around every corner and every step of the way. I tried to talk his probation officer out of doing his job. I hired expensive lawyers.

I argued, begged, threatened, and bargained. The whole ball of wax. I followed him around in the car, pleading with him to get in. I showed up at his school and walked him to his classes, just to make sure he got there. I begged him to stay away from friends who I knew were drug users.

I threatened him with calling the police, calling his probation officer, telling his grandparents about his drug use. I even threatened him with my own health. "Don't you care about what this is doing to me?" I'd ask him.

"If you stay clean for a month," I told him, "I'll buy you a pool table." I bought the pool table, but he kept on using.

I protected him from every negative consequence I could. I lied like a rug, hoping to protect him. I lied to everybody. I lied until I just couldn't lie anymore.

I just got tired. Tired of fighting, arguing, worrying. And I realized that whatever happened would happen whether I was worried about it or not. I could put hurdles in front of him, but he would jump over them if he wanted to. I realized I couldn't live his life for him, so I decided to let him make his own decisions and his own mistakes and then live with the consequences.

I feel a freedom now that I never felt before. I don't spend my days worrying about what is going to happen. If something happens, I deal with it the best way I know how. I keep repeating to myself the Serenity Prayer and try to accept the things I cannot change and change the things I can.

In her interactions with probation officers, counselors, educators, teachers, and other parents, this mother learned what she could do to help her son and what was beyond her reach as a mere human being. She decided to stop lying and covering up for her son, and in the process she discovered freedom.

Interventions in all their different shapes and forms put a stop to the lying, deceiving, protecting, arguing, bargaining, and threatening. Rather than allowing drugs to control their lives, the family members begin to fight back. As they become educated about drugs and substance-use problems, they can see how their enabling behaviors allow the drug use to continue and escalate. Understanding that the adolescent is ill and does not recognize that fact, they are able to abandon punitive, moralistic, and judgmental approaches and, with compassion and conviction, begin to enforce their "bottom lines."

Bottom Lines

Bottom lines are really enabling behaviors turned inside out. If you have been giving your son money, which he then uses to buy drugs or to go places where he hangs out with other drug-using kids, you make a firm decision to stop financing his addiction.

If you lied to your daughter's teacher in order to help her get a passing grade, you make a commitment to tell the truth from now on.

If you blamed your son's problems on his friends, you refuse to participate in the blame game anymore and focus instead on accepting responsibility for your role in protecting your child.

You take away your child's driving privileges until he agrees to get help for his drug problem.

You tell your child that if she takes the car again without asking, you will call the police—and then, when she takes the car, you call the police.

You stop making excuses for your child's behavior.

Bottom lines work because they take away the protective screens that the family members have erected and, at the same time, they force adolescents to face the harmful consequences of their drug use. Bottom lines are not punishment—they signal your refusal to continue to lie and cover up.

One mother, a recovering alcoholic herself, explains why she decided to "bring the bottom up."

> I wasn't going to wait until my daughter hit bottom. I'm an alcoholic myself, and I know all about bottoms—you can die down

there at the bottom. So I brought the bottom up. I told her she couldn't live in my house anymore if she continued to use drugs. I took her house and car keys away. It wasn't easy, but I am convinced my actions and tough love saved her life.

"Alcoholics and addicts get help not because they see the light, but because they feel the heat," write Jeff and Debra Jay in their book *Love First: A New Approach to Intervention for Alcoholism and Drug Addiction*.

How can parents and others apply the heat? Intervention happens in different ways.

Brief Interventions

When family members, friends, teachers, coaches, or other meaningful people in the adolescent's life express their concerns with honesty and compassion, they are conducting a brief intervention. These brief, informal, and sometimes spontaneous interventions can make a difference if they are presented with love and concern. Here's an example of a close friend expressing her concerns.

> Kate, you are my best friend and that's why I feel the need to talk to you. I'm concerned about your drinking and marijuana use. You told me you were almost raped at a party the other night because you got so drunk. I love you, and I don't want to see terrible things happen to you. Would you be willing to talk to someone? I'll go with you if you want.

If the adolescent refuses your offer of help, experts advise you to respect his or her response and simply repeat that you will always be there if he or she ever wants to talk. In the groundbreaking book *Changing for Good* authors James Prochaska, John Norcross, and Carlos DiClemente explain that helping another person to change requires effort, patience, and strength. They offer an overview of what *not* to do when trying to help:

- **DON'T PUSH SOMEONE INTO ACTION:** Change does not necessarily mean action, and pushing someone into action too soon can backfire. Instead, encourage the person's internal inclination to consider changing.
- **DON'T NAG:** Constant criticism and fault-finding usually backfire and can weaken your special relationship with the person you want to change.
- **DON'T GIVE UP:** If you give up, you send a signal to the adolescent that the problem is not really all that serious after all. Your apathy may be interpreted as unspoken approval of the adolescent's behavior.
- **DON'T ENABLE:** By your well-meaning attempts to soften the damage, you are colluding with the adolescent and strengthening his or her denial. "Enabling continues when the helper fears that any challenge to the [adolescent's] behavior will risk a break in the relationship," the authors conclude. "If the problem is ever to be resolved, however, it will be because the helper dares to intervene."

Brief interventions can happen spontaneously, initiating a dramatic process of internal change that results in a completely new outlook on life. The following story is told by Joanna, seventeen, who started using marijuana and smoking cigarettes in seventh grade and then turned to inhalants, alcohol, prescription painkillers and muscle relaxants, and methamphetamines. Joanna should be graduating from high school this year, but because of her drug problems, she is a beginning sophomore.

I'd been going to a drug class for six months, and my counselor introduced me to Heather, a college student who became my mentor and friend. We have coffee and talk. She's clean, and I really respect that. Well, one day Heather invited me to a poetry reading by Maya Angelou. That was deep for me. Maya was talking about how you can compose your life so that you are fully able to learn, and how others can help you so you can become the best person you can be. I felt like I was hit by lightning. "This is my life," I thought—"what am I doing with it? Where am I going? And if I keep using drugs, will I go where I want and need to go?"

I knew right then I needed to change, and I got serious about staying clean. It hasn't been easy, but it's not the hardest thing either. I enjoy things way more now that I'm clean. I'm happier. It's a genuine happiness, not a fake, drug-induced happiness. I appreciate everything. I notice everything. Like the sun is out. I'm so glad I'm here to see the sun.

Brief interventions by doctors or other health care professionals in a medical setting or emergency room can be extremely effective in motivating adolescents to change. Physicians in the Adolescent Medicine Program at the State University of New York in Syracuse have developed the "Heads First" approach for physicians, emphasizing the need to "get into the adolescent's head" during routine medical examinations. The table below summarizes this holistic approach, which is intended to reveal the nature and consequences of the adolescent's substance use, identify additional problems including screening for conflict or abusive behavior at home, assess specific strengths, and develop a plan for ongoing care.

TABLE 1. The "HEADS FIRST" Approach to Gathering and Organizing Information About the Psychosocial-Medical Issues of Adolescence

Home	Separation, support, "space to grow"
Education	Expectations, study habits, achievement
Abuse	Emotional, verbal, physical, sexual
Drugs	Tobacco, alcohol, marijuana, others
Safety/Sexuality	Hazardous activities, safety belts, helmets, sexual activity, and acting out
Friends	Confidantes, peer pressure, interaction
Image	Self-esteem, looks, appearance
Recreation	Exercise, relaxation, TV, video games

Spirituality	Values, beliefs, identity
Threats/Violence	Harm to self or others, running away

SOURCE: This table, which appears in "Principles of Addiction Medicine" (American Society of Addiction Medicine, 2003), was adapted by Deborah Poteet-Johnson, M.D., and Philomena Dias, M.D., from the "Heads First" mnemonic developed by the Adolescent Medicine Program, State University of New York at Syracuse.

Crisis Interventions

Crisis interventions are more immediate and forceful. When the adolescent or a family member is in crisis—an emergency room admission for an overdose, suicide attempt, drunk driving arrest, minor-in-consumption (MIC) or minor-in-possession (MIP) charge—an intervention can be arranged to provide immediate emergency assistance. The purpose of the crisis intervention is to focus attention on the underlying cause of the emergency—alcohol and/or other drug problems—and direct the adolescent into treatment for the primary problem rather than get sidetracked by mistaken diagnoses, legal entanglements, or court battles.

Court orders and deferred prosecution are extremely effective forms of crisis intervention. Intervention specialists Jeff and Debra Jay tell a story about a family who used a court order to help their daughter:

> A mother was unable to control her seventeen-year-old daughter. The girl had been in trouble with the police and was skipping school. She was addicted to illegal drugs and running off with a twenty-four-year-old boyfriend who was her supplier. The girl was on probation, so we advised the mother to contact the probation officer and bring the girl into court. As is usual in these cases, the judge offered the alternative of treatment instead of juvenile detention. The daughter quickly agreed. The boyfriend disappeared when he learned the parents weren't afraid to use the criminal justice system.

Formal Interventions

And then there are formal interventions, which generally involve several weeks or months of planning and preparation. The first step is to find a counselor or intervention specialist who can guide you through the intervention process, educate you about the disease of addiction, encourage you to build up a support system, and act as a clearinghouse for various resources, including information about successful, disease-based treatment centers and community programs specifically designed to help families cope with drug-related problems.

Thirty years ago, Vernon Johnson, a recovered alcoholic and founder of the Johnson Institute in Minneapolis, detailed the concept and process of intervention in *I'll Quit Tomorrow*. As Johnson explains in his book, intervention is a process of education and enlightenment designed to "bring the bottom up" before drugs destroy everything of value in the addicted person's life. "Early intervention is a must," he writes. "Earlier intervention means less destruction to the chemically dependent person's life and body. More important, it produces a greater likelihood of recovery."

The process of intervention involves several basic rules:

1. **MEANINGFUL PEOPLE must present the facts.** Meaningful people include family members, siblings, and friends; professionals who possess useful information about the adolescent's drug use, such as physicians, clergy members, educators, or probation officers; and, if the adolescent is employed, employers or fellow employees.

   Every member of the intervention team should be an important and respected person in the adolescent's life. Furthermore, each member should be (or become) well informed about the disease, available and ready to help when needed, and emotionally stable so that he or she can assist with the intervention in a positive, constructive way. If the team members decide to employ a professional interventionist, everyone must agree to cooperate and work together with the interventionist.

2. **CAREFUL PREPARATION AND REHEARSAL is essential.** The intervention team selects a chairperson to direct and oversee the formal intervention. All members of the team work together, often over a period of weeks, to prepare and rehearse the sequence of events that will take place and what they will say, both individually and as a team. With the same compassionate, nonjudgmental voice, the team will ask the adolescent to get help for his or her drug problem.

3. **SPECIFIC, FIRSTHAND EVIDENCE is especially convincing.** The most powerful evidence describes specific events that happened in the recent past or that continue to exist. Opinions ("You need to quit"), generalizations ("You've been drinking too much"), and speculations ("I think you might be involved with drug dealers") should be avoided.

Nicholas Pace, M.D., tells about an intervention he arranged for the sixteen-year-old son of one of his patients.

Jacob was using cocaine on a daily basis, and his father and mother suspected the problem was serious. We talked about what we could do, and his parents decided to hire a retired New York City detective to find out exactly what was going on. The detective took photographs of Jacob riding his bicycle to his drug dealer's house and buying the cocaine.

A few days later, Jacob came to see me, thinking he was going to have a routine physical examination. His mother and father were in my office, along with Frank, the detective, who showed Jacob the photographs of his interactions with the drug dealer.

"Your drug dealer is being arrested this afternoon," Frank said. "Out of respect for your mother and father, I'm willing to give you a break. If you agree to go immediately into the treatment program your parents have arranged for you, we won't press charges and you will not be prosecuted."

Jacob agreed to enter treatment, completed the program, and

stayed clean. That was twenty years ago. He's now a successful businessman, happily married and the father of two young boys.

4. **EVERYONE INVOLVED IN THE INTERVENTION** should avoid moral judgments and any tone of censure. Anger and blame must be replaced by honesty and love. A pamphlet published by the Christopher D. Smithers Foundation explains why it's important to verbalize "the love side of intervention."

There have been good times. Recall some of the better of them. There have been triumphs together. . . . Put them in simple, concrete words and mix them into the intervention. . . .

Also, simply tell the loved one that it takes a lot of love and caring to do an intervention at all. Say that it is a sign of how much you really care. Love isn't just for the good times. It is for the bad times as well. And now you are showing love in the bad times by helping him or her to get into treatment. When one is willing to "sweat it out," that's love. Say so.

5. **ALL THE FACTS SHOULD BE USED** to support the reasons why the family members and friends are concerned. These should include both the harmful consequences and the actual chemical consumption. Here's an example:

Jeremy, last Saturday you came home at two in the morning—three hours past your curfew—and when I asked you why you were late, you began to yell at me and swear at me. You even raised your fist as if you were going to hit me. I could smell alcohol on your breath. You drove the car that night.

Your mother and I found beer bottles hidden in your room and an empty bottle of gin in your car.

I am here because I care about you, and I want you to get help before something terrible happens to you.

6. **THE FACTS SHOULD CENTER ON** the adolescent's alcohol and/or other drug use. Highlighting the contradictions or conflicts in values caused by the adolescent's drug use helps to make the point even stronger. For example:

Alison, you are a beautiful, gentle, loving person who would never hurt another soul. But when you started using cocaine, you became a completely different person. Last Saturday night, you told me you hated me. You called me awful, hurtful names, and you threatened to kill me if I told your probation officer that you broke curfew. I love you. I don't want to lose you. Will you get help now?

Keeping a diary of past and present drug-related behaviors and events is extremely helpful. In your diary, list the behaviors you personally witnessed, and the feelings you had about those behaviors. Specific behaviors might include:

- Selfishness, thoughtlessness, carelessness (insensitivity to others, breaking promises).
- Unreliability (neglect of chores, forgotten or broken appointments, overspending money).
- Relinquishing of responsible decision making (procrastination, avoidance).
- Defending alcohol and/or other drug behaviors (denying, minimizing, rationalizing, alibis, blaming, excuses).
- Poor communication (repeating stories, rambling, monopolizing conversations, refusal to discuss issues in a reasonable way).
- Job or school problems (missing school/work, suspended/fired, tardy/late, failing courses).
- Broken promises and disrupted plans due to alcohol or other drug use.

- Emotional and spiritual changes (lack of self-confidence, withdrawal from others, fear, despair, shame, guilt, lack of trust).
- Embarrassing social situations (loud, aggressive, or rude talk, falling asleep at someone's home).
- Dangerous situations (driving under the influence, car accidents, physical fights, falls, head injuries, arrests, overdoses).
- Blackouts and memory blanks (complete or partial loss of memory about events, confusion while under influence).
- Verbal abuse (name calling, cursing, belittling, judging).
- Physical abuse (beating, punching, unnecessary use of force).
- Destruction of property (punching holes in walls, vandalism, breaking furniture).
- Financial irresponsibility (neglecting bills, borrowing money without repayment, writing bad checks).
- Changes in morals/values (dishonesty, stealing, lying, violating personal values).
- Inappropriate sexual behavior (promiscuity, incest, forcing sex, sexual overtures to friends).
- Deterioration in self-care (neglect of personal hygiene, sloppy physical appearance, refusing medical or dental care).
- Differences in personality between intoxication and sober states (Jekyll and Hyde personalities).

7. **THE GOAL OF THE INTERVENTION is to help the adolescent see reality so that he or she can accept help.** Adolescents and adults who are addicted to drugs are out of touch with reality. In the following passage from Vernon Johnson's book, we have changed the word *alcoholic* to *chemically dependent adolescent*:

The people around a chemically dependent adolescent do not realize how little he knows of himself and of his own behavior. He is not confronted by his own actions; many of them he is not even aware of, although those around him assume that he is. They believe that he sees himself as they see him. In point of fact, as the disease runs its course, he is increasingly deluded. He lives with increasing impairment of his judgment, and eventually loses touch with his emotions entirely. He has a conscious and unconscious way of forgetting painful experiences. It is a matter of self-survival. If a person is drug-addicted, by definition he is unable to recognize the fact.

8. **EVERY EXPRESSION OF CARING AND CONCERN should be followed by a suggestion to get help, along with a specific plan for treatment.** It is not enough to tell addicted adolescents that you love them and want to help them—you must have a treatment plan ready.

9. **MAKE PREPARATIONS FOR TREATMENT.** Intervention specialists advise families to make the following preparations far in advance of the actual intervention: (1) Identify financial resources for covering treatment costs; (2) evaluate treatment centers; (3) choose a treatment center; (4) talk to an intake counselor and answer pre-intake questions; (5) make all travel arrangements for the adolescent to get to treatment; (6) determine who should drive the adolescent to the treatment center; (7) pack a bag with everything the adolescent will need in treatment; and (8) after the intervention, call the admissions staff and let them know whether the adolescent has agreed to treatment and when you expect to arrive.

When interventions follow these simple rules, they work. They *always* work—even if the adolescent refuses to go into treatment or relapses soon after treatment. They work because, in the process of learning about drugs and the disease of addiction, family members are released from ignorance, confusion, guilt, shame, and fear. They learn how the drug use has affected their own lives, and they make a commitment to themselves and to each other to stop lying and hiding from the truth. Educated about the disease, they know what must be done to free themselves from its influence. They learn how to communicate with each other and how to talk about their feelings. They discover the importance of community and the need to reach out to others for help and support.

And, as so often happens, the expressions of love and concern break through the adolescent's denial to initiate the process of internal coercion—the inner voice that keeps repeating phrases like "I'm sick and tired of being sick and tired" and "There's help available if I'm willing to consider it."

As you enter this arena and prepare to fight for your child's life, you might find these thoughts comforting.

Many people think intervention is a dirty word. But intervention is an essential part of the recovery process, and if it is set up properly, it never fails. The pain in the family is huge, and if it is left untended—if nothing changes within the family system—it is excruciatingly difficult for the addicted person to get clean and sober and then stay in a recovery program. Intervention opens up everyone in the family to a new way of life.

After I do an intervention, I often accompany the addicted person to treatment. As we sit together and talk, I hear this amazing sense of relief. It's almost as if they are saying, "Thank God. Finally you are here. What took you so long?"

I've actually had people say to me, "Couldn't they have found you earlier? Then I might have been able to keep my job, stay in school, hold on to the people I love, retain my self-respect."

The good news is that once the person is in recovery, he or she can begin to work on all these issues. Intervention leads them to the path—and guides everyone in the family along the way to forgiveness.

—BILL TEUTEBERG
Intervention Specialist with the
Caron Foundation's treatment centers

Treatment

My life was hell, but people kept telling me it could be better. All I
had to do was stay clean, and eventually that's what I did.

I feel so much better now. I want to talk to other kids in trouble with drugs so they can see that they can make it, too. Because
now that I'm doing good, I want everyone to do good.

—MICHELLE, *fifteen*

Maybe one in twenty adolescents actually wants to go to treatment. Most adolescents insist they don't need treatment.
They say they can quit on their own, anytime they want, but they
just don't want to quit. Not yet, anyway. Maybe sometime.

Maybe when I'm 18, I'll cut back.
Maybe when I get a steady job.
Maybe when I get married and have kids.

Not yet, not now, because just the thought of giving up drugs is
frightening, and the idea of treatment makes it all the more terrify-
ing. Having someone stick a label on you—"drug abuser," "alcoholic," "drug addict"—and then forcing you to get help is
downright humiliating and unfair. "Who," adolescents think, "has
a right to judge me, to presume to know what is going on inside
me?"

My mother is making me go to inpatient treatment. I don't want to
go. I hear they make you talk about your feelings there. That's a
bunch of bull. I don't need treatment. I'm not addicted to drugs—
I'm only sixteen! I hate everybody interfering with my life.

—JUAN, *sixteen*

Kids don't like the very idea of treatment. Listening to boring
lectures. Filling out questionnaires. Having counselors dig into
your past. Sitting in a circle with people you've never seen before
in your life and being forced to talk about your feelings. Being separated from friends and family. Getting yanked out of school and
pulled away from everything else that is familiar for weeks or even
months. Losing control over your life. Adolescents think:

Who knows? Maybe these people in treatment are nut cases, religious fanatics, control freaks, or brainwashing experts. Maybe
they'll stereotype me as a typical drug addict, just like every other
drug addict, and never take the time to get to know me as a unique
individual. Maybe they'll think I'm weak-willed, abnormal, or just
plain bad. Maybe they'll say I have a mental problem, or tell me
I'm a lost cause and need to be locked up somewhere. Who are
these people, anyway, and what right do they have to tell me what
to do?

If I go to treatment, all my relatives, friends, teachers, and
coaches will know that I'm being forced to get help. They'll think
I'm weak-willed, that I have no guts, no courage, that I can't
control myself. They'll say I can't handle drugs. It's embarrassing,
stupid, useless. I don't need help. I can quit on my own.

Getting help *is* scary, for all these reasons and more. Perhaps the most frightening part of all is the feeling of being trapped
and powerless. The idea that the school system, probation officers, lawyers, judges, and even their own parents gang up on
them and force them to get help makes adolescents mad. "Who,"
they ask with indignation, "has the right to take away my free
choice?"

It just made me so mad. I couldn't believe it. Who are these people that they think they can make me stop using? Go ahead, lock me up for a month and I'll stop using, no problem. I've stopped for months at a time, it's no sweat for me. But guess what I'm gonna do when I get out of that treatment center? You got it, I'm gonna use drugs. And nobody, nowhere, no matter what they do or say, can stop me.

—BJ, *seventeen*

Drugs, kids will tell you, are the solution, not the problem. Drugs make them feel better, less anxious, more relaxed, happier, calmer. Drugs are the friend—maybe even the best friend—and not the enemy.

Hey, you can't pin my problems on drugs. I wasn't high when I was caught stealing a case of beer. I wasn't fiending for alcohol. I just liked the thrill of stealing and getting away with something. Only this time a grocery store clerk tackled me and now I'm locked up in detention for thirty days.

—JORDAN, *seventeen*

I do much stupider things when I'm not using than when I'm using. I like to jump off cliffs and roofs and second-floor windows, stuff like that. I've messed myself up pretty good, but I was never high when I did those things. Oh, maybe I was high once or twice, but most of the times I do crazy things, I do them sober.

—MARIO, *sixteen*

Parents also have a hard time connecting the dots between the adolescent's drug use and the problems that are related directly or indirectly to using drugs. "How," they wonder, "can I know for sure if my child really needs help? What kind of treatment works best? What exactly goes on in treatment? What if treatment doesn't work after I've spent hundreds, even thousands of dollars?

How do I measure success, since so many kids get out of treatment and start using again in months, weeks, even days?"

In this chapter, we will answer these questions and concerns as we look at the who, what, where, when, why, and how of adolescent treatment and recovery programs:

- Who needs treatment?
- What happens in treatment?
- Where can I find appropriate, effective treatment?
- When should I seek help for my child?
- Why is a formal program of recovery necessary?
- How do I know if treatment "worked"?

Who Needs Treatment?

Here's a general rule: Adolescents and their families need to take action when alcohol and/or other drug use causes serious, recurring problems in their lives.

Getting wasted once a month does not necessarily mean that your child is in serious trouble with drugs. Alcohol and other drugs are toxic—poisonous—to the brain and body, and millions of kids who are not regular users or addicts get into trouble with them. First-time users are often in special danger because they don't know what to expect and they don't know when to stop. For example, approximately 20 percent of the kids who die from sudden sniffing death after inhaling toxic chemicals such as hair spray, air freshener, paint thinner, gasoline, or glue are first-time users.

Drugs are clearly dangerous for all kids, but the key words to remember in determining who needs a structured treatment and recovery program are *continued use despite negative consequences or recurring problems*. What kind of problems are we talking about? Here is a general but by no means all-inclusive list:

- **FAMILY PROBLEMS:** Fights and violent disagreements at home. Deteriorating relationships with parents, siblings, grandparents, and other relatives. Regularly breaking house rules (ignoring curfews; disrespectful language or behavior).

- **FRIENDSHIP CHANGES:** Drops old (straight) friends. Wants to spend all free time away from home. Gives up school and sports activities to just "hang out" or "chill" with friends. Frequent overnights. Refuses to talk about activities with friends. Strong allegiance to and/or defense of friends who are known drug users.

- **PERSONALITY CHANGES:** Gradual or abrupt changes in personality, including irritability, anxiety, depression, belligerence, anger, resentment, defiance, hostility, paranoia, and/or apathy (not caring about what happens in life).

- **PROBLEMS AT SCHOOL:** Skips school (truancy). Numerous sick days. Frequent tardy (late) slips. Gradual decline or rapid deterioration in grades. Teacher complaints about attitude and/or performance. Suspended or expelled from school.

- **CHANGES IN PHYSICAL APPEARANCE:** Lack of interest in appearance. Clothing and hairstyles change dramatically. Lack of concern (or excessive concern) about physical hygiene.

- **ABUSIVE LANGUAGE:** Swearing, slang, or gangster talk. Uses hostile or threatening language with family members.

- **VIOLENT BEHAVIOR:** Physical attacks on family members. Fights at school. Bullying peers or younger children. Cruelty toward animals. Unexplained bruises, black eyes, broken bones, cuts on parts of his or her body. Gang activity.

- **SELF-INJURY:** Scars, blisters, scabs, or infections from burns or cuts, especially on the arms, wrists, legs. Suicidal thoughts or attempts.

- **EATING DISORDERS:** Rapid or excessive weight loss or weight gain. Preoccupation with body image and perceived physical flaws or defects. Starving to lose weight (anorexia). Bingeing on food and then using laxatives or throwing up (bulimia).

- **INCREASED SEXUAL ACTIVITY:** Multiple sex partners. Unprotected sex. Sexually transmitted diseases.
- **LEGAL PROBLEMS:** Arrests for truancy, probation violations, shoplifting, burglary, physical or sexual assault, minor-in-possession (MIP) or minor-in-consumption (MIC) charges. Time spent in detention or on probation. "Dirty UAs" (drug use shows up on urine screens) and altered UAs (indicating attempts to hide or disguise drug use by drinking small amounts of bleach or massive amounts of water, or using goldenrod or other so-called "vascular flush" products easily available on the Internet).

Kids who have a history of regular drug use, who experience multiple and ongoing problems related to using drugs, and who are unable to stop despite these problems need intensive treatment. But they are not the only ones who need help.

In a recently published scholarly work on adolescent drug problems, Ken Winters, Ph.D., director of the Center for Adolescent Substance Abuse Research at the University of Minnesota, argues persuasively that intervention and treatment are also needed when children or adolescents:

- **USE CERTAIN DRUGS:** "The use of some drugs (e.g., crack cocaine) is sufficiently dangerous that, by itself and in the absence of any other personal consequences or diagnostic symptoms, it is a cause for intervention."
- **START USING DRUGS AT AN EARLY AGE:** ". . . Any regular use (apart from other considerations) in a child or very young adolescent (e.g., twelve or thirteen years old) may be a warning flag for further drug involvement, so that these individuals should be referred for early intervention." A child or adolescent who huffs inhalants even in the absence of other drug use, for example, should be referred for assessment and possible treatment.
- **USE LARGE QUANTITIES OF DRUGS:** "Prolonged use of

intermediate quantities of drugs or acute ingestion of large quantities of drugs at any age is sufficiently risky that such behavior probably justifies intervention."

- **USE IN INAPPROPRIATE SETTINGS:** "Use in particularly inappropriate settings (e.g., prior to driving or during school hours) may be considered 'abuse' even in the absence of the overtly negative consequences of such use; it makes no sense to delay intervention until the person advances to more serious consequences, such as getting arrested or involved in an automobile accident."
- **EXPERIENCE NEGATIVE SOCIAL OR PSYCHOLOGICAL EFFECTS:** ". . . In the event that an ambiguous pattern of risky substance use exists, intervention is warranted when the individual has experienced negative social or psychological effects of use."
- **HAVE CERTAIN RISK FACTORS EVEN IN THE ABSENCE OF DRUG PROBLEMS:** ". . . The case in which drug use and consequences are absent but several drug use risk factors are present, such as a family history of drug addiction or alcoholism, drug involvement by older siblings, presence of conduct disorder or ADHD . . . and so forth."

What Happens in Treatment?

What happens in a structured treatment program depends, of course, on the specific kind of program the adolescent enters. And there are enough choices to make your head spin, with more than eleven thousand specialized drug treatment facilities in this country and hundreds of treatment programs specifically targeted to adolescents.

Rather than detail the multitude of treatment approaches and therapies, we will focus briefly on the two basic kinds of structured treatment—outpatient and inpatient (both short and long term).

Outpatient Programs

Outpatient treatment is the most frequently used level of care for adolescents. The types and intensity of services offered vary from one program to the next. Services generally take place in a treatment center or counseling office, and adolescents meet once a week, several times weekly, or on a daily basis for drug education classes, individual counseling, group counseling, or a combination of programs. Meetings are usually held after school or on weekends.

Adolescents with more severe problems are placed in intensive outpatient programs (IOPs), which meet between two and five times weekly, with each session lasting between one and three hours.

Outpatient programs typically include the following components: evaluation and assessment, identification of emotional and behavioral obstacles in recovery; alcohol and other drug education; individualized treatment planning; short- and long-term continuing care and transition planning; access to a variety of community resources, including self-help groups, vocational agencies, and multicultural resources; introduction to Twelve Step recovery principles and self-help groups; drug screens when required; coordination with physicians, therapists, employers, teachers, probation officers, and so on; and relapse prevention techniques. Counselors and other staff members meet regularly to assess the adolescent's progress and ongoing treatment needs.

The advantages of outpatient programs include their lower cost, often covered by insurance, and the fact that they allow adolescents to stay in their homes, attend school, and keep their jobs. These programs tend to work best with adolescents who do not have co-occurring emotional or behavioral disorders; are highly motivated to quit; have significant levels of support (family, school, extracurricular, community); are able to resist peer influence; have not experienced serious problems related to their drug use; and can be carefully monitored.

When kids are not yet ready to change and are therefore resistant to treatment, outpatient education and counseling programs can help motivate them. During treatment sessions, counselors and educators gauge the adolescent's attendance record, attitude, willingness to abide by the rules, participation in groups, and general progress. If the adolescent cannot comply with the rules or complete the program, the next level of care may be required—intensive outpatient treatment, which generally consists of at least six hours a week of structured programming, or inpatient treatment.

Adolescents with significant emotional or behavioral problems may be referred to a partial hospitalization program (PHP), where they have access to medical and psychiatric services. Partial hospitalization programs offer twenty or more hours of intensive programming a week and provide daily monitoring and supervision; some PHPs also offer school-based programs and activities.

Residential Treatment Programs (Short Term)

Most adolescent inpatient programs consist of three to four weeks of highly structured programming. Daily schedules vary, but the following schedule, based on programs offered at several treatment centers, will give you a general idea what to expect:

Morning

6:30–7:30	Wake-up/showers
7:30–8:00	Breakfast
8:00–8:30	Bed and room cleanup
8:30–9:00	Meditation exercise/community meeting
9:00–10:00	Morning lecture and discussion
10:00–11:30	Primary counseling group
11:30–11:45	Free time
11:45–12:30	Lunch

Afternoon

12:30–1:30	Afternoon lecture and discussion
1:30–2:00	Study hall or problem-specific groups (ADHD, grief, anger, nicotine cessation)
2:00–3:00	School/tutoring

| 3:00–4:30 | Primary counseling group |
| 4:30–5:30 | Recreational activity (exercise, team games) |

Evening

5:30–6:30	Dinner and free time
6:30–7:30	Lecture, movie, or life skills
7:30–8:00	Snack, free time
8:00–9:45	Twelve Step meeting or Big Book study groups
9:45–10:30	Closure groups, meditation
10:30	In rooms
11:00	Lights-out

Looking at this schedule, adolescents often have many questions they want to know the details. Here are some answers to questions adolescents and their parents often ask.

What happens in counseling and group therapy? Adolescents spend several hours a day in group therapy with six to eight peers. The group facilitator helps the group members process lecture materials and worksheets, discuss their experiences, share their doubts and fears, and get feedback on their future recovery plans.

In group, adolescents learn how to identify and express their feelings—a scary undertaking for many adolescents, who have learned to cover up their innermost emotions with a cool, "I don't care" attitude. Sharing your innermost thoughts and feelings is uncomfortable for adults, too. Aerosmith's Steven Tyler, a recovering alcoholic/addict, describes how facing your fears can help dispel them.

We all went around the room and talked about ourselves. I was scared to death. I stood up. It's one of those things that I like to jump into. If something bugs me a little and I'm afraid of it, I have to jump in there and face it. You get right back on the horse after it throws you. That can be the most frightening thing to do; my heart was pounding out of my chest.

One of the easy things now is I immediately say, "I'm scared to death." I talk about what's going on in my mind. If you hold things in, you kind of internally hemorrhage, whereas if you get it out and talk about what you're feeling at the moment, it really breaks the ice.

In group, adolescents rediscover the morals and values that were twisted and torn by their addiction. The group changes over time, as some kids graduate from the treatment program and others who have just been admitted into treatment join the group. Thus, in a month-long program, adolescents will have the opportunity to know dozens of people from diverse backgrounds and cultures, all suffering from the same basic problems related to their substance use. These interactions are invaluable in teaching honesty, humility, trust, tolerance, gratitude, forgiveness, and, perhaps most important of all, self-forgiveness.

As the body and mind heal over time, so does the soul. Recovering alcoholic/addict Nils Lofgren, guitarist for Bruce Springsteen's E Street Band, explains what spiritual healing means to him.

The hardest part for me in this whole process is to really heal and get well. You can't just stop drinking and using drugs. You have to heal as a human being spiritually. I can no longer sit on the fence. If I don't do some kind of healing on a regular basis, I backslide. It doesn't mean I have to use drugs, but I get miserable and that's a threatening thing. I think that's what keeps many people from getting help. It's about getting in touch with your feelings, starting to embrace who you are and all that goes on with that. This includes not only the good parts of you, but all the bad parts and facing up to it, wading through it and not running away from it anymore.

Why all those lectures? In daily lectures, the treatment staff and outside experts cover a wide variety of topics. At Milam Recovery Center's adolescent program in Burien, Washington, for example, lecture subjects include the disease and recovery process, effects on the family, medical aspects, Twelve Step program philosophy and mechanics, sponsorship, spirituality, nutrition, relapse prevention, denial, defenses, depression, rational emotive therapy, self-discipline, behavior management, anger management, self-esteem, and grief. All lectures include follow-up worksheets specifically geared to the developmental level of adolescents, for use in later discussion and process groups.

What about school? Most adolescent inpatient programs have a school-based program, with regularly scheduled educational activities. Students work on assignments from their home schools or complete a semester credit in a certain area such as science, math, and language skills. Tutors are often available for individualized education, and adolescents are monitored in study hall. In some programs, kids receive English or sociology credits for journal writing, participation in group counseling, and completion of written assignments. Adolescents also receive physical education credits for participation in the recreational program.

An exciting, relatively new option now available to adolescents in recovery is the creation of "recovery schools" around the country. These programs are designed to support the recovery of teenagers who have been through a formal treatment program or who have made a conscious decision to stop using drugs. They are not treatment facilities. Students receive a full range of academic services while also working on a daily program of recovery. All students agree to be drug-free (that includes alcohol, of course); most recovery schools give students a second chance if they are honest about relapses.

Most recovery schools are small, ranging from six to seventy students. Staff-to-student ratios are low, allowing small classes and individualized attention from teachers, counselors, and program staff. Family involvement in the program and curriculum is considered essential. Funding sources vary from one school to the next, but most recovery schools receive a mix of public and private funds.

Nineteen recovery high schools are currently in operation, with four more scheduled to open in the next two years. The chief goal of these programs is to:

> . . . build a supportive community and provide the peer support vital to a young person's attempts to avoid alcohol and other drugs. Connecting with a peer who not only has struggled with many of the same life issues, but also has found a way to both cope and *have fun* without alcohol and other drugs, is one of the most valuable accomplishments of these schools.
>
> —ANDY FINCH
> *Director of the Association of Recovery Schools*

Three colleges—Augsburg College in Minnesota, Rutgers University in New Jersey, and Texas Tech in Lubbock—also offer programs specifically designed to support students in recovery. (For more information on recovery high schools and college programs, visit the Web site www.recoveryschools.org.)

What are "recreational activities" and why is exercise considered important in recovery? Virtually all adolescent inpatient facilities offer recreational programs, and many feature well-equipped gymnasiums with basketball courts, indoor jogging tracks, aerobic exercise areas, weight rooms, Ping-Pong or pool tables, and outdoor exercise areas such as jogging paths, playing fields, and volleyball courts.

Michael Osbourne, a teacher and physical education instructor who works at Sundown M Ranch's adolescent treatment program in Selah, Washington, sums up the general philosophy underlying regular exercise and recreational activities.

> Entering a twenty-eight-day inpatient treatment program is a frightening experience for most adolescents. Withdrawal from chemicals often causes irritability. Denial and delusions ("I don't have a problem") can produce anger and blaming.

A structured exercise and recreational program can have a positive effect on unhealthy moods. Students often enter physical education class sullen and complaining about everything from their parents to their physical ailments. After fifty minutes of fitness and a structured activity emphasizing running and cooperation, amazingly, they leave laughing and talking with their fellow students.

This phenomenon, of course, has a physiological base. We know, for instance, that running increases brain serotonin synthesis. Serotonin is a neurotransmitter that has a positive mood affect. Exercise also produces endorphins, natural opiates in the brain that mediate our pain response and promote feelings of well-being.

Besides a daily fitness program, we play a variety of games in our physical education classes, giving adolescents an opportunity to deal with inappropriate responses to healthy competition. Prior to treatment, when confronted with conflict, the adolescent's response has been to "use." Because using is not possible in treatment, the game or activity becomes the format for the student to deal with conflict and experiment with concepts being learned in the lectures and group therapy sessions. In a sense, the physical education class becomes the real world for people in treatment.

Why do I have to go to Twelve Step and "Big Book" meetings? In approximately 90 percent of all treatment programs, patients are introduced to AA and NA, including the programs' history and traditions, the concept of a higher power, and the Twelve Steps. Dozens of scientific studies with adults show that regular attendance at AA or NA meetings is the greatest predictor of a stable long-term recovery.

When plans are made for continuing care, attention should focus on the support groups available in the community and the specific groups where adolescents feel most at home. Not all adolescents are comfortable in traditional Twelve Step groups, and a significant number may do better in church- or school-based recovery programs, gender-based trauma groups, values clarification groups, or other mutual aid support groups. Different groups match up with different kids, and different kids may use different groups or other sobriety-based structures at different points in their recovery career.

The challenge for parents and the community as a whole is to offer adolescents a wide variety of support groups so that they can discover where they fit and belong or move comfortably from one group to the next as their needs and developmental issues change.

What happens during free time? The daily schedule leaves adolescents with very little free time. Some adolescent programs have eliminated free time from their daily schedule, substituting life skills and recreational activities during those times. Life skills activities might include refusal skills, anger management skills, and behavior modification skills.

When free time is offered, adolescents are expected to work on letters, journals, or other therapy-related assignments. If they are able to keep up with their assigned work, they often use the thirty or forty minutes of free time daily to read, exercise, play musical instruments, or talk to friends.

Why is everything scheduled hour by hour? Many adolescents come from chaotic, unstructured family or social environments. Inpatient treatment programs externally enforce structure in an effort to stabilize their routine and daily life. The hope is that they will internalize some of this structure, which helps to establish time management skills, self-regulation, and, most important of all, self-esteem.

The security of knowing that the day is carefully mapped out for them, with carefully explained rules and expectations for attending classes, meals, school, groups, and recreational activities, gives adolescents a sense of safety and stability and prevents unnecessary worrying about what is going to happen next. With a structured schedule that varies little from one day to the next, adolescents soon become comfortable with the routine and learn to focus all their attention on their recovery program.

Why do I have to have a roommate? When adolescents share a room, secrets are harder to keep. Peer influence is extremely important in motivating the adolescent to become interested and invested in the treatment process. Isolation can lead to loneliness, doubts about treatment, fears, and resentments that can undermine the treatment and recovery process. For these reasons, very few treatment programs offer private rooms.

What's this family program all about? When family members bring the adolescent to treatment, they are usually required to attend an orientation program where they are introduced to the treatment staff and offered information about what will happen in treatment. Orientation may last several hours or several days and, in most treatment programs, at least one family member is required to attend.

During treatment, most programs allow family members to visit one or two days a week, usually on the weekends during scheduled visiting hours. A typical schedule for visitors might be Saturday and Sunday afternoons from one to five o'clock.

Toward the end of treatment, many programs offer a residential family program, generally consisting of two or three days of educational programs (lectures, discussion groups), therapy (individual, group, and family), relapse prevention strategies, and continuing care planning. The cost of the family program may or may not be included in the cost of the adolescent's treatment.

Adolescent addiction experts and treatment specialists universally agree that family involvement in the treatment and recovery process is essential for long-term success.

> A simultaneous focus on the family and the individual adolescent is an important ingredient for successful treatment of adolescent drug abuse.
>
> —DR. HOWARD LIDDLE
> *Director of the Center for Treatment Research on*
> *Adolescent Drug Abuse at the University of Miami*

Involving the family is the most critical part in our treatment program with adolescents. We treat the adolescent and family as one in most cases, and we focus on putting the families back together. Family stability, involvement, and commitment will make or break the recovery process for most kids.

—DAVID ROSENKER
Executive Vice President of Treatment
Services at the Caron Foundation

There is no stronger interpersonal bond in a young person's life than his or her family. Consequently, working with the family is an integral part of the recovery process. There is frequently a need to address substance use disorders in other family members and how the families understand and respond to the problem.

—STEPHEN A. WYATT
Medical Director, Stonington Institute

Adult and adolescent substance use disorders infect every area of family life from adult intimate relationships, each parent-child relationship, all sibling relationships, as well as family roles, rules, rituals, and the nature of family interaction with the outside world. Families achieve an unhealthy "normality" around these abnormal adaptations and require significant help to get through the crisis of recovery. With such help, the whole family can recover; without such help, individual recovery can precipitate a further deterioration in family relationships. Family programs are needed because individual recovery is strengthened by family recovery and because individual recovery does not automatically generate family recovery.

—WILLIAM L. WHITE
Chestnut Health Systems

Families frequently get stuck in how they solve problems and they keep doing the same things over and over expecting different results. Family Week creates an opportunity for both the patient and the family members to recognize and restructure their relationship with each other and receive new methods and techniques as to how they address problems.

—COTTONWOOD DE TUCSON, INC.

Family involvement is critical to positive outcomes. We work intensively with the parents and the family system as a whole in order to educate them, provide support, and begin a healing process.

—JAMES STEINHAGEN
Executive Director of Hazelden
Center for Youth and Families

Long-Term Residential Treatment

The community is the healer. The community brings all the parts of the person together.

—TONY GELORMINO, *Director of Staff*
Development at Daytop, Inc.

Boot camps, wilderness camps, adventure programs, recovery houses, and therapeutic communities designed specifically for adolescents with substance-use disorders abound. Treatment philosophies, staffing ratios, educational opportunities, counseling approaches, and daily schedules vary dramatically from one program to the next, so parents will need to research these options carefully.

Therapeutic communities (TCs), originally designed to treat hard-core addicts, offer highly structured, drug-free residential programs lasting from three months to two years. Some programs take a tough love approach, others function as modified boot camps, and still others offer daily Bible study and emphasize moral and ethical development.

Personal accountability is an essential element of all therapeutic communities. "Particularly useful in the treatment of adolescents are the core elements of the therapeutic community, the focus on behavior and an orderly lifestyle, and the values of work, honesty, and responsibility for others," explains Mitchell S. Rosenthal, M.D., president of Phoenix House, the nation's largest private, nonprofit drug treatment organization.

Phoenix House runs twelve residential programs for adolescents; called Phoenix Academies, they are located in California, Texas, New York, and New England. "Phoenix Academies are boarding schools for teens in treatment, offering an accelerated academic program that allows students to make up school work lost to drugs," says Dr. Rosenthal. "Teachers and counselors work together, so that social learning and academic learning occur simultaneously, and school life reflects the therapeutic community's clearly articulated value system, with its emphasis on honesty and responsibility." Residents are expected to meet community norms, abide by explicit rules, and meet behavioral expectations that range from making their beds and conforming to the community's standards of personal hygiene to the prohibition against any form or threat of violence.

Daytop, Inc., offers adolescent residential programs providing "in-depth, full-time exposure to a structured lifestyle and positive peers" in New Jersey and California, and Odyssey House runs a long-term residential program for adolescents in New York City.

Teen Challenge, founded in 1958, "endeavors to teach a whole new way of living" through a Christ-centered program that helps troubled kids and their families address addictions, interpersonal and community relationships, work attitudes, social issues, peer pressure, and self-image. Participants in the one-year residential program are expected to follow strict rules and attend chapel and Bible classes daily.

Where Can I Find Appropriate, Effective Treatment?*

Because not all treatment programs are the same—and some programs base their treatment philosophy on myths and misconceptions

---

*For help locating a treatment program or facility in your area, see "Resources" at the back of this book.

that can be harmful, even self-defeating—parents should research programs carefully. As you consider the different treatment choices that might be available to you, it is absolutely essential that you keep the following key elements in mind. These standards, which have been developed by addiction medicine specialists, are based on the most current scientific knowledge about adolescent substance-use disorders.

Assessment: Accurate assessment is an essential first step in diagnosing substance-use disorders. According to Ken Winters, Ph.D., Todd Estroff, M.D., and Nicole Anderson in *Principles of Addiction Medicine*:

> Assessing adolescent alcohol and other drug [problems] can be a daunting task. It is clear that, in adolescents, substance abuse problems rarely occur in isolation. Issues related to school performance, family and peer functioning, psychiatric and psychological status, physical health, and delinquency are widely cited as factors that can predispose, precipitate, or perpetuate the use of alcohol and drugs by youth. . . . Assessment strategies must be multifaceted and comprehensive in order to address such complex patient and environmental problems.

Professionals in substance use and emotional and behavioral disorders administer various assessments to adolescents before they are admitted to a specific treatment program, and additional assessments are conducted in the first days of treatment. At Visions Adolescent Treatment Program in Malibu, California, for example, the admission process involves comprehensive assessments of the youth's medical, psychiatric, academic, and psychosocial status. Depending on the results of these assessments, additional assessments may be conducted including psychiatric evaluation, trauma assessment, psychological testing, eating disorder assessment, educational assessment, sexual compulsivity assessment, and neurological testing.

Treatment matching: The treatment plan should match the severity of the adolescent's physical, emotional, and behavioral problems. Factors that should be considered include the adolescent's readiness and willingness to change; potential for relapse; and the stability and safety of the home and living environment.

Important note: If your child does not respond well to one level of care, we strongly recommend that you advocate for a higher or more intensive level of care.

Integrated treatment: Scientific studies show that between 50 and 90 percent of adolescents in trouble with drugs also suffer from co-occurring emotional and behavioral disorders such as depressive disorders, anxiety disorders, attention deficit hyperactivity disorder (ADHD), conduct disorders, and eating disorders.

Kenneth Minkoff, M.D., an expert in dual diagnosis, outlines the following key principles of integrated treatment:

- When substance-use disorders and emotional or behavioral disorders coexist, both diagnoses should be considered primary, requiring simultaneous treatment for each.
- Addiction treatment requires modification when people also have psychiatric disabilities and disorders.
- The most significant predictor of success is an empathic, hopeful, continuous care relationship, in which integrated treatment and coordination of care can take place through multiple treatment episodes.

Family involvement in treatment: Parents, grandparents, siblings, and other relatives have a profound influence on the adolescent's development. Research shows that family involvement in treatment dramatically increases the adolescent's chances for a successful, long-term recovery.

Family members also need special care and attention as they deal with their own emotions and seek to understand what has happened to their child and their family as a whole. Says Jeanette Friedman, director of adolescent services at Caron Foundation of New York:

All family members are affected by the particular problems of even just one member. The inability to acknowledge the existence and rights of others—to essentially share the planet with others—can make life with an addicted person very challenging. Resentments on the part of family members who feel neglected, often for years, make family work essential to the emotional health and survival of everyone involved.

Developmentally appropriate program: Adolescents differ from adults in their physical, emotional, mental, social, and spiritual development, and treatment must be tailored to their specific developmental needs. The *SAMHSA/CSAT Treatment Improvement Protocols*, for instance, note:

> In treatment, adolescents must be approached differently than adults because of their unique developmental issues, differences in their values and belief systems, and environmental considerations (e.g., strong peer influences). At a physical level, adolescents tend to have smaller body sizes and lower tolerances, putting them at greater risk for alcohol-related problems even at lower levels of consumption. The use of substances may also compromise an adolescent's mental and emotional development from youth to adulthood because substance use interferes with how people approach and experience interactions.
>
> The treatment process must address the nuances of each adolescent's experience, including cognitive, emotional, physical, social, and moral development. An understanding of these changes will help treatment providers grasp why an adolescent uses substances and how substance use may become an integral part of an adolescent's identity.

Individual assessment, staff education, low staff-to-patient ratio, increased structure, and creative programming are often key elements of a developmentally appropriate program. "The key is educating our staff and providing clinical supervision at a level that allows clinicians to be sophisticated and knowledgeable so they can meet the youth where they are, not where others think they should be," says James Steinhagen, executive director of the Hazelden Center for Youth and Families.

Engage and retain teens in treatment: In general, adolescents require greater intensity of treatment and more external assistance and support to engage them in the recovery process. Treatment is regarded as a dynamic process rather than a single episode of care, and relapses indicate the need for a higher level of care and/or a change in approach. A "never give up" attitude is essential in treating substance-use disorders, as it is in all chronic disorders.

Qualified staff: Treatment staff must be knowledgeable about adolescent stages of development, substance-use disorders, neurological addiction, and co-occurring emotional and behavioral disorders.

Gender and cultural differences: Prevention, treatment, and recovery support programs must be designed to reflect gender and cultural differences in patterns of drug use, development of problems, obstacles to treatment, and pathways of long-term recovery.

Continuing care is an essential element of any treatment plan. Adolescent treatment specialists explain why:

> Most adolescents are precariously balanced between recovery and relapse in the months following treatment. The period of greatest vulnerability for relapse is in the first 30 days following treatment. . . . The stability of recovery is enhanced by post-treatment monitoring and periodic recovery checkups. Assertive continuing care is characterized by sustained continuity of contact and support, and assumption of responsibility for such contact by the service professional rather than the adolescent.

—RICK RISBERG AND WILLIAM WHITE
Chestnut Health Systems Lighthouse Institute

That last phrase bears repeating—*responsibility for such contact is assumed by the service professional rather than the adolescent.* Adolescent addiction experts emphasize the critical importance of continuing care and intensive support systems to protect adolescents during early recovery, when they are most vulnerable to relapse.

Relapse prevention: Relapse is common in adolescents with substance-use disorders—approximately a third of adolescents who have completed a twenty-eight-day inpatient program will relapse within three months. Plans should be made in treatment for continuing care to reduce the incidence of relapse and/or provide support and assistance if relapse occurs.

Relapses must be treated not as signs of treatment failure but as indications that a higher intensity of care or different treatment approaches may be necessary. "The emphasis should be on what the adolescent can learn from the lapse," writes Steven Jaffe, M.D. "For example, avoiding high-risk situations such as the company of 'using peers,' or seeking out a sponsor for help in dealing with intense thoughts and urges to use."

Treatment outcomes: At this point in time, relatively few adolescent programs adequately or scientifically evaluate their effectiveness. The situation will change, however, as treatment programs adopt the principles of effective treatment outlined by the American Society of Addiction Medicine and strengthen their assessment, treatment matching, integrated care, and continuing care programs.

When Should I Seek Help for My Child?

This question is often phrased in this way: "How bad does it have to get before I ask for help?"

The answer is clear and unequivocal. If you think your adolescent has a problem with drugs, you are probably right. Get help now. Do not wait until the problem is so obvious that your friends, relatives, or neighbors have worked up the courage to tell you that they are concerned. While it may seem, at times, that the great majority of people are gossips and busybodies, most people are actually afraid to speak up about drugs and addiction because they do not want to stigmatize drug users and their family members—or they may fear a defensive backlash that could destroy their friendship with the adolescent and/or family members. When it comes to drugs and drug users, unfortunately, people are much more likely to keep their concerns to themselves—or confide their suspicions to others, but not to those most directly involved.

We urge you to listen to your heart. Do not wait until you are absolutely sure that your child is in trouble with drugs, because by the time you are absolutely sure, your child could be absolutely dead. That statement is intended to be frightening. If you knew the risks your child takes every time he or she gets drunk, stoned, baked, broiled, roasted, blasted, or fried, you would not wait one moment before getting help.

Please—heed the wisdom and experience of others who have been through the pain and anguish of watching their children's lives destroyed by drugs and who offer their heartfelt experience in the hope of influencing others to act before it is too late. In his book *Terry: My Daughter's Life and Death Struggle with Alcoholism*, former U.S. senator and presidential candidate George McGovern struggles to make sense of his daughter's short life and unexpected death. In one of the book's most moving passages, Senator McGovern reflects on what he would have done if he had a second chance to save his child.

> As I have traced Terry's life and reflected on what I would do differently with the benefit of hindsight, several thoughts have emerged. I would make a greater effort to share in her life and development from the beginning. I would watch over her more carefully—especially in the adolescent, high school years. I would, if I detected signs of alcoholism, inform myself thoroughly about this disease and do everything in my power to get her into a sound recovery program as quickly as possible.
>
> In Terry's case, once the disease had fastened on to her, I

would stay in close communication with her, expressing my love and concern for her at all times. I would call her every few days in a nonjudgmental manner, just to let her know I shared and understood her pain.

I regret more than I can describe the decision Eleanor [his wife] and I made under professional counsel to distance ourselves from Terry in what proved to be the last six months of her life. No matter how good the intentions or great the wisdom of the counselor, this was not the right course. Terry had become so ill as the disease took its deadly toll in her final months that she needed all the attention, concern, love, and intelligent action we could have brought to bear. She should have been confined to long-term care with no opportunity to leave until she was in recovery. This method might not have worked. But we will never know that, because at the end, when she was the most helpless, it wasn't tried. It wasn't tried because we were not aware of how her disease had accelerated so rapidly in the last months.

But if I could recapture Terry's life, I would never again distance myself from her no matter how many times I had tried and failed to help her. Better to keep trying and failing than to back away and not know what is going on. If she had died despite my best efforts and my close involvement with her life up to the end, at least she would have died with my arms around her, and she would have heard me say one more time: "I love you, Terry."

Why Is a Formal Program of Recovery Necessary?

If you bring forth what is within you,
what you do bring forth will save you.
If you do not bring forth what is within you
what you do not bring forth will destroy you.

—THE GOSPEL OF THOMAS, *Verses 69–70*

Treatment in all its varied forms helps kids "bring forth" what is within them so that they can find the strength and wisdom to free themselves from the physical, emotional, and spiritual devastation caused by drugs and addiction.

In treatment and recovery programs, adolescents come into contact with concerned, compassionate adults who understand the stresses inherent in adolescence and the serious risks associated with drug use and addiction. Knowing that someone understands them and, perhaps more important, believes in them, gives kids hope and faith that change is possible.

Interactions with other adolescents who are struggling to change or who are successfully involved in recovery programs teach and inspire them. In the process of identifying with the struggles and triumphs of others, their motivation to change intensifies.

Group and individual counseling help adolescents feel comfortable in discussing their personal experiences and expressing their innermost feelings. They learn social and communication skills that will help them work through problems in their interpersonal relationships.

Behavioral modification therapies teach teenagers how to avoid situations associated with drug use, control their cravings and impulses, and recognize specific thoughts, feelings, attitudes, and actions that can lead to relapse.

In educational sessions, adolescents learn the importance of personal responsibility and self-care in various areas, including nutrition, personal hygiene, proper weight management, and exercise.

Family involvement in treatment helps every member of the family deal with anger, resentment, shame, guilt, and grief. Relationships within the family often improve dramatically, and the home becomes a safer, more stable environment.

As myths and misconceptions are replaced with facts, kids are released from shame and self-blame.

Talking about values, dreams, and goals puts adolescents in touch with their souls and their own unique spirituality, which can be defined broadly as the individual search for truth and meaning.

In individual and group counseling, in lectures and readings, and in Twelve Step groups, adolescents learn about tolerance, gratitude, humility, honesty, and forgiveness. They discover how alcohol and other drugs destroy their most cherished values, causing profound despair, and they learn the central importance of forgiving themselves and others.

Treatment gives adolescents hope, faith, and belief in the promise of life itself. And treatment—good treatment, effective treatment—helps adolescents understand that happiness is not a temporary emotional state but a way of being and acting, of making certain choices and living your life in a way that is honestly, steadfastly true to your most cherished values. For the joy that we discover in life is determined not by our feelings, not even by our thoughts, but by the activities we engage in, the way we behave toward others, and, of course, the way we treat ourselves. As the Greek philosopher Aristotle put it more than two thousand years ago:

> [We] acquire a particular quality by constantly acting a particular way. [We] become just by performing just actions, temperate by performing temperate actions, brave by performing brave actions.

For all these reasons, and for so many more, treatment is necessary. Adolescents can and do stop using on their own, but for far too many kids, the decision to get help comes only after they have suffered devastating physical, emotional, or legal consequences.

Are you willing to wait until drugs have eaten holes in your child's body, mind, and soul? For most of us, of course, the answer to that question is an unequivocal no.

How Do I Know if Treatment Worked?

Treatment doesn't work. The day my son got out of treatment, he got drunk. He's been drinking, smoking marijuana, and doing God knows what else ever since. Sometimes he'll stop using for a month or two, but then he'll start up again. I've had it with treatment. For the money I've put into inpatient and outpatient treatment, I could have put both my children through college.

—MARIA, *forty-eight*

"Treatment doesn't work." You have undoubtedly heard that refrain from friends and family members, and there are plenty of treated-but-still-using adolescents around to prove the point. In fact, sometimes it seems as if adolescents who go to treatment end up even worse off. They stay clean for a few days or a few weeks (or even just a few hours), and then they relapse and slide right back into the disease. This time, however, they have an extra grenade to toss at you: "I already tried treatment, and it didn't work."

Of all the myths and misconceptions surrounding adolescent drug use and addiction, the most damaging of all may be the belief that treatment doesn't work if the adolescent relapses or experiences continuing drug-related problems. Treatment works—but it takes time. Treatment works in the same way that seeds planted in a garden take months, even years, to grow to full maturity. With patience and tender, ongoing care, the seeds will take root; with time, the roots will become firmly entrenched.

Everyone involved in the lives of children who use drugs must understand that treatment is not a single, discrete event that stops when the adolescent leaves a structured inpatient or outpatient program. Adolescents (and adults) require a continuum of care involving ongoing assessment, intervention, and treatment at various levels of intensity, depending on the individual's present needs. Such a program of continuing care "reinforces the need for chronic attention and vigilance in response to a chronic vulnerability, even in the improved patient," writes Marc Fishman, M.D. "Ongoing treatment at less intensive levels of care to consolidate gains initiated at more intensive levels of care is a critical feature of successful treatment across a continuum of care."

Once we recognize and understand the need for *a continuum of care*, we can reframe the way we view adolescents who experience setbacks or full-blown relapses. Rather than considering them treatment "failures," we can redouble our efforts by changing our strategies, developing a new treatment plan, and/or involving the adolescent in more intensive treatment and continuing care programs.

For when treatment is viewed as active and ongoing, it works—

it may not work miracles, at least not all at once or right away, but over time miracles do happen.

Listen to the kids talking.

I got all A's and B's my freshman year, and then I got D's and F's my sophomore year. I was drinking and smoking lots of weed after my freshman year, but do you think I connected the two? No way—I was convinced that I suffered from depression and I was only using drugs to help me cope. I was just so sad and I felt so much better when I used drugs. So I figured drugs were the solution, not the problem. I thought I would use marijuana and alcohol until the day I died. I said I would never be without my drugs.

But I became more and more depressed. I wanted to kill myself. I hated everything about myself. My mother was so worried about me. She sent me to a counselor who sent me to a doctor, who decided that I had a mental health problem and put me in a mental hospital. I spent a week there before they realized I had a drug problem and not a mental problem and sent me to an inpatient treatment center. But I still didn't think I belonged there, and I couldn't wait to get out.

It wasn't until my third week in treatment that my brain cleared up and I could see the truth. I suddenly understood that my depression, mood swings, anger, and irritability were all connected to my drug use. I stayed in treatment for twenty-eight days and then spent another month in a recovery house.

I've been sober now for three years. I'm in college, and I want to become a drug counselor so I can help other kids like me. I have my life back.

—LUCY, *nineteen*

I'm a methamphetamine addict. Treatment raised my self-esteem. It helped me get connected with God. When I got out of treatment, I used again, and I felt really bad about myself. But somehow, I was still able to find some good in myself, something I could believe in and work toward. I know there is a place I want to go back to—a place inside me. Treatment helped me find that place. I'm going to find it again.

—SAMANTHA, *seventeen*

I believe that treatment works for those who want it to. You basically get what you give. If you give 75 percent out of changing your life and the world around it, that is how much you will receive in return. Treatment worked for me because I felt that I had nothing to lose for I had already been to hell and back. I was tired of all that pain that comes with drugs and its lifestyle. I learned that I would have to make many sacrifices and continue to have faith in God (my higher power) no matter what. Something had obviously been wrong with the choices I had made and the way I was thinking. I just had to focus on not just the problem but the solution as well and have enough willingness to go through with it.

Treatment changed my whole perspective on things, including the way I had been perceived by others. It opened up my eyes to the way life really was supposed to be and that I had a purpose in it. It showed the pain I had caused not only to myself but to others as well.

I now see life in color instead of black and white.

—JAVI, *eighteen*

Relapses

Sometimes I have failed. But I am
not a failure; I have made mistakes,
but I am not a mistake.

—FROM THE AA BOOKLET
Came to Believe

Relapse tendencies are a normal and
natural part of the recovery process.
They are nothing to be ashamed of.
They need to be dealt with openly
and honestly. If they are not, they
grow stronger.

—TERENCE GORSKI
AND MERLENE MILLER
Staying Sober

Relapses happen. We all wish they didn't, but they do.
The most important fact to remember is this: A relapse is
not a failure but a temporary setback, part of the learning curve.
We learn the most important lessons in life from experience, and
the experience of relapse teaches us that sobriety is more than mere

abstinence. Staying clean and sober requires a commitment to living a different kind of life and becoming a different kind of person. If we stay the same—if we are not willing and open to change—we will use drugs again.

Relapse is part of every chronic disease—from eating disorders to asthma, diabetes, and heart disease—and the recovery process involves learning how to make different choices. With substance-use disorders, that process requires learning how to live without the drug or drugs that would always make you feel better, at least for a little while. Learning, as we all know, comes from experience, and experience can be a tough teacher.

> I was so pumped up after I got home from treatment. I loved treatment. The food was grubbing and the people were awesome. I learned so much about addiction and about myself. So for the first two weeks I did great. I was committed to staying clean. I told my drug-using friends I wasn't going to use and not to offer me drugs. Then, after two weeks, something happened. I don't know what it was. I just hit a low point, and I really wanted to use again. Things weren't going right for me at home, my mom and dad were in the middle of a divorce, my sister was partying all the time, and I felt like life sucked. So I smoked some weed. But this time it wasn't the same. I woke up feeling terrible—guilty, ashamed. I hated myself. I felt ripped in two. I wanted to use and I didn't want to use. I needed to use, and I hated myself for needing it so much.
>
> I don't know how this will work out, but I just wish I could stay clean. I really want that. I really want to stay clean.
>
> —ROSS, *sixteen*

Why Relapses Happen

Researchers and clinicians who specialize in adolescent substance-use disorders identify four major pathways that increase the recovering teenager's risk of relapse.

The most common is involvement with peers who use alcohol or [other] drugs. Even if the adolescent is committed to sobriety, spending time with using peers becomes too tempting and the teen relapses. A second pathway is the presence of comorbid psychiatric disorders. Adolescents with substance abuse disorders have a high incidence (50 to 90 percent) of other psychiatric disorders, especially mood, behavior, and anxiety disorders. In this pathway, the teen experiences depression, rage, or panic, and relapses in an effort to deal with those symptoms. A third pathway is denial, in which the recovering adolescent decides that he or she is not an addict and can use alcohol or other drugs in moderation. The fourth pathway involves subconsciously arranging one's life to be in proximity to alcohol or other drugs.

—STEVEN JAFFE, M.D.
Addiction Medicine Specialist

Learning how to live without alcohol and/or other drugs can be extremely stressful. We live in a drinking and drugging society. Adolescents in recovery are even more vulnerable than adults, for most of their friends continue to use. Virtually everywhere they go—school, parties, other kids' homes—there are drugs.

Even adolescents who are committed heart and soul to recovery sometimes struggle on a daily basis with temptation to use.

I've been sober for almost a year, but I notice I've been falling into some of my addict behaviors. It scares me to death and trips me out. I really need to set some of my priorities straight. I don't know. But I do know that whatever is going on with me, I am not the only one who has experienced it.

The addict behaviors are like not wanting to help around the house and finding excuses when it comes to why I can't help clean. I haven't been spending that much time with my extended family, either. I see them around and they tell me that they are so happy to see me and that I should visit them sometime but the only time I have is on the weekends and I spend that time with my friends and all.

I still have trouble sometimes dealing with life on life's terms. I sometimes want to take things into my own hands and fix them, whether that is the proper way to deal with it or not.

The biggest problem that I have been experiencing is my gangster mentality. I sometimes feel like I am superior to others and that I can do things a certain way because I am me. I have brought back some more slang into my vocabulary and have even been in the presence of people while they were under the influence of one drug or another.

I just miss the easy way of life some days, but I know that if I wasn't working right now, I would have too much time on my hands. I wish that I were back in rehab sometimes, because I was so sheltered in there and it was so much easier to stay clean. I didn't have to worry about so much stuff then, stuff that I'm worrying about right now. I just miss the treatment center. There was so much more unity and love shown there. Sometimes I also sit back and think about the days that I was in detention. It is kind of weird to admit it, but I miss detention sometimes, too. I don't know why. I guess that I love the easy life too much.

—FRANCISCO, *eighteen*

Recovering teens are often confused by the fact that they feel depressed, anxious, lost, and out of control even though they are not using drugs. Like so many adults, they conclude that their problems are primarily psychological, and they berate themselves for their weakness and wavering resolve. Their hopelessness and despair are, at times, overwhelming, and they are haunted by questions that they believe can only be answered with yes.

- "Am I simply an emotionally unstable person who uses drugs to solve my problems?"
- "Will I always return to drugs because I am so weak and psychologically sick?"
- "Am I abnormal?"
- "Am I a lost cause?"

When the depression, anxiety, and fear persist, even during long periods of sobriety, adolescents experience extreme frustration and fear. They may begin to think that they were far better off when they were using drugs, for drugs always seemed to ease their problems. They may conclude that they are losers and that nothing they can do will make any difference. Their options appear to be few and their future precarious.

In despair, they may give in to their cravings for drugs, reasoning that they are too weak, too stupid, or too damaged to make it.

> I used last night. It felt good to use, because I thought I was going to blow up. So I just gave in. But even when I was high I felt awful, and when I woke up, I just hated myself. I kept saying to myself, "You are so weak, you are so stupid, you are such a loser." Because I did what I didn't want to do. Oh, sure I wanted to get high. I wanted to avoid the pain for a little while.
>
> But I want even more to stay sober, to be happy, to get back into school and straighten out my crooked life. And I can't seem to do it. I keep thinking that I'm hopeless. I will never have what it takes to stay sober. That thought fills me with despair and self-hatred. It makes me want to die.
>
> —ALICIA, *fifteen*

Lingering symptoms of depression, anxiety, insomnia, mental confusion, and craving for drugs are often clear signs that the adolescent's brain and body are still suffering from the damage caused by months or years of drug use. Drugs are toxins—poisons—and a brain that has been soaked in poison needs time to recover. While the brain is healing, many adolescents go through a period of mental and emotional turmoil that experts call "post acute withdrawal" or PAW.

Post Acute Withdrawal

Post-acute withdrawal is a bio-psycho-social syndrome. It results from the combination of damage to the nervous system caused by alcohol or [other] drugs and the psychosocial stress of coping with life without drugs.

—TERENCE GORSKI AND MERLENE MILLER
Staying Sober

Understanding the long-term effects of alcohol and other drugs on the central nervous system will help protect adolescents' recovery and guard against relapses. Rather than jumping to the conclusion that they are weak-willed, bad, or abnormal people who can't enjoy life without drugs, they will gain a deeper appreciation for the devastating, slow-to-fade effects of drugs on diverse brain functions. They will learn to see that their emotional symptoms are temporary states, directly linked to disruptions in neurochemistry.

And they will understand that time is their friend, not their enemy. Given time to heal, the toxic brain will return to normal functioning. *Time* is the key word, however, for many adolescents will continue to experience post acute withdrawal for weeks, months, and possibly years after they stop using drugs.

Symptoms

The major symptoms of the protracted withdrawal syndrome are:

Disrupted thought patterns: In the first weeks and months of sobriety, adolescents may express concern about their thick or foggy brains and complain about symptoms such as difficulty concentrating, memory problems, and circular or obsessive thoughts.

Their minds feel like they are racing, and they have difficulty constructing logical chains of thought. They make bad decisions and then can't figure out why. Theoretical or abstract concepts—like math problems or philosophy discussions—drive them crazy because they can't seem to put their thoughts together in a way that makes sense.

Memory gaps are characterized by short-term memory loss, the inability to remember significant events from the past, and/or difficulty learning new skills.

Emotional hypersensitivity is evident when an event that would normally evoke a minor emotional reaction stimulates an extraordinarily intense response. Emotional overreactions are common in early recovery, and many adolescents find themselves constantly on the verge of tears or ready to explode in anger and frustration. After a while, this extreme hypersensitivity can lead to emotional exhaustion and a sense of being numb and not caring anymore about what happens. The adolescent may say, "Nothing really matters anymore," "I just don't care what happens," or "I can't seem to feel anything."

> I know if I use again, I could die. Believe me, after using meth and cocaine and heroin and combining drugs, I know that. But do I care? I just don't. My life isn't worth much one way or the other. What does it matter if I live or die?
>
> —COLIN, *sixteen*

Sleep problems typically show up in disturbing dreams or nightmares. Many recovering adolescents have extremely disturbing dreams about using again—the dreams seem so real that they often wonder if they really did use and experience great anxiety and fear. Other sleep problems include general restlessness, inability to fall asleep, fragmented sleep, and waking up frequently during the night.

Physical coordination problems include dizziness, problems with balance and hand-eye coordination, and slow reflexes, all of which can contribute to physical clumsiness and accident-proneness.

Adolescents and adults recovering from alcohol addiction are even more prone to injury than people recovering from cocaine, heroin, methamphetamine, and marijuana addictions. One recent study shows that alcoholics are approximately twice as likely to suffer a serious injury—falls, fractures, head injuries, traffic accidents, stab and gunshot wounds—than illicit drug users. In the study, the pattern of higher injury rates to alcoholics persisted for two years after detoxification.

Causes

The major causes of the protracted or post-acute withdrawal syndrome are neurotransmitter depletion, malnutrition, and hypoglycemia.

- **NEUROTRANSMITTER DEPLETION:** Research shows that many chemically dependent people inherit certain genetic variations that interfere with the synthesis of feel-good brain chemicals such as dopamine, serotonin, norepinephrine, and GABA. In addition, alcohol and other drugs disrupt the normal actions of feel-good brain chemicals, leading to imbalances that can cause anxiety, irritability, depression, sleep disturbances, and cravings for drugs. These imbalances and disruptions can persist for months or even years after the adolescent stops using drugs.
- **NUTRITIONAL PROBLEMS:** Adolescents are notorious for bad eating habits. Most adolescents load up on high-sugar foods such as soda pop and candy, high-fat snacks and meals, and fast foods. Relatively few teenagers eat the recommended daily doses of fresh fruits and vegetables. Thus, the typical adolescent diet is low in fiber and whole grains and high in sugar and fat—exactly the opposite of what it should be.

  Adolescents who drink alcohol often experience nutritional problems because alcohol interferes with the absorption, digestion, and utilization of nutrients in the body.

Chronic or excessive alcohol use can lead to widespread vitamin and mineral deficiencies. Alcohol also severely damages the organs responsible for processing, using, and distributing nutrients, most notably the liver and pancreas.

Regular use of marijuana, cocaine, methamphetamines, Ecstasy, heroin, and other illegal drugs will also create nutritional problems. Each drug affects the body differently. Stimulants (cocaine, Ecstasy, methamphetamines), for example, reduce appetite, thus cutting back on healthy food intake, while marijuana usually increases the appetite for high-sugar and high-fat foods.

■ **HYPOGLYCEMIA:** Heavy alcohol intake disrupts blood sugar levels in the body, leading to steep spikes and sudden drops in glucose levels. When the blood sugar drops, the body releases epinephrine, an emergency hormone that instructs the liver to release more glucose into the bloodstream. As epinephrine surges through your body, your heartbeat speeds up and your blood pressure rises, causing symptoms such as anxiety, fear, nausea, intense hunger, shakes, sweats, and a pounding heart.

The brain depends on glucose for its primary energy source. When blood glucose levels drop abruptly, the brain signals its distress through symptoms such as mental confusion, headaches, irritability, nervousness, depression, and an intense craving for alcohol or high-sugar foods. If the adolescent drinks or eats foods with a high sugar content, the blood sugar levels will rise steeply, temporarily relieving the symptoms. But what comes up must come down, and as the blood sugar drops again, the symptoms return with a vengeance.

Being sober for thirty, sixty, or ninety days will not always fix the problem, unfortunately. If adolescents in recovery rely on sweets and other high-sugar foods to reduce their craving for alcohol, they are unknowingly creating an even greater craving. For when the blood sugar eventually drops, as it must, it brings along with it anxiety, nervousness, insomnia, panic, fear, nausea, mental confusion, irritability, depression, and craving for alcohol and/or other drugs.

We should mention two additional disorders that can contribute to protracted withdrawal symptoms—autonomic nervous system dysfunction and cortical atrophy. Both conditions are fairly common in late-stage adult alcoholics who have been drinking heavily for many years. Adolescents who regularly combine drugs or who use drugs in excessive amounts, however—even over a relatively short period of time—may experience these problems to one degree or another.

- **AUTONOMIC NERVOUS SYSTEM DYSFUNCTION:** The autonomic nervous system governs the glands, cardiac muscle, and smooth muscles of the digestive and respiratory systems, controlling such functions as blood pressure, pulse, temperature, sweating response, and muscle tone. Symptoms of dysfunction in the autonomic nervous system include excessive perspiration, rapid pulse, increased heart rate, and tremor (involuntary movements such as shaking or trembling caused by muscle contractions). These symptoms will lessen as sobriety lengthens, but lingering problems can persist for months or even years.
- *CORTICAL ATROPHY* is a term used to describe a measurable loss of function in the cerebral cortex area of the brain. This is the brain area that controls the highest levels of human functioning—analytical and abstract reasoning, speech production, facial recognition, working memory, and conscious movements. Of all the drugs, alcohol in particular targets the cortex, and excessive or prolonged drinking can lead to reduced cortical activity and symptoms such as memory lapses, difficulty reasoning, sensory deficits, muscle weakness, and coordination problems.
  Even after months of abstinence, many recovering people continue to experience problems with obsessive or

circular thinking, irrational thought patterns, and forgetfulness. Rather than label them as uncooperative, irrational, thoughtless, or irresponsible, we can learn to appreciate the underlying physiological changes that make recovery such a challenge and understand the need for patience and support as the body works to heal the widespread damage inflicted by drugs.

Understanding the causes and symptoms of the post-acute withdrawal syndrome will help you know what to do if and when your child relapses. Remember—relapse is common with every chronic disease. Remember, too, that when relapses occur, adolescents are likely to be especially hard on themselves. They may feel as if they are failures. If the people they love the most give up on them, it is far too easy for them to give up on themselves.

As parents, you will make mistakes. You will say things in disappointment, anger, and frustration that you will regret later.

Not one of us can claim perfection. We all make mistakes. The trick is to recognize when we make a mistake and try to make amends. Apologize to your child, but make sure your apology is sincere. Ask for your child's help, but be willing to listen and learn when advice is offered. Never, never give up, even when it seems that there is no reason left to hope. And always remember these words, which are as meaningful for parents as they are for children:

Sometimes I have failed, but I am not a failure; I have made mistakes, but I am not a mistake.

The Relapse Process

Recovery from addiction is like walking up a down escalator. It is impossible to stand still. When you stop moving forward, you find yourself moving backward.

—TERENCE GORSKI AND MERLENE MILLER
Staying Sober

Relapse is a process that begins long before the adolescent starts using again. Like a swell in the ocean, the energy begins to build up long before the wave crashes on the shore.

In their groundbreaking book *Staying Sober: A Guide for Relapse Prevention*, Terence Gorski and Merlene Miller offer a detailed look at the phases of relapse. With their permission, we offer a condensed and slightly adapted version of the relapse phases.

PHASE 1: INTERNAL CHANGE. You begin to feel increased stress, along with changes in thinking, feeling, and behavior. Emotions begin to swing around, from euphoria to depression, and the highs and lows often have nothing to do with what is happening in real life.

PHASE 2: DENIAL. You worry about the changes in your thinking, emotions, and behavior but try not to think about them, or you try to persuade yourself that everything is fine.

PHASE 3: AVOIDANCE AND DEFENSIVENESS. This phase involves a dual process of avoiding concerns about what's going on inside you and telling others to back off and leave you alone because there is nothing wrong. You don't want to discuss your personal problems because you fear criticism. Your behavior becomes compulsive, as you monopolize conversations, take over the care of others ("playing therapist"), and always try to maintain control. You get overinvolved in activities in order to avoid confronting your problems. You act impulsively, without thinking through your actions beforehand, and you tend to blame others for the problems your behavior creates. You spend more time alone because you are uncomfortable being with others, and you begin to feel lonely and misunderstood.

PHASE 4: CRISIS BUILDING. Your problems begin to pile up. You start focusing on one small part of your life and stop thinking about everything else. You feel depressed, listless, unmotivated. You stop planning ahead and engage in wishful thinking that things were different than they really are, or you make unrealistic plans and then feel frustrated because you can't implement them. Life seems unfair, and you feel powerless to do anything about it.

PHASE 5: IMMOBILIZATION. Nothing seems to be going your way and you feel powerless to change things. You want to give up. You spend a good part of your time daydreaming or fantasizing about escaping from your problems. You begin to feel like a failure, and you blow things out of proportion, telling yourself that you are helpless to solve your problems and nothing is going your way.

PHASE 6: CONFUSION AND OVERREACTION. You feel mentally confused and irritable. You have difficulty thinking clearly. Your feelings and emotions are often out of control. You have problems remembering things, and your mind races at times, and wanders at other times. You can't decide what to do next. At times you feel extremely emotional and at other times you feel numb, as if you have no feelings at all. Your mood swings vary dramatically, ranging from depression to anxiety to fear. You get angry with yourself for not being able to solve your problems. Your relationships are strained, and you often get in arguments or conflicts with your family and friends. Irritability and frustration increase. You lose your temper and then feel guilty about it. Your inability to control your emotions adds to your stress.

PHASE 7: DEPRESSION. You begin to wonder if life is worth living. You wonder if using alcohol or other drugs again might help you feel better. Your eating habits change as you overeat or lose your appetite and eat mostly junk food. You feel anxious, fearful, uneasy, trapped with no way out. You have difficulty falling asleep, and disturbing dreams often wake you up. Even after a good night's sleep, you feel tired. The structure of your day changes as you start skipping meals, missing appointments, and finding it difficult to plan a social life. You alternate between feeling stressed about obligations and bored with nothing to do.

As time goes by, your depression worsens and other people begin to notice and comment on the changes in your behavior. You are most depressed when you have no plans or structured activities. When you are hungry, angry, lonely, or tired (the H.A.L.T. symptoms often associated with relapse), you feel even more depressed. You begin to isolate yourself and convince yourself that no one understands you or cares about you.

PHASE 8: BEHAVIORAL LOSS OF CONTROL. Life becomes increasingly chaotic, as you have difficulty controlling your thoughts, feelings, and behavior. You can't stick to a daily schedule, and find excuses to miss counseling or Twelve Step meetings. You hide feelings of helplessness and loss of self-confidence with an "I don't care" attitude. When people offer to help, you reject them or find reason to criticize them. You think often about using again, reasoning that things can't get much worse. You feel powerless to change your life and wonder if there is no way out.

PHASE 9: RECOGNITION OF LOSS OF CONTROL. Things have gotten so bad that you can't deny them anymore. With a growing sense of fear and despair, you realize that your life has become unmanageable. At times you feel dizzy, uncoordinated, off balance, and clumsy. You feel sorry for yourself and wallow in self-pity. You feel ashamed, thinking you might be emotionally disturbed or mentally ill. You feel guilty because you know you should be attending meetings or support groups and involving yourself in activities. Your situation seems hopeless, and you find yourself thinking more and more about using again, telling yourself that you can handle it this time. Alcohol or other drugs seem like the only rational solution to your problems—you're afraid that if you don't find some relief, you'll go crazy or even kill yourself. You feel out of control and can't stop yourself from lying to others and saying or doing things that violate your most cherished values. Concluding that you are useless and incompetent, you begin to feel powerless and hopeless.

PHASE 10: OPTION REDUCTION. In this phase, you feel as if your options are running out, and the only choices left to you are insanity, suicide, or a return to alcohol and/or other drug use. Feeling trapped by pain and helplessness, you become angry with yourself, with friends and strangers, and with the world itself. Resentment and bitterness threaten to overwhelm you. As you progressively cut yourself off from others, you experience unbearable loneliness. Frustration, anger, and tension mount, and you wonder if you are truly going crazy. You seem to have no control over your thoughts, emotions, and behaviors, and you begin to experience serious problems in all areas of your life, including your health.

PHASE 11: ALCOHOL AND DRUG USE. You start using again, convincing yourself that drugs will help you solve your problems or at least allow you to escape from them for a while. In the beginning, you think you can control your drug use through social drinking or short-term binges. As time goes on, however, you realize that your addiction is once again controlling your life. You feel disappointed by your inability to control your drug use, guilty because you started using again, and ashamed. Your drug use creates serious problems in your life, damaging your relationships with family and friends, interfering with school or work, threatening your physical health, and creating severe emotional turmoil and mental confusion.

What can you do if you notice any of these warning signs in your child? How can you interrupt the process and prevent relapse from occurring? In the next chapter, we will look at the essential elements of a strong recovery program. The basic principles are simple, really, although the adolescent's journey may be slow and full of challenges. In a 1955 letter, AA cofounder Bill W. describes the hope embedded in the difficult journey:

> You are asking yourself, as all of us must: "Who am I?" . . . "Where am I?" . . . "Whence do I go?" The process of enlightenment is usually slow. But in the end, our seeking always brings a finding.

Staying Clean and Sober

Give me those days with heart in
riot,
The depths of bliss that touched on
pain,
The force of hate, and love's
disquiet—
Ah, give me back my youth again.

—GOETHE, *Faust*

Recovery takes time. A lifetime. And that's good, not bad, because recovery is more than just getting clean and sober. In its broadest, most meaningful sense, recovery is the process of becoming the person you want to be . . . the person you are meant to be.

This lifelong journey requires hard work and consistent effort. No one is going to hand you a new identity. No one—not even God—can erase your resentments, fear, shame, and guilt. Only you can do that, with patience, persistence, and determination. And, of course, time.

Adolescents, with their hearts "in riot" as German poet Goethe put it, are capable of great acts of moral courage. To be thirteen, fifteen, or seventeen and consciously, boldly begin the process of reconstructing a life that has not yet been fully lived requires a strong and resilient spirit.

> I want a different life. I don't want to live like this anymore. I want something different. I don't know what it is, exactly, or how to get it. But I want it, and somehow I'm going to try to find it.
>
> —CURTIS, *sixteen*

In recovery, adolescents learn to accept responsibility for their actions. They know they can't blame anyone else for what happens to them. They ask for help, and they do everything within their power to listen to the answers they receive. Ask a roomful of teenagers in trouble with drugs if they pray, and almost every hand will go up.

> I say my prayers every night. I ask God to help me. But I can't blame God when things go wrong. He gives me a path to run down, and if I keep going down the wrong path, He ain't gonna help me. Only thing He can do is give me choices. Maybe I don't notice all the choices, but if I take the wrong path, I can't blame it on God.
>
> —MARC, *fourteen*

As parents, educators, and helping professionals, we must be there whenever our children need us to help them find their way. If we believe in our children, they will show us a strength of character and innate goodness that we could not have imagined they possessed. We must at all times, as psychologist Bruno Bettelheim urged, "retain our conviction of their inherent goodness."

If we offer adolescents the tools they will need to stay clean and sober, they will use them. If we do not give up on them, they will not give up on themselves. They will stumble and fall, at times, for that is the way of all human beings, but with our faith, hope, knowledge, and support, they will pick themselves up, dust themselves off, and keep walking the walk.

Recovery is not magical, but it is miraculous. Magical events happen instantly, without effort, and they are always an illusion. Miracles develop gradually, over time, as shattered lives are pieced back together again. This process of healing and reconstruction—of putting the pieces back together again so that the jagged edges are smoothed out and each piece fits and belongs—comes about by paying attention to the needs of your body, mind, and spirit.

The essentials of recovery include:

- Spiritual development.
- Regular exercise.
- Good nutrition.
- Healthy relationships.
- Service to others.

Spiritual Development

It is a normal part of a child's development to begin to question his or her spiritual teachings as they grow older. It does not mean that the parent has done a poor job of teaching spiritual values; rather, it is the child or teenager's attempt to explore his or her own spiritual self. Spirituality is vital to helping one to learn to solve problems and to have a sense of well-being and purpose in life. Parents can help children and teenagers when they question their spiritual teachings by being good listeners and allowing them to express their thoughts.

—DEBORAH J. POTEET-JOHNSON, M.D.
Addiction Medicine Specialist

The question is always asked—"Why do recovering drug addicts need AA, NA, or any kind of spiritual program? Why, if addiction is a physical disease, is spirituality necessary for long-term recovery?"

Here's the simplest answer we can offer. Drugs are as toxic to the soul as they are to the liver or the brain. By *soul*, we mean all those intangible realities that give meaning and value to human life—goodness, kindness, mercy, love, empathy, courage, trust, respect, responsibility, honesty, and simple human decency.

Under the influence of alcohol and other drugs, adolescents have said and done things that create inside them great, deep wells of shame and guilt. Their morals and ethics have been twisted and torn. They have come to believe that they are not normal, good, or decent human beings, that they are, in fact, somehow defective and therefore real happiness will elude them forever. While the physical damage caused by drug addiction usually clears up within several months, the spiritual damage can last for a much longer time.

> I'm hurting. I ache inside. I've been sober for eight months, but I still feel lost. I kept thinking about these deep questions like, "Who am I? What do I want in life? Where am I going? Why should I keep trying? *What is the point of all of this?*" And I don't know the answers. I don't know how to find myself. I'm searching, I really am, but I'm not finding.
>
> —MONICA, *seventeen*

"Who am I? Where do I belong? What's the point?" These are spiritual questions, and they are as old as the hills. From the beginning of time, men and women, young and old, have been asking themselves these same questions. They are the questions we ask when we are most troubled and afraid, when we are wandering in the dark, lost, in despair, about to give up hope.

More than a hundred years ago, Russian writer Count Leo Tolstoy asked the same kind of questions. He was fifty years old at the time.

> What will be the outcome of what I do today? Of what I shall do tomorrow? What will be the outcome of all my life? Why should I love? Why should I do anything? Is there in life any purpose which the inevitable death which awaits me does not undo and destroy?
>
> These questions are the simplest in the world. From the stupid

child to the wisest old man, they are in the soul of every human being. Without an answer to them it is impossible, as I experienced, for life to go on.

We find the answers to these universal questions in different places. Some of us find what we need in organized religion. Others find what we are looking for in the simplest of prayers (*"Help me!"* *"Thank you!"*) or in nature, silent meditation, loving relationships, or service to others. Where we find the answers is not nearly as important as asking the questions, for the questions themselves take us where we need to go. Spiritual in nature, the questions have to do with *being real*, with wanting to become a *real* person.

For adolescents who are addicted to drugs, being real means that you don't have to lie to yourself anymore. Being real is about knowing and accepting yourself for who you really are, with all your faults, flaws, and imperfections. Recovery—and spirituality—is all about being real.

You know, there are a lot of questions people my age ask. I mean, what is there to do? What is left in life after alcohol is taken away from you? Also questions like, "I'm only nineteen, what am I going to do when I turn twenty-one? How am I not going to go out at night and get drunk? What am I going to do at my wedding or my prom?" But your thoughts change. . . .

If I hadn't stopped drinking, I wouldn't be where I am today. I wouldn't have the job I have or the boyfriend or the wonderful friends and relationships with my parents and stepparents. Everything is better because my head's clear and I'm more in touch with myself. I really only have me. I realize I only have me and I have to be nice to people. If I find a friend that I really like, I have to give them all I got. I can't imagine where I'd be if I was still drinking.

What really made me want to get sober is I started coming out of denial and realizing that my reality was completely fake. What I thought I was, was fake. What I thought school was, was fake. What I thought friends were, was fake. It's really hard to explain, but I would get drunk like every other alcoholic—to get out of my-self and get back into that unreality quick so I wouldn't have to deal with the reality imposing on me. I was trying to find this dreamland and I finally realized it is not the way to live. You can't live this way your whole life. You can't live in this fake world that you're creating in your head; it's being created by alcohol.

—CHINA KANTNER, *recovering alcoholic*

The real world is nothing like the dreamland of drugs. Being real means connecting to other real people who want—who *need*—to stop lying to themselves. And that's why people go to meetings and support groups, because that's where they connect with a whole roomful of people whose whole purpose at that moment, in that hour, is to "be real" with other people who also desperately want and need to be real.

I sought my soul, but my soul I could not see. I sought my God, but He eluded me. I sought my brother—and found all three.

—ANONYMOUS

"God," it is said, "works through others." In meetings and sup-port groups, adolescents in recovery discover what those words mean. They learn that everyone is searching for answers to the same basic spiritual questions—"Who am I? Where do I fit and be-long? How can I live my life? What is to become of me?" And slowly, over time, they begin to identify with others who may be outwardly different—in age, sex, ethnic group, manners, speech, economic class—but who suffer from the same basic problems and who are working toward the same basic goals.

In AA language, they learn to *identify not compare. Identification* is the act and process of recognizing yourself in other people's sto-ries. With identification comes hope, for adolescents see that other people who have struggled with the same basic problems are now living sober, happy lives.

Here is one description of how identification works.

I don't understand it, exactly. One of my best friends, his name is Francisco, went to this treatment center for sixty days, and he came back a different person. He used to be a wild man, and he could be mean, you know, get in fights, pick on people smaller than him. But now he's different. Nicer. He cares about his friends; he wants to help them.

He told me I should get help for my drinking problems. I don't know, maybe I should. I'm kind of tired of this life. I look at Francisco, and he seems happy, like he knows what he wants and he'll do whatever he needs to do to get it. That seems like a good thing, a good way to be. I'd like to be like that.

—JOSÉ, *eighteen*

Regular Exercise

I've been in detention for a week or so, and I just realized that I kind of like this life. We have a routine, you know, a schedule, like there are certain things we can do and other things we can't do without getting into trouble.

One thing they do is get us up early and make us exercise. When I exercise, I feel good about myself, good about my body. It's a high—you know, a natural high. And I've been thinking—if I feel this good inside a detention center, wearing orange overalls, sleeping on a hard bed, eating prison food, separated from my family and friends—think what it would be like if I could get into this kind of routine on the outs. Exercising instead of sleeping until noon and then getting high and playing video games all day. I don't know. It's something I've been thinking about.

—JOLAN, *seventeen*

Regular exercise helps adolescents feel better about themselves. Studies show that adolescents who exercise score higher in positive personality traits and social acceptance than those who don't.

I'm a really good hockey player. I should be playing hockey. I feel like I'm letting myself down, and my parents, too, because I could probably get a college scholarship if I keep playing. I don't know why I don't. I guess I'm too lazy. Unmotivated, smoking too much weed. I miss it, though. And I feel bad, because my parents want me to play. It's a disappointment to them. To me, too. I guess I just feel bad about the whole thing. I'm trying to stay clean and sober and I'm doing pretty well, but I wish I'd get back on the ice.

—TODD, *eighteen*

Feeling bad about yourself—feeling unmotivated, fearing that you have let yourself and others down—is dangerous to sobriety. Exercise is an effective antidote to feeling bad, for it reduces stress and tension and offers immediate physical and emotional benefits. Muscle tension eases, heart rate stabilizes, mental confusion clears, and energy increases. Regular exercise also confers long-term health benefits, including a stronger heart, increased muscle strength, greater bone density, an improved immune system, more efficient neurological functioning, and protection against weight gain and obesity.

I feel strong after I run or take a long walk. I don't like feeling weak and lazy, just sitting around all the time. That's boring. If I exercise, I have the motivation to get up and do something.

—SABRINA, *fourteen*

It makes me feel good when I play football and basketball. I'm moving, not just sitting around. After I exercise, I like myself better.

—DERRICK, *seventeen*

Nearly half of adolescents between the ages of twelve and twenty-one are not vigorously active on a regular basis, and about 14 percent of adolescents report that they do not exercise at all—statistics that are linked directly to the staggering rise in obesity among children and adolescents.

Since 1976, obesity has increased by more than 50 percent among our country's children and teenagers. According to the U.S. surgeon general, "The most immediate consequence of overweight as perceived by the children themselves is social discrimination. This is associated with poor self-esteem and depression."

The mother of a sixteen-year-old boy recovering from marijuana and alcohol addiction offers this perspective on the problem of obesity:

> Don't let your kids get fat! The child then suffers from poor self-esteem, poor peer relationships, and they'll do anything to overcome the lack of self-esteem. This is my sixteen-year-old son's biggest hurdle. The way he sees himself is so vital, and so all-consuming.

And then, of course, there is the problem of getting too thin. Many adolescent girls and an increasing number of boys use stimulant drugs—cocaine, methamphetamines, Ritalin, Adderall—to lose weight, fast. Drugs give them a magical way to get skinny without investing any effort at all.

> I used to be really, really fat. So I started taking over-the-counter diet pills. Then a friend told me about meth and I thought, "Well, I'll just use a little, enough to lose ten pounds or so." On my last binge, I didn't eat or drink for three weeks, and I went from a size eleven to a size three.
>
> —GENEVA, *sixteen*

In recovery, adolescents need to discover how exercise can help them control their weight in a healthy way, while simultaneously strengthening their bodies, sharpening their minds, and lifting their spirits. How often should adolescents exercise? What type of exercise is best? Most fitness experts agree that adolescents need to exercise at least three to four times a week, for twenty to thirty minutes at a time. Those who participate in team sports will get at least that much exercise.

Both aerobic and anaerobic exercises are important.

- **AEROBIC EXERCISE**, which depends on oxygen for energy, and conditions the lungs and heart. Continuous activities such as running, swimming, bicycling, in-line skating, rowing, basketball, soccer, or fast walking are forms of aerobic exercise.
- **ANAEROBIC EXERCISE**—repeated short intervals of high-intensity exercise such as weight lifting and strength training—burns stored sugar for energy and contributes to strength, bone density, and muscle tone.

Good Nutrition

Food can act as drugs, and we must be aware of how our moods and physiology—mental and physical—are so inextricably intertwined that what and how we eat can have an enormous impact on our lives.

—CANDACE B. PERT, Ph.D.
Author of Molecules of Emotion

What we eat and drink has both immediate and long-lasting effects on our moods, emotions, our ability to think and reason, and our self-esteem.

Unfortunately, most treatment programs spend little if any time teaching adolescents about the central role diet and nutrition play in recovery. That means parents will need to educate themselves and consistently remind their children to follow the simple but extremely important rules of good nutrition.

General Rules for Good Nutrition

RULE 1: EAT THREE NUTRITIOUS MEALS EVERY DAY.
Concentrate on natural, whole, unprocessed, and unrefined foods such as fresh vegetables, fresh fruits, and whole grains. Avoid sugar, white flour, white bread, white pasta, white rice, fast foods, high-sugar foods, and high-fat foods whenever possible.

Remember—don't skip breakfast! "But I'm not hungry in the morning!" adolescents often say. Explain to your children that a nutritious breakfast speeds up metabolism, helping you burn calories and giving you the energy needed to motivate yourself, think clearly, and reason effectively. Studies show that children and adolescents who eat breakfast have fewer discipline problems, fewer visits to the school nurse, and higher test scores.

Breakfast doesn't have to be toast, cereal, pancakes, or bacon and eggs. Sliced lunch meat, soup, leftover mashed potatoes heated in the microwave, yogurt, and trail mix (without the M&M's) are all healthy breakfast choices.

RULE 2: EAT THREE NUTRITIOUS SNACKS EVERY DAY.
Space the snacks several hours apart, between meals—one in mid-morning, another in mid-afternoon, and a final snack in the evening, an hour or so before bedtime. Snacks will keep your blood sugar at a steady level, which will, in turn, keep your energy high; prevent hypoglycemic reactions that can affect mood, concentration, and focus; and reduce cravings for alcohol and other drugs.

Here are some easy-to-prepare, nutritious snacks that kids can fix for themselves:

- Whole-grain bread, crackers, or melba toast with peanut butter, tuna fish, egg salad, or cheese.
- Sliced apples, carrot sticks, and cheese.
- Nonfat or low-fat yogurt.
- Milk and a peanut butter sandwich.
- Almonds, seeds, peanuts, walnuts, or other nuts.
- Energy bars.
- Popcorn sprinkled with wheat germ.
- Low-fat milk and graham crackers.
- Whole wheat muffin with tomato sauce and cheese.
- Low-sugar cereal with low-fat or nonfat milk.

RULE 3: CUT BACK ON SWEETS. High-sugar foods—desserts, candy, soft drinks, high-sugar cereals—flood the body with a sudden surge of glucose, leading to a sharp rise in blood sugar, followed by a steep crash. This blood sugar roller coaster, called hypoglycemia, brings on many distressing symptoms.

Physical symptoms include body tremors (internal and external trembling), heart palpitations, headaches, muscle pain, backache, numbness, chronic indigestion, cold hands and feet, sighing, yawning, ringing in the ears, dry mouth, hot flashes, and noise and light sensitivity.

Psychological symptoms include moodiness, exhaustion, insomnia, depression, anxiety, irritability, headaches, forgetfulness, intense cravings for sweets, memory problems, nervousness, constant worrying, indecisiveness, mental confusion, crying spells, phobias, difficulty concentrating, and temper tantrums.

RULE 4: CUT BACK ON CAFFEINE. Caffeine is a powerful stimulant capable of upsetting blood sugar control and causing the physical and psychological symptoms listed above. Caffeine can also cause or aggravate gastrointestinal disorders, leading to nausea, diarrhea, and indigestion.

Caffeine is found in caffeinated coffee and teas, chocolate, cocoa, most soft drinks, and certain over-the-counter drugs such as Midol and No-Doz.

RULE 5: TAKE VITAMIN, MINERAL, AND AMINO ACID SUPPLEMENTS. Nutritional supplements will speed up your body's ability to repair cells and tissues, restore nutrients depleted by heavy drinking or other drug use, and fight infections and diseases. Adolescents can safely take the following supplements: a high-potency multivitamin and mineral supplement once a day, and a B-50 or B-100 complex one to three times daily.

Important reminder: Taking a nutritional supplement is not a replacement for eating nutritious foods. Be sure to ask your physician or health care practitioner for advice before taking nutritional supplements.

RULE 6: CUT BACK ON SOFT DRINKS (SODAS). Soft drinks are the leading source of added sugar in our diets. The annual consumption of soft drinks in the United States averages more than fifty-six gallons for every man, woman, and child.

Adolescents consume lots of soft drinks. Teenage boys drink more than girls—65 percent of adolescent girls and 74 percent of adolescent boys consume soft drinks daily. Boys between the ages of thirteen and eighteen average three or more cans a day, with 10 percent of boys drinking five or more cans a day. Girls between thirteen and eighteen average two cans a day, with 10 percent of girls drinking five or more cans a day.

A twelve-ounce soft drink contains from 140 to 200 calories and about eight teaspoons of sugar in addition to other unhealthy ingredients such as caffeine and phosphoric acid. Drinking two or more soft drinks a day can have a profound effect on our children's health (and, of course, our own), causing or contributing to the following health problems:

- **OBESITY:** A recent study published in the prestigious British journal *Lancet* links soft drink consumption to obesity in children and concludes that for every can or bottle of soda a child drinks, his or her chances of becoming obese *increase 60 percent.* (In the United States, obesity rates increased 61 percent from 1990 to 2000, and they continue to rise.)
- **TOOTH DECAY:** Sugar and sugar-rich foods cause tooth decay, and the acids in soft drinks compound the problem by dissolving protective tooth enamel.

- **CAFFEINE OVERLOAD:** Many soft drinks contain caffeine. Daily use can disturb brain chemistry, create spikes and steep drops in blood sugar, and induce caffeine withdrawal with symptoms such as headaches, irritability, stomach problems, nervousness, anxiety, insomnia, and increases in blood pressure.
- **WEAK BONES:** Phosphoric acid, a common ingredient in soft drinks, weakens the bones by promoting the loss of calcium. A twelve-ounce can of soda contains approximately thirty milligrams of phosphoric acid. A recent Harvard study showed that girls who drink soft drinks are five times more likely to have broken bones.

  Because the peak bone-building years are during adolescence, any weakening or damage to our bones can have lifelong consequences. Researchers warn that the phosphoric acid in soft drinks is a major contributor to the rising increase in osteoporosis in this country.
- **VITAMIN AND MINERAL DEPLETION:** Twenty years ago, teenagers in the United States drank twice as much milk as soda—today's adolescents drink twice as many soft drinks as milk and, as a result, are less likely to get the recommended levels of vitamins A, C, and magnesium. The calories supplied in soft drinks can contribute to vitamin and mineral depletion by reducing the appetite for nutritious foods.

Diet soft drinks are equally bad for your health. Diet sodas contain aspartame, which has been linked to depression, insomnia, anxiety, irritability, weakness, dizziness, migraine headaches, and seizures; artificial flavors and colorings, which can have adverse effects on health; phosphoric acid; and caffeine. We strongly advise you to avoid them.

> **RULE 7: DRINK LOTS OF WATER.** Researchers believe that dehydration is the number one cause of daytime

fatigue. When we're dehydrated—when we don't have enough water in our bodies—we feel tired and drained of energy. Our short-term memory is fuzzy, and we have difficulty concentrating. Our metabolism also slows down as our bodies work to conserve energy.

As parents, we should push water on our children, offering them a glass of water at every meal and giving them bottled water to take to school and extracurricular activities. Be sure to emphasize the facts about drinking water that are especially important to teens. Drinking eight or more glasses of water a day, for example:

- Helps control weight gain. When we are thirsty, our bodies translate thirst pains into hunger pains. In other words, we may feel hungry when we are really thirsty. If we drink water, the hunger pains disappear.
- Improves concentration, memory, and abstract thinking.
- Significantly reduces the risk of cancer, including colon, breast, and bladder cancers.
- Eases back and joint pain.

RULE 8: AVOID FAST FOODS—AND NEVER CHOOSE THE HUGE PORTIONS LABELED "SUPERSIZE." Fast foods are low in fiber, vitamins, minerals, and whole grains—and high in fat and sugar. Avoid them whenever you can. Supersizing can double, triple, or even quadruple the regular portions, adding extra grams of fat and hundreds of calories.

Healthy Relationships

It's tough to be a tulip when you're growing up with weeds.

—PETER, *eighteen*

Healthy relationships are essential to maintaining sobriety. If adolescents are involved in relationships in which they feel misunderstood, used, abused, or unappreciated, their recovery is in jeopardy.

For adolescents, of course, the main risk in relationships is hanging out with friends who still use. If most of your child's friends continue to use drugs, the risk of relapse is extremely high. In fact, hanging out with drug-using friends can be viewed as a way of setting up a relapse. "If everyone I know uses drugs, how am I supposed to stay clean?" the adolescent might reason.

In treatment, adolescents are often encouraged to write letters to their old drug-using friends.

In my third week of treatment, I wrote to all my friends and told them I couldn't hang out with them anymore if they continued to use drugs. That was the hardest thing I had to do, because all my friends used drugs!

When I got home, some of my friends stopped by to see me. I asked them if they were still using, and they said they were, so I told them not to come by anymore. Eventually I made new friends, but that first year was really hard. I spent a lot of time in AA and NA meetings, talking often with my sponsor and studying hard.

It's weird, though. About a year later, two of my old friends decided to go into treatment. They were just tired of their lives. I think sometimes it comes to that—you just get tired of using and feeling bad all the time. So now I have old sober friends. That feels good. I feel like I was kind of a model to them. Like they saw what I did and thought, "Hey, maybe I can do that, too." And now we support each other. It's pretty cool.

—LUCY, *eighteen*

Kids can do everything right—go to meetings, exercise, eat nutritious foods—but if their relationships are unhealthy, their physical and mental health will suffer. Staying away from friends who use drugs is absolutely essential. It is also incredibly difficult, for drugs are everywhere and so are the kids who use them. All too often, avoiding drug-using friends means staying at home alone, night after night.

> I was sober for eight months, with just two relapses, one on my birthday and one on the Fourth of July. Every day I'd go to school and then I'd come home and play video games or watch TV. Every day it was the same thing. Look—I want to stay sober, I really do, but life without alcohol—which means life without my old friends and life without parties—is just so incredibly dull. I don't know how I'm going to keep doing this.
>
> —JASON, *seventeen*

As parents, probation officers, teachers, and community members, we need to work together to create opportunities for adolescents to meet new friends and engage in healthy activities. Talk to your child and find activities that he or she enjoys. A part-time job or volunteer position can be a lifesaver. Joining an outdoor or adventure club, becoming involved in church, participating in YMCA or YWCA activities, taking music or dance lessons, joining a youth group, or helping out with community service projects offer opportunities for adolescents to stay busy, meet new people, expand their horizons, and feel good about themselves.

Relationships are never easy, for interpersonal skills—learning how to be flexible and adaptable, surrendering your own will to another person's needs or desires, being honest always and at all times, expressing thoughts and emotions openly and compassionately, being a good listener—are developed over a lifetime. Many adolescents, particularly those who started using drugs when they were nine, ten, eleven, or twelve years old, have little experience or practice in these areas. Nor do they always have good models.

Here again is the value of Twelve Step and other support groups, where adolescents learn how to relate to others who are also suffering and struggling. In groups, teens discover that they can develop close relationships with people with whom they may have nothing in common other than their drug problems.

On the very last page of her book *Drinking: A Love Story*, recovering alcoholic Caroline Knapp describes an AA meeting, in which a woman named Megan talked about losing her job and custody of her son, a guy named Bill talked about his fear of starting over again, and a young man named John told his story about his first year of sobriety and how grateful he was to be alive. In the book's concluding paragraph, Knapp (who died of lung cancer from cigarette smoking at age forty-two) discusses the feelings evoked by these simple, heartfelt stories:

> I sat near the back and looked out over the room. Familiar faces, unfamiliar faces, all of us more or less like John, pulling in the same direction. Then I had an image of every person in that room climbing into bed that night, all fifty of us getting into our beds clean and sober, another day without a drink behind us. It was a simple image but it filled me with a range of complicated feelings: appreciation for the simple presence of all those people; admiration for their courage and strength; a tinge of melancholy for the amount of pain it must have taken each and every one of them to put down the drink; affection for their humanity.
>
> I didn't realize until hours later that there was a name for that feeling. It's called love.

In Twelve Step meetings and recovery support groups, adolescents learn what it means to feel safe, protected, understood, at home. The challenge confronting all of us who care about the world we are leaving to our children is to expand that sense of fitting into and belonging in the larger community, creating places where all children feel safe and protected. We cannot leave that task to our civic leaders and community activities. We have to care enough about our children and their children and all the generations of children to come to roll up our sleeves and start digging. We have to understand what we must do to create safe havens for our children:

> Children are like the tiny figures at the center of the nesting dolls for which Russian folk artists are famous. The children are cradled

in the family, which is primarily responsible for their passage from infancy to adulthood. But around the family are the larger settings of neighborhood, school, church, workplace, community, culture, economy, society, nation, and world, which affect children directly or through the well-being of their families.

Each of us participates in several of these interlocking layers of the village. Each of us, therefore, has the opportunity and responsibility to protect and nurture children. We owe it to them to do what we can to better their lives every day—as parents and through the myriad choices we make as employers, workers, consumers, volunteers, and citizens. We owe it to them to set higher expectations for ourselves. We must stop making excuses for why we can't give our children what they need at home and beyond to become healthy, well-educated, empathetic, and productive adults

—HILARY RODHAM CLINTON
It Takes a Village

Service to Others

The spiritual approach was as useless as any other if you soaked it up like a sponge and kept it to yourself.

—DR. BOB, *AA cofounder*

In recovery, we learn a vital spiritual lesson: *You get what you give, and when you give something away, you will surely get something back.*

This insight runs contrary to so much of what adolescents learned during their months or years of drug use. For drugs focus us in on ourselves—they make us greedy. Drunk, high, stoned, baked, burned, blasted, ripped, or roasted, we think only of *our* needs, *our* wants, *our* cravings.

Self-centeredness always and inevitably accompanies regular drug use and addiction, and adolescence itself is a self-absorbed phase of life in which kids struggle to know who they are and where they fit and belong. Is it any wonder, then, that drug-using teenagers think first and often only of themselves? In *The Varieties of Religious Experience*, psychologist/philosopher William James makes the point that we grow into a spiritual life and that this growth is a normal and natural phase of adolescence:

> The age is the same, falling usually between fourteen and seventeen. The symptoms are the same—sense of incompleteness and imperfection; brooding, depression, morbid introspection, and sense of sin; anxiety about the hereafter; distress over doubts, and the like. And the result is the same—a happy relief and objectivity, as the confidence in self gets greater through the adjustment of the faculties to the wider outlook.

As we develop this wider outlook, we stop thinking only about ourselves and start thinking about others. Shifting the focus off ourselves and onto others, we discover that there is more to happiness than feeling good. *Feeling good*, after all, is a momentary thrill—adolescents feel good when they use drugs, but after several minutes or hours, the feeling goes away. *Being good*, on the other hand, is a way of life that focuses us and keeps us directed, guiding us through life's inevitable ups and downs. *Being good* is the only pathway to true and long-lasting feeling good.

Adolescents often talk about wanting to be good even as they tell their stories about being bad. The following conversation took place among four adolescent boys locked up in detention.

"I want a reputation for being a ladies' man," said Luis, sixteen, with a big smile.

"Yeah, that's good." Mario, fifteen, laughed. "I want that reputation, too. But I also want to be known as a risk taker, someone who is not afraid of anything or anybody."

"Me? I want people to be scared of me, to say, 'He's got no conscience, watch out for him,'" said Doug, seventeen.

When it was his turn to speak, sixteen-year-old Derrick hesitated. He looked at his hands, folded in front of him, and then he began to speak softly, so the rest of the group had to lean forward to hear him.

"I want to be known as a person that follows God," he said. "I want to be a good person. I think that there's a reason for everything—like, there's a reason I'm here right now. I need to understand the reason and then try to follow what God would want me to do."

Luis nodded his head. "Yeah, I know what you mean," he said. "I've been praying. I never prayed before. But I pray now, every day, every night, I ask for help. And I feel like God is helping me."

"I don't know if I believe in God," said Mario. "But I want to be a good person, too."

"Me, too, I guess," Doug said. "I'd like to be a better person. I just don't know how to do it."

Learning how to be good is a process that develops over time. Drugs interfere with that process. As we seek to help our children find their way in life, can we teach them how to be good? Yes, but only by our own example. Child psychiatrist Bruno Bettelheim, author of *A Good Enough Parent*, explains:

A child is rarely *convinced* that something is wrong simply because his parents say it is. It *becomes* wrong to him because he wishes to be loved by his parents, to be thought well of by them. Since the best way to be loved, in the short run, is to do what the parents approve of and in the long run to become like them, he identifies with their values. This identification is thus the result of loving and admiring one's parents, not of being punished by them.

Teaching our children about values—goodness, kindness, mercy, tolerance, forgiveness, gratitude, humility, faith, hope, love—is one of the greatest challenges facing adults. So often we focus on the negative and neglect the positive. We tell our kids what *not* to do without talking to them about the virtues and values that can help them believe in their own goodness and in the inherent goodness of others.

I hear all the time how bad I am. But never once have my parents praised me for trying to do good, for trying to be good.

—DJ, *seventeen*

My mother has never, not once in her life, told me she was sorry for something she said or did. She is always right, in her mind. I can't imagine what it would feel like to hear her say "I'm sorry." I just can't imagine what that would be like.

—BRENDA, *thirteen*

Perhaps the greatest service we can perform for our children is to believe in them, to see the good in them, to willingly and openly admit our own limitations and imperfections, and—most important of all—to live our own lives in concert with the values and moral principles that we set forth for our children. For then they will know that we mean what we say.

L.I.S.T.E.N.

Adolescence—the only time we ever
learned anything

—MARCEL PROUST

I go to school to youth to learn the
future.

—ROBERT FROST

Literally millions of words have been written on parenting, with hundreds of experts offering advice about how best to raise our children.

But let's keep things simple. Life is too complicated, and drug problems overlaid on the already difficult and challenging task of parenting an adolescent can create a hopeless muddle.

If you keep in mind the acronym *L.I.S.T.E.N.*, you will always be able to remember the most important lessons about raising children:

L: Learn
I: Inspire
S: Set Limits
T: Teach Values
E: Empathize
N: Negotiate

Learn

Effective parenting is a learned skill. Work to learn all you can.

—DANIEL AMEN, M.D.

When we show a willingness to learn from our children—to really, truly learn from them by listening with an open heart and mind—we establish a foundation of honesty and trust. We convey the message that we value what they have to say, and we honor their willingness to speak openly and honestly with us. Most important of all, we let them know that we are teachable—that we do not have all the answers.

When an interviewer asked comedian Bill Cosby why kids trust him, he answered:

> Because I understand them. When I talk to them, I give them a
> chance to think and answer. Many adults don't have the patience
> for that.

If we want to have real conversations with our children, we need to accept certain ground rules. The first requirement is an open mind. If we think we've learned everything there is to learn and if we believe that good parenting consists of imposing our hard-earned lessons on our children, we close the door to learning and growing. If we shut our eyes to other perspectives, including the wisdom and experience of our own children, we cannot hope to have a healthy relationship with our offspring.

Keeping an open mind is challenging, for when we consciously work to understand our child's perspective, we must temporarily suppress our own point of view. This active effort to enter another person's inner world takes hard work and discipline, especially when we are dealing with a hostile, angry, or rebellious teenager.

The second essential element involved in learning from our children is the willingness to admit that we do not have all the answers. If your child asks you a question and you don't know the answer, don't try to pretend you do. Your child will know you are not being honest. Be willing to answer truthfully and say, "I don't know"—words that convey your humility and your refusal to coerce or control your child with bogus information.

Finally, an open mind requires a willingness to admit that you have made—and will continue to make—mistakes. We all learn from experience, and we learn best from painful experiences. That's one reason parenting is such a difficult and demanding occupation—we learn how to do it as we do it. We learn from experience, which is to say that we learn from our mistakes. As Bruno Bettelheim wrote in the preface to his best-selling book *A Good Enough Parent*:

> . . . in order to raise a child well one ought not to try to be a perfect parent, as much as one should not expect one's child to be, or to become, a perfect individual. Perfection is not within the grasp of ordinary human beings.

You are not a perfect parent. No one is. You will make little mistakes, and you will also make some whoppers. Learn from those mistakes. Learn how to admit that you are not perfect and that you are not perfectly in control. Through these admissions, you will convey your willingness to learn and in the process become a better person yourself.

If you keep your mind open, you will learn that adolescents are great teachers. Their wisdom is simple and straightforward—they may not have the big words, the perfect sentence structure, or the emotional maturity to put into words everything they are thinking and feeling, but each and every adolescent has much to teach us.

Here are several specific ways that you can convey your willingness to learn from your children:

- **STOP EVERYTHING ELSE YOU ARE DOING:** Most of us have become adept at doing two things at once—talking on the phone and doing the dishes, listening to a ball game while weeding the garden, checking our e-mail while our children are talking to us, cleaning the house with headphones on, driving a car and talking on the cell phone.

Multitasking may make us feel more efficient, but when we split our attention between two chores, we necessarily lower our effectiveness at each task. If we really want to learn from our children and, by learning, strengthen our relationship with them, we must stop everything else we are doing and listen. (This is good advice for all our relationships, not just those with our children.)

For there is listening, and then there is *listening*. When we really listen—with an open mind and without an attempt to convince or control—we stop what we are doing and focus all our attention where it matters, on our child. A story makes the point better than a thousand words.

One Sunday I was entertained in a farm home of a member of a rural church. The intelligence and unusually good behavior of the only child in the home, a little four-year-old boy, impressed me.

Then I discovered one reason for the child's charm. The mother was at the kitchen sink, washing the intricate parts of the cream separator, when the little boy came to her with a magazine.

"Mother," he asked, "what is this man in the picture doing?" To my surprise she dried her hands, sat down on a chair, and taking the boy in her lap, she spent the next few minutes answering his questions.

After the child had left, I commented on her having interrupted her chores to answer the boy's question, saying, "Most mothers wouldn't have bothered."

"I expect to be washing cream separators for the rest of my life," she told me, "but never again will my son ask me that question."

—AUTHOR UNKNOWN *(the story appeared in a Marquette, Michigan, church bulletin)*

■ **ENTER YOUR CHILD'S WORLD:** Listen to your teenager's favorite music—you can bear it for a few minutes, and that is often all it takes to make your children feel that you are willing to pay attention to something that matters to them. Ask what your child likes about the music—the beat? the lyrics? the band members?—and be willing to talk about the kind of music you used to listen to when you were an adolescent. Chances are that your music was just as strange and jarring to your parents' ears as your child's music is to yours.

Talk to your child's friends. Get to know them; show an interest in what they are doing. Ask questions but try to avoid judging them by asking questions with hidden (or not-so-hidden) judgments such as, "How did your mother feel when you came home with that tattoo?" or "Was your father upset when you flunked chemistry?"

These questions carry extra baggage, for they imply an already formed opinion—"I can imagine how your mother must have felt!" and "Your father must have been furious!" Ask open-ended questions instead, such as "I always wondered what it felt like to get a tattoo—was it painful?" or "I took chemistry when I was in high school, and it was my toughest class—will you be able to repeat the course?"

- **WATCH OUT FOR THE "WHY" QUESTIONS,** which can be particularly offensive to adolescents who hear criticism even when it is not intended, as Bruno Bettelheim explains.

The fact is that it is most children's experience that we rarely ask them to explain conduct of which we thoroughly approve; we ask for reasons when we are dissatisfied, and children know this. For example, most of us are not in the habit of asking, "Why did you work so hard to make such excellent grades in school?" We ask, "Why didn't you do your homework?" not "Why did you come in to do your homework when you were having such a good time playing outside?" We rarely, if ever, ask, "Why are you so nice to your brother?" or "Why did you pick up your room so well?" We may be ready to lavish praise on a well-behaved child, but we are unlikely to question his motives—even though these may be as complex and even questionable as those that underlie bad behavior. So he knows a question usually implies disapproval.

- **DON'T BE IN SUCH A HURRY:** We're always rushing from one thing to the next, and our kids are caught up in the maelstrom. "Hurry up!" "Get a move on!" "Come on!" And, in exasperation, "Why are you always so slow?"

A study conducted many years ago in an obstetric ward shows that we start the "hurry up" process almost immediately after our children are born. Mothers in this study hurried their babies, often in critical voices, to wake up, eat, burp, and perform. The most frequent remark was, "Come on."

"Come on, wake up!" "Come on, you have to drink more than an ounce!" "Come on, open your mouth!" "Come on and burp!" "Come on, show off for the lady!"

The message we give our children, almost from birth, is that we don't believe they will do what is good for them unless we push and prod them along.

- **ADOPT A LISTENING POSTURE:** The way you sit or stand, the gestures you make, and the facial expressions you wear when you talk to your child convey an attitude of respect—or one of disrespect. Watching you, your child will learn important lessons about how to listen and learn from others.

In *The Power of Empathy*, clinical psychologist Arthur Ciaramicoli describes how he learned to listen well by watching his father.

I learned to listen from my father, who understood both the power of the spoken word and the even greater authority contained in the silent spaces created when we listen with wholehearted attention. I watched my father as he listened to others, observing the way he consciously focused his attention. I saw how he took great care in the phrasing of his questions, in the pauses that signified his reluctance to come up with quick or easy answers, and in the small gestures that told his listeners he was paying wholehearted attention.

My father had what I call a *listening posture* that conveyed his total absorption in the conversation. Like someone in prayer, he had a way of consciously stilling himself, focusing his mind, and making sure that nothing distracted him from the task at hand. Leaning forward, his eyes intent, his hands folded together, he would ask a question, and then he would listen without interrupting.

When the speaker was finished, my father would be quiet. He might light a cigarette or sip his coffee, taking a moment to reflect on what had been said. Then he would ask a question. And another and another. Afterward he would make sure that the other person had a chance to say everything in his or her mind. Then and only then would he offer his carefully considered thoughts.

Inspire

Our children pay close attention to what we say and do, and they seem to know immediately when we are being evasive or dishonest. If we tell them not to swear but use bad language ourselves, they know we are living a lie. If we insist they stay away from drugs because drugs are bad for them but drink alcohol, smoke marijuana, or snort cocaine ourselves, they see the hypocrisy and learn well from it. If we lie and deceive, why shouldn't they?

We learn our most important lessons in life not from books or belief systems but from people, in the give-and-take of ordinary conversations and experiences. From other people's stories—especially our parents' stories—we learn how to be a particular kind of person. Identifying with our parents, we internalize what they have taught us and use these lessons as a map for our own lives.

Knowing how another human being lives and functions on the inside—how he or she handles the vicissitudes of life, copes with its joys and frustrations, faces critical choices, meets failure and defeat as well as challenge and success—is what enables us to feel prepared for life.

It is the availability of appropriate individuals with whom we can identify, individuals who also permit us to do so, which quiets the inner yearning for preparedness, for an external model that may serve as an internal guide for the self.

—GERSHEN KAUFMAN
Shame: The Power of Caring

And so we must ask ourselves several very difficult questions: Are we appropriate models for our children? Are we inspiring our children by our own behavior, teaching them how to handle the ups and downs of life and cope with both joy and frustration, success and failure?

Are we, our children's parents, appropriate individuals with whom our child can identify? This is a critically important question that can also be phrased in this way: "Do I want my children to identify with me and use me as an external model that will then serve as an internal guide for their own development?"

Though essential, the question is also a bit unfair. For not one person on this earth is finished with the process of becoming the person he or she wants to be. But perhaps we can focus our attention and energy on the word *becoming*, for we are all in the process of becoming and in that lifelong journey we will make many mistakes. We are all, even the most emotionally balanced, compassionate, and self-respecting among us, imperfect.

Rather than trying to inspire our children by being perfect—always right, always in control, always effective, always having the final word—we might try to inspire by way of imperfection. This would mean that we openly acknowledge our struggles and our failures and that we are honest about our past mistakes. Admitting our own imperfections, we are automatically wary of taking an authoritarian stance—"You will do this or else"—for we understand that our children will stumble and fall, as we have. Rather than inspiring our children through fear of punishment, we encourage them to develop self-control and self-discipline based on the idea that "I want to do the right thing because then I will be like my parent who struggles (but does not always succeed) to do the right thing."

Foster Cline, coauthor of *Parenting Teens with Love and Logic*, calls this the concept of "hurting from the inside out":

> There are two ways of hurting: from the outside in, and from the inside out. Hurting from the outside in only goes skin deep. It occurs when someone else is angry or when teens can't make a connection between the infraction and the parent's response. It just doesn't sink in. This occurs when the response is not something that would happen to an adult in the real world [such as being grounded].
>
> Instead of punishment, we use "the concept of hurting from the inside out." We allow children to suffer the consequences of their decisions so that every time they ask themselves this question—"Who's making me hurt like that?"—they have to turn around and say, "Oh, me."
>
> . . . When teens hurt from the inside out by correctly suffering the consequences of their actions, they examine their actions. This takes some thought, because laying down consequences is not always a natural thing for us [parents]. We may have to stop and reflect on what would happen in the real world in order for us to identify what the consequences should be for our teen.
>
> As an alternative to punishment, give a lot of thought to how you can reinforce positive behavior, look for solutions, help your child reach his or her own conclusions, and allow the natural consequences to occur.

As we inspire our children by reinforcing their positive behaviors, laying down consequences fairly and consistently, and being

willing to listen, learn, and admit our own mistakes, we also motivate them with honesty. In all our interactions with our children,
we can repeatedly stress honesty as a core value.

Tell your children what you think, deep down. Be emotionally
honest with them. Let them know that their behavior has an emotional impact on you. Respond to them with real, honest feelings
and responses.

"But how honest should I be about my own past?" you might
ask. A father's answer to this question, published in *Time* magazine's "Viewpoint," offers some guidance.

> We problem drinkers who've put away the bottle know well how
> little others' warnings affect us (except, perhaps, to make us more
> defiant) and are doubtful about the impact of our own words. . . .
> But we can at least be honest. When it comes to conditioning chil-
> dren's behavior with words, maybe that's the most a parent can
> wish for: to preserve his own integrity and pray that his child is
> duly impressed. . . . I'll try to teach [my child] by my own abstinent
> example and take solace in not having lied about my own youth. . . .

If we use alcohol and/or other drugs and if, in an attempt (usually subconscious) to minimize our own drug problems, we make
excuses and rationalizations for our children, we are creating an external model for their future development. If we voice disrespect
for "the system" or try to absolve our children of responsibility for
their own behavior, we teach our children to be disrespectful and
irresponsible. If we deny our own problems, our children will learn
to deny theirs.

And if we impose our way of life on their lives, they may never
have the opportunity to discover who they really are. As British
psychiatrist R. D. Laing observed:

> Others tell one who one is. Later one endorses, or tries to discard,
> the way others have defined one. It is difficult not to accept their
> story. One may try not to be what one "knows" one is, in one's

heart of hearts. . . . [But all too often,] we learn to be whom we are told we are.

Inspiring our children to become their own true selves, through our own honesty and openness, may be the ultimate goal of parenting.

Set Limits

Even as we give our children freedom to make their own mistakes and chart their own pathway in life, so should we draw the boundaries that will serve as the outer limits of acceptable behavior. Setting firm boundaries and consistently enforcing them gives our children a sense of security, for they know what is expected of them. If we do not establish boundaries, the very real danger exists that our children might assume that we don't care about them.

> Here's my advice for parents—set boundaries. Everyone needs boundaries, chores, responsibilities. But don't go overboard. Don't expect too much and don't argue with every petty little thing.
>
> —MANDEN, *sixteen*

Here are some specific suggestions that may help you in setting limits:

- **DON'T SWEAT THE SMALL STUFF:** Choose your battles and focus your energy on the behaviors and attitudes that put your children at real risk of physical or emotional harm. You will have to decide for yourself what really matters, but one guide might be to ask if a particular behavior will cause long-term pain or suffering. Is it worth fighting over piercing her belly button or dyeing his hair green? Might it help to loosen your boundaries in some areas, giving your children freedom to express themselves, and then draw the line when it comes to behaviors that are harmful and self-destructive?

- **PROTECTION, NOT PUNISHMENT:** Explain to your children that the point of setting limits is not to punish but to teach. When talking to your children about drugs, you might want to follow these examples, adapted from the Office of National Drug Control Policy's booklet "Keeping Your Kids Drug Free":

  - The rule in our house is that nobody uses drugs.
  - If you're at a party and you see that drugs or alcohol are being used, the rule is to leave that party. Call me and I'll come and get you.
  - I love you and I want the best for you, so I don't want you using alcohol, marijuana, or any other drug.
  - I don't want you riding in a car with a driver who's been using drugs or who's been drinking.
  - I love you, but you've got to know I'm your parent, not one of your friends. As your parent, I will not put up with you being in a place where drugs are being used.
  - It's my job as a parent to keep you safe, so I'm going to ask you questions about who you're with and what you are doing.

- **HELP YOUR CHILDREN FIND WAYS TO AVOID RISKY SITUATIONS:** Talk to your children about what they can say to friends or acquaintances who offer them drugs. Ask them what they would say or do in certain situations. You might want to offer some examples of words or phrases they could use if someone offers them drugs. Here are some examples offered by the National Youth Anti-Drug Media Campaign:

  - I like you, but I don't like drugs.
  - No, thanks. It's not for me.

- I'd get kicked off the soccer [baseball, football, basketball] team if I were caught doing drugs.
- I have a big game tomorrow.
- I'm up for a scholarship and don't want to blow it.

And here are some additional ideas:

- I've got addiction all through my family and I'm not willing to take the risk.
- I've seen what drugs do to people, and I don't want to lose everything that matters to me.
- It's not worth the risk.
- Drugs mess with your body and your mind. I'm not willing to throw away what I've got.

- **ESTABLISH CONSEQUENCES IF YOUR CHILD DOES NOT FOLLOW THE RULES:** Rules are rules, and parents need to be clear and consistent. Clearly state the rules you expect your children to follow, establish the consequences that will be imposed if the rules are broken, and list the privileges your children will enjoy if they follow the rules. Discuss the rules, consequences, and privileges in advance, and make sure your children agree with them and understand exactly what will be expected of them.

  You can create rules regarding curfews, chores, behavior at school, grades, alcohol and other drug use, telephone use, computer time, driving privileges, profanity, and attendance at counseling sessions or meetings with probation officers, but try not to go overboard—decide on the four or five most important rules you expect your children to follow and then stick to them.

- **TEACH SELF-CONTROL AND SELF-DISCIPLINE:** Our ultimate goal as parents is to help our children develop self-control and self-discipline. Self-control requires that we think through our behaviors and act on our own decisions.

We develop self-control not by being told what to do or being punished if we don't do what is expected of us, but by thinking through our behaviors, acting on our own decisions, and accepting the consequences for our actions.

If we act in ways that run contrary to our own values, we end up feeling bad about ourselves. Living according to our values, however, increases our self-respect, which strengthens our desire—in fact, our need—to do well, to act honorably, and to be a good person. As self-esteem and self-confidence grow, adolescents are better able to find their own solutions to their problems.

"One of the ironies of parenting," advise Foster Cline and Jim Fay in *Parenting Teens with Love and Logic*, "is that the best way to influence teens to become irresponsible and fail at life is to become highly involved in making sure that they *do* make it. This is because the implied message in that involvement is, 'I don't think you're going to succeed, so I'd better get in here.' And the teen lives up to that."

Teach Values

Whatever is true, whatever is honorable, whatever is right, whatever is pure, whatever is lovely, whatever is of good repute, if there is any excellence and anything worthy of praise, let your mind dwell on it.

—SAINT PAUL

We live in a world where values don't seem to mean very much anymore. "What good are values?" adolescents wonder. "How can old-fashioned values like honesty, trust, respect, gratitude, forgiveness, tolerance, faith, and humility protect us in such a violent, unpredictable world? Why turn the other cheek when you're likely to get hit again?"

Teaching values to children and adolescents who have been deeply wounded by life is not a simple or easy task. Many parents are skeptical about the practical nature of values and wonder if it is even possible to discuss morality with children. As one father put it:

> I learned through experience. I was an angry, mixed-up kid and I was cruel to people, even the people I loved the most. It was only when I got older that I realized it is better to be kind than cruel. But I couldn't have learned that from a book or a class, and I certainly wouldn't have learned it from my father or mother trying to pound values into my head.

This father makes a good point. It is true that we learn how to be honest, patient, kind, compassionate, and forgiving through experience, and that we learn best from painful experiences. *Growth through suffering* is a motto that can be applied to every life, for adolescents, like adults, have to fall on their faces to learn the most essential and enduring lessons in life. Sometimes we have to fall in the same hole, time and time again, before we can see how to walk around it.

Experience is a great teacher, but we can also learn valuable life lessons from people we admire and respect. Adolescents who have been using drugs for months or years crave information about basic moral values. If you sit down with them and listen, they will tell you that they want to be good people, normal people. They want to be responsible, dependable, respectable, honest, humble, trustworthy, likable, lovable, and wise. Ask what means the most to them in the world, and they will say: Love. Freedom. Respect. God.

Adolescents want to know who they are, where they fit and belong. Life has knocked them flat dozens of times, and they yearn for ways to make sense of the world and themselves. Bruised and bloodied, twisted and torn, they want to feel good, but even more important they want to *be* good. When they trust you, they will tell you, in choked voices, with tears streaming down their faces, about their fears and dreams. They will admit where they have failed. They will ask for your help. And they will accept responsibility for turning their lives around.

> I feel like I have lied and cheated my way through life. I'm sick and tired of lying and cheating and doing things my own way. I'm tired

of blaming everyone else for my problems. It's not anyone else's fault. I know I need to blame myself, and I have to be able to deal with the shame and guilt. I have to work the steps.

I want to be normal. Can you tell me how to be normal?

—LEO, *sixteen*

If we do not talk to adolescents about their values, helping them to look deep inside themselves and refusing to flinch from the truths they find there, we leave them alone and adrift. They want and need our help, for they are desperate to talk about the fears that haunt them. Although they may seem sullen and unapproachable, hostile and defensive, they long to explore their doubts and fears. If they trust you, if they feel your respect and compassion, they will open up to you. In the act and process of revealing their hearts and souls to others, they can begin to discover who they are and where they fit and belong.

The best way to talk to children and adolescents about their values is to ask them questions. Then listen—just listen. Do not offer advice, do not try to fix them or "make it all better," and do not judge them. Just listen. The values are there, deep inside all of us— they need to be listened into life.

Here are some questions that can be used to begin a discussion about values. Teachable moments can occur at any hour of the day—before school, after church, driving in the car, at dinnertime or bedtime. You might begin the discussion with a story you read in the newspaper, a story from your own past, or a passage from a book you are reading, but keep the story short and then ask your child for his or her thoughts. After asking the questions, focus all your attention on listening to your child's answer.

Honesty

- Why is honesty important in relationships?
- How do you feel when people lie to you and you find out about it after the fact?
- Is it okay to steal from a place like Wal-Mart or Target,

because they are big chain stores and they can afford the loss?
- Talk about a lie you told in the past—why did you tell it? How did you feel about it? Did you ever admit the truth?
- Who are the most honest people you know—and why do you consider them honest? Who are the most dishonest people you know, and why do you consider them dishonest?
- Are your friends honest or dishonest in their dealings with you, with their parents, with authority figures?
- If honesty is important in relationships, do we need to be honest with everyone at all times, or is it okay to lie and deceive at certain times?

Trust

- What does it mean to trust someone?
- How is trust developed between people?
- Can you have a good relationship with people you don't trust? Why or why not?
- Who is someone you trust completely? Why do you trust that person?
- Name someone who trusts you. What do they find in you that is trustworthy?

Kindness

- What does it mean to be kind?
- Suppose a student who received special help in school was called "a retard" by another student and you heard it; how would you react?
- How do you feel when you see someone bullied? How do you feel about the person who is doing the bullying?
- Has anyone ever been unkind to you? If so, how did you feel?
- Why do you think people are unkind to each other?

Relationships

- Who do you love the most in the world? What is it about that person that you love?
- What do we need to do to have strong relationships with our friends, parents, relatives, and teachers?
- Have you ever had a relationship with someone you cared deeply about fall apart? What happened, and could it have been prevented?
- Are there any adults in your life whom you respect and admire and who respect and admire you?
- Do you have a good relationship with your parents? Why or why not?
- What do you think is difficult about being a parent?
- What are the most important things you think parents can do to improve their relationships with their children?

Forgiveness

- Do you believe that cruel or hateful behaviors can be forgiven?
- Who can forgive you?
- What do you think people mean when they say forgiveness begins with forgiving yourself?
- Can you ask for forgiveness?
- If someone you hurt forgives you, why is it sometimes hard to accept it?
- What if you ask for forgiveness and someone refuses to forgive you?
- Can you forgive someone who has hurt you in the past? If your answer is no, what obstacles stand in your way?
- Is there anything in life that is truly unforgivable? Why?

Respect

- Do you agree or disagree with the statement that people

who respect themselves do not need to demand respect
from others?
- What does respect mean to you?
- Why is self-respect important?
- Who is someone you respect and why?
- Who is someone you don't respect and why?
- What are some things you respect about yourself?
- What are some things about yourself that you don't respect?

Responsibility

- Do we need to accept responsibility for how our behavior
  affects others or do other people need to be less sensitive?
- Is responsibility a sign of maturity and irresponsibility a sign
  of immaturity?
- When you blame other people or life circumstances for
  something you have done or said, what happens?
- Have you said or done anything recently that you consider
  irresponsible?
- Do you accept responsibility for your actions and behaviors
  or do you sometimes try to foist the blame onto others?
- Have you ever lied about something you did and let
  someone else take the rap?
- Why do you think it is so hard to accept responsibility?

All these questions focus attention on the adolescent and his or
her feelings and thoughts about the world. Because these questions
do not contain hidden answers or judgments, they help you communicate to your children that you want to listen to them, you appreciate their ideas and emotions, and you respect their thoughts
no matter how different those thoughts are from your own. With
these questions, and with our refusal to insist on formulaic answers,
we teach our children the most important value of all, the core
value from which all our most meaningful experiences take root—
trust.

If it is difficult for you to talk to your child about values, we encourage you to ask others for help. Church youth groups, school or community service clubs, Big Brother/Big Sister programs, and Twelve Step meetings are often safe, supportive places where your child can talk openly and honestly about values, morals, and ethics. Ask your school administrators or teachers if there are opportunities during or after school for children to talk about values. If your child is involved with the juvenile justice system, ask his or her probation officer if there is a group available—or if there might be an opportunity to start a group—where adolescents can share their ideas and thoughts about values.

Empathize

Numerous studies by child researchers have demonstrated that from early years onward, children are capable of tremendous empathy; they have a desire to nurture and a real need to make others feel better. While you're in the midst of haggling over every little detail of life around the house, this may seem like the furthest thing from the truth. But a recognition of the tremendous potential for connection in all children helps fight the "us-against-them" attitude that's so easy to fall into. It also helps us envision that even though today is filled with acrimony, tomorrow may bring some peace and goodwill.

—RON TAFFEL, Ph.D.

Empathy is the capacity to understand and respond to another human being's unique experience. Our ability to empathize with each other leads us to ask these questions: "Who are you? What do you feel? How do you think? What values and experiences in life mean the most to you?"

These are the questions that allow us to develop meaningful relationships with each other—meaningful in the sense that we put honesty and respect at the heart of every interaction. With these questions, we step back from our own feelings, set aside our biases and judgments, and work to understand what our children are really feeling and thinking.

Empathy is hard work, for it requires a willingness to learn, change, and grow in all our interactions with all kinds of people. Empathy says "Teach me," which reaffirms the fact that "I am willing to learn."

But how do we develop empathy? How do we feel it, use it, and practice it in our own lives? The first step is to ask open-ended questions. Most people ask closed-ended questions—for example: "I can see that you're frightened, Amanda. Can you tell me about your feelings?"

This question may sound good, even empathic, but look at the way it answers itself. The question says: "You're frightened. Now tell me about it." You're not really asking Amanda for an answer; you're giving the answer to her and then asking her to expand on your perception.

An open-ended question is: "I can see that you're feeling pretty emotional about this, Amanda. Can you tell me what you're thinking?" This question is truly empathic, seeking to understand another person without presuming to know his or her thoughts and feelings.

Here's an example of an empathic, open-ended encounter between a mother and her adolescent son.

Ben, sixteen, returned home from an evening with his friends. He was upset about something and started to tell his parents, who were getting ready for bed, about an interaction with Sandra, his friend Tony's girlfriend.

"I had a fly on my arm, so I turned to slap it, and the baseball bat on my lap fell off and hit the PlayStation controls," Ben said. His voice was shaking, and he was close to tears. "Sandra started yelling at me and said I meant to do it. She called me stupid and said I broke the PlayStation. Why would she call me stupid? I didn't do anything to her! I didn't break the stupid PlayStation! I got mad and told her to go away, and she said I'd never get a girlfriend because I'm so immature.

"I hate her," he said, finishing his story. "You have no idea how much I hate her. Sometimes I just want to hit her."

Tired after a long day, Ben's mother became upset with him. She tried to stay calm but her irritation was obvious in her voice.

"Honey, you keep putting yourself into these situations," she said. "Why do you get so upset? Why can't you just ignore Sandra, or just stay away from her?"

"She's always over at Tony's house," Ben said, getting agitated. "How am I going to stay away from her?"

Then, suddenly, he exploded. "I hate talking to you! You never listen to me!"

Quickly realizing her mistake, Ben's mother apologized. "You're right," she said. "I didn't listen to you. I'm sorry. Can we start over again?"

Although he was extremely upset, Ben eventually agreed to talk. This time his mother took an empathic approach, listening carefully, acknowledging his feelings, avoiding judgment, and refusing to try to "fix" the problem by offering advice. As they talked, Ben admitted that he was feeling frustrated and sad because he didn't think he would ever have a friend who would stand by him and always be there for him.

"Tony always supports Sandra, even when he knows she's being a jerk," he said. Then he began to cry and talked for a long time about his best friend, who died in a car accident one year earlier.

Later, kissing his mother good night, Ben thanked her for taking the time to listen.

"I just needed to talk so I could try to understand myself," he said.

When we experience empathy for another person's experience, we slow ourselves down, avoid snap judgments, and allow the story to unfold in its own time, at its own pace. Empathy strengthens our relationships by broadening our perspective and expanding our sense of connection to others and to the world itself. As mythologist Joseph Campbell put it: "At such moments, you realize that you and the other are, in fact, one."

Negotiate

A tree that is unbending is easily broken. . . .

—TAO TE CHING (76)

The ability to negotiate with our children brings together all the skills we have explored in this chapter. For to be skilled negotiators, we must first be willing to learn from our children's needs, desires, fears, and dreams. When we show a willingness to negotiate, we inspire our children to be flexible and adaptable in their relationships. Setting limits is an essential part of negotiating, as we develop a partnership with our children by agreeing to give up control in some areas while maintaining firm boundaries in others. Teaching values is critical, for the art of negotiation requires honesty, trust, responsibility, and respect. And empathy allows us to set aside our biases and judgments, step back from our emotions, and take our children's perspective so that we understand what they are really thinking and feeling.

Being willing to negotiate with our children means that we are willing to listen, discuss, and compromise. Negotiating does not mean, however, that we are willing to bargain for anything and everything. Here are one mother's words of advice:

When I used to shop with my toddler son, he would reach for something on the shelves and then start crying and wailing if I said he couldn't have it. So I got in the habit of giving him something little, just to keep him quiet. I realize now what a terrible strategy that was. I rewarded him for being a pain in the neck. Basically, I taught him that if you make a big enough stink, eventually you'll get what you want.

Now he's sixteen, and he still thinks he can talk me into anything. But I'm learning—we're both learning. When it comes to keeping him safe, I'll say no and stick to my guns. But most times, we'll discuss things. If I treat him like a real person and show that I respect his opinions, we don't get into arguments and shouting matches. We talk and we listen and we both give a little and take a little. It works.

When we show that we are willing to negotiate, we model for our children how to be flexible, adaptable, and open-minded. Negotiation is really a matter of giving our children a choice between alternatives rather than dictating to them, word for word, what they should do or say. Through negotiation we teach our children to make their own independent decisions, even as we provide guidance and set limits.

A poem by Kahlil Gibran offers parents an image to live by:

And a woman who held a babe against her bosom said, Speak to us of
*   Children.*
And he said:
Your children are not your children.
They are the sons and daughters of Life's longing for itself.
They come through you but not from you,
And though they are with you yet they belong not to you.

You may give them your love but not your thoughts.
For they have their own thoughts.
You may house their bodies but not their souls,
For their souls dwell in the house of tomorrow, which you cannot visit,
*   not even in your dreams.*
You may strive to be like them, but seek not to make them like you.
For life goes not backward nor tarries with yesterday.

You are the bows from which your children as living arrows are sent
*   forth.*
The archer sees the mark upon the path of the infinite,

and He bends you with His might that His arrows may go swift
and far.
Let your bending in the archer's hand be for gladness:
For even as He loves the arrow that flies, so He loves also the bow that
is stable.

If we distill it all down, perhaps those are the words and the im-age that we must always keep in our minds and our hearts: *Be the stable bow.*

Kids Talking

Children begin by loving their parents. As they grow older, they judge them. Sometimes they forgive them.

—AUTHOR UNKNOWN

Good people are good because they've come to wisdom through failure.

—WILLIAM SAROYAN

"*What advice would you give to parents raising kids these days?*" For the last three years we have been asking kids this question. These are kids who are locked up in detention or juvenile institutions, who are on probation or in treatment programs, alternative schools, recovery schools, support groups, and youth camps.

They are kids who use or have used drugs. They have been there. They have suffered and lost and yet, in so many ways, they have triumphed. They are alive, thinking, wondering, yearning. They are walking the walk.

When we first ask the question, they are taken aback, for they are used to taking advice, not giving it. So they sit for a while, thinking. Then, tentatively, one person offers an insight from his or her own experience, and then another builds on those words, and suddenly everyone has something to say.

Their words are simple, but they come straight from the heart. Here's what they have to say:

- Parents need to be there for their kids. Most of the time, they are just not there.
- Try to talk to your kids more. Every chance you get try to find a way to spend time with them. Go to a movie or a ball game. Go camping. My dad goes to the bar so I just leave and go to my friends' houses. My dad tries, but he always just drinks.
- Parents need to discipline their kids—good, old-fashioned discipline.
- If you discipline your kids when they're young, they'll learn to obey you. It's just something they know inside.
- My parents didn't discipline me. Now all they do is yell at me.
- I wish I'd been brought up on a farm because the discipline would be part of life. You know, feeding the animals, getting on the tractor, getting up early and going to bed early—a hardworking kind of life. I like to work because you get a sense of pride from it. But I've never had to work. So I don't have much pride.
- Give your kids chores to do and make sure they do them. If you live in the city, tell them to vacuum, clean their rooms, wash the car, take out the garbage, walk the dog. If you live in the country, they could chop wood or whatever. Then if they don't do it, take away their privileges. That's what they do in juvenile detention centers, and it works. You take away what they want, take away phone privileges or computer privileges or dessert. But don't ground them. Grounding doesn't work. You just leave, climb out the window, run away, whatever.
- Don't let kids always get their way. Don't spoil them.

- Don't beat them when they're just little kids.
- Don't hit your kids. If you hit them, it makes them want to hang out more with their friends. If you hit them, they just want to get away from you.
- Don't hit me no more.
- Instead of constantly harping on kids, talk to kids in ways they can understand.
- Don't argue with every petty little thing.
- Don't speak in high voices all the time. My father yells at me; he yells so hard he spits in my face. I hate that. I lose respect for him then.
- Express yourself to your kids as a human being. You can yell at them or you can talk to them. It's much better just to talk to them.
- Be a parent and a friend. If you're always in parent mode, you're nagging, and your kids just rebel.
- My mom can't be wrong, ever. That's not right.
- You need to say sorry to kids when you've been fighting.
- Don't blame your problems on us. Don't use us as an excuse for your own problems.
- Always keep things positive and on the right track.
- Listen to what we have to say. Don't assume you always know what's going on.
- I knew all about drugs at six, and I started using when I was eight. You need to talk to your kids about drugs when they're little, five or six years old. Tell them that drugs are bad for them, that drugs can kill them.
- Tell your kids what drugs do to you. But tell them the whole truth—that drugs can make you feel good but the bad part lasts a lot longer.
- Keep your kids away from people who would influence them to use drugs. Even their brothers, sisters, cousins—sometimes you have to keep them away from their own family.
- Don't try to get your kids out of trouble. If they're doing something bad, let them take responsibility for their actions

so they know that if they get into trouble again, they'll have to face the consequences.

- Don't be hypocrites. If you've done drugs before, tell your kids. Be honest. When your parents drink or smoke cigarettes or marijuana, and then tell you not to use drugs—well, that's hypocritical. How are we supposed to listen to our parents when they're hypocrites?
- Don't tell your kids they're bad kids because they use drugs.
- If your kids' friends use drugs, don't look at them and say they're bad. Everyone is a good person. They're just lost. They've taken a detour.
- A lot of parents just give up on their kids. They say, "My kid is a druggie, that's how they're going to be, there's nothing I can do." Don't give up on your kids.
- Yeah. Never give up.

Epilogue

In the introduction to this book, we emphasized the most important words parents need to hear: *You are not alone.*

When words fail . . . when patience is lost . . . when hope is nowhere to be found . . . when faith wavers and forgiveness seems impossible . . . remember these words.

You are not alone.

Notes

Part One: Why Kids Get Hooked

Chapter 1: The Road Less Traveled

Page 8: The treatment gap: The most recent National Household Survey on Drug Abuse (NHSDA) reports that 1.1 million children between the ages of twelve and seventeen have problems with alcohol and other drugs. Only about 122,000 adolescents received treatment in 2000, leaving an estimated "treatment gap" of 1 million children. The study, released in September 2002 by the Substance Abuse Mental Health Services Administration (SAMHSA), can be seen at www.samhsa.gov/oas/TXgap/toc.htm.

Page 9: Treatment works. Muck, R., et al., "An Overview of the Effectiveness of Adolescent Substance Abuse Treatment Models," in Herr, K. (editor), *Bringing Restorative Justice to Adolescent Substance Abuse*, special issue of *Youth & Society* 33 (December 2001): 143–68. (Thousand Oaks, Calif.: Sage Publications). See also:

Hser, Y. I.; C. Grella, R. Hubbard, et al., "An Evaluation of Drug Treatment for Adolescents in Four U.S. Cities," *Archives of General Psychiatry* 58(7) (2001): 689–95. You can find a discussion of this research ("Adolescent Treatment Programs Reduce Drug Abuse, Produce Other Improvements") in NIDA's Research Findings 17(1) (April 2002), available on-line at www.drug abuse.gov/NIDA_Notes/NNVol17N1/Adolescent.html.

Chapter 2: "If You Could Only See Inside Me"

Page 13: Cisco is quoted in Fremon, C., *Father Greg and the Homeboys: The Extraordinary Journey of Father Greg Boyle and His Work with the Latino Gangs of East LA* (New York: Hyperion, 1995), p. 43.

Research on stigma:

Page 15: Goffman, E., *Stigma: Notes on the Management of a Spoiled Identity* (New York: Prentice Hall, 1963), pp. 2–3.

Page 15: 1979 survey: "The General Mills American Family Report: Family Health in an Era of Stress," conducted by Yakelovich, Skelly, and White, Inc.

1998 survey: "The Road to Recovery: A Landmark National Study on Public Perceptions of Alcoholism and Barriers to Treatment," conducted by Peter D. Hart Research Associates, Inc. (October 1997 to February 1998). For more information on the survey, contact The Rush Recovery Institute, P.O. Box 254, 33 Wall Street, Madison, CT 06443, 203-318-8597.

Page 16: October 2001 survey: Peter D. Hart Research Associates organization conducted a national poll of individuals in recovery from addiction and their families. The Robert Woods Johnson Foundation funded the survey research.

Page 17: Barton, Judith, "Parental Adaptation to Adolescent Drug Abuse: An Ethnographic Study of Role Formulation in Response to Courtesy Stigma," *Public Health Nursing* 8(1) (1991): 39–45.

Barton, J., P. Allderdice, and L. Campbell, "Parental Responses to Adolescent Drug Abuse," National Institute of Nursing Research Grant; contact Judith.Barton@UCHSC.edu.

Pages 16–19: "The Stigma of Substance Use: A Review of the Literature," Centre for Addiction and Mental Health (Toronto, Canada, 1999). You can view the article on-line at http://sano.camh.net/stigma/litrev.htm.

Pages 18–20: "Blamed and Ashamed: The Treatment Experiences of Youth With Co-occurring Substance Abuse and Mental Health Disorders and Their Families," published by the Federation of Families for Children's Mental Health (FFCMH) and Keys for Networking, Inc. Copies are available from FFCMH: 703-684-7710, or visit www.ffcmh.org, or e-mail ffcmh@ffcmh.org.

Chapter 3: Why Kids Get Hooked

Page 24: Every year since 1975, the University of Michigan's Institute for Social Research, funded by the National Institute on Drug Abuse (NIDA), has studied the extent of alcohol and other drug use among high school twelfth-graders. In 1991 the annual Monitoring the Future (MTF) Survey was expanded to include eighth- and tenth-graders. The data reported in this chapter and in other sections of the book are taken from the 2002 MTF survey, available on-line at www.monitoringthefuture.org.

Page 25: "Teen Tipplers: America's Underage Drinking Epidemic" is published by Columbia University's National Center on Addiction and Substance Abuse (CASA) and is available on-line at www.casacolumbia.org/publications1456/publications.htm.

Page 27: Blum, K., *Alcohol and the Addictive Brain* (New York: The Free Press, 1991), p. 237.

Page 27: Data on current drinkers in the United States is taken from the 2001 National Household Survey on Drug Abuse (see www.samhsa.gov).

Pages 28–29: Preference: For an excellent review of studies on preference, see Blum, *Alcohol and the Addictive Brain*, pp. 92–95.

Page 29–30: Adoption studies: For an excellent overview, see Heath, A. C., "Genetic Influences on Alcoholism Risk, a Review of Adoption and Twin Studies," *Alcohol Health & Research World* 19(3) (1995): 166–71.

Page 30. Brain wave abnormalities:
Begleiter, H., and B. Kissin, *The Genetics of Alcoholism* (New York: Oxford University Press, 1995).

Begleiter, H., and B. Porgesz, "Potential Biological Markers in Individuals at High Risk for Developing Alcoholism," *Alcoholism: Clinical and Experimental Research* 12 (1988): 488–93.

Pages 30–31: Acetaldehyde buildup: Charles S. Lieber, chief of the research program on liver disease and nutrition at the Bronx Veterans Administration Hospital in New York, has been researching the metabolism of alcohol for several decades. See his book *Medical and Nutritional Complications of Alcoholism: Mechanisms and Management* (New York: Plenum, 1992). See also:

Lieber, C., "Microsomal Ethanol Oxidizing System (MEOS), the First 30 Years (1968–1998)—a Review," *Alcoholism: Clinical & Experimental Research* 23 (1999): 991–1007.

Page 31: Dopamine deficiencies: See Blum, *Alcohol and the Addictive Brain*, and research by Ernest Noble, M.D., Ph.D., Pike Professor at UCLA:

Noble, E., "Addiction and Its Reward Process Through Polymorphisms of the D2 Dopamine Receptor Gene: A Review," *European-Psychiatry* 15(2) (2000): 7–89.

Noble, E., "The D2 Dopamine Receptor Gene: A Review of Association Studies in Alcoholism and Phenotypes," *Alcohol* 16(1) (1998): 35–45.

Page 32: Nora Volkow's research projects are listed on her Web page, www.bnl.gov/medical/Personel/Volkow/Volkow.htm. See also *NIDA Notes* 17(6) (March 2003), www.drugabuse.gov/NIDA_notes/NNVol17N6/Volkow .html.

Pages 33–34: Low-intensity reaction: Marc Schuckit's research is discussed in his book *Educating Yourself About Alcohol and Drugs: A People's Primer* (New York: Plenum Press, 1995). See also:

Schuckit, M. et al., "A genome-wide search for genes relating to a low level of response to alcohol," *Alcoholism: Clinical and Experimental Research* (in press).

Schuckit, M., and T. Smith, "The Relationships of a Family History of Alcohol Dependence, a Low Level of Response to Alcohol, and Six Domains of Life Functioning to the Development of Alcohol Use Disorders," *Journal of Studies on Alcohol* (in press).

Chapter 4: Beyond the Genes

Page 35: Ting-Kai Li, M.D., current director of the National Institute on Alcohol Abuse and Alcoholism (NIAAA), is quoted by Hal Kibbey in an article posted on www.indiana.edu.

Page 36: Prenatal exposure: U.S. Department of Health and Human Services, *Substance Abuse and Mental Health Statistics Source Book* (Rockville, Md.: Substance Abuse and Mental Health Services Administration, 1998).

See the "Booze News Fact Sheet" on fetal alcohol syndrome (www.cspinet .org/booze/fas.htm), published by the Center for Science in the Public Interest (CSPI).

Page 37: Young pregnant women drinking: Centers for Disease Control and Prevention study; see: "CDC Data Show Younger Women Less Likely to Stop Using Alcohol and Tobacco During Pregnancy," www.cdc.gov/od/oc/ media/pressrel/r2k1101.htm (October 31, 2000).

Pages 38–39: Age of first drink: Grant, B., "The Impact of Family History of Alcoholism on the Relationship Between Age at Onset of Alcohol Use and DSM-III Alcohol Dependence," *Alcohol Health and Research World* 22 (1998): 144–47.

McGue, M., et al., "The Origins and Consequences of Age at First Drink, I: Associations with Substance-use Disorders, Disinhibitory Behavior and Psychopathology, and P3 Amplitude," *Alcoholism: Clinical and Experimental Research* 25 (2001): 1156–65.

McGue, M., et al., "The Origins and Consequences of Age at First Drink, II: Familial Risk and Heritability," *Alcoholism: Clinical and Experimental Research* 25 (2001): 1166–73.

Page 42: Adolescent brain development: Jay Giedd quote is from a PBS interview, 2002, www.pbs.org/wgbh/pages/frontline/shows/teenbrain/ interviews/giedd.html.

Pages 42–44: In December 2002, the American Medical Association (AMA) released a comprehensive compilation of two decades of scientific research on how alcohol affects the adolescent's developing brain and causes possibly irreversible damage. "Harmful Consequences of Alcohol Use on the Brains of Children, Adolescents, and College Students" dispels the myth that youths are more resilient than adults to the adverse effects of drinking alcohol. You can view the report on-line at www.alcoholpolicysolutions.net/pdf/RUDC_dec_nr.pdf.

See also: Brown, S., et al., "Neurocognitive Functioning of Adolescents: Effects of Protracted Alcohol Use," *Alcoholism: Clinical and Experimental Research* 24(2) (1999): 164–71.

Page 44: Insensitivity: For a review of the literature on adolescent brain development and neural alterations, see: www.collegedrinkingprevention.gov/reports/Journal/spear.aspx.

Page 47: Victimization and maltreatment: Funk, R., et al., "Maltreatment Issues by Level of Adolescent Substance Abuse Treatment: The Extent of the Problem at Intake and Relationship to Early Outcomes," *Child Maltreatment* 8(1) (2003): 36–45.

Titus, J., et al., "Gender Differences in Victimization Severity and Outcomes Among Adolescents Treated for Substance Abuse," *Child Maltreatment* 8(1) (2003): 19–35.

A recent study shows that girls who witness or experience violence (robbery, assault, rape) are two to three times more likely than girls with no exposure to violence to use legal and illegal drugs and three to four times more likely to engage in risky health behaviors such as having sex at an early age, having multiple sex partners, or having sex with strangers.

See: Berenson, A., C. Wiemann, and S. McCombs, "Exposure to Violence and Associated Health-Risk Behaviors Among Adolescent Girls," *Archives of Pediatric and Adolescent Medicine* 155 (2001): 1238.

Pages 48–50: Emotional disorders: For an excellent overview of recent studies in this area, see Armentano, M., and R. Solhkhah, "Co-Occurring Disorders in Adolescents," chapter 8 in *Principles of Addiction Medicine*, 3rd ed. (Chevy Chase, Md.: American Society of Addiction Medicine, Inc., 2003), pp. 1573–80.

Bert Pepper, M.D., is founder and executive director of the Information Exchange, Inc., based in New City, New York, a national nonprofit agency created in 1983 to improve treatment of mentally and emotionally troubled persons. He is quoted in the Mental Health Roundtable Fact Sheet (see www.drugstory.org/pdfs/MentalHealth_YouthFS.pdf).

For an overview of the research on the interaction between drugs and specific mental health disorders, see the fact sheets published by the National Youth Anti-Drug Media Campaign, www.drugstory.org/feature/mentalhealth.asp.

Pages 51–52: Eating disorders: Columbia University's Center on Addiction and Substance Abuse (CASA) 231-page report "The Formative Years: Pathways to Substance Abuse Among Girls and Young Women Ages 8–22" is available from CASA, www.casacolumbia.org, or call 212-841-5200.

For a detailed list of eating disorders resources, see: www.addiction resourceguide.com/specpop/anorexia.html.

Pages 52–54: ADHD: Biederman, J., et al., "Pharmacotherapy of attention-deficit/Hyperactivity Disorder Reduces Risk for Substance Use Disorder," *Pediatrics* 104(2) (1999): 20.

Milberger, S., et al., "Familial Risk Analysis of the Association Between Attention-deficit/Hyperactivity Disorder and Psychoactive Substance Use Disorders," *Archives of Pediatric and Adolescent Medicine* 152 (1998): 945–51

See also Amen, D., *Change Your Brain, Change Your Life: The Breakthrough Program for Conquering Anxiety, Depression, Obsessiveness, Anger, and Impulsiveness* (New York: Three Rivers Press, 1998).

Pages 54–55: Learning disabilities: See CASA's September 2000 report, "Substance Abuse and Learning Disabilities: Peas in a Pod or Apples and Oranges," on-line at: www.casalibrary.org/CASA%20Publications/Learning.pdf.

Pages 55–57: For more information on head injuries and a detailed list of references, see the Family Caregiver Alliance Web site at www.caregiver.org/factsheets/tbi_stats.html.

Page 57: Hingson, R., et al., "Magnitude of Alcohol-Related Mortality and Morbidity Among U.S. College Students Ages 18–24," *Journal of Studies on Alcohol* 63 (2002): 136–44.

Page 57: Stress: National Institute on Drug Abuse news release May 28, 2002, "Substance Abuse Increases in New York City in Aftermath of September 11," www.nida.nih.gov/MedAdv/02/NR5-28.html.

McBride, W., and A. Noronna, "Central Nervous System Mechanisms in Alcohol Relapse," *Alcoholism: Clinical and Experimental Research* 25(2) (2002): 287–93.

Pages 58–59: PTSD: For an excellent review of the research on PTSD and substance abuse, see the Addiction Technology Transfer Centers (ATTC) Web site at www.nattc.org/hpsb/trauma/f.html. ATTC is a nationwide, multidisciplinary resource that draws upon the work of recognized experts in the addiction field.

Pages 59–60: Green Eyes and Turtle are quoted in Fremon, *Father Greg and the Homeboys*, pp. 135, 258.

The Office of Juvenile Justice and Delinquency Prevention (OJJDP) conducts an annual National Youth Gang Survey. See www.ncjrs.org/html/ojjdp/97_ygs/survey_7.html.

Pages 61–62: Poverty: Payne, R., *Understanding Poverty* (Baytown, Tex.: RFT Publishing, 1998) www.rftpub.com.

See also the National Center for Children in Poverty (NCCP) Web site at www.nccp.org.

Pages 62–65: Gender: See CASA's report, "The Formative Years" (see note for pages 51–52).

See also: Morse, Jodie, "Women on a Binge: Many Teen Girls Are Drinking as Much as Boys. More College Women Regularly Get Drunk. Is This a Case of Girl Power Gone Awry?" *Time* 159(13) (2002).

Part Two: The Drugs

The facts and statistics in chapters 5 through 14 are collected from various sources, including:

Centers for Disease Control and Prevention (CDC): www.cdc.gov/scientific.htm.

Center for Science in the Public Interest (CSPI): www.cspinet.org/booze/fctindex.htm (index for "Booze News" fact sheets).

Monitoring the Future: www.monitoringthefuture.org.

National Center for Addiction and Substance Abuse (CASA) at Columbia University: www.casacolumbia.org.

National Council on Alcoholism and Other Drug Addictions (NCADD): www.ncadd.org.

National Institute on Alcoholism and Alcohol Abuse (NIAAA): www.niaaa.nih.gov.

National Institute on Drug Abuse (NIDA): www.nida.nih.gov—see Info-Facts for specific information for each drug.

Substance Abuse and Mental Health Services Administration (SAMHSA): www.drugabusestatistics.samhsa.gov.

See also: Kuhn, C., S. Swartzwelder, W. Wilson, *Buzzed: The Straight Facts About the Most Used and Abused Drugs from Alcohol to Ecstasy* (New York: W. W. Norton, 1998),

Falkowski, Carol, *Dangerous Drugs: An Easty-to-Use Reference for Parents and Professionals*, pp. 163–64, 2nd ed. (Center City, Minn.: Hazelden, 2003).

Chapter 5: Alcohol

Page 69, 75: Joseph Califano's statements on release of CASA report, "Teen Tipplers: America's Underage Drinking Epidemic," February 2002, are reported in Reuter's Health news release, February 26, 2002.

Page 74: See CASA report (above) on-line at www.casacolumbia.org/publications1456/publications.htm.

The Youth Risk Behavior Survey is conducted by the Centers for Disease Control and Prevention: www.cdc.gov/mmwr/preview/mmwrhtml/ss5104a1 .htm.

Pages 76–77: Ozzy Osbourne is quoted in Dodd, D. *Playing It Straight: Personal Conversations on Recovery, Transformation and Success* (Deerfield Beach, Fla.: Health Communications, Inc., 1996), pp. 208–09.

Page 77: Blackouts: White, A., "Prevalence and Correlates of Alcohol-Induced Blackouts Among College Students: Results of an E-mail Survey," *Journal of American Health* 5(3) (November 2002): 117–31.

Page 77: Brain damage in binge-drinking rats: Obernier, J., T. Bouldin, F. Crews, "Binge Ethanol Exposure in Adults Rats Causes Necrotic Cell Death," *Alcoholism: Clinical and Experimental Research* 26 (2002): 547–57.

Page 83: Doug Fieger, quoted in Dodd, *Playing It Straight*, p. 85.

Chapter 6: Nicotine

Page 91: "Popular" kids more likely to smoke: "Drinking, Smoking, Drug Use, and Gambling Are More Associated with the Popular Kids than the Unpopular Ones," press release from the University of Pennsylvania's Annenberg Public Policy Center, July 2002. Dan Romer is the study's lead researcher.

See also: Simons-Morton, B. G., "Prospective Analysis of Peer and Parent Influences on Smoking Initiation Among Early Adolescents," *Prevention Science* 3(4) (December 2002): 275–83.

Page 91: Lowry, R., et al., "Weight Management Goals and Practices Among U.S. High School Students: Associations with Physical Activity, Diet, and Smoking," *Journal of Adolescent Health* 31 (2002): 133–44.

Pages 96–97: The National Center for Tobacco-Free Kids, January 3, 2002, Fact Sheet: www.tobaccofreekids.org/research/factsheets/pdf/0106.pdf.

Page 97: UCLA study on brain blood flow in cocaine addicts who smoke is cited in Amen, *Change Your Brain, Change Your Life*, pp. 226–27, and on his Web site at www.brainplace.com.

Page 98: Rapid addiction in youth: DiFranza, et al., "Development of Symptoms of Tobacco Dependence in Youths: 30 Month Follow Up Data from the DANDY Study," *Tobacco Control* 11 (2002): 228–35.

See also: DiFranza, J., et. al., "Measuring the Loss of Autonomy Over Nicotine Use in Adolescents: The DANDY (Development and Assessment of Nicotine Dependence in Youths) Study," *Archives of Pediatrics & Adolescent Medicine*, April 2002.

Page 98: Female smokers more susceptible to addiction: "Women and Smoking: A Report of the Surgeon General 2001." View on-line at Centers for Disease Control and Prevention Web site at www.cdc.gov/tobacco/sgr/sgr_for women/ataglance.htm.

Page 100: Gidwani, P., et. al., "Television Viewing and Initiation of Smoking Among Youth," *Pediatrics* 110(3) (September 2002): 505–08.

Chapter 7: Marijuana

Page 107: Marijuana and driving: Professor Olaf Drummer, a forensic medicine expert at Monash University in Australia, presented his findings at a government committee on family and community affairs. See "Pot Smoking Called Driving Danger," Join Together news releases, September 26, 2002; www.jointogether.org.

Page 107–08: Amen, D., *Change Your Brain, Change Your Life*, p. 239.

Page 110: Heart attack risk increases: Mittleman, M., et al., "Triggering of Myocardial Infarction by Marijuana," *Circulation* 103 (2001): 2805–09.

Page 110–11: Medical marijuana: Nahas, G., K. Sutin, D. Harvey, S. Agurell, N. Pace, R. Cancro, *Marijuana and Medicine* (Totowa, N.J.: Humana Press, 1999).

Page 112: Is marijuana a gateway drug? See:

Adams I., B. Martin, "Cannabis: Pharmacology and Toxicology in Animals and Humans," *Addiction* 91 (1996): 1585–1614.

Kandel, D. B., "Stages in Adolescent Involvement with Drugs," *Science* 190 (1975): 912–14.

"Marijuana: Facts Parents Need to Know," brochure published by National Institute on Drug Abuse, revised 1998; available on-line at www.nida .nih.gov/MarijBroch/MarijIntro.html.

Monitoring the Future Survey (www.monitoringthefuture.org): Perceived harmfulness of regularly smoking marijuana decreased from 74.8 percent to 72.2 percent among eighth-graders.

"RAND Corporation Study Casts Doubt on Claims That Marijuana Acts as 'Gateway' to the Use of Cocaine and Heroin" (December 2002), www.rand.org.

Page 113. National surveys on perceived risk of marijuana use. These surveys include the annual Monitoring the Future Surveys conducted by the University of Michigan's Institute for Social Research (www.monitoringthe future.org), the PRIDE surveys (www.pridesurveys.com), and the National Household Survey on Drug Abuse (www.samhsa.gov/oas/nhsda).

Page 114: Australian twin study: Lynskey, M., et al., "Escalation of Drug Use in Early-onset Cannabis Users vs. Co-twin Controls," *Journal of the American Medical Association*, 289(4) (2003): 427–33, with accompanying editorial on 482–83.

Page 114: Interview with Tom Farley, www.freevibe.com/hangtime/chris-farley.shtml. See www.chrisfarleyfoundation.com.

Page 115: The Office of National Drug Control Policy, "Kids and

Marijuana: The Facts." See www.mediacampaign.org/marijuana/kids_and_marijuana.html.

Pages 117–19: Withdrawal symptoms:

Budney, A., et al., "Marijuana Abstinence Effects in Marijuana Smokers Maintained in Their Home Environment," *Archives of General Psychiatry* 58(10) (2001): 917–24.

Haney, M., et al., "Abstinence Symptoms Following Smoked Marijuana in Humans," *Psychopharmacology* 141 (1999): 395–404.

Kouri, E., et al., "Changes in Aggressive Behavior During Withdrawal from Long-term Marijuana Use," *Psychopharmacology* 143 (1999): 302–08.

Page 119: Glen Hanson, Ph.D., D.D.S., acting director of the National Institute on Drug Abuse, is quoted in *Cannabis News*, November 14, 2002; see www.cannibisnews.com. See also NIDA's research report: www.nida.nih.gov/ResearchReports/Marijuana.

Chapter 8: Inhalants

Page 122: Harvey Weiss quoted on www.drugstory.org, "Huffing—An Interview with Harvey Weiss." See the National Inhalant Prevention Coalition Web site at www.inhalants.org.

Page 128: Falkowski, *Dangerous Drugs*.

Page 130: Dr. Richard Heiss's story appears on www.drugstory.org. See also "Poison in the House" by Tracy McCarthy, *USA Today*, March 21, 1999 (www.usaweekend.com).

Page 131: British study of inhalant deaths is reported in Kuhn, et al., *Buzzed*, pp. 121–22.

Pages 131–32: Five teenagers die: See Center for Parent Youth Understanding (CPYU) summer 1999 newsletter, on-line at www.cpyu.org/news/99summert.htm.

Page 132: Kuhn, et al., *Buzzed*, p. 121.

Chapter 9: Methamphetamines

Page 136: Hitler, Churchill, JFK on amphetamines: Plant, S., *Writing on Drugs* (New York: Picador, 1999), p. 123.

Air force pilots on speed: For a comprehensive list of media articles on this subject, see www.isi.edu/geoworlds/geotopics/bydate2003/date20030102800/barchart_places_world_world09.html.

Pages 140–41: Joseph (teenage boy) and Caroline are featured on the tape *Life or Meth: What's It Cost?* distributed by Northwest High Intensity Drug Trafficking Area (HIDTA, 1-800-562-1240); quoted with permission from Steve Freng, director of the program.

Pages 145–46: Nora Volkow, Brookhaven National Laboratory, March 1, 2001, press release, "Researchers Document Brain Damage, Reduction in Motor and Cognitive Function from Methamphetamine Abuse: 'Speed' Shows More Neurotoxic Effects than Heroin, Cocaine, or Alcohol." See www.bnl .gov. See also: Volkow, N., et al., "Low Level of Brain Dopamine D_2 Receptors in Methamphetamine Abusers: Association with Metabolism in the Orbitofrontal Cortex," *American Journal of Psychiatry* 158 (2001): 2015–21.

Volkow, N., et. al., "Higher Cortical and Lower Subcortical Metabolism in Detoxified Methamphetamine Abusers," *American Journal of Psychiatry* 158 (2001): 383–89.

Volkow, N., et al., "Association of Dopamine Transporter Reduction with Psychomotor Impairment in Methamphetamine Abusers," *American Journal of Psychiatry* 158 (2001): 377–82.

Chapter 10: LSD and Other Hallucinogens

Page 151: George Harrison and Ringo Starr quotes: See www.geocities.com/ sunsetstrip/8015/quotes.html.

Page 154: Carl Jung is quoted in Plant, *Writing on Drugs*, p. 130.

Chapter 11: Ecstasy and Other Club Drugs

Page 166: Ecstasy and sex: Female therapist quoted in Beck and Rosenbaum, *The Pursuit of Ecstasy*, p. 74.

Page 167: Marsha Rosenbaum is quoted in Davidow, Julie, "The Age of Ecstasy," a three-part series in *The Reporter*, Vacaville, Calif.

Page 169: Ricaurte is quoted in "Recreational Use of Ecstasy Causes New Brain Damage," Johns Hopkins *Gazette Online* 32(5) (September 30, 2002). Ricaurte's study appears in the September 27, 2002, issue of *Science*.

Chapter 12: Cocaine

Page 179: The natives of South America: Quote in Kuhn, et al., *Buzzed*, p. 197.

Page 184: Arthur Siegel, M.D., quote: May 8, 2002, press release, McLean Hospital, "Frequent Cocaine Use Linked to Heart Attack and Stroke." Dr. Siegel's research appeared in *American Journal of Cardiology* 89: 1133–35.

Page 185: Decreased blood flow: For an overview of the research on cocaine and decreased cerebral blood flow, see NIDA Notes 13(3) (July 1998), "Cocaine Abuse May Lead to Strokes and Mental Deficits," available on-line at www.drugabuse.gov/NIDA_Notes/NNVol13N3/Cocaine.html.

Page 185: Amen, D., *Change Your Brain, Change Your Life*, p. 226.

Page 186: University of Michigan study: Little, K., D. Krolewski, L. Zhang, and B. Cassin, "Loss of Striatal Vesicular Monoamine Transporter Protein (VMAT2) in Human Cocaine Users," *American Journal of Psychiatry* 160 (2003): 47–55.

Pages 186–87: Qureshi, A. I., et al., "Cocaine Use and the Likelihood of Nonfatal Myocardial Infarction and Stroke: Data from the Third National Health and Nutrition Examination Survey," *Circulation* 103 (January 30, 2001): 502–06.

Page 187: University of Maryland study on violent injuries: Dischinger, P., et al., "A Longitudinal Study of Former Trauma Center Patients: The Association Between Toxicology Status and Subsequent Injury Mortality," *Journal of Trauma* 51(5) (November 2001).

Page 188: Gregory Harrison is quoted in Dodd, *Playing It Straight*, p. 61.

Pages 188–90: Cohen, S., *Cocaine: The Bottom Line* (American Council for Drug Education, 1985), chapter 4: "A Dozen Ways to Die with Cocaine," pp. 17–19.

Pages 190–191: Cohen, *ibid.*, p. 14.

Page 191: Marijuana and cocaine: see *Columbia University Record* 20(10) (November 18, 1994), or see on-line article at www.columbia.edu/cu/record/record2010.24.html.

Page 192: Gregory Harrison is quoted in Dodd, *Playing It Straight*, pp. 60–61.

Chapter 13: Heroin

Page 196: Carol Falkowski is quoted in Ramirez, M., "High-profile Rockers Spotlight Addiction—and Treatment Programs That Are Saving Lives," *Seattle Times*, May 2, 2002.

Page 197: Baum, L., *The Wonderful Wizard of Oz*, chapter 8: "The Deadly Poppy Field."

Page 198: Erin Artigiana is quoted in a story published in "Heroin Use on Rise in U.S.," *Join Together Online* (March 7, 2001); see: www.jointogether.org/sa/news/summaries/reader/0,1854,266290,00.html.

Pages 199–200: Anthony Kiedis is quoted in Dodd, *Playing It Straight*, pp. 88–89.

Page 200: Amen, *Change Your Brain, Change Your Life*, p. 235.

Pages 201–202: Kiedis is quoted in Dodd, *Playing It Straight*, p. 93.

Page 204: Kurt Cobain is quoted in "Cries from the Heart," *Newsweek* (October 28, 2002), pp. 60–63; see Cobain, *Journals* (New York: Riverhead Books, 2002).

Pages 204-205: William Burroughs, *Junky* (New York: Viking, 1985).

Chapter 14: OxyContin, Ritalin, and Other Prescription Drugs

Page 207: Wurtzel, E., *More, Now, Again: A Memoir of Addiction* (New York: Simon & Schuster, 2002), p. 120.

Page 208: Julie Zito is quoted in Vedantam, S., "More Kids Receiving Psychiatric Drugs," *Washington Post* (January 14, 2003). See also Zito, J., et al., "Psychotropic Practice Patterns for Youth: A 10-year Perspective," *Archives of Pediatric and Adolescent Medicine* 157 (January 2003): 17–25.

Page 209: OxyContin addict quoted in Rosenberg, D., "How One Town Got Hooked," *Newsweek* (April 9, 2001), p. 48.

Page 211: The Partnership Attitude Tracking Study (PATS) is published by the Partnership for a Drug Free America (PDFA); see www.drugfreeamerica.org.

Page 217: Middle school students treated for Xanax: See: "Information Brief: Prescription Drug Abuse and Youth" (August 2002) on U.S. Department of Justice Web site, www.usdoj.gov/ndic/pubs/1765/.

Page 218: Wurtzel, *More, Now, Again*, p. 116.

General note: For a comprehensive scholarly review of the benzodiazepines and other sedative-hypnotic drugs, including medical management of intoxication and withdrawal, see the following chapters in *Principles of Addiction Medicine*, 3rd ed. (Chevy Chase, Md.: American Society of Addiction Medicine, Inc., 2003):

Juergens, S., and D. Cowley, "The Pharmacology of Benzodiazepines and Other Sedative-Hypnotics," pp. 119–38.

Dickinson, W., M. Mayo-Smith, and S. Eickelberg, "Management of Sedative-Hypnotic Intoxication and Withdrawal," pp. 633–49.

Wesson, D., D. Smith, and W. Ling, "Pharmacologic Interventions for Benzodiazepine and Other Sedative-Hypnotic Addiction," pp. 721–33.

Part Three: What Parents Can Do

Introduction to Part 3

Page 222: Prochaska, J., J. Norcross, and C. DiClemente, *Changing for Good: A Revolutionary Six-Stage Program for Overcoming Bad Habits and Moving Your Life Positively Forward* (New York: Quill, 2002), p. 77.

Page 223: Coerced treatment: See Miller, N., and J. Flaherty, "Effectiveness of Coerced Addiction Treatment (Alternative Consequences): A Review of Clinical Research," *Journal of Substance Abuse Treatment* 18 (2000): 9–16.

Pages 223–24: Pickett, M., P. Rogers, and R. Cavanaugh, "Screening for

Alcohol, Tobacco, and Drug Use in Children and Adolescents," *Principles of Addiction Medicine*, pp. 1511–1521.

Chapter 15: Seeing the Problem

Page 225: Marc Fishman is quoted in Markel, H., "Tailoring Treatments for Teenage Drug Users," *New York Times* (January 7, 2003).

Page 226: Anthony Kiedis is quoted in Dodd, *Playing It Straight*, p. 92.

Page 233: Lynd, H., *On Shame and the Search for Identity* (New York: Science Editions, 1966), p. 20.

Chapter 16: Getting Help: Follow the L.E.A.D. Guidelines

Page 239: Fishman, M., "Placement Criteria and Strategies for Adolescent Treatment Matching," chapter 7 in *Principles of Addiction Medicine*, p. 1565.

Pages 239–40: Stages of change model: See Prochaska, J., et al., *Changing for Good*.

Page 242: Rogers, C., *On Becoming a Person: A Therapist's View of Psychotherapy* (Boston and New York: Houghton Mifflin, 1961), pp. 332–33.

Pages 243–47: Twelve lessons for parents: Risberg, R., and W. White, "Adolescent Substance Abuse Treatment: Expectations Versus Outcomes," *Student Assistance Journal* 15(2) (2003): 16–20.

Page 248: Bert Pepper quoted in "Blamed and Ashamed," published by FFCMH (see note for pages 17–18).

Page 252: "Home" quote from Kurtz, E., and K. Ketcham, *The Spirituality of Imperfection: Storytelling and the Search for Meaning* (New York: Bantam, 1992), pp. 191–92.

Chapter 17: Intervention

Page 259: Jay, Jeff, and D. Jay, *Love First: A New Approach to Intervention for Alcoholism and Drug Addiction* (Center City, Minn.: Hazelden Foundation, 2000), p. 4.

Pages 259–60: Prochaska, Norcross, and DiClemente, *Changing for Good*, pp. 96–97.

Pages 261–262: "Heads First" table appears in Poteet-Johnson, D., and P. Dias, "Office Assessment of the Substance-Using Adolescent," chapter 3 in *Principles of Addiction Medicine*, p. 1526. Published here with the author's permission.

Pages 262–63: Jay and Jay, *Love First*, pp. 73–74.

Page 263: "Early intervention is a must . . .": Johnson, V., *I'll Quit Tomorrow* (New York: Harper & Row, 1973), p. 43.

Page 265: "Alcoholism Intervention: How to Get a Loved One into Treatment," published by the Christopher D. Smithers Foundation, P.O. Box 67, Mill Neck, NY 11765, 516-676-6007, www.smithersfoundation.org.

Pages 267–68: "The people around . . .": Johnson, *I'll Quit Tomorrow*, p. 4.

Page 269: From telephone interviews conducted in February–March 2003 with Bill Teuteberg, national director/special projects with Caron Foundation in Wernersville, Penn. For more information on Caron Foundation's adolescent treatment programs, see www.caron.org.

Chapter 18: Treatment

Page 273: The American Council for Drug Education (ACDE) reports that Great Britain has been tracking inhalant-related deaths for several years and has found that first-time inhalant users account for one in five of the deaths recorded.

Pages 275–76: Winters, K., "Assessing Adolescent Substance Use Problems and Other Areas of Functioning: State of the Art," in Monti, P., S. Colby, and T. O'Leary (editors), *Adolescents, Alcohol, and Substance Abuse: Reaching Teens Through Brief Interventions* (New York: Guilford Press, 2001), p. 84.

Page 276: "More than eleven thousand specialized drug treatment facilities": Adler, M., A. Barthwell, and L. Brown, "The Treatment of Drug Addiction: A Review," in *Principles of Addiction of Medicine*, p. 419.

Pages 279–280: Steven Tyler quoted in David Dodd, *Playing It Straight*, p. 227.

Page 280: Nils Lofgren quoted in *ibid.*, p. 236.

Pages 283: For a comprehensive and entertaining overview of AA, see Kurtz, E., *Not God: A History of Alcoholics Anonymous* (Center City, Minn.: Hazelden, 1979).

See also: Ringwald, C., *The Soul of Recovery*.

Page 287: Gelormino is quoted in Ringwald, C., *The Soul of Recovery: Uncovering the Spiritual Dimension in the Treatment of Addictions* (New York: Oxford University Press, 2002), p. 199.

Page 287: Mitchell Rosenthal, M.D., quotation is taken from e-mail correspondence with Dr. Rosenthal and Ira Mothner of Phoenix House.

Page 288: Teen Challenge quote is from the Web site www.teenchallenge .net.

Pages 288–93: Addiction medicine specialists present the standards of effective, appropriate treatment in *Principle of Addiction Medicine* (2003).

Page 289: Assessment: Winters, K., T. Estroff, and N. Anderson, "Adolescent Assessment Strategies and Instruments," in *Principles of Addiction Medicine*, p. 1535.

Page 290: Emotional and behavioral disorders and integrated treatment: See note for pp. 48–50.

Page 290: Kenneth Minkoff, M.D., articulates his key principles of integrated treatment in numerous publications. See his Web site at www.kenminkoff.com.

Page 291: "Treatment of Adolescents with Substance Use Disorders: *Treatment Improvement Protocol (TIP) Series 32*, Executive Summary and Recommendations."

The Center for Substance Abuse Treatment (CSAT) of the Substance Abuse and Mental Health Services Administration (SAMHSA) publishes a series of "treatment improvement protocols" designed to help treatment providers design and deliver better services to adolescent clients with substance-use disorders. These protocols are an excellent resource for parents, teachers, health care providers, probation officers, and others interested in the most recent research on adolescent treatment methods and effectiveness. They are free and can be ordered from the Web site www.treatment.org/Externals/tips.html or from the National Clearinghouse for Alcohol and Drug Information (NCADI), SAMHSA's information service. Call 1-800-729-6686.

Page 292: Risberg, R., and W. White, "Adolescent Substance Abuse Treatment: Expectations Versus Outcomes," *Student Assistance Journal* 15(2) (2003): 16–20. See also: White, W., M. Dennis, and M. Godley, "Adolescent Substance Abuse Disorders: From Acute Treatment to Recovery Management," *Reclaiming Children and Youth*, 11(3) (2002): 172–75.

Pages 294–95: McGovern, G., *Terry: My Daughter's Life and Death Struggle with Alcoholism* (New York: Villard Books, 1996), pp. 189–90.

Page 297: Aristotle is quoted on the quotations Web page, www.quotations page.com.

Pages 297–300: "Treatment works": See Hser, Y-I, et al., "An Evaluation of Drug Treatment for Adolescents in Four U.S. Cities," *Archives of General Psychiatry* 58(7) (2001):689–95.

In a review of this study, the National Institute on Drug Abuse (NIDA) concludes: "In the first large-scale study designed to evaluate drug abuse treatment outcomes among adolescents in age-specific treatment programs, NIDA-supported researchers have found that longer stays in these treatment programs can effectively decrease drug and alcohol use and criminal activity as well as improve school performance and psychological adjustment." See www.drugabuse.gov/NIDA_Notes/NNVol17N1/Adolescent.html.

Page 298: Fishman, M., *Principles of Addiction Medicine*, p. 1570.

Chapter 19: Relapses

Page 301: "Sometimes I have failed . . .": *Came to Believe: The Spiritual Adventure of A.A. as Experienced by Individual Members* (New York: Alcoholics Anonymous World Services, 2003), p. 49.

Page 301: "Relapse tendencies": Gorski, T., and M. Miller, *Staying Sober: A Guide for Relapse Prevention* (Independence, Mo.: Herald House/Independence Press, 1986), p. 35.

Pages 302–03: Jaffe, S., "Adolescent Treatment and Relapse Prevention," in *Principles of Addiction Medicine*, p. 1551.

Pages 306–11: "Post acute withdrawal . . .": Gorski and Miller, *Staying Sober*, p. 58.

Page 308: Alcoholics twice as likely to suffer serious injury: Rees, V., et al., "Injury Among Detoxification Patients: Alcohol Users' Greater Risk," *Alcoholism: Clinical and Experimental Research* 26 (2002):212–17.

Pages 308–11: Causes of protracted withdrawal syndrome: James Milam, Ph.D., was the original architect of many of these ideas. See Milam, J., and K. Ketcham, *Under the Influence: A Guide to the Myths and Realities of Alcoholism* (New York: Bantam, 1983).

Page 311: "Recovery from Addiction": Gorski and Miller, *Staying Sober*, p. 129.

Pages 312–16: The eleven relapse phases are discussed in detail in Gorski and Miller, *Staying Sober*, pp. 139–55. For more information on relapse and recovery, see Terence Gorski's Web site at www.tgorski.com.

Page 316: "You are asking yourself . . .": Bill Wilson, letter, 1955, quoted in *Came to Believe*, p. 53.

Chapter 20: Staying Clean and Sober

Page 318: Bettelheim, B., *A Good Enough Parent: A Book on Child Rearing* (New York: Vintage Books, 1988), p. 131.

Page 320: Tolstoy is quoted in James, W., *The Varieties of Religious Experience* (New York: Touchstone, 1997), p. 134. James cites the source as Tolstoy's *Confessions*, published in 1882.

Pages 321–22: China Kantner is quoted in Dodd, *Playing It Straight*, p. 149.

Pages 323–26: Obesity: The quotation is from "The Surgeon General's Call to Action to Prevent and Decrease Overweight and Obesity," www.surgeongeneral.gov/topics/obesity/calltoaction/fact_adolescents.htm-STOP.

Page 326: Candace Pert quotation is taken from her foreword to Des-Maisons, K., *Potatoes Not Prozac* (New York: Simon & Schuster, 1998), p. 12.

Page 334: Knapp, C., *Drinking: A Love Story* (New York: Dial Press, 1996), p. 254.

Pages 334–35: Rodham Clinton, H., *It Takes a Village* (New York: Touchstone, 1996), p. 317.

Page 335: Dr. Bob on spirituality: From the obituary "Dr. Bob," in the *AA Grapevine* 7:7 (January 1951):22.

Page 336: James, W., *The Varieties of Religious Experience* (New York: Touchstone, 1997), p. 167.

Page 337: Bettelheim, *A Good Enough Parent*, pp. 113–14.

Chapter 21: L.I.S.T.E.N.

Page 340: Effective parenting is a learned skill: This is rule number 110 of Dr. Daniel Amen's "135 Best Things You Can Do for Your Child." See Dr. Amen's Web site at www.amenclinic.com/ac/news/135_things.asp.

Page 340: Bill Cosby is interviewed in *Reader's Digest*, May 2003, p. 78.

Page 341: Bettelheim, Bruno, *A Good Enough Parent*, p. xi.

Pages 343–44: Bettelheim on "why questions": *Ibid.*, p. 95

Page 344: Hurrying our children: *Ibid.*, p. 109.

Pages 344–45: Ciaramicoli, A., and K. Ketcham, *The Power of Empathy: A Practical Guide to Creating Intimacy, Self-understanding, and Lasting Love in Your Life* (New York: Dutton, 2000), p. 66.

Page 346: Kaufman, G., *Shame: The Power of Caring* (Cambridge, Mass.: Schenkman, 1980), p. 60.

Page 347: Cline, F., and J. Fay, *Parenting Teens with Love and Logic: Preparing Adolescents for Responsible Adulthood* (Colorado Springs, Colo.: Pinon Press, 1992), pp. 146–47.

Page 348: Father's story about alcohol addiction: Kern, Walter, "What Do You Tell the Kids?" *Time* (June 18, 2001): p. 49.

Pages 348–349: Laing, R. D., *Self and Others*, 2nd ed. (London: Tavistock Publications, 1969), p. 94.

Pages 350–351: "Keeping Your Kids Drug Free: A How-to Guide for Parents and Caregivers," by the National Youth Anti-Drug Media Campaign, Office of National Drug Control Policy. For ordering information, see the Web site www.theantidrug.com.

Page 352: "One of the ironies . . .": Cline, and Fay, *Parenting Teens with Love and Logic*, p. 139.

Pages 354–57: Questions about values: Parents, educators, counselors, and others will find the following guide useful: DeMarco, J., *Adolescent Group Facilitator's Guide: Dynamic Discussion Starters* (Center City, Minn: Hazelden, 2001).

Page 358: Taffel, R. with M. Blau, *Parenting by Heart: How to Stay Connected to Your Child in a Disconnected World* (Cambridge, MA: Perseus, 2002), p. 287.

Pages 362–63: Gibran, K., *The Prophet* (New York: Random House, 2001), pp. 17–18.

Resources

Recommended Reading

AA, NA, and the Twelve Steps

Alcoholics Anonymous (New York: Alcoholics Anonymous World Services, 2001).

As Bill Sees It: The A.A. Way of Life . . . Selected Writings of AA's Co-Founder by Bill Wilson (New York: A.A. World Services, Inc., 1974).

Codependents' Guide to the Twelve Steps by Melody Beattie (New York: Fireside, 1993).

It Works How and Why: The Twelve Steps and Twelve Traditions of Narcotics Anonymous (Chatsworth, Calif.: NA World Services, Inc., 1993).

Narcotics Anonymous (Van Nuys, Calif.: World Service Office, Inc., 1988).

Addiction: Biological and Environmental Influences

Alcohol and the Addictive Brain by Kenneth Blum (New York: The Free Press, 1991).

Alcoholism: The Genetic Inheritance by Kathleen Whalen Fitzgerald (Friday Harbor, Wash.: Whales Tales Press, 2002).

Beyond the Influence: Understanding and Defeating Alcoholism by Katherine Ketcham and William Asbury (New York: Bantam, 2000).

Change Your Brain, Change Your Life: The Breakthrough Program for Conquering Anxiety, Depression, Obsessiveness, Anger, and Impulsiveness by Daniel Amen (New York: Three Rivers Press, 1998).

Educating Yourself About Alcohol and Drugs: A People's Primer by Marc Schuckit (New York: Plenum Press, 1995).

Framework for Understanding Poverty by Ruby Paine (Highlands, Tex.: Aha! Process, Inc., 2001).

The Natural History of Alcoholism Revisited by George Vaillant (Cambridge, Mass.: Harvard University Press, 1995).

Under the Influence: A Guide to the Myths and Realities of Alcoholism by James Milam and Katherine Ketcham (New York: Bantam, 1983).

Drugs

Buzzed: The Straight Facts About the Most Used and Abused Drugs from Alcohol to Ecstasy by Cynthia Kuhn, Scott Swartzwelder, and Wilkie Wilson (New York: W. W. Norton, 1998).

Dangerous Drugs, 2nd ed., by Carol Falkowski (Center City, Minn.: Hazelden, 2003).

Ecstasy: The Complete Guide: A Comprehensive Look at the Risks and Benefits of MDMA by Julie Holland (editor), (Rochester, Vt.: Inner Traditions, 2001).

LSD, My Problem Child by Albert Hoffman (Los Angeles: Jeremy P. Tarcher, 1983).

Marihuana and Medicine by Gabriel Nahas, Kenneth Sutin, David Harvey, Stig Agurell (editors); Nicholas Pace and Robert Cancro (co-editors), (Totowa, N.J.: Humana Press, 1999).

The Doors of Perception by Aldous Huxley (New York: HarperCollins, 1990).

The Pursuit of Ecstasy: The MDMA Experience by Jerome Beck and Marsha Rosenbaum (Albany, N.Y.: SUNY Press, 1994).

Writing on Drugs by Sadie Plant (New York: Picador, 1999).

Intervention

Getting Them Sober: You Can Help by Toby Rice Drews (Deerfield Beach, Fla.: Health Communications, Inc., 1998).

I'll Quit Tomorrow by Vernon Johnson (New York: Harper & Row, 1973).

Love First: A New Approach to Intervention for Alcoholism and Drug Addiction by Jeff Jay and Debra Jay (Center City, Minn.: Hazelden, 2000).

Nutrition

Eating Well for Optimum Health: The Essential Guide to Bringing Health and Pleasure Back to Eating by Andrew Weil (New York: Quill, 2001).

Potatoes Not Prozac by Kathleen DesMaisons (New York: Simon & Schuster, 1998).

Seven Weeks to Sobriety: The Proven Program to Fight Alcoholism Through Nutrition by Joan Mathews (New York: Fawcett Columbine, 1992).

Spontaneous Healing: How to Discover and Enhance Your Body's Natural Ability to Maintain and Heal Itself by Andrew Weil (New York: Ballantine, 1996).

Staying Healthy with Nutrition: The Complete Guide to Diet and Nutritional Medicine by Elson Haas (Berkeley, Calif.: Celestial Arts, 1993).

The Sugar Addict's Total Recovery Program by Kathleen DesMaisons (New York: Ballantine, 2000).

Parenting Books

A Good Enough Parent: A Book on Child Rearing by Bruno Bettelheim (New York: Vintage Books, 1988).

Another Chance: Hope and Health for the Alcoholic Family by Sharon Wegsheider Cruse (Palo Alto, Calif.: Science and Behavior Books, 1989).

From Anger to Forgiveness by Earnie Larsen (Center City, Minn.: Hazelden, 1992).

Get Out of My Life, but First Could You Drive Me & Cheryl to the Mall: A Parent's Guide to the New Teenager by Anthony Wolf (New York: Farrar, Straus and Giroux, 2002).

How to Talk So Kids Will Listen & Listen So Kids Will Talk by Adele Faber and Elaine Mazlish (New York: Avon Books, 1999).

Kids Power, Too! Words to Grow By by Cathey Brown, Betty LaPorte, and Jerry Moe (Dallas, Tex.: Imagin Works, 1996).

Parenting 911 by Charlene Giannetti and Margaret Sagarese (New York: Broadway Books, 1999).

Parenting Teens with Love and Logic: Preparing Adolescents for Responsible Adulthood by Foster Cline and Jim Fay (Colorado Springs, Colo.: Pinon Press, 1992).

Queen Bees and Wannabes: Helping Your Daughter Survive Cliques, Gossip, Boyfriends, and Other Realities of Adolescence by Rosalind Wiseman (New York: Crown, 2002).

Raising Cain: Protecting the Emotional Life of Boys by Daniel Kindlon and Michael Thompson (New York: Ballantine, 2000).

Reviving Ophelia: Saving the Selves of Adolescent Girls by Mary Pipher (New York: Ballantine, 1995).

The Primal Teen: What the New Discoveries About the Teenage Brain Tell Us About Our Kids by Barbara Strauch (New York: Doubleday, 2003).

Uncommon Sense for Parents with Teenagers by Michael Riera (Berkeley, Calif.: Celestial Arts, 1995).

Yes, Your Teen Is Crazy: Loving Your Kid Without Losing Your Mind by Michael J. Bradley (Gig Harbor, Wash.: Harbor Press, 2003)

Personal Accounts

A Monk Swimming by Malachi McCourt (New York: Hyperion, 1998).

Betty: A Glad Awakening by Betty Ford and Chris Chase (New York: Jove, 1988)

Drinking: A Love Story by Caroline Knapp (New York: Dial Press, 1996).

Father Greg and the Homeboys: The Extraordinary Journey of Father Greg Boyle and His Work with the Latino Gangs of East LA by Celeste Fremon (New York: Hyperion, 1995).

Go Ask Alice: A Real Diary by Anonymous (New York: Aladdin Paperbacks, 1998).

John Barleycorn or, Alcoholic Memoirs by Jack London (New York: Signet, 1990).

Journals by Kurt Cobain (New York: Riverhead Books, 2002).

Junky by William Burroughs (New York: Viking, 1985; reissued by Penguin, 2003).

More, Now, Again: A Memoir of Addiction by Elizabeth Wurtzel (New York: Simon & Schuster, 2002).

Playing It Straight: Personal Conversations on Recovery, Transformation and Success by David Dodd (Deerfield Beach, Fla.: Health Communications, Inc., 1996).

Terry: My Daughter's Life and Death Struggle with Alcoholism by George McGovern (New York: Villard Books, 1996).

Relapse and Recovery

Changing for Good: A Revolutionary Six-Stage Program for Overcoming Bad Habits and Moving Your Life Positively Forward by James Prochaska, John Norcross, and Carlo DiClemente (New York: Quill, 2002).

Passages Through Recovery: An Action Plan for Preventing Relapse by Terence Gorski (Center City, Minn.: Hazelden, 1997).

Stage II Recovery: Life Beyond Addiction by Earnie Larsen (San Francisco: Harper & Row, 1985).

Staying Sober: A Guide for Relapse Prevention by Terence Gorski and Merlene Miller (Independence, Mo.: Herald House/Independence Press, 1986).

The Miracle of Change: The Path to Self-Discovery and Spiritual Growth by Dennis Wholey (New York: Pocket Books, 1997).

The Recovery Book by Al Mooney, Arlene Eisenberg, and Howard Eisenberg (New York: Workman Publishing Co., 1992).

Spirituality

Came to Believe: The Spiritual Adventures of AA as Experienced by Individual Members (New York: AA World Services, Inc., 1973).

Not God: A History of Alcoholics Anonymous by Ernest Kurtz (Center City, Minn.: Hazelden, expanded edition 1991).

The Promise of a New Day by Karen Casey and Martha Vanceburg (New York: HarperSanFrancisco, 1996).

The Prophet by Kahlil Gibran (New York: Random House, 2001).

Spiritual Literacy: Reading the Sacred in Everyday Life by Frederic and Mary Ann Brussat (New York: Scribner, 1996).

The Soul of Recovery: Uncovering the Spiritual Dimension in the Treatment of Addictions by Christopher Ringwald (New York: Oxford University Press, 2002).

The Spirituality of Imperfection: Storytelling and the Search for Meaning by Ernest Kurtz and Katherine Ketcham (New York: Bantam, 1992).

The Varieties of Religious Experience by William James (New York: Touchstone, 1997).

Treatment

Adolescent Substance Abuse Treatment in the United States, Sally Stevens and Andrew Morral (editors), (New York: Haworth Press, 2002).

Principles of Addiction Medicine, 3rd ed., by Allan Graham, M.D., Terry Schultz, M.D., Michael Mayo-Smith, M.D., Richard Ries, M.D., and Bonnie Wilford (editors), (Chevy Chase, Md.: American Society of Addiction Medicine, Inc., 2003).

Slaying the Dragon: The History of Addiction Treatment and Recovery in America by William White (Bloomington, Ill.: Chestnut Health Systems, 1998).

Web Sites for Parents and Teens

Al-Anon/Alateen

www.al-anon.alateen.org

Al-Anon helps families and friends of alcoholics recover from the effects of living with the problem drinking of a relative or friend. Alateen is a similar program for teens.

Alcoholics Anonymous (AA) and Narcotics Anonymous (NA)

www.alcoholics-anonymous.org
www.na.org

AA and NA are fellowships of men and women (young and old) "who share their experience, strength, and hope with each other that they may solve their common problem and help others to recover" from alcoholism and other drug addictions. The AA and NA Web sites offer information and resources for people who want to know more about Twelve Step programs.

American Society for Addiction Medicine (ASAM)

www.asam.org

ASAM is the nation's medical specialty society "dedicated to educating physicians and improving the treatment of individuals suffering from alcoholism and other addictions." To find a physician specializing in addiction medicine, see the American Medical Association Web site at www.ama-assn.org/aps/amahg.

Association of Recovery Schools (ARS)

www.recoveryschools.org

ARS is dedicated to creating a community of young people, their parents, and helping professionals to support students in recovery from alcohol and other drug dependencies. ARS advocates for strengthening and expanding high school and college programs dedicated to helping youth achieve both academic and recovery goals. High school and college programs are listed on the Web site.

Center of Alcohol Studies at Rutgers University
www.rci.rutgers.edu/~cas2/online
The "Online Facts" section lists hundreds of helpful resources for children, parents, educators, and community activists.

Center for Science in Public Interest (CSPI)
www.cspinet.org
CSPI is a nonprofit educational and advocacy organization whose stated purpose is "to promote health through educating the public about nutrition and alcohol." The "Booze News" fact sheets, available on the Web site, are particularly informative.

Families Anonymous
www.familiesanonymous.org
A Twelve Step, self-help, recovery fellowship of support groups for relatives and friends of those who have alcohol, drug, or behavioral problems.

Join Together Online (JTO)
www.jointogether.org
JTO "supports community-based efforts to reduce, prevent, and treat substance abuse across the nation" and focuses attention "on strengthening community capacity to expand the demand for and supply of high quality drug and alcohol treatment." If you subscribe to "JTO Direct," you will receive daily or weekly information about recent research findings, grant announcements, action alerts, and stories in the news.

Mothers Against Drunk Driving (MADD)

www.madd.org

A volunteer advocacy and education organization, MADD was established to stop drunk driving, support the victims of drunk drivers, and prevent underage drinking.

National Association for Children of Alcoholics (NACoA)

www.nacoa.org

NACoA is a national nonprofit voluntary membership dedicated to helping the more than twenty-eight million people in this country whose lives have been affected by family alcohol addiction—eleven million of whom are under the age of eighteen. As NACoA executive director Sis Wenger writes: "If we are ever to break the intergenerational transmission of alcoholism, we must come to terms with the impact on the children who live in the addicted home environment during their critical developmental years."

National Center for Addiction and Substance Abuse (CASA) at Columbia University

www.casacolumbia.org

A think tank and action organization headed by former Health, Education and Welfare secretary Joseph Califano Jr., CASA's mission is to "inform Americans of the economic and social costs of substance abuse and its impact on their lives" and to "remove the stigma of abuse and replace shame and despair with hope." CASA's informative and enlightening research reports on subjects ranging from binge drinking to the role of spirituality in recovery can be downloaded directly from the Web site.

National Clearinghouse for Alcohol and Drug Information

www.health.org

The clearinghouse is the information service for the Center for Substance Abuse Prevention (CSAP) in the Department of Health and Human Services. The world's largest resource for current information and materials concerning drugs and addiction, the clearinghouse distributes free or low-cost fact sheets, brochures, pamphlets, posters, and videotapes.

National Council on Alcoholism and Drug Dependence (NCADD)

www.ncadd.org

Founded in 1944 by Marty Mann, the first woman to find long-term sobriety in Alcoholics Anonymous, NCADD is a voluntary, nonprofit health organization with a network of affiliates that provide education and information about prevention, intervention, and treatment of alcoholism and other drug addictions.

National Families in Action

www.nationalfamilies.org

NIFA's mission is to help families and communities prevent drug use among children by promoting policies based on science. This colorful Web site is filled with useful information including illustrated fact sheets on specific drugs, tips, and advice for parents, and sections on drug prevention and education.

National Inhalant Prevention Coalition

www.inhalants.org

NIPC serves as an inhalant referral and information clearinghouse designed to educate youth and adults about inhalants.

National Institute on Alcohol Abuse and Alcoholism (NIAAA)

www.niaaa.nih.gov

NIAAA supports and conducts research on the causes, consequences, treatment, and prevention of alcoholism and alcohol-related problems and disseminates research findings to health care providers, researchers, policymakers, and the general public.

National Institute on Drug Abuse (NIDA)
www.nida.nih.gov

NIDA's mission is "to lead the Nation in bringing the power of science to bear on drug abuse and addiction." The Parents and Teachers section (www.drugabuse.gov/parent-teacher.html) is particularly helpful and informative.

Office of National Drug Control Policy
www.whitehousedrugpolicy.gov

Look up the drug facts, prevention, and treatment sections of this Web site.

Parents—the Anti-Drug
www.antidrug.com

This Web site was created by the National Youth Anti-Drug Media Campaign and serves as a drug prevention information center and a "supportive community for parents to interact and learn from each other."

Students Against Destructive Decisions (SADD)
www.saddonline.com

SADD (originally Students Against Drunk Driving) is dedicated to "preventing destructive decisions, particularly underage drinking, other drug use, impaired driving, teen violence and teen depression and suicide."

Substance Abuse and Mental Health Services Administration (SAMHSA)
www.samhsa.gov

SAMHSA is the federal agency charged with improving the quality and availability of prevention, treatment, and rehabilitative services in order to reduce illness, death, disability, and costs to society resulting from substance abuse and mental illnesses. The Web site offers a wealth of data and statistics. SAMHSA's treatment facility locator (http://findtreatment.samhsa.gov/facilitylocatordoc.htm) offers detailed information on programs available in your city and state.

Finding a Treatment Center

Treatment for substance-use disorders should be readily available to any and all who need it. In the addiction field, this is called "treatment on demand." Treatment on demand is not just humanitarianism or utopianism—it's a matter of economics, for drug treatment programs are cost-effective, saving approximately seven dollars for every dollar spent.

Yet despite these immediate and impressive savings, treatment for drug problems and addiction is subject to a higher level of management than other health care services. Managed care restrictions limit the amount of time adolescents (and adults) can spend in treatment and restrict access to certain kinds of treatment or specific treatment programs. In many cases, insurance benefits are denied because drug problems are classified under the category of mental health, and mental health disorders are not covered under the policy.

Despite the cutbacks and closed doors, there are dozens of high-quality treatment programs with facilities and programs *specifically tailored to adolescent needs*. If you are not familiar with the facilities in your area or state, try one or all of the following options. Once you've narrowed your search to one or more treatment centers, schedule a time to talk to the director or a qualified staff member. Be sure to ask detailed questions about the program's philosophy, staff, services, and various programs.

- Call your county human services agency; the address and phone number should be listed in a special "government pages" section of the phone book.
- Look in the yellow pages under "Alcoholism Information and Treatment" or "Drug Abuse Information and Treatment" and call the counseling offices, help lines, or treatment programs· listed. If you need more information, be sure to ask for brochures, referrals, and/or additional resources.
- To find a physician in your area who specializes in addiction medicine, contact the American Society of Addiction Medicine (ASAM), 4601 North Park Ave, Arcade Suite 101, Chevy Chase, Maryland 20815; 301-656-3920; fax: 301-

656-3815; E-mail@asam.org; www.asam.org. Or visit the American Medical Association's "doctor finder" Web site at www.amaassn.org/aps/amahg.html and follow the simple directions to find a specialist in your city or state.

- The National Council on Alcoholism and Drug Dependence has two help lines offering information on intervention, counseling, and treatment. Call 1-800-NCA-CALL or 1-800-475-HOPE.

- The Substance Abuse Mental Health Services Administration (SAMHSA) offers a "treatment locator" listing the more than eleven thousand addiction treatment programs, including residential centers, outpatient programs, and hospital-based programs for both adolescents and adults. The Web site is http://findtreatment.samhsa.gov/, or you can e-mail info@samhsa.gov or call 301-443-5700.

- A comprehensive guide to adolescent treatment programs was just published by Drug Strategies, a nonprofit research institute "that promotes more effective approaches to the nation's drug problems." You'll find "Treating Teens: A Guide to Adolescent Drug Problems" at www.drugstrategies.org/teens/programs.html. Call 202-289-9070 or send an e-mail to dspolicy@aol.com.

- If you're searching for detailed information about programs geared to specific problems such as codependency, dual diagnosis, eating disorders, cocaine addiction, and so on, try the Addiction Resource Guide at www.addictionresourceguide.com. The Web site also includes a long list of Internet community resources. E-mail info@addictionresourceguide.com or call 914-725-5151.

- To learn more about the options available for long-term residential treatment programs, visit the following Web sites:

www.daytop.org/adolescent.html
www.odysseyhouseinc.org/Programs/youth.html
www.phoenixhouse.org/treatment/adolesc.asp
www.teenchallenge.com/main/centers/adolescent.cfm

Index

MAO inhibitors, Ecstasy and, 171
marijuana, 101–21
  bad effects, 105–11
  drug combinations, 112–14
  Ecstasy and, 171
  effects long-term, 107–10
  effects short-term, 106–7
  as the gateway drug, 112–13
  the high, 102–4
  medical use of, 110–11
  overdose and death, 111–12
  physical dependence, 19–20, 115–19
  signs and symptoms, 119–21
  who uses, 104–5
memory problems
  alcohol abuse and, 76
  marijuana and, 106
mental health, nicotine and, 94
mescaline, 162
  See also LSD
methamphetamines, 135–50
  bad effects, 143–46
  dangerous combinations, 147–48
  effects long-term, 144–45
  effects short-term, 143–44
  the high, 138–41
  overdose and death, 147
  physical dependence, 148–49
  signs and symptoms, 149–50
  who uses, 141–43
Miller, Merlene, 301, 306, 311, 312
Minkoff, Kenneth, 290
money problems, drug use and, 231
Monitoring the Future Survey
  adolescent illegal drug use, 24–25
  alcohol use, 24–25, 75
  cocaine/crack cocaine use, 183–84
  Ecstasy use, 167–68
  heroin use, 199
  inhalant use, 126
  LSD use, 154
  marijuana/hashish use, 104–5

methamphetamine use, 141–43
nicotine use, 24–25, 91
prescription drugs, 213–14
More, Now, Again (Wurtzel), 207, 218
Morral, Andrew, 113
muscle problems
  alcohol abuse and, 79
  cocaine and, 184
  inhalants and, 129

National Center on Addiction and
  Substance Abuse (CASA), 74
National Drug Assessment Threat
  (NIDC), 196
National Household Survey on Drug
  Abuse, 134
National Youth Gang Survey, 60
nervousness, drug use and, 231–32
New England Journal of Medicine, 113
Nexus or 2CB, 176
nicotine, 89–100
  bad effects, 92–95
  drug combinations, 96–97
  effects long-term, 92–94
  effects short-term, 92
  the high, 90
  overdose and death, 96
  physical dependence, 98–99
  secondhand and sidestream smoke,
    94–95
  signs and symptoms, 99–100
  who uses, 90–91
Noble, Ernest, 32
Norcross, John, 222, 239–40, 259–60
nose and throat problems
  cocaine and, 184, 187
nutritional problems
  cocaine and, 185
NyQuil, 160

oblivion, drug use and, 232
obsessive-compulsive behavior, 49

About the Authors

Katherine Ketcham is the coauthor of eleven books, including the bestselling classic *Under the Influence: A Guide to the Myths and Realities of Alcoholism* with James Milam, Ph.D. (Bantam, 1983), *The Spirituality of Imperfection: Storytelling and the Search for Meaning* with Ernest Kurtz, Ph.D. (Bantam, 1992), and *Beyond the Influence: Understanding and Defeating Alcoholism* with William F. Asbury (Bantam, 2000). Over one million copies of her books are currently in print.

In addition to her writing career, Kathy works part time at the Juvenile Justice Center and the alternative high school in Walla Walla, Washington, where she has developed an educational curriculum for teenagers with alcohol and/or other drug problems.

Kathy and her husband, Patrick Spencer, a professor of geology at Whitman College in Walla Walla, are the parents of three children: Benjamin, seventeen; Alison, nineteen; and Robyn, twenty-one.

Nicholas A. Pace, M.D., is an associate professor of medicine at New York University's School of Medicine, and a medical consultant to General Motors and other corporations. Dr. Pace is the founding director of Pace Health Services, past chair of New York State Governor's Advisory Committee on Alcoholism, founding director and past vice-chair of the American Council on Drug Education, and co-founder and past president of the Alcoholism Council of New York. A life member of the board of directors of the National Council on

Alcoholism and Drug Dependence, and a fellow in the American Society of Addiction Medicine, he was an advisor to President Ford's White House physician, and assisted First Lady Nancy Reagan with the Chemical People Project. He is the author of *Safe Drinking* (McGraw Hill, 1984).

Dr. Pace lives in Westchester County, New York, and maintains a private practice in New York City. He and his wife, Carolyn, have three children, Victoria, Gregory, and Anthony, and two grandchildren, Nicholas and Stefani.